Your friend, as ever
A. Lincoln

THE LIFE OF
ABRAHAM LINCOLN

BY

ISAAC N. ARNOLD

Fourth Edition

Introduction to the Bison Book Edition
by James A. Rawley

University of Nebraska Press
Lincoln and London

Introduction to the Bison Book Edition copyright © 1994
by the University of Nebraska Press
Manufactured in the United States of America

The paper in this book meets the minimum requirements of
American National Standard for Information Sciences—
Permanence of Paper for Printed Library Materials, ANSI
Z39.48–1984.

First Bison Book printing: 1994
Most recent printing indicated by the last digit below:
10   9   8   7   6   5   4   3   2

Library of Congress Cataloging-in-Publication Data
Arnold, Isaac Newton, 1815–1884.
The life of Abraham Lincoln / by Isaac N. Arnold;
introduction by James A. Rawley.
p. cm.
ISBN 0-8032-5924-7 (pbk.)
1. Lincoln, Abraham, 1809–1865.   2. Presidents—United
States—Biography.   I. Title.
E457.A754   1994
973.7′092—dc20
[B]
94-17449   CIP

Originally published in 1884 by A. C. McClurg & Company,
Chicago.

INTRODUCTION TO THE BISON BOOK EDITION

By James A. Rawley

"I hope . . . I may, to some extent, aid you in forming a just and true estimate of Abraham Lincoln. I knew him, somewhat intimately, in private and public life for more than twenty years. We practiced law at the same bar, and during his administration, I was a member of Congress, seeing him and conferring with him often, and therefore, I may hope without vanity, I trust, that I shall be able to contribute something of value in enabling you to judge him." The words are by Isaac Newton Arnold who in 1884 produced a notable biography of the sixteenth president that for years stood as the best available life.

Arnold, lawyer and congressman, was born in Hartwick, Otsego County, New York, November 30, 1815. His parents, Dr. George Washington Arnold and Sophie M., were Rhode Islanders who had migrated to New York about 1800. His grandfather, Thomas Arnold, served in the American Revolution. Young Arnold studied in the local schools until age fifteen, when he became self-dependent, and enterprisingly taught school and studied law. At twenty he was admitted to the bar, and within a short time, he volunteered to defend a black man named Dacit, accused of murdering his brother in a jealous rage because the two were rivals for the love of the same woman. Believing his client innocent, Arnold won an acquittal—the start of a notable career as a criminal (as well as a civil) lawyer.

In 1836 with only some law books and a few hundred dollars Arnold migrated to Chicago, then a prairie village, and opened a law office. The next year, when Chicago was incorporated, he was elected city clerk, but soon resigned because of the pressure of his burgeoning practice. About those days he later recalled dangerous journeys by foot and horse over the prairies, escaping wolves and Indians.

Taking an interest in politics in 1842, concerned that Illinois might repudiate its state debt, he won election to the legislature. As chairman of the committee on finance, he helped push through a plan to effect payment of the debt and assure bondholders of the Illinois and Michigan Canal in the future of a pledge of repayment. A Democrat, he preferred Van Buren to Polk in 1844, but he reluctantly served as a presidential elector for Polk. In the next presidential election he followed Van Buren in the Free Soil Party, becoming a delegate to the Buffalo nominating convention and helping organize the party. With others he called a state convention launching the formal antislavery movement in Illinois. He stumped Cook County, which gave its vote to the Free-Soilers. When in 1850 Congress enacted a new Fugitive Slave law, he served on a Chicago committee to draw up protest resolutions.

Leaving the legislature in 1845, Arnold devoted himself to the law until 1855, when as a Republican he returned to the legislature and came within three or four votes of being elected speaker. Lincoln called Arnold "a talented and practiced debater." Eager to enter the national stage of politics, Arnold ran unsuccessfully for Congress in 1858, tried again two years later and won a seat that he held for two terms—during the whole of Lincoln's administration.

Early in 1860 Arnold and Lincoln faced one another in a Chicago courtroom, Arnold among counsel for the

Illinois Central Railroad and Lincoln among counsel for the defense, which won the verdict. Later in the year Arnold spoke for "Lincoln and Liberty"; and Arnold is said to have remarked to Lincoln as the candidate was leaving town, "Next time I see you I shall congratulate you on being President-elect." Lincoln responded, "And I you on being Congressman-elect." Arnold won handily, garnering seventy-six more votes than the Republican electors did. Following the election, in late November, Arnold and Lincoln together attended St. James Church in Chicago.

Lincoln was the first Republican to be elected president; a consequence was a rush of Republicans to secure public office. Patronage was a source of political strength to both the president and the congressman. Arnold urged Lincoln to appoint his candidate as Chicago postmaster, with its many employees, perhaps the lushest plum, in his district. But Lincoln, fatefully as it turned out, named John Locke Scripps, editor of the *Chicago Press and Tribune,* who in the summer of 1860 had written a campaign biography of Lincoln. Arnold was grieved to learn that Lincoln had not only failed to name his nominee but had also given the office to a man he disliked.

The Thirty-seventh Congress did not meet until the Fourth of July in 1861, after the Confederates had reduced Fort Sumter and Lincoln had called out the militia, beginning the Civil War. During the first important clash of arms, at nearby Bull Run, Arnold served as aide to Colonel David Hunter. Later in the year he conferred with Lincoln on conditions in the Northwest. During the war Arnold saw Lincoln frequently, and loyally supported the president's policies.

The Republican Party originated in opposition to the extension of slavery, and made it the cardinal principle. To carry out this aim Arnold, a fervent antislavery man,

on March 24, 1862, introduced a bill to prohibit slavery
in all places where the national government had exclusive jurisdiction, including military installations and
vessels on the high seas. Strong objection from conser-
vatives to its sweeping character caused him to accept a
substitute proposed by his Illinois colleague, Owen
Lovejoy, reducing the scope to all territories. The bill
passed both houses by a partisan vote and became law
on June 19. Meanwhile Congress, waging war against
the rebels, had proposed strengthening earlier legislation to confiscate enemy property, including slaves. On
May 23, 1862, Arnold spoke in favor of the measure,
which became law on July 17.

While Congress was attacking slavery by its ban on
slavery in the territories and confiscaton of enemy-
owned slaves, Lincoln had proposed a moderate scheme
to entice the loyal slave states to emancipate their
slaves with financial aid from the Federal government.
Congress had passed an enabling act, but the border
states had not budged. After successive efforts to per-
suade Border State congressmen to favor compensated
emancipation by state authority, Lincoln began to contemplate emancipation by his personal decree.

On July 13 Lincoln told two of his cabinet members,
Secretary of State Seward and Secretary of the Navy
Welles, that he intended to free rebel-owned slaves if the
war did not end soon. That night Arnold and Lovejoy
called on their fellow Illinoisan at the Soldiers Home
outside Washington, where the Lincoln family sought
relief from the summer heat. The president voiced his
deep anxiety about the border states. "Oh, how I wish
the border states would accept my proposition. Then
you, Lovejoy, and you, Arnold, and all of us, would not
have lived in vain. . . . You would live to see the end of
slavery."

When Congress adjourned, with McClellan's Peninsula Campaign a failure and recruiting flagging, Arnold spoke with Lincoln. "You used to maul rails," he reminded the president, "now you must maul rebels."

"Tell the people of Illinois that I'll do it," Lincoln assured him. On September the railsplitter president used the maul of his Emancipation Proclamation to strike a blow for freedom of the rebels' slaves.

Returned to Congress by a two thousand majority, unlike other Republicans who suffered losses because of the proclamation, Arnold stayed loyal to Lincoln, while General Ambrose Burnside failed at Bloody Fredericksburg, and Republican politicians schemed against both the president and Seward. Gloom spread throughout the North, foreign opinion appeared hostile, and General Joseph Hooker declared, "Both the army and the government need dictators." With perhaps some exaggeration, Congressman Albert Riddle of Ohio recalled of Lincoln's fallen popularity, "At the end of the Thirty-seventh Congress, there were in the House but two men, capable of being heard, who openly and everywhere defended him—Mr. Arnold of Illinois and Mr. Riddle of Ohio."

In the spring of 1863, after Hooker, appointed to succeed Burnside by Lincoln with some reservations, had suffered a costly defeat at Chancellorsville, and U. S. Grant was slowly moving against Vicksburg, criticism of management of army operations by General Henry W. Halleck mounted.

Arnold joined in the clamor for Haleck's head, on May 18, 1863, urging Lincoln "as one of your old & true friends" to replace Halleck whom the public thought responsible for driving various generals from public service. In a "private & confidential" reply, the president remarked that what the public was said to believe was false; and chiding Arnold with an uncommon bluntness observed, "My position enables me to understand my duty in all these matters better than you possibly can." Lincoln signed his letter, "Your friend, as ever."

The two men remained steadfast friends, and Halleck continued to be general in chief, developing a harmonious relationship with Grant and Lincoln. Meanwhile Burnside blundered again by suspending publication of the *Chicago Times*. In early June, Arnold and others forwarded a petition from prominent Chicagoans asking Lincoln to revoke the order. Lincoln complied, saying the request strongly influenced him in doing so. Later in the year when the ladies in charge of the Northwestern Sanitary Fair in Chicago sought the original of the Emancipation Proclamation for auction, Arnold urged the president to donate it as a fund-raising trophy. Toward the year's end Lincoln, with an unwonted intervention in non-military legislation in his annual message, endorsed Arnold's pet project to enlarge water communication between the Mississippi River and Chicago and on to the northeastern seaboard. Two days later Arnold spent an evening with the president, listening to "a magnificent Western law story about a steam doctor's bill," and discussing the annual message.

Soon after the Thirty-eighth Congress opened, Arnold introduced a bill "for . . . carrying into more complete and immediate execution" the Emancipation Proclamation by banning reenslavement of any person declared free by the proclamation. It did not pass, but not long after he earned a place in history books by moving the amendment to abolish slavery in the United States. Between these moves he delivered an address in Congress on "The Power, Duty and Necessity of Destroying Slavery in the United States." In March 1864 he gave a speech in praise of Lincoln and his reconstruction policy that became a campaign pamphlet, which he said was "in greater demand than any other document" published by his party.

When foes to Lincoln's renomination suggested post-poning the party's nominating convention, Arnold stoutly fought the suggestion in an influential letter to the *New York Evening Post*. Days later, after the *New York Tribune* published a critical article on the failed battle of the Wilderness, Arnold and others spoke for the Union party at the Cooper Institute, where in 1860 Lincoln had given his memorable address.

Arnold's own bid for renomination fell afoul of John Locke Scripps, whom Lincoln had appointed Chicago postmaster over Arnold's protest. Arnold's role in Lincoln's reversal of Burnside's suspension order had antagonized Chicago Germans, causing "much excitement of which I am the special object," Arnold lamented to Lincoln. Scripps sought Arnold's seat in the House, and unscrupulously used his postoffice patronage in his own behalf.

Caught between loyalty to his biographer and his friend, Lincoln intervened in the excitement by a letter saying Arnold had merely forwarded the petition and in a personal communication had stated he was not expressing an opinion that the order should be revoked. Arnold read the letter to a Republican mass meeting in Chicago. As to Scripps and the patronage, Lincoln wrote directly to him to vote as he pleased, but not to "constrain any of your subordinates" to do other than vote their own preferences. At the end of August Arnold withdrew his candidacy for the seat, giving way to John Wentworth.

A lame duck, Arnold continued to sustain the antislavery cause. When the joint resolution that became the Thirteenth Amendment was read in the House, Arnold rose to say, "In view of the long catalogue of wrongs which it has inflicted upon the country, I demand to-day the death of African slavery." As Arnold's term was expiring, Lincoln offered him appointment as auditor of the treasury for the postoffice department. At first hesitant, Arnold accepted, holding the office under President Andrew Johnson until the end of September the next year.

Arnold was among the last persons to speak with Lincoln. While the president was entering his carriage to ride to Ford's Theater, he and Arnold exchanged a few words. Within a short while after Lincoln's death, Arnold had become a zealous biographer of his martyred friend and fellow Illinoisan.

Lincoln's biographer fittingly presented a scholarly appearance, with his high-domed forehead, trim mustache, and tall, thin frame. Though untrained, he was as well scholarly in outlook, concerned about historical accuracy and skeptical in examining evidence. He drew on primary published material, including the *Congressional Globe;* corresponded with the many persons who had known Lincoln, particularly Lincoln's law partner, William H. Herndon; invoked his own recollections; and benefited from having known many of the figures in Lincoln's acquaintance. His sketches of congressional colleagues like James A. Garfield and Thaddeus Stevens are finely drawn. He had seen Lincoln in the courtroom, on the circuit, in Lincoln's Springfield home and the Executive Mansion, and in his own home in Chicago. He had importantly participated in framing the momentous legislation of the Civil War years. As a member of Congress, he had taken a leading part in its assault on slavery.

Arnold, moreover, was an able writer, employing a clear readable style, with an occasional, enjoyable flair for literary craftsmanship. By the time he wrote his *Life of Abraham Lincoln* he had extensive experience with his pen, having published books on Lincoln and slavery and on Benedict Arnold, who was not a relative, as well as articles.

Arnold's first book on Lincoln, *The History of Abraham Lincoln and the Overthrow of Slavery,* appeared in 1866. Written in haste, heavily freighted with history, it was not squarely a biography. Others rushed in to publish biographical material. Lincoln's law partner, William H. Herndon, delivered a series of lectures, in one of which he stated that Lincoln's acquaintance with Ann Rutledge was the only romance in his life. Herndon portrayed his partner as ambitious, greedy, not warm-hearted, and a man who "read less and thought more than any man in America." Herndon's work disturbed Arnold, who wrote Herndon of his disappointment, "I know you could not intentionally do him injustice."

When Ward Hill Lamon in 1872 brought out his *Life of Abraham Lincoln,* Arnold was shocked. The book made Lincoln a religious hypocrite—attending public services but doubting Christian doctrine—and a husband beset by a shrewish spouse. "Do not you and I owe it to the memory of the dead to vindicate him [Lincoln] of these charges?" Arnold demanded of Lincoln's friend Orville H. Browning.

Arnold set to work to correct misapprehensions and present Lincoln as he saw him. Unlike Herndon, who had known Lincoln only up to the presidency, Arnold could draw on his relationship with Lincoln during the momentous years of the Civil War as well as earlier. Unlike Lamon and the numerous popularizers, Arnold had a scholarly bent, avoided sensationalism, was intent on truth, and held a strong sympathy and admiration for an undoubtedly eminent historical figure. Also unlike Lamon, Arnold had a keen analytical mind and a sense of history. Though his love for his subject "as a brother" lured him from the full objectivity a later century demands, Arnold made a judgment many present-day scholars would agree with: Lincoln was "the greatest,

take him all in all [and] best man, our country has produced."

Contemporary critics hailed the new work; the distinguished librarian and historian W. F. Poole, writing in
The Dial, pronounced, "Of the lives of President Lincoln
which have thus far appeared, Mr. Arnold's is the most
satisfactory. . . . The book must therefore take rank
without question as the standard life of Lincoln." The
London Spectator judged, "Mr. Arnold has done his work
in a manner worthy of his subject."

Despite the advance of the historians' craft, later
scholars have continued to praise Arnold's biography.
Writing in 1928, Theodore C. Pease saw in the book "the
value of a source. . . . Compared with the standards of
his time, his historical workmanship is generally competent."

Lincoln specialists acknowledged the book's merits.
Paul Angle in 1946 found the work "valuable today
chiefly for his [Arnold's] own comments and impressions." Benjamin P. Thomas the next year observed,
"Because he knew the men of whom he wrote, his char-
acterizations of members of Congress and officials of the
government are valuable. . . . The book concludes with
a fine character sketch and an estimate of Lincoln's
place in history." The next year David Potter, assaying
the Lincoln theme in American historical writing,
judged that Arnold's *Life* "remains one of the best early
biographies." A more recent student, Mark A. Neely Jr.,
found the book "still valuable for Arnold's first-hand
views of the Lincoln administration."

Biographers and historians have frequently drawn on
Arnold's *Life.* James G. Randall, whom some authorities
believe to have written the greatest life of Lincoln, not
only made numerous references to Arnold and his book,
but also cited it heavily in discussing passage of the
Thirteenth Amendment. Writers retell Arnold's story of

his encounter with the acid-tongued Thaddeus Stevens, who told an editor in 1864 that Arnold was the only Lincoln member of Congress. Other common references are to Lincoln's anguished talk with Arnold and Lovejoy about the refusal of the border states to accept gradual, compensated emancipation by the state action. Ida Tarbell, a turn-of-the century biographer, availed herself of Arnold's description of Lincoln's private office and his relation of his conversation with Mary Todd Lincoln about her husband's request, made at a country graveyard, "Lay my remains in some quiet place like this."

At the same time, the book, written well over a century ago, should be read not only for its clear merits but also with awareness of the march of Lincoln scholarship. Sources are available today that were not at hand for Arnold. Present-day biographers benefit from several generations of scholarship, more exacting standards, and new interests such as Lincoln's relationship to women and especially his wife, his legal career, and his views on race as well as slavery. It is easy today to point to such slips as making Lincoln's illiterate mother a fluent reader, having Lincoln write his Gettysburg Address on a "rough sheet of foolscap" in pencil on his way to Gettysburg, and holding a lifelong ambition to free the slaves.

More pertinent is Arnold's very evident admiration of his subject and his neglect to mention important qualifications to Lincoln's antislavery views. Lincoln was not an abolitionist; he was reluctant to join the antislavery Republican party; he was willing not only to uphold the Fugitive Slave Law but would amend it; and he gave official support in his First Inaugural to a proposed constitutional amendment that would forever have guaranteed slavery in the United States. Arnold also scanted the friction in the Republican party and the hostility of abolitionists to Lincoln.

Such shortcomings may be expected from a book published in 1884. Today the book may be read for its strengths: a classic in Lincoln historiography; an eyewitness account of Lincoln and his contemporaries; an engagingly written book; and a concentration on the years of Lincoln's greatness—his presidency.

The Life of Abraham Lincoln

INTRODUCTION.

By the Hon. E. B. Washburne.

This work —"The Life of Abraham Lincoln"—was completed only a few days before the death of the distinguished author, the Hon. Isaac N. Arnold. He did not live to oversee its publication. That was entrusted to competent and friendly hands; and the work, with its chapter heads and its full and elaborate index, is herewith presented to an indulgent public.

Few had known Mr. Lincoln better than had Mr. Arnold, and no man was more familiar with his life or had studied more profoundly his personal and political character, or his public career. They had been personal friends for a quarter of a century. They were much together in the courts and often associated in the trial of causes, and had been opposing counsel in important litigation. Their long acquaintance and association had made them to know each other well and had engendered mutual respect and mutual regard.

From the time that Mr. Arnold entered Congress, at the breaking out of the War of the Rebellion, he became one of the most trusted advisers of Mr. Lincoln, and few men outside of the Cabinet were more frequently consulted by him in important matters. No one knew better Mr. Lincoln's thoughts and intentions than Mr. Arnold, and no one enjoyed his confidence to a higher degree. It may be truly said that no man was better qualified to write a serious and authoritative life of Mr. Lincoln, and to enlighten the public in respect to the character, career and services of that illustrious man.

There is no doubt that for some time prior to the assassination of Mr. Lincoln, Mr. Arnold had contemplated writing his life. Previous to that event, and while yet a member of Congress, he had commenced to write the " History of Abraham Lincoln and the Overthrow of Slavery," which he completed and published in 1867. He brought to the preparation of that work the qualities of an able and conscientious historian, who wrote very largely from personal knowledge and personal observation. It is a book of real interest and exceptional historic value. Important and valuable facts are to be obtained therein which are not to be found elsewhere.

This work was never entirely satisfactory to Mr. Arnold, so far as it related to Mr. Lincoln, and hence some two years since he determined to write in a stricter sense the life of Mr. Lincoln, in the light of additional material he had gathered, and disconnected with the history of the overthrow of slavery, except in so far as the subject was connected generally with the administration of Mr. Lincoln.

Stimulated by his admiration and friendship for Mr. Lincoln, Mr. Arnold entered on his work *con amore*, and devoted to it his most earnest thoughts and great labor. He undertook his self-imposed task with the idea and purpose that it would be the finishing work of his life. His great object was to write a life worthy of the man. He has taken the utmost pains to procure reliable material, to verify all statements of fact, and to bring out the incidents of Mr. Lincoln's life, with candor, fairness, and accuracy.

Mr. Arnold has shown in his life of Mr. Lincoln that he has a full and just appreciation of the true province of history. He was guided by that spirit which governed the greatest historian of modern times, M. Adolph Thiers. M. Xavier Marmier, in his admirable discourse before the French Academy, quotes M. Thiers as saying :

"I have for the mission of history such a respect, that the fear of alleging an inexact fact fills me with a sort of consternation. I have no repose till I have discovered the proof of the fact, the object of my doubt. I seek it wherever it ought to be, and I never stop till I have found it, or when I have acquired the certainty that it does not exist."

In the present volume Mr. Arnold has shown himself, in this regard, a worthy disciple of M. Thiers.

CONTENTS.

CHAPTER I.

ANCESTRY AND EARLY LIFE.

Early History of the Family.—Removal of the President's Grandfather from Virginia to Kentucky.—He is Killed by the Indians.—Autobiography of the President.—His Father's Marriage.—His Mother. —Their Children.—Death of His Mother.—His Education.—Books He Read.—Father's Second Marriage.—Trip to New Orleans.

CHAPTER II.

LIFE AT NEW SALEM.

The Lincoln Family Remove to Illinois.—Second Trip to New Orleans. —Life at New Salem.—Jack Armstrong and the Clary Grove Boys. —Black Hawk War.—Acquires the Name of "Honest Abe."—Postmaster at Salem. — Trust Funds. — Studies Law.—A Surveyor.— Story of Anne Rutledge.—Elected to the Legislature.

CHAPTER III.

THE ILLINOIS LEGISLATURE.

Lincoln at Twenty-Five.—At Vandalia.—Re-elected in 1836.—Replies to Forquer. — To Dr. Early. — To Col. Taylor. — State Capital Removed from Vandalia to Springfield. — Anti-Slavery Protest.— Re-elected in 1838.—Removes to Springfield.—Re-elected in 1840.— Partnership with John T. Stuart.—Riding the Circuit.

CHAPTER IV.

MISCELLANEOUS SPEECHES AND MARRIAGE.

CHAPTER V.

CONGRESS AND THE BAR.

CHAPTER VI.

THE IRREPRESSIBLE CONFLICT.

CHAPTER VII.

THE STRUGGLE FOR KANSAS.

CHAPTER VIII.

THE ORGANIZATION OF THE REPUBLICAN PARTY.

CHAPTER IX.

THE LINCOLN AND DOUGLAS DEBATE.

CHAPTER X.

LINCOLN BECOMES PRESIDENT.

CHAPTER XI.

LINCOLN REACHES WASHINGTON.

CHAPTER XII.

LINCOLN IN THE WHITE HOUSE.

CHAPTER XIII.

EXTRA SESSION OF CONGRESS.

CHAPTER XIV.

EFFORTS FOR PEACEFUL EMANCIPATION.

CHAPTER XV.

THE EMANCIPATION PROCLAMATION.

CHAPTER XVI.

MILITARY OPERATIONS IN 1861-1862.

CHAPTER XVII.

ANTIETAM AND CHANCELLORSVILLE.

CHAPTER XVIII.

THE TIDE TURNS.

CHAPTER XIX.

AFTER GETTYSBURG.

CHAPTER XX.

THE AMENDMENT PROPOSED.

CHAPTER XXI.

PASSAGE OF THE AMENDMENT.

CHAPTER XXII.

GRANT AND SHERMAN.

CHAPTER XXIII.

THE SECOND TERM.

CHAPTER XXIV.

THE APPROACHING END.

CHAPTER XXV.

VICTORY AND DEATH.

CHAPTER XXVI.

LIFE OF ABRAHAM LINCOLN.

CHAPTER I.

ANCESTRY AND EARLY LIFE.

HISTORY furnishes the record of few lives at once so
eventful and important, and ending so tragically, as that of
Abraham Lincoln. Poets and orators, artists and historians, have tried to depict his character and illustrate his
career, but the great epic of his life has yet to be written.
We are probably too near him in point of time fully to com-
prehend and appreciate his greatness, and the influence he
is to exert upon his country and the world. The storms
which marked his tempestuous career have scarcely yet fully
subsided, and the shock of his dramatic death is still felt ;
but as the clouds of dust and smoke which filled the air during his life clear away, his character will stand out in bolder
relief and more perfect outline. I write with the hope that
I may contribute something which shall aid in forming a just
estimate of his character, and a true appreciation of his
services.

Abraham Lincoln was born to a very humble station in life, and his early surroundings were rude and rough, but his ancestors for generations had been of that tough fiber, and vigorous physical organization and mental energy, so often found among the pioneers on the frontier of American civilization. His forefathers removed from Massachusetts to Pennsylvania, in the first half of the seventeenth century; and from Pennsylvania some members of the family moved to Virginia, and settled in the valley of the Shenandoah, in the county of Rockingham, whence his immediate ancestors came to Kentucky. For several generations they kept on the crest of the wave of Western settlement. The family were English, and came from Norfolk County, England, in about the year 1638, when they settled in Hingham, Massachusetts. Mordecai Lincoln, the English emigrant who thus settled in Massachusetts, removed afterwards to Pennsylvania, and was the great-great-grandfather of the President. His son John, who was the great-grandfather of the President, moved to Virginia, and had a son Abraham, the grandfather of the President. He and his son Thomas moved, in 1782, from Rockingham County, Virginia, to Kentucky.[1] It was in the same year that General George

---

1. The following statement, of which a fac-simile is now before me, was drawn up by Mr. Lincoln, at the request of J. W. Fell, of Bloomington, Illinois :

I was born Feb. 12, 1809, in Hardin County, Kentucky. My parents were both born in Virginia, of undistinguished families—second families, perhaps I should say. My mother, who died in my tenth year, was of a family of the name of Hanks, some of whom now reside in Adams, and others in Macon Counties, Illinois. My paternal grandfather, Abraham Lincoln, emigrated from Rockingham County, Virginia, to Kentucky, about 1781 or '2, where, a year or two later, he was killed by Indians, not in battle, but by stealth, when he was laboring to open a farm in the forest. His ancestors, who were Quakers, went to Virginia from Berks County, Pennsylvania. An effort to identify them with the New England family of the same name, ended in nothing more definite than a similarity of Christian names in both families, such as Enoch, Levi, Mordecai, Solomon, Abraham, and the like.

My father, at the death of his father, was but six years of age, and he grew up literally without education. He removed from Kentucky to what is now Spencer County, Indiana, in my eighth year. We reached our new home about the time the state came into the Union. It was a wild region, with many bears and other wild animals still in the woods. There I grew up. There were some schools,so called,but no qualification was ever required of a teacher beyond "*readin', writin', and cipherin'*" to the Rule of Three. If a straggler supposed to understand Latin happened to sojourn

Rogers Clark captured Kaskaskia, and on the 12th of September, 1782, Patrick Henry, Governor of Virginia, appointed John Todd commandant of the county of Illinois, then a part of Virginia. These ancestors of the President were rough, hardy, fearless men, and familiar with woodcraft ; men who could endure the extremes of fatigue and exposure, who knew how to find food and shelter in the forest ; brave, self-reliant, true and faithful to their friends, and dangerous to their enemies.

The grandfather of the President and his son Thomas emigrated to Kentucky in 1781 or 1782, and settled in Mercer county. This grandfather is named in the surveys of Daniel Boone as having purchased of the United States five hundred acres of land.[1]

A year or two after this settlement in Kentucky, Abraham Lincoln, having erected a log cabin near " Bear Grass

in the neighborhood, he was looked upon as a wizard. There was absolutely nothing to excite ambition for education. Of course, when I came of age I did not know much. Still somehow, I could read, write, and cipher to the Rule of Three, but that was all. I have not been to school since. The little advance I now have upon this store of education, I have picked up from time to time under the pressure of necessity.

I was raised to farm work, which I continued till I was twenty-two. At twenty-one I came to Illinois, and passed the first year in Macon County. Then I got to New Salem, at that time in Sangamon, now in Menard County, where I remained a year as a sort of clerk in a store. Then came the Black Hawk war, and I was elected a Captain of Volunteers—a success which gave me more pleasure than any I have had since. I went [through] the campaign, was elated, ran for the Legislature the same year (1832), and was beaten—the only time I have ever been beaten by the people. The next, and three succeeding biennial elections, I was elected to the Legislature. I was not a candidate afterwards. During this legislative period I had studied law, and removed to Springfield to practice it. In 1846 I was once elected to the Lower House of Congress. Was not a candidate for re-election. From 1849 to 1854, both inclusive, practiced law more assiduously than ever before. Always a Whig in politics, and generally on the Whig electoral tickets, making active canvasses. I was losing interest in politics, when the repeal of the Missouri Compromise aroused me again. What I have done since then is pretty well known.

If any personal description of me is thought desirable, it may be said, I am in height, six feet, four inches, nearly ; lean in flesh, weighing, on an average, one hundred and eighty pounds : dark complexion, with coarse black hair, and gray eyes. No other marks or brands recollected.   Yours very truly,

                                                                A. LINCOLN.

1. " Abraham Lincoln enters 500 acres of land on a Treasury warrant on the south side of Licking Creek or River, in Kentucky." See the original Field Book of Daniel Boone, in possession of the Wisconsin Historical Society.

Fort," the site of the present city of Louisville, began to open up his farm. Shortly after this, he was one day, while at work in the field, waylaid, shot, and instantly killed, by a party of Indians. Thomas Lincoln, born in 1778, and the father of the President, was in the field with his father when he fell. Mordecai and Josiah, his elder brothers, were near by in the forest. Mordecai, startled by the shot, saw his father fall, and, running to the cabin, seized the loaded rifle, rushed to one of the loop-holes cut through the logs of the cabin, and saw the Indian who had fired; he had just caught the boy, Thomas, and was running towards the forest. Pointing the rifle through the logs, and aiming at a silver medal on the breast of the Indian, Mordecai fired. The Indian fell, and the boy, springing to his feet, ran to the open arms of his mother, at the cabin door. Meanwhile, Josiah, who had run to the fort for aid, returned with a party of settlers, who brought in the body of Abraham Lincoln, and the Indian who had been shot. From this time throughout his life, Mordecai was the mortal enemy of the Indians, and, it is said, sacrificed many in revenge for the murder of his father.

It was in the midst of such scenes that the ancestors of the President were nurtured. They were contemporaries of Daniel Boone, of Simon Kenton, and other border heroes and Indian fighters on the frontiers, and were often engaged in those desperate conflicts between the Indians and the settlers, which gave to Kentucky the suggestive name of " the dark and bloody ground." [1]

These Kentucky hunters, of which the grandfather and the father of the President are types, were a very remarkable class of men. They were brave, sagacious, and self-reliant, ready in the hour of danger, frank, generous and hospitable. Tough and hardy, with his trusty rifle always in his hands or

1. It is a curious fact that the grandfather of the President should have been a comrade of Daniel Boone in Kentucky, and that the President and a grandson of Boone should have been fellow soldiers in the Black Hawk war; both volunteers from Illinois. See Major Robert Anderson's manuscript sketch of the Black Hawk war (quoted hereafter), in possession of the Chicago Historical Society.

by his side, his long, keen knife always in his belt, and his faithful hunting-dog his constant companion, of greater endurance and of far superior intellect, the Kentucky hunter could outrun his Indian enemy, or whip him in a man to man fight. This man, who has driven away or killed the Indian, who has cleared the forests, broken up and reclaimed the wilderness, and whose type still survives in the pioneer, is one of the most picturesque figures in American history. From this sort of ancestry have sprung Andrew Jackson and David Crockett, Benton and Clay, Grant and Lincoln.

Thomas Lincoln was married on the 2d of September, 1806, to Nancy Hanks, she being twenty-three and he twenty-eight years of age. They were married by the Rev. Jesse Head, a Methodist clergyman, near Springfield, Kentucky. She has been described as a brunette, with dark hair, regular features, and soft, sparkling hazel eyes. Her ancestors were of English descent, and they, like the Lincolns, had emigrated from Virginia to Kentucky. Thomas and his wife settled on Rock Creek farm, in Hardin County; and here, on the 12th of February, 1809, Abraham Lincoln was born. He was the second child, having an older sister, named Sarah. He had, besides, a younger brother, named Thomas, who died in infancy.

The ancestors of President Lincoln for several generations were farmers, and, as has already been stated, his grandfather purchased from the United States five hundred acres of land. His father, Thomas, on the 18th of October, 1817, entered a quarter-section of government land; and President Lincoln left, as a part of his estate, a quarter-section which he had received by patent from the United States for services rendered as a volunteer in the Black Hawk war. So that this humble pioneer family for three generations owned land, by direct grant from the government, and in that sense may be said to have belonged to "the landed gentry."

It is curious to note in this race of Lincolns many of the same strong and hardy traits of character which have marked the founders of influential historic families in older nations,

2

and especially among the English.   Had Abraham Lincoln
been born in England or in Normandy, or on the Rhine, some
centuries ago, he might have been the founder of a baronial
family, perhaps of a royal dynasty.   He could have wielded
with ease the battle-axe of "Richard of the Lion Heart," or
the two-handed sword of Guy, the first Earl of Warwick,
some of whose characteristics were his also.   Indeed, the
difference between such men as Boone, and Kenton, and
Abraham Lincoln, the grandfather of the President, on the
one hand, and the early Warwicks, the Douglases and the
Percys on the other, is that the Kentucky heroes were far
better men and of a more advanced civilization.

In 1816, the year in which Indiana was admitted into
the Union, the family of Lincoln removed from Kentucky
to Spencer County, in the former state.   It was a long, hard,
weary journey.   Many streams were to be forded, and a part
of the way was through the primeval forest, where they were
often compelled to cut their path with the axe.   At the time
of this removal the lad Abraham was in his eighth year, but
tall, large and strong of his age.   The first things he had
learned to use were the axe and the rifle, and with these he
was already able to render important assistance to his parents
on the journey, and in building up their new home.   The
family settled near Gentryville, and built their log-cabin on
the top of an eminence which sloped gently away on every
side.   The landscape was beautiful, the soil rich, and in a
short time some land was cleared and a crop of corn and
vegetables raised.   The struggle for life and its few comforts was in this wilderness a very hard one, and none but
those of the most vigorous constitution could succeed.   The
trials, privations, and hardships incident to clearing, breaking up, and subduing the soil and establishing a home, so far
away from all the necessaries of life, taxed the strength and
endurance of all to the utmost.   Bears, deer and other sorts
of wild game were abundant, and contributed largely to the
support of the family.

Mrs. Lincoln, the mother of the President, is said to have been in her youth a woman of beauty. She was by nature refined, and of far more than ordinary intellect. Her friends spoke of her as being a person of marked and decided character. She was unusually intelligent, reading all the books she could obtain. She taught her husband, as well as her son Abraham, to read and write.[1] She was a woman of deep religious feeling, of the most exemplary character, and most tenderly and affectionately devoted to her family. Her home indicated a degree of taste and a love of beauty exceptional in the wild settlement in which she lived, and, judging from her early death, it is probable that she was of a physique less hardy than that of most of those by whom she was surrounded. But in spite of this she had been reared where the very means of existence were to be obtained but by a constant struggle, and she had learned to use the rifle and the tools of the backwoods farmer, as well as the distaff, the cards, and the spinning wheel. She could not only kill the wild game of the woods, but she could also dress it, make of the skins clothes for her family and prepare the flesh for food. Hers was a strong, self-reliant spirit, which commanded the respect as well as the love of the rugged people among whom she lived. She died on the 5th of October, 1818, aged thirty-five years. Two children, Abraham, and his sister, Sarah, alone survived her.

The country burying-ground where she was laid, half a mile from their log cabin home, had been selected perhaps by herself, and was situated on the top of a forest-covered hill. There, beneath the dark shade of the woods, and under a majestic sycamore, they dug the grave of the mother of Abraham Lincoln. The funeral ceremonies were very plain and simple, but solemn withal, for nowhere does death seem so deeply impressive as in such a solitude. At the time no clergyman could be found in or near the settlement to perform the usual religious rites. But this devoted mother had carefully instructed Abraham to read the Bible,

1. John Hanks.

and to write; and perhaps the first practical use the boy made of the acquisition was to write a letter to David Elkin, a traveling preacher whom the family had known in Kentucky, begging him to come and perform religious services over his mother's grave. The preacher came, but not until some months afterwards, traveling many miles on horseback through the wild forest to reach their residence; and then the family, with a few friends and neighbors, gathered in the open air under the great sycamore beneath which they had laid the mother's remains. A funeral sermon was preached, hymns were sung, and such rude but sincere and impressive services were held as are usual among the pioneers of the frontier.

His mother's death and these sad and solemn rites made an impression on the mind of the son as lasting as life. She had found time amidst her weary toil and the hard struggle of her busy life, not only to teach him to read and to write, but to impress ineffaceably upon him that love of truth and justice, that perfect integrity and reverence for God, for which he was noted all his life. These virtues were ever associated in his mind with the most tender love and respect for his mother. "All that I am, or hope to be," he said, "I owe to my angel mother."

The common free schools which now so closely follow the heels of the pioneer and settler in the western portions of the republic had not then reached Indiana. An itinerant teacher sometimes "straggled" into a settlement, and if he could teach "readin', writin', and cipherin'" to the rule of three, he was deemed qualified to set up a school. With teachers thus qualified, Lincoln attended school at different times; in all about twelve months. Among anecdotes relating to this period, there is one that peculiarly illustrates his kindness and his readiness of invention. A poor, diffident girl, who spelled *definite* with a *y*, was threatened and frightened by the rude teacher. Lincoln, with a significant look, putting one of his long fingers to his eye, enabled her to change the letter in time to escape punishment. He early manifested the most eager desire to learn. He acquired knowledge with great facility. What he learned he learned thoroughly, and everything he had once acquired was always at his command.

There were no libraries, and but few books, in the "back settlements" in which he lived. Among the few volumes which he found in the cabins of the illiterate families by which he was surrounded were the Bible, Bunyan's "Pilgrim's Progress," Weems' "Life of Washington," and the poems of Robert Burns. These he read over and over again, until they became as familiar as the alphabet. The Bible has been at all times the *one* book in every home and cabin in the republic; yet it was truly said of Lincoln that no man, clergyman or otherwise, could be found so familiar with this book as he. This is apparent, both in his conversation and his writings. There is hardly a speech or state paper of his in which allusions and illustrations taken from the Bible do not appear. Burns he could quote from end to end. Long afterwards he wrote a most able lecture upon this, perhaps next to Shakespeare, his favorite poet.

His father afterwards married Mrs. Sally Johnson, of Kentucky, a widow with three children. She was a noble woman, sensible, affectionate, and tenderly attached to her step-son. She says of him: "He read diligently. * * * He read everything he could lay his hands on, and when he came across a passage that struck him, he would write it down on boards, if he had no paper, and keep it until he had got paper. Then he would copy it, look at it, commit it to memory, and repeat it." He kept a scrap-book, into which he copied everything which particularly pleased him. His step-mother adds: "He never gave me a cross word or look, and never refused, in fact or appearance, to do anything I requested of him." He loved to study more than to hunt, although his skill with the rifle was well known, for while yet a boy he had brought down with his father's rifle, a wild turkey at which he had shot through an opening between the logs of the cabin.

The family consisted now of his father and step-mother, his sister Sarah, sometimes called Nancy, the three children of his step-mother, and himself. The names of Mrs. Johnson's children were John, Sarah, and Alexander. They all went to school together, sometimes walking four or five miles, and taking with them for their dinner, cakes made of the coarse meal of the Indian corn (maize), and known as "corn dodgers." The settlers used the phrase "corn dodgers and common doings," to indicate ordinary fare, as distinguished from the luxury of "white bread and chicken fixings." In these years he wore a cap made from the skin of the coon or squirrel, buckskin breeches, a hunting shirt of deerskin, or a linsey-woolsey shirt, and very coarse cowhide shoes. His food was the "corn dodger" and the game of the forests and prairies. The tools he most constantly used were the axe, the maul, the hoe and the plough. His life was one of constant and hard manual labor.

The settlers on the frontier, both in Indiana and Illinois, whose homes dotted the edges of the timber, or were pitched along the banks of streams, were so far apart at that time that they could rarely see the smoke from each other's cabins. The mother with her own hands carded and spun the rolls of flax and wool on her own spinning-wheel. She and her daughters wove the cloth, dyed it, and made up the garments her children wore. The utensils of the farm and the furniture of the cabin were rude, primitive, and often home-made. Pewter plates and wooden trenchers were used. The tea and coffee cups were made of japanned tin; these, and the shells of the gourd, were the usual drinking-vessels. In those days Lincoln ate his

> "Milk and bread
> With pewter spoon and bowl of wood,
> On the door-stone, gray and rude."

The wild thorn and the acacia furnished a good substitute for pins. The axe, the rifle, the maul, and the plough were the farmer's tools and means of livelihood. Every child, boy or girl, was early trained to habits of industry. The people were kind and neighborly, always ready to help one another, and were frugal, industrious, and moral. There was a quick sense of justice among them. No gross wrong, fraud, or injustice, but was promptly punished, and, if too often repeated, the offender was expelled from the community.

Young Abraham borrowed of the neighbors and read every book he could hear of in the settlement within a wide circuit. If by chance he heard of a book that he had not read, he would walk many miles to borrow it. Among other volumes, he borrowed of one Crawford, Weems' "Life of Washington." Reading it with the greatest eagerness, he took it to bed with him in the loft of the cabin, and read on until his nubbin of tallow candle had burned out. Then he placed the book between the logs of the cabin, that it might be at hand as soon as there was light enough in the morning to enable him to read. But during the night a violent rain came on, and he awoke to find his book wet through and through. Drying it as well as he could, he went to Crawford and told him of the mishap, and, as he had no money to pay for it, offered to work out the value of the injured volume. Crawford fixed the price at three days' work, and the future President pulled corn three days, and thus became the owner of the fascinating book. He thought the labor well invested. He read, over and over again, this graphic and enthusiastic sketch of Washington's career, and no boy ever turned over the pages of Cooper's "Leather Stocking Tales" with more intense delight than that with which Lincoln read of the exploits and adventures and virtues of this American hero. Following his plough in breaking the prairie, he pondered over the story of Washington and longed to imitate him. Perhaps there is no biography in the language better calculated to exert a lasting influence on an ingenuous and ambitious boy, situated as he then was, than this of Weems'. Its enthusiasm was contagious, and

Lincoln began to dream of being himself a doer of great deeds. Why might not he also be a soldier and a patriot? Bred in solitude, brooding and thoughtful, he began very early to study the means of success, and to prepare himself for a life which, as we shall see by and by, he early had a presentiment was to be an eventful one.

He now set himself resolutely to learn, to educate himself. It has been a matter of surprise that, with such meagre opportunities, he became a man of such general intelligence and culture. But when it is remembered that, united with an intense desire to learn, he had great facility in acquisition; that he early formed the important habit of learning thoroughly and going to the bottom of everything he studied; and that his memory was both ready and tenacious enough to enable him to retain forever what he had once learned; it will not seem so surprising. His habits of study, of constant investigation and acquisition, he retained up to the day of his death. He studied Euclid, Algebra, and Latin, when traveling the circuit as a lawyer. He began early to exercise himself in writing prose and in making speeches. One of the companions of his boyhood says: " He was always reading, writing, cyphering, writing poetry." "He would go to the store of an afternoon and evening, and his jokes and stories were so odd, so witty, so humorous, that all the people of the town would gather around him." [1] * * * * " He would sometimes keep his crowd until midnight." [2] " He was a great reader, and a good talker."

In after life, when pronouncing a eulogy on Henry Clay, whose opportunities for education at schools were little better than his own, Lincoln said: " His example teaches us that one can scarcely be so poor, but that, if he will, he can acquire sufficient education to get through the world respectably." [3] A truth of which he himself furnished a still more striking illustration.

1. Dennis Hanks.

2. " I would get tired, want to go home, curse him for staying."—Dennis Hanks.

3. See Lincoln's Eulogy on Henry Clay, in July, 1852.

In practicing his speeches on political and other subjects, he made them so amusing and attractive that his father had to forbid his speaking during working hours, "for," said he, "when Abe begins to speak, all the hands flock to hear him."

He attended court at Boonville, the county seat of Warwick County, to witness a trial for murder, at which one of the Breckenridges, from Kentucky, made a very eloquent speech for the defence. The boy was carried away with intense admiration, and was so enthusiastic, that, although a perfect stranger, he could not refrain from expressing his admiration to Breckenridge. He wished he could be a lawyer, and went home and dreamed of courts, and got up mock trials, at which he would defend imaginary prisoners. Several of his companions at this period of his life, as well as those who knew him after he went to Illinois, declare that he was often heard to say, not in joke, but seriously, as if he were deeply impressed, rather than elated with the idea: " I shall some day be President of the United States." [1]

In March, 1826, Lincoln was seventeen years old. At that time, from specimens of his writing in the possession of the author, he wrote a clear, neat, legible hand, which is instantly and easily recognized as his by those familiar with Lincoln's handwriting when President. He was quick at figures, and could readily and accurately solve any and all problems of arithmetic up to, and including, the "rule of three." [2] He studied, at about this time, the theory of surveying. Afterwards, and after his removal to Illinois,

1. I have myself heard from many of Lincoln's old friends, that he often said, while still an obscure man : " Some day I shall be President." He undoubtedly had, for years, some presentiment of this.

2. I have in my possession, a few pages from his manuscript "Book of Examples in Arithmetic." One of these is dated March 1, 1826, and headed "Discount," and then follows in his careful handwriting, *first;* "A definition of Discount," *second;* "Rules for its computation," *third;* "Proofs and Various Examples," worked out in figures etc.; then " Interest on money" is treated in the same way, all in his own handwriting. I doubt whether it would be easy to find among scholars of our common or high schools, or any school of boys of the age of seventeen, a better written specimen of this sort of work, or a better knowledge of figures than is indicated by this book of Lincoln's, written at the age of seventeen.

as we shall see, he became like Washington, a good practical surveyor.[1]

In the spring of 1828, young Lincoln, in the employ of the proprietor of Gentryville, and in company with Allen, a son of Mr. Gentry, made a trip to New Orleans. They made the descent of the Mississippi in a flat-boat loaded with bacon and other farm produce. This was his first opportunity of seeing the world outside of the little settlement in which he lived. Having disposed very successfully of their cargo and boat, the young adventurers returned home by steamboat.

Living thus on the extreme frontier, mingling with the rude, hard-working, simple, honest backwoodsmen, while he soon became superior in knowledge to all around him, he was at the same time an expert in the use of every implement of agriculture and woodcraft. As an axe-man he was unequalled. He grew up strong in body, healthful in mind, with no bad habits, no stain of intemperance, profanity or vice. He used neither tobacco nor intoxicating drinks, and thus living, he grew to be six feet and four inches high, and a giant in strength. In all athletic sports he had no equal. His comrades say "he could strike the hardest blow with axe or maul, jump higher and further, run faster than any of his fellows, and there was no one, far or near, could lay him on his back."[2]

Among these rough people he was always popular. He early developed that wonderful power of narration and story-telling, for which he was all his life distinguished. This, and his kindness and good-nature, made him a welcome guest at every fireside and in every cabin. A well authenticated incident illustrating his kindness occurred while he lived near

1. I have also in my possession, the book from which he learned the art of surveying. It is entitled, "The Theory and Practice of Surveying, by Robert Gibson." It was published by Evert Duyckinck, New York, in 1814, as appears from the title page. Lincoln's name, in his own handwriting, appears in several places and on blank leaves of the book.

2. "He could strike with an axe," says old Mr. Wood, "a heavier blow than any man." * * "He could sink an axe deeper than any of his fellows."

Gentryville. Going home with a companion, late on a cold night, they found an acquaintance dead drunk in the road. Although his companion refused assistance, young Lincoln would not leave the drunken man, but, lifting him in his long, stalwart arms to his shoulders, he carried him a considerable distance to the cabin of Dennis Hanks, and there warmed him and brought him to consciousness. The poor fellow often afterwards declared : " Abe Lincoln's strength and kindness saved my life."

CHAPTER II.

LIFE AT NEW SALEM.

THE LINCOLN FAMILY REMOVE TO ILLINOIS.— ABRAHAM'S SECOND
TRIP TO NEW ORLEANS.— LIFE AT NEW SALEM.— JACK ARM-
STRONG AND THE CLARY GROVE BOYS.— BLACK HAWK WAR.—
LINCOLN ACQUIRES THE NAME OF "HONEST ABE."—POSTMASTER
AT SALEM.— TRUST FUNDS.— STUDIES LAW.— A SURVEYOR.—
STORY OF ANNE RUTLEDGE.— ELECTED TO THE LEGISLATURE.

IN the spring of 1830, the Lincoln family removed from
Indiana to Illinois, and settled near Decatur, in Macon
County.   The family and their personal effects were transported by an ox-team, consisting of four yoke of oxen,
which were driven by the future President.

Young Lincoln helped to build a cabin for his father, and
to break up, fence, and plant a portion of the farm—splitting
the rails for the enclosure himself.   He was now in his
twenty-second year, and living in the land of the Illinii,
which signifies the land of full grown men ; as an example
of such in size, strength, and capacity, one might search the
country through and not find his equal.   Up to this time all
his earnings, with the exception of his own very frugal support, had gone to the maintenance of his father and family.
Ambitious to make his way in the world, he now asked permission to strike out for himself, and to seek his own
fortune.

His father, after several changes, finally settled near
"Goosenest Prairie," in Coles County.   There he made his
home, until his death, in 1851, at the age of seventy-three.
He lived to see his son one of the most prominent lawyers,

and one of the most distinguished men of the state. During his life this son was continually performing for him acts of kindness and generosity. He shared in the prosperity, and his pride was gratified in the rising fortunes of his son, who often sent money and other presents to his father and mother, bought land for them, and always treated them with the kindest consideration.

When, in 1830, Lincoln became a citizen of Illinois, this great commonwealth, now the third or fourth state in the Union, and treading fast upon the heels of Ohio and Pennsylvania, was on the frontier, with a population a little exceeding one hundred and fifty thousand. In 1860, when Lincoln was elected President, it had nearly two millions, and was rapidly becoming the center of the republic.

Perhaps he was fortunate in selecting Illinois as his home. Touching on the northeast the vast chain of lakes through which passes to the Hudson and to the St. Lawrence the commerce of the valley of the Mississippi, and having that river along its entire western boundary, more than five hundred miles in length ; on the south the Ohio, reaching eastward to the mountains of Pennsylvania and Virginia ; while from the west comes to its shores the Missouri, bringing for three thousand miles the waters of the springs of the Rocky Mountains ; this was the Illinois in which he settled ; then a wilderness, but destined to become in the near future the keystone of the Federal arch. Being thus situated, the National Union was to this state an obvious necessity, and Lincoln, as we shall see, early and always recognized this fact. He realized that his own state, with its vast products, must seek the markets of the world by the Mississippi and the Gulf of Mexico, as well as by the Great Lakes and the Hudson, but never through foreign territory. He early declared that no foreign flag or custom house must ever intervene between Illinois and salt water. To these lakes and rivers encircling her with their mighty arms, is Illinois indebted for her prosperity. Her rich soil, her emerald prairies, her streams fringed with stately forests, have made her the emigrant's paradise. And this land so attractive and beautiful, lacked not the charm of early historic association. Before Penn had pitched his tent on the banks of the Delaware, LaSalle had found his way around the chain of lakes to Chicago, and erected Fort St. Louis on the banks of the Illinois. The settlement of Kaskaskia and Cahokia was contemporaneous with the founding of Philadelphia.

Young Lincoln, although a thoughtful, dreamy youth, would, when brooding over the future, have been almost as unlikely to anticipate the marvelous growth of the state, as to foresee his own still more wonderful elevation. When the sturdy blows of his axe resounded through the primeval forests, or while he lay on the grass at his nooning, with his ear to the earth, one would like to know whether he heard

> " The sound of that advancing multitude,
> Which soon should fill these deserts ; from the ground
> Come up the laugh of children, the soft voice
> Of maidens, and the sweet and solemn hymn
> Of Sabbath worshippers."

Did he hear this ? If so, he was soon awakened to the stern necessities of the hour. Day dreams would bring neither food nor clothing.

Leaving his father's cabin and seeking abroad for employment, he was engaged by one Denton Offutt to aid in taking a flat-boat loaded with provisions to New Orleans. In April, 1831, the boat reached New Salem, on the Sangamon, and lodged on the dam which had been erected across the stream. When the owner had given up all hope of being able to get the craft over the dam, Lincoln, by the exercise of that ingenuity of invention for which he was ever distinguished, devised a means for the extrication of the boat, and it passed on safely to the Illinois and down the Mississippi to New Orleans.

On this his second visit, he for the first time observed slavery in its most brutal and revolting form. New Orleans was a slave mart, and his companion[1] reports that Lincoln then

1. John Hanks.

witnessed for the first time the spectacle of the chaining together and whipping of slaves. He saw families sold, the separation forever of husband and wife, of parent and child. When we recall how deeply he always sympathized with suffering, brute as well as human, and his strong love of justice, we can realize how deeply he was affected by these things. His companions on this trip to New Orleans have attempted to describe his indignation and grief. They said, " his heart bled," * * * " he was mad, thoughtful, abstracted, sad and depressed."

Lincoln often declared to his intimate friends that he was from boyhood superstitious. He said that the near approach of the important events in his life were indicated by a presentiment or a strange dream, or in some other mysterious way it was impressed upon him that something important was to occur. There is a tradition that on this visit to New Orleans he and his companion, John Hanks, visited an old fortune teller, a Voudou negress. Tradition says that during the interview she became very much excited, and after various predictions exclaimed: " You will be President, and all the negroes will be free." That the old Voudou negress should have foretold that the visitor would be President is not at all incredible. She doubtless told this to many aspiring lads, but the prophecy of the freedom of the slaves requires confirmation.[1]

On his return from New Orleans, in July, 1831, he was employed by Offutt to take charge of a country store at New

1. The author wrote to William H. Herndon, the partner of the President, inquiring if he had heard of the tradition referred to in the text. In the reply, dated October 21, 1882, Herndon said: " It *seems* to me *just now* that I once heard of the fortune-telling story, but can not state when I heard it, nor from whom I got it. It *seems* that John Hanks, who was with Lincoln at New Orleans in 1831, told me the story. At that time and place Lincoln was made an anti-slavery man. He saw a slave, a beautiful mulatto girl, sold at auction. She was *felt over, pinched, trotted* around to show to bidders that said article was sound, etc. Lincoln walked away from the sad, inhuman scene with a deep feeling of *unsmotherable* hate. He said to John Hanks this: 'By God! If I ever get a chance to hit that institution, I'll hit it hard, John.' He got his chance, and *did hit it hard.* John Hanks, who was two or three times examined by me, told me the above facts about the negro girl and Lincoln's declaration. There is no doubt about this. As to the fortune-telling story, I do not affirm anything or deny anything."

Salem, a small village near the Sangamon River. In August of the same year, he acted as clerk of the election. He remained as a salesman with Offutt until the spring of 1832. He was a great favorite, both with his employer and his customers. Anecdotes of his scrupulous honesty and his bravery in protecting women from annoyance by bullies, are so numerous that we have not space to relate them. Offutt often declared that his clerk, or salesman, knew more than any man in the United States, and that he could outrun, whip or throw any man in the county. These boasts came to the ears of "The Clary Grove Boys," a set of rude, roystering, good-natured fellows, who lived in and around "Clary's Grove," a settlement near New Salem. Their leader was Jack Armstrong, a great, square-built fellow, strong as an ox, and who was believed by his partisans to be able to whip any man on the Sangamon River. The issue was thus made between Lincoln and Armstrong as to which was the better man, and although Lincoln tried to avoid such contests, nothing but an actual trial could settle the question among their partisans. And so they met and wrestled for some time, without any decided advantage on either side. Finally Jack resorted to some foul play which roused Lincoln's indignation. Putting forth his whole strength, he seized the great bully by the throat, and holding him at arm's length, shook him like a boy. The "Clary Grove Boys," who made up most of the crowd of the lookers-on, were ready to pitch in, on behalf of their champion, and a general onslaught upon Lincoln was threatened. Lincoln backed up against Offutt's store, and was ready, calmly awaiting the attack of the whole crowd. But his cool courage touched the manhood of Jack Armstrong. He stepped forward, seized Lincoln's hand and shook it heartily as he declared; "Boys! Abe Lincoln is the best fellow that ever broke into this settlement. He shall be one of us." From that time on, Jack Armstrong was Lincoln's man and his most willing thrall. His hand, his table, his purse, his vote, and that of the "Clary Grove Boys," belonged to Lincoln. Lincoln's popularity with them was unbounded, and his rule was just. He would have fair play, and he repressed the violence and brutality of these rough fellows to an extent which would have been impossible to another man. He could stop a fight and quell a riot among these rude neighbors when all others failed.

What made Lincoln so popular with the " Clary Grove Boys " ? He did not use tobacco, nor drink, nor gamble, nor fight except when he was obliged to, and yet the rough fellows almost worshipped him. Why ? He was brave, he could fight, and physically he was their superior, but he indulged in none of their vices, nor did he flatter them. Although he was their companion, he made them respect him. He treated them like men, and always brought out the best there was in them. They felt his moral and intellectual superiority, but they also felt that he did not despise them, and that he sympathized with them. In a certain sense he was one of them, but he was their ideal, their hero.

A fellow-clerk in Offutt's store, a Mr. Green, declares that Lincoln's talk showed that he was, even then, dreaming of " a great life, and a great destiny." He, at this time, although extremely poor, took, and read, the Louisville *Journal*, edited by George D. Prentice, a man who for wit and repartee has, perhaps, never had his superior among the editors of the United States.

In the spring of 1832, Offutt having failed, Lincoln was again out of employment. During the spring and summer, great excitement and alarm prevailed in Northern Illinois, on account of the Black Hawk war. There is nowhere a more beautiful, fertile, and picturesque valley, than the valley of Rock River, in Northern Illinois. It had been the hunting-ground and home of the Sac tribe of Indians of which Black Hawk was the chief. The tribe for several years had been living on their reservation, west of the Mississippi, but this brave warrior and skillful leader, uniting several tribes under his leadership, determined to return to the old home, and re-occupy the old hunting-grounds. Crossing the Miss-

3

issippi with his warriors, several white families were murdered, and the whole state was alarmed. John Reynolds, Governor of Illinois, issued his proclamation, calling for volunteers to help the Federal troops drive the Indians out of the state. Lincoln promptly volunteered, and his friends, the " Clary Grove Boys," soon made up a company.

The volunteers gathered at Rushville, in Schuyler County,—at which place they were to be organized—and elected officers. Lincoln was a candidate for the place of captain, and in opposition to him was one William Kirkpatrick. The mode of election was novel. By agreement, each candidate walked off to some distance, and took position by himself ; the men were then to form, and those who voted for Lincoln were to stand in a line with him, and those who voted for Kirkpatrick to range on a line with their candidate. When the lines were formed, Lincoln's was three times as long as that of Kirkpatrick, and so Lincoln was declared elected. Speaking of this when President, he said that he was more gratified with this, his first success, than with any other election of his life. Neither Lincoln nor his company was in any engagement during the campaign, but there was plenty of hardship and fatigue, and some incidents occurred to illustrate his courage and power over men. Perhaps the most notable event in the campaign, so far as Captain Lincoln was concerned, was his determined and successful effort to save the life of an Indian from the infuriated soldiers.

One day there came into camp, a poor, old, hungry Indian. He had in his possession, General Cass's " safe-conduct," and certificate of friendship for the whites. But this he did not at first show, and the soldiers, suspecting him to be a spy, and exasperated by the late Indian barbarities, with the recent horrible murder by the Indians of some women and children still fresh in their minds, were about to kill him. Many of these soldiers were Kentuckians with the hereditary Indian hatred, and some, like their captain, could recall the murder by the red men, of some ancestor, or other member of their own families. In a phrensy of excitement

and blind rage, they believed, or affected to believe, that the
"safe-conduct" of the old Indian, which was now produced,
was a forgery, and they were approaching the old savage,
with muskets cocked, to dispatch him, when Lincoln rushed
forward, knocked up their weapons, and standing in front of
the victim, in a determined voice ordered them not to fire,
declaring that the Indian should not be killed. The mob,
their passions fully roused, were not so easily to be
restrained. Lincoln stood for a moment between the
Indian and a dozen muskets, and, for a few seconds, it
seemed doubtful whether both would not be shot down.
After a pause, the militia reluctantly, and like bull-dogs
leaving their prey, lowered their weapons and sullenly turned
away. Bill Green, an old comrade, said: "I never in all my
life saw Lincoln so roused before."

The time for which the company had volunteered having
expired, the men were discharged. But Black Hawk and
his warriors being still east of the Mississippi, Governor Reynolds issued a second call for troops, and Lincoln at once
responded by volunteering again, and this time he served as
a private in a company of which Elijah Iles, of Springfield,
was elected captain. This company did service as a company
of mounted rangers, and in it Lincoln served until the close
of the war. Here he met as a fellow soldier, John T. Stuart,
afterwards member of Congress, and others, who became
prominent citizens of Illinois.[1]

In their camp on the banks of Rock River, near where
the city of Dixon is now situated, there met at this time,

1. In a letter to the author, dated Springfield, Ills., December 7, 1868, Captain Iles
says: * * * "I have yours asking whether Mr. Lincoln was a member of my company in the Black Hawk war, etc. In reply, I answer he was a member of my
company during a portion of the time, and received an honorable discharge. The first
call for volunteers, Mr. Lincoln volunteered, and was elected captain. The term of
Governor Reynolds' first call being about to expire, he made a second call and the first
was then disbanded. * * * I was elected a captain of one of the companies. I
had as members of my company, General James D. Henry, John T. Stuart, and
A. Lincoln, and we were mustered into the service on the 29th of May, 1832, by
Lieutenant *Robert Anderson*, Assistant Inspector General. We reported to Colonel
Zachary Taylor, at Dixon's Ferry (on Rock River). Mr. Lincoln remained with the
company to the close of the war."

Lieutenant Colonel Zachary Taylor, Lieutenant Jefferson Davis, Lieutenant Robert Anderson, and private Abraham Lincoln of Captain Iles's company of Illinois Mounted Rangers.[1]

Lincoln and Anderson did not meet again until sometime in 1861, and after Major Anderson had evacuated Fort Sumter. He then visited Washington, and called at the White House to pay his respects to the President. After having expressed his thanks to Anderson for his conduct in South Carolina, Mr. Lincoln said: "Major, do you remember of ever meeting me before?" "No, Mr. President, I have no recollection of ever having had the pleasure before." "My memory is better than yours," said Mr. Lincoln. "You mustered me into the service of the United States, in 1832, at Dixon's Ferry, in the Black Hawk war."[2]

Father Dixon, who, as below stated, was attached to this company of mounted rangers as guide, says that in their marches, when approaching a grove or depression in which an Indian ambush might be concealed, and when scouts were sent forward to examine the cover, Lincoln was often selected for that duty, and he adds that while many, as they approached the place of suspected ambush, found an excuse for dismounting to adjust girths or saddles, Lincoln's saddle was always in order. He also states that at evening, when off duty, Lincoln was generally found sitting on the grass, with a group of soldiers eagerly listening to the stories of

1. John Dixon, who then kept the ferry across Rock River, was a guide attached to the troops. The Indians gave him the name of *Na-chu-sa*, or "White-Head." He told the author of the curious meeting mentioned in the text.

2. The author happened to be present at this interview. Colonel Robert Anderson, in a manuscript sketch of the Black Hawk war, now before me, dated May 10, 1870, and addressed to the Hon. E. B. Washburne, to whom the manuscript belongs, says: "I also mustered *Abraham Lincoln* twice into the service, and once out. He was a member of two of the Independent Companies. * * * I mustered him into the service at the mouth of Fox River (Ottawa), May 29, 1832, in Captain Elijah Iles's company. I have no recollection of Mr. Lincoln, but when President he reminded me of it. * * * William S. Hamilton, son of Alexander Hamilton, joined us with a small party of friendly Indians. * * * The Rock River country was beautiful beyond description, surpassing any thing I' ever saw in our country, Mexico, or in Europe."

which his supply seemed inexhaustible, and that he invariably declined the whiskey which his comrades, grateful for the amusement he afforded, pressed upon him.

When a member of Congress, Mr. Lincoln made a very amusing campaign speech, in which, alluding to the custom of exaggerating the military service of candidates, and ridiculing the extravagant claims to heroism set up for General Lewis Cass, then a candidate for the Presidency against General Zachary Taylor, he referred with great good humor to his own services in the Black Hawk war in the following terms:

" By the way, Mr. Speaker, did you know I am a military hero? Yes, sir; in the days of the Black Hawk war I fought, bled, and came away. Speaking of General Cass's career reminds me of my own. I was not at Stillman's defeat, but I was about as near it as Cass was to Hull's surrender; and, like him, I saw the place very soon afterwards. It is quite certain I did not break my sword, for I had none to break; but I bent my musket pretty badly on one occasion. If Cass broke his sword, the idea is he broke it in desperation. I bent my musket by accident. If General Cass went in advance of me in picking whortle-berries, I guess I surpassed him in charges upon the wild onions. If he saw any live fighting Indians, it was more than I did ; but I had a good many bloody struggles with the musquitoes, and, although I never fainted from loss of blood, I can truly say I ˙was often very hungry. Mr. Speaker, if I should ever conclude to doff whatever our democratic friends may suppose there is of black-cockade federalism about me, and thereupon they shall take me up as their candidate for the Presidency, I protest they shall not make fun of me, as they have of General Cass, by attempting to write me into a military hero."

The volunteers returned from the Black Hawk war a short time before the state election. In this expedition Lincoln had rendered himself so popular that his comrades and others insisted upon his being a candidate for the Legislature. Although not elected, he received the unanimous vote of New Salem. For member of Congress both candidates together received 206 votes, while Lincoln alone received 207 votes for the Legislature.

Left again without employment, he was induced, in association with one Berry as partner, to become the purchaser of a small store at New Salem. Berry turned out to be a dissipated, worthless fellow, and within a few months the enterprise failed, leaving Lincoln responsible for the purchase money. It was six years before he was able entirely to pay off the liabilities thus incurred.

It was while he was salesman for Offutt, and proprietor of this little store, that Mr. Lincoln acquired the *sobriquet* of " Honest Abe." Of many incidents illustrating his integrity one or two may be mentioned. One evening he found his cash overrun a little, and he discovered that in making change for his last customer, an old woman who had come in a little before sundown, he had made a mistake, not having given her quite enough. Although the amount was small, a few cents only, he took the money, immediately walked to her house, and corrected the error. At another time, on his arrival at the store in the morning, he found on the scales a weight which he remembered having used just before closing, but which was not the one he had intended to use. He had sold a parcel of tea, and in the hurry had placed the wrong weight on the scales, so that the purchaser had a few ounces less of tea than had been paid for. He immediately sent the quantity required to make up the deficiency. These and many similar incidents are told, exhibiting his scrupulous honesty in the most trifling matters, and for these the people gave him the name which clung to him through life.

In the course of the great debate between Lincoln and Douglas, in 1858, at their joint discussion at Ottawa, Douglas alluded to Lincoln's store-keeping. He said :

" I have known him for nearly twenty-four years. There were many points of sympathy between us. When we first got acquainted, I was a school-teacher at Winchester, and he a flourishing grocery-keeper at Salem." * * * " He soon got into the Legislature. I met him then, and had a sympathy with him because of the up-hill struggle we both had in life."[1]

On the 7th of May, 1833, he was appointed postmaster at New Salem. This was a small office with a weekly mail.

1. Lincoln and Douglas Debates, p. 69.

He kept the office until the station was discontinued and the place of delivery changed to Petersburg. The balance in his hands at the time of the discontinuance of the office was sixteen or eighteen dollars. This small sum was perhaps overlooked by the post-office department and was not called for until some years after Lincoln had removed to Springfield. During these years he had been in debt and very poor. So poor, indeed, that he had often been compelled to borrow money of his friends to pay for the very necessaries of life. One day an agent of the post-office called on Dr. Henry, with whom Lincoln at that time kept his law office. Knowing Mr. Lincoln's poverty, and how often he had been pressed for money, Henry says :[1] "I did not believe he had the money on hand to meet the draft, and I was about to call him aside and loan him the money, when he asked the agent to be seated a moment, while he went over to his trunk at his boarding-house, and returned with an old blue sock with a quantity of silver and copper coin tied up in it. Untying the sock, he poured the contents on the table and proceeded to count the coin, which consisted of such silver and copper pieces as the country-people were then in the habit of using in paying postage. On counting it up there was found the exact amount, to a cent, of the draft, and in the identical coin which had been received. He never used, under any circumstances, trust funds." The anecdote will recall an incident narrated by Sir Walter Scott, in the famous "Chronicles of the Canongate."[2] On the return of Craftengry, who had been absent twenty years, honest "Shanet," in triumph, hands him the fifteen shillings, she has kept sacred for him, saying: "Here they are, and Shanet has had siller, and Shanet has wanted siller, mony a time since that. The gauger has come, and the factor has come, and the butcher, and the baker. Cot bless us—just like to tear poor ould Shanet to pieces, but she took good

1. Dr. Henry gave me the details of this incident at Washington when Mr. L. was President.

2. "Waverley Novels," Black's Ed., v. 19, p. 384.

care of Mr. Craftengry's fifteen shillings." So with Mr.
Lincoln, the tailor came, the boarding-house keeper came,
and the law bookseller came, but Lincoln took good care of
Uncle Sam's post-office money.

In 1832, Lincoln bought at auction, in Springfield, a second hand copy of Blackstone's Commentaries, and began to
study law. A few weeks hard study, and he had mastered
this elementary work, and laid the foundation of a good
lawyer's education ; he then resolved to make the law his
profession. But he had neither books, nor any means of
buying them. In this dilemma he sought the advice of his
old friend, comrade and fellow soldier in the Black Hawk
war, John T. Stuart. Mr. Stuart was a prosperous and successful lawyer at Springfield, and had, for a new country, a
respectable law library. Stuart encouraged him to go on,
and generously offered to loan to him all the law books he
needed. And now, with an application which showed that
he had at last found a congenial pursuit, he devoted himself
to study.

He still lived at New Salem, some fourteen miles from
Springfield ; he walked into town to exchange one book for
another, and, it is said, he would often master thirty or forty
pages of the new book on his way home. He was often
seen seated against the trunk of a tree, or lying on the grass
under its shade, poring over his books, changing his position
as the sun advanced, so as to keep in the shadow. So
intense was his application, and so absorbed was he in his
study, that he would pass his best friends without observing
them, and some people said that Lincoln was going crazy
with hard study. He very soon began to make a practical
application of his knowledge. He bought an old form-book,
and began to draw up contracts, deeds, leases, mortgages,
and all sorts of legal instruments for his neighbors. He also
began to exercise his forensic ability in trying small cases
before justices of the peace and juries, and he soon acquired
a local reputation as a speaker, which gave him considerable
practice.

But he was able in this way to earn scarcely money enough for his maintenance. To add to his means, he again took up the study of surveying, and soon became, like Washington, a skillful and accurate surveyor. John Calhoun, an intelligent and courteous gentleman, was at that time surveyor of the County of Sangamon. He became interested in Lincoln, and appointed him as his deputy. His work was so accurate, and the settlers had such confidence in him, that he was much sought after to survey, fix and mark the boundaries of farms, and to plot and lay off new towns and villages. Among others, he plotted and laid off the town of Petersburg. His accuracy must have been attained with some difficulty, for the old settlers who survive say that when he began to survey his chain was a grape-vine. He did not speculate in the land he surveyed. Had he done so, the rapid advance in the value of real estate would have made it easy for him to make good investments. But he was not in the least like one of his appointees when President—a surveyor-general of a western territory, who bought up much of the best land, and to whom the President said: "I am told, sir, you are monarch of all you survey."

By surveying, and his small law practice, he earned his very frugal livelihood, and made some progress in reducing the debts incurred by the purchase of the store. But, in 1834, one of the notes which he had given for it was put in judgment, and the impatient creditor seized his horse, saddle and bridle, and surveying instruments, and sold them under execution. Lincoln was, it is said, somewhat discouraged, but his friends bid in and restored to him the property. One of them, who had often befriended him, and whose name was Bolin Greene, was especially kind and generous. He bid in and restored the horse, saddle, and bridle, and waited Lincoln's convenience for payment. Lincoln was a very grateful and warm-hearted man, and Bolin Greene's friendship and repeated acts of kindness touched him. Bolin Greene died a short time thereafter, and Lincoln tried to deliver a funeral oration over his remains. "When he rose to speak his voice was choked with deep emotion."[1] The tears ran down his cheeks, and he was so overcome that he could not go on. His tears were more eloquent than any words he could have spoken.

Lincoln had not grown up to manhood without the usual experiences of the tender passion. Like most young men, he had his youthful fancies ; perhaps on one occasion something which approached a " grand passion." There is more than a mere tradition, that, while residing at New Salem, he became very much attached to a prairie beauty, with the sweet and romantic name of Anne Rutledge. Irving, in his " Life of Washington," says: " before he was fifteen years old, he had conceived a passion for some unknown beauty, so serious as to disturb his otherwise well regulated mind, and to make him really unhappy." Lincoln was less precocious than Washington, or perhaps his heart was better shielded by the hard labor to which he was subjected. Something sensational and dramatic has been printed in regard to this attachment. Gossip and imagination have represented this early romance as casting a shadow over his whole after life, and as having produced something bordering upon insanity. The picture has been somewhat too highly colored, and the story made rather too tragic.

James Rutledge, one of the founders of New Salem, and who is said to have been of the distinguished South Carolina family of that name, one of whom was a signer of the " Declaration of Independence," was a warm personal friend of Lincoln. He was the father of a large family, and among the daughters was Anne, born January 7th, 1813. She is described as being a blonde, with golden hair, lips as red as the cherry, a cheek like the wild rose, with blue eyes, as sweet and gentle in manners and temper as attractive in person. Lincoln was among her suitors, and they were engaged to be married as soon as he should have finished his legal studies, and he should be admitted to the bar of the Supreme Court. But in August, 1835, she died. Her beauty and

1. W. H. Herndon.

attractions, and her early death, made a very deep impression upon him. He idealized her memory, and in his recollections of her, there was a poetry of sentiment, which might possibly have been lessened had she lived, by the prosaic realities of life.

With all his love of fun and frolic, with all his wit and humor, with all his laughter and anecdotes, Lincoln, from his youth, was a person of deep feeling, and there was always mingled with his mirth, sadness and melancholy. He always associated with the memory of Anne Rutledge the plaintive poem which in his hours of melancholy he so often repeated, and whose familiar first stanzas are as follows:

> "Oh, why should the spirit of mortal be proud?
> Like a swift fleeting meteor, a fast flying cloud,
> A flash of the lightning, a break of the wave,
> He passeth from life to his rest in the grave.

> "The leaves of the oak and the willow shall fade,
> Be scattered around, and together be laid,
> And the young and the old, and the low and the high
> Shall moulder to dust and together shall lie." [1]

Lincoln loved at twilight, or when in the country, or in solitude, or when with some confidential friend, to repeat this poem. I think he exaggerated its merits, and I attribute his great love of the poem to its association with Anne Rutledge. Several years passed after the sad death of Miss Rutledge before he married. It is not impossible that his devotion to her memory may have been, in part, the cause of so long a delay.

An old friend [2] of Lincoln long years afterwards, on one occasion when they were talking of old times at New Salem, of the Greenes and Armstrongs and Rutledges, ventured to ask him about his early attachment, to which he replied: " I loved her dearly. She was a handsome girl, and would have made a good, loving wife. She was natural, and quite intellectual, though not highly educated."

1. See Carpenter's "Six Months in the White House."

2. Isaac Cogswell.

In 1834, Lincoln was again a candidate for the Legislature, and was now elected, receiving a greater number of votes than any other man on either ticket. This is the more remarkable as among his colleagues was his old friend and comrade, John T. Stuart. Thus, at the age of twenty-five, this plain, rough, sturdy son of a pioneer found himself a member of the Illinois Legislature, and the most popular man in Sangamon County.

CHAPTER III.

THE ILLINOIS LEGISLATURE.

LINCOLN AT TWENTY-FIVE.—AT VANDALIA.—RE-ELECTED IN 1836.—
REPLIES TO FORQUER.—TO DR. EARLY.—TO COL. TAYLOR.—
STATE CAPITAL REMOVED FROM VANDALIA TO SPRINGFIELD.—
ANTI-SLAVERY PROTEST.—RE-ELECTED IN 1838.—REMOVES TO
SPRINGFIELD.—RE-ELECTED IN 1840.—PARTNERSHIP WITH JOHN
T. STUART.—RIDING THE CIRCUIT.

Up to this time Lincoln's work had been up-hill, and his
humble life had been a constant struggle with difficulties.
By heroic endeavor, by persevering effort, by fortitude and
constancy, and a resolute will, he had overcome these
difficulties, and had at length found his true vocation. He
was now to enter upon a new career. What he was he had
made himself. What he knew he owed to his own exertions.
Let us pause for a moment, and see what he was and what
were his acquirements.

We find him now, at the age of twenty-five, a vigorous,
well-developed man, with a constitution inured to toil and
hardened by exposure—a sound body upon which he could
rely for almost any amount of physical or mental labor, and
great powers of endurance. He knew the Bible by heart.
There was not a clergyman to be found so familiar with it
as he. Scarcely a speech or paper prepared by him, from
this time to his death, but contains apt allusions and striking
illustrations from the sacred book. He could repeat nearly
all the poems of Burns, and was familiar with Shakespeare,
In arithmetic, surveying, and the rudiments of other branches

45

of mathematics, he was perfectly at home. He had mastered Blackstone, Kent, and the elementary law books. He had considerable knowledge of physics and mechanics. He showed how much better it is to know thoroughly a few books, than to know many superficially. Such had been his education. He was manly, gentle, just, truthful, and honest. In conduct, kind and generous; so modest, so considerate of others, so unselfish, that every one liked him and wished him success. True, he was homely, awkward, diffident; but he was, in fact, strictly a gentleman—" in substance, at least, if not in outside polish." [1]

From the books named, and especially from the Bible, he had acquired that clear, concise, simple, nervous, Anglo-Saxon style so effective with the people, and in this he was scarcely equalled by any American writer or speaker. It is wonderful how many sentences can be found in his writings, short, striking, clear and emphatic, in which every word consists of a single syllable.

His residence at Vandalia during the session of the Legislature, and his removal to Springfield, brought him into association with many families of culture and refinement. He now met as associates men of learning and intellect. He had access to all the books he could read, and the world of English literature, history and science lay open before him. He became and continued through life a student, always seeking and constantly acquiring knowledge. He was never ashamed to acknowledge his ignorance of any subject, and he rarely lost an opportunity to remedy it. At the first session of the Legislature he took no very active part in the discussions, but was studious and observant. He said little, and learned much.

In 1836, he was again a candidate for the Legislature, and in this canvass he greatly distinguished himself. On

1. In his reply to Douglas, at Springfield, July 17, 1858, he said: " I set out in this campaign with the intention of conducting it strictly as a gentleman, in substance, at least, if not in outside polish. The latter I shall never be, but that which constitutes the inside of a gentleman, I hope I understand, and I am not less inclined to practice than another." (Lincoln and Douglas Debates, p. 57.)

one occasion there was to be a public discussion among the opposing candidates, held at the Court House at Springfield, and Lincoln, among others, was advertised to speak. This was his first appearance " on the stump " at the County Seat. There lived at this time in the most pretentious house in the town a prominent citizen with the name of George Forquer. He had been long in public life, had been a leading whig, the party to which Lincoln belonged, but had lately gone over to the democrats, and received from the democratic administration an appointment to the lucrative post of Register of the Land Office at Springfield. Upon his handsome new house he had lately placed a lightning rod, the first one ever put up in Sangamon County. As Lincoln was riding into town with his friends they passed the fine house of Forquer, and observed the novelty of the lightning rod, discussing the manner in which it protected the house from being struck by lightning.

There was a very large meeting, and there was great curiosity to hear the orator from New Salem, who, as the " Clary Grove Boys " insisted, could make a better stump speech than any man at the County Seat. A Kentuckian,[1] then lately from his native state, and who had heard Clay, Rowan, and many of the orators for which that state was then so distinguished, says: " I stood near Lincoln and heard his speech, and it struck me then, and it seems to me now, I never heard a more effective speaker."   *   *   *   " The crowd seemed to be swayed by him, as he pleased."[2]

There were seven whig and seven democratic candidates for the lower branch of the Legislature, and after several had spoken, it fell to Lincoln to close the discussion. He did it with great ability. Forquer, though not a candidate, then asked to be heard for the democrats in reply to Lincoln. He was a good speaker, and well known throughout the county. His special task that day was to attack and ridicule

1. Joshua F. Speed.

2. Joshua F. Speed. See the Lincoln Memorial Album, pp. 144, 145.

the young countryman from Salem. Turning to Lincoln, who stood within a few feet of him, he said : "This young man must be taken down, and I am truly sorry that the task devolves upon me." He then proceeded, in a very overbearing way, and with an assumption of great superiority, to attack Lincoln and his speech. He was fluent and ready with the rough sarcasm of the stump, and he went on to ridicule the person, dress, and arguments of Lincoln with so much success that Lincoln's friends feared that he would be embarrassed and overthrown. The "Clary Grove Boys," who were present to cheer, applaud, and back Lincoln, could scarcely be restrained from getting up a fight in behalf of their favorite. They and all his friends, felt that the attack was ungenerous and unmanly.

Lincoln, however, stood calm, but his flashing eye and pale cheek indicated his indignation. As soon as Forquer had closed, he took the stand and first answered his opponent's arguments, fully and triumphantly. So impressive were his words and manner that a hearer [1] believes that he can remember to this day, and repeat, some of the expressions. Among other things, he said : "The gentleman commenced his speech by saying that 'this young man,' alluding to me, must be taken down. I am not so young in years, as I am in the tricks and the trades of a politician, but," said he, pointing to Forquer, "live long or die young, I would rather die now, than, like the gentleman, change my politics, and with the change receive an office worth three thousand· dollars a year, and then," continued he, "then feel obliged to erect a lightning-rod over my house to protect a guilty conscience from an offended God."

It is difficult to-day to appreciate the effect on the old settlers, of this figure. This lightning rod was the first which most of those present had ever seen. They had slept all their lives in their cabins, in conscious security. Here was a man who seemed to these simple-minded people to be afraid to sleep in his own house, without special and extra-

1. Joshua F. Speed. Letter of 1882.

ordinary protection from Almighty God. These old settlers thought that nothing but the consciousness of guilt, the stings of a guilty conscience, could account for such timidity. Forquer and his lightning-rod were talked over in every settlement from the Sangamon to the Illinois and the Wabash. Whenever he rose to speak thereafter, they said "there is the man who dare not sleep in his own house, without a lightning-rod to keep off the vengeance of the Almighty."

Lincoln's reply to Dr. Early, a prominent democratic leader, in the same canvass, has been often spoken of as exhibiting wonderful ability, and a crushing power of sarcasm and ridicule. When he began he was embarrassed, spoke slowly, and with some hesitation and difficulty, but soon becoming warm, and excited by his subject, he forgot himself entirely, and went on with argument and wit, anecdote and ridicule, until his opponent was completely crushed.[1]   Old settlers of Sangamon County, who heard this reply, speak of his personal transformation as wonderful. When Lincoln began, they say, he seemed awkward, homely, unprepossessing. As he went on, and became excited, his figure rose to its full height, and became commanding and majestic. His plain face was illuminated and glowed with expression. His dreamy eye flashed with inspiration, and his whole person, his voice, his gestures, were full of the magnetism of powerful feeling, of conscious strength and true eloquence.

Among the democratic orators who canvassed Sangamon County in 1836, was Colonel Dick Taylor. He was a small, but very pompous little gentleman, who rode about in his carriage, neatly dressed, with many and very conspicuous ruffles to his shirt, with patent leather boots, kid gloves, some diamonds and gold studs in his linen, an immense watch-chain with many seals, charms, and pendants, and altogether in most striking contrast with the simple, and plainly clad people whom he addressed. The Colonel was a very amiable man, but pompous. Vain, and affecting to be, withal, an ex-

1. Holland's Life of Lincoln.

4

treme democrat, he had much to say of "the bone and sinew" of the land, "the hard-handed yeomanry." He was very sarcastic on the whig "aristocracy," the "rag barons," the "silk stocking gentry." Lincoln, the candidate of this so-called aristocracy, was dressed in Kentucky jeans, coarse boots, checkered shirt buttoned round his neck without a neck-tie, an old slouched hat, and certainly the last thing he or his appearance could suggest, would be that of anything aristocratic.

On one occasion when Lincoln was present, Taylor, in the midst of a most violent harangue against the whig aristocrats, made a gesture so forcibly, that he tore the buttons off his vest, and the whole magnificence of his ruffles, gold watch chain, seals, etc., burst forth, fully exposed. Taylor paused in embarrassment. Lincoln stepping to the front, and turning to Taylor, pointed to his ruffles and exclaimed, " Behold the hard-fisted democrat. Look, gentlemen, at this specimen of the bone and sinew. And here, gentlemen," said he, laying his great bony hand bronzed with work, on his own heart, "here at your service," bowing, "here is your aristocrat! here is one of your silk stocking gentry!" 'Spreading out his hands. " Here is your rag baron with his lily-white hands. Yes, I suppose," continued he, " I, according to my friend Taylor, am a bloated aristocrat." The contrast was irresistibly ludicrous, and the crowd burst into shouts of laughter and uproar. In this campaign the reputation of Lincoln as a speaker was established, and ever afterwards he was recognized as one of the great orators of the state.

The Sangamon delegation to the Legislature, there being two senators and seven members of the House—nine in all, and each over six feet high—was known as the "Long Nine," and Lincoln, being tallest of all, was called the " Sangamon Chief." Among his colleagues from Sangamon, were Edward D. Baker, afterwards member of Congress and United States Senator,—killed at Balls Bluff, and Ninian W. Edwards, son of Governor Ninian Edwards. Among his fellow-members of the House, were Stephen Arnold

Douglas, John J. Hardin, James Shields, William A. Richardson, John Logan, John A. McClernand, and others who became prominent in the state and nation. In this canvass he had received, as in 1834, the highest vote given to any man on the ticket. At the first session (1836-7), he advocated and voted for measures for opening the great ship canal from Lake Michigan to the Illinois River. This work, which would bring into exchange the commerce of the Lakes and the Mississippi, by cutting through the short portage between Lake Michigan and the Illinois River, needs but to be enlarged to the size contemplated in its original plan, to realize all, and more, than was expected from it. He also voted for a system of internal improvements by means of railroads, far, very far, in advance of the needs of the state at that time, and very much exceeding the ability of the people to pay for; yet such was the popular delusion, that the people of Sangamon County instructed their delegation to vote "for a general system of internal improvement," and not only Lincoln, but Douglas, and nearly all the prominent members, voted for this extravagant measure.[1] Orville H. Browning, then senator from Adams County, and afterwards United States senator, had the honor of opposing this system.

For the immediate constituents of Sangamon County, Lincoln and the "Long Nine " succeeded in getting a law passed removing the capital from Vandalia to Springfield. A fellow member, one of the " Nine," speaking of this measure says: "When our bill to all appearance was dead, and beyond resuscitation, * * and our friends could see no hope, Lincoln never for a moment despaired, but collecting his colleagues in his room for consultation, his practical common sense, his thorough knowledge of human nature, made him an overmatch for his compeers, and for any man I have ever known."[2]

At this session, and on the 3d of March, 1837, he began that series of anti-slavery measures which were ended and

1. See Ford's History of Illinois.
2. Robert L Wilson. See Journal of House of Representatives, 1836-7.

consummated in the "Proclamation of Emancipation," and the "Amendment of the Constitution," abolishing and prohibiting slavery forever throughout the republic. At this time it required courage to speak or write against slavery. Resolutions of an extremely violent pro-slavery character, and denunciatory of "abolitionists" and all efforts to abolish or restrict slavery, were carried through the Legislature by overwhelming majorities. The people of Illinois at that time, were made up largely of emigrants from the slave states, filled with the prejudices of that section, and the feeling against anti-slavery men was violent, and almost universal. There then existed in Illinois a body of laws against negroes, called "The Black Code," of most revolting cruelty and severity. Under these circumstances Lincoln jeopardized his popularity by drawing up and signing a solemn protest against these resolutions. But among all the members of the House, over one hundred in number, he found only one who had the courage to join him. Abraham Lincoln and Dan Stone were the only ones who had the nerve to express and record their protest against the injustice of slavery. This protest, qualified as it was to meet, if possible, the temper of the times, declared that slavery is founded on injustice and bad policy.[1]

1. The following is the protest in full. *See* House Journal of Illinois Legislature, 1836–7, pp. 817, 818.

"March 3, 1837.

" The following protest was presented to the House, which was read and ordered to be spread on the journals, to wit :

"Resolutions upon the subject of domestic slavery having passed both branches of the General Assembly at its present session, the undersigned hereby protest against the passage of the same.

" They believe that the institution of slavery is founded on both injustice and bad policy, but that the promulgation of abolition doctrine tends rather to increase than to abate its evils.

" They believe that the Congress of the United States has no power, under the ' Constitution' to interfere with the institution of slavery in the different States.

"They believe that the Congress of the United States has the power, under the ' Constitution,' to abolish slavery in the District of Columbia, but that that power ought not to be exercised, unless at the request of the people of said district.

"The differences between these opinions, and those contained in the said resolutions, is their reason for entering this protest.

"DAN STONE,

"A. LINCOLN,

"*Representatives from the county of Sangamon.*"

In 1838, Lincoln was again elected to the Legislature. One of his colleagues,[1] who made the canvass in a part of the county with him, says: " We called at nearly every house. * * * Everybody knew Lincoln. It was, then, the universal custom to keep whiskey in the house, for private use, and to treat friends. Everywhere the master of the house, addressing Lincoln, would say: ' *You* never drink, but may be your friend will take a little.'" " I never saw Lincoln drink, and he told me he never drank." [2]   He was now the acknowledged leader of his party, and they made him their candidate for speaker; but his party, the whigs, being in a minority, he was not elected.

The great service he had rendered the town of Springfield, in carrying through the law for removing the capital to that place, was gratefully appreciated, and his many friends urged him to come there to live and practice law. His old friend, John T. Stuart, a lawyer of established position and in good practice, offered him a partnership.   This offer he gladly accepted, and in April, 1837, he removed to, and made his home in Springfield.   He had been admitted to the bar of the Supreme Court in the fall of 1836, but his name does not appear on the roll of attorneys until 1837. On the 27th of April of that year he entered into partnership with Stuart, under the name of Stuart and Lincoln, and this partnership continued until the 14th day of April, 1841.[3]

His friend Speed, speaking of his entry into Springfield, says: " He rode into town on a borrowed horse, without

1. Robert L. Wilson.

2. Robert L. Wilson.

3.   "SPRINGFIELD, ILL., September 7, 1882.
" HON. ISAAC N. ARNOLD.

" *Dear Sir:*—I have received your favor of the 4th inst., and I answer.

" The partnership, between myself and Mr. Lincoln, was entered into, on the 27th day of April, 1837, and continued until the 14th day of April, 1841.

" The partnership, between Judge Logan and Mr Lincoln, was entered into on the 14th of April, 1841, and continued until about the 20th of September, 1843.

"About the 20th of September, 1843, Mr. Lincoln and William H. Herndon, entered into partnership, which continued until the death of Mr. Lincoln.

" Mr. Lincoln never had any other partner in Sangamon County, his home, and so far as I am informed, never had one elsewhere.

                    " Respectfully your friend,   JOHN T. STUART."

earthly goods, but a pair of saddle-bags, two or three law-books, and some clothing in his saddle-bags.   He came into my store, set his saddle-bags on the counter, and said:

" ' Speed, tell me what the furniture for a single bed-room will cost.'

" I took my pencil, figured it up, and found it would cost seventeen dollars.

" Lincoln replied: ' It is cheap enough, but I want to say, cheap as it is, I have not the money to pay.   But if you will credit me until Christmas, and my experiment here is a success, I will pay you then. If I fail, I will probably never be able to pay you.'

" The voice was so melancholy, I felt for him."

Lincoln was evidently suffering from one of his fits of depression and sadness.   Speed kindly replied:

" I have a very large double bed which you are perfectly welcome to share with me, if you choose."

" Where is your bed ? " said Lincoln.

" Up-stairs," replied Speed.

He took his saddle-bags on his arm, went up stairs, placed them on the floor, and came down, laughing, saying: " Speed, I am moved." [1]   The ludicrous idea of "moving " all his goods and chattels, by taking his saddle-bags up-stairs, made him as mirthful as he had been melancholy.

From that time on, Springfield was his home until when, twenty-three years thereafter, he left his humble residence to occupy the White House as President of the United States. He and Speed took their meals with William Butler, a mutual friend, and afterwards Treasurer of the State of Illinois.   In a short time, by his close application and indus-try, and by his association with Stuart, he had a good prac-tice, and attended courts in all the counties near Springfield.

We are indebted to Mr. Speed for another incident, illus-trating his kindness of heart.   Lincoln and the other mem-bers of the bar from the capital had been attending court at Christiansburg, and Speed was riding with them towards

1. Joshua F. Speed, Lincoln Memorial Album, pp. 145, 146.

Springfield. He tells us that there was quite a party of these lawyers, riding, two by two, along a country lane. Lincoln and John J. Hardin[1] brought up the rear of the cavalcade. "We had passed through a thicket of wild plum and crab-apple trees, and stopped to water our horses. Hardin came up alone.

"'Where is Lincoln,' we inquired.

"'Oh,' replied he, 'when I saw him last, he had caught two young birds, which the wind had blown out of their nest, and he was hunting the nest to put them back.'

"In a short time, Lincoln came up, having found the nest and placed the young birds in it.

"The party laughed at him, but he said; ' I could not have slept if I had not restored those little birds to their mother.'"[2]

The act was characteristic, and illustrates a tenderness of heart which never failed him. To that tenderness in after life, many a mother appealed in behalf of a wayward son, and rarely in vain.

When Lincoln began the practice of law in Springfield, all the federal courts in the state were held there. John McLean, Justice of the Supreme Court of the United States, was the circuit, and Nathaniel Pope the district judge. Both were good lawyers, and very able men. The Supreme Court of the state then held all its sessions at the capital, and the judges were sound lawyers and men of high personal character. The Springfield bar was especially distinguished for its able lawyers and eloquent advocates. The state was sparsely settled, with a hardy, fearless, and honest, but very litigious, population.

The court house was sometimes framed and boarded, but more frequently of logs. The judge sat upon a raised platform, behind a rough board, sometimes covered with green baize, for a table on which to write his notes. A small table stood on the floor in front, for the clerk, and another

---

1. Killed in the Mexican war at the battle of Buena Vista.

2. Speed. Lincoln Memorial Album, p. 147.

larger one in front of the clerk, and in the area in the center of the room, around which in rude chairs the lawyers were grouped, too often with their feet on top of it. Rough benches were placed there for the jury, parties, witnesses, and by-standers. The court rooms were nearly always crowded, for here were rehearsed and acted the dramas, the tragedies, and the comedies of real life.

The court house has always been a very attractive place to the people of the frontier. It supplied the place of theatres, lecture and concert rooms, and other places of interest and amusement, in the older settlements and towns. The leading lawyers and judges were the star actors, and had each his partisans. Hence crowds attended the courts to see the judges, to hear the lawyers contend with argument, and law, and wit for success, victory, and fame. The merits and ability of the leading advocates ; their success or discomfiture in examining or cross-examining a witness ; the ability of this or that one to obtain a verdict, were canvassed at every cabin-raising, bee or horse-race, and at every log house and school in the county. Thus the lawyers were stimulated to the utmost exertion of their powers, not only by controversy and desire of success, but by the consciousness that their efforts were watched with eagerness by friends, clients, partisans, and rivals.

From one to another of these rude court houses, the gentlemen of the bar passed, following the judge around his circuit from county to county, traveling generally on horseback, with saddle-bags, brushes, an extra shirt or two, and perhaps two or three law books. Sometimes two or three lawyers would unite and travel in a buggy, and the poorer and younger ones not seldom walked. But a horse was not an unusual fee, and in those days when horse thieves, as clients, were but too common, it was not long before a young man of ability found himself well mounted. There was great freedom in social intercourse. Manners were rude, but genial, kind, and friendly. Each was always ready to assist his fellows, and selfishness was not tolerated. The relations between the bench and bar were familiar, free, and easy, and flashes of wit, humor, and repartee were constantly exchanged.

Such was the life upon which Lincoln now entered, and there gathered with him, around those pine tables of the frontier court house, a very remarkable combination of men ; men who would have been leaders of the bar at Boston or New York, Philadelphia or Washington ; men who would have made their mark in Westminster Hall, or upon any English circuit. At the capital were John T. Stuart, Stephen T. Logan, [1] Edward D. Baker, Ninian W. Edwards, Josiah Lamborn, attorney-general, and many others. Among the leading lawyers from other parts of the state, who practiced in the Supreme and Federal Courts at the capital, were Stephen Arnold Douglas ; Lyman Trumbull, for many many years chairman of the judiciary committee of the United States Senate ; O. H. Browning, senator and member of the cabinet at Washington ; William H. Bissell, member of Congress, and governor of the state ; David Davis, justice of the Supreme Court, senator, and Vice-President of the United States ; Justin Butterfield, [2] of Chicago, and many others almost, or quite, equally distinguished.

1. A man whom Judge McLean pronounced the ablest *nisiprius* lawyer in the United States.

2. Justin Butterfield was among the ablest lawyers of Chicago. I insert the following incidents connected with him and illustrating life at that time:

In Presence of the Pope, Angels, Prophet, and Apostles.—In December, 1842, Governor Ford, on the application of the executive of Missouri, issued a warrant for the arrest of Joseph Smith, the apostle of Mormonism, then residing at Nauvoo in this state, as a fugitive from justice. He was charged with having instigated the attempt, by some Mormons, to assassinate Governor Boggs of Missouri. Mr. Butterfield, in behalf of Smith, sued out, from Judge Pope, a writ of *habeas corpus*, and Smith was brought before the United States District Court. On the hearing it clearly appeared that he had not been in Missouri, nor out of Illinois, within the time in which the crime had been committed, and if he had any connection with the offence, the acts must have been done in Illinois. Was he then a fugitive from justice? It was pretty clear, that if allowed to be taken into Missouri, means would have been found to condemn and execute him. The Attorney General of Illinois, Mr. Lamborn, appeared to sustain the warrant. Mr. Butterfield, aided by B. F. Edwards, appeared for Smith, and moved for his discharge. The prophet (so called) was attended by his twelve apostles, and a large number of his followers, and the case attracted great interest. The court room was thronged with prominent members of the bar and public men. Judge Pope was a gallant gentleman of the old school, and loved nothing better than to be in the midst of youth and beauty. Seats were crowded on the judge's platform on both sides and behind the judge, and an array of brilliant and

It was with these men that Lincoln now came into constant collision and competition.   It was in conflict with
these intellectual giants at the bar and on the stump that he
was trained and disciplined for the great work before him.
In those days law libraries were small, and comparatively

beautiful ladies almost encircled the court. Mr. Butterfield, dressed *a la Webster*, in
blue dress-coat and metal buttons, with buff vest, rose with dignity, and amidst the
most profound silence. Pausing, and running his eyes admiringly from the central
figure of Judge Pope along the rows of lovely women on each side of him, he said:
  "May it please the Court,
  "I appear before you to-day under circumstances most novel and peculiar. I am
to address the 'Pope' (bowing to the judge) surrounded by angels (bowing still lower
to the ladies), in the presence of the holy apostles, in behalf of the prophet of the
Lord."
  Among the most lovely and attractive of these "angels," were the daughters of
Judge Pope, a daughter of Mr. Butterfield, Mrs. Lincoln, Miss Dunlap, afterwards
Mrs. Gen. Jno. A. McClernand, and others, some of whom still live, and the tradition
of their youthful beauty is verified by their lovely daughters and grandchildren.
  General Shields and the Shot that Killed Breese.—All the old members of the bar
will recall with pleasant recollections a gallant and genial Irishman, James Shields, of
Tyrone County, Ireland. He was, however, more distinguished as a politician and
soldier, than as a lawyer and judge. In 1848, he was elected to the United States
Senate, succeeding Senator Breese, who was a candidate for re-election. At the battle of Cerro Gordo, in the war against Mexico, he was shot through the lungs, the
ball passing out at his back. His nomination over a man so distinguished as Judge
Breese was a surprise to many, and was the reward for his gallantry and wound. His
political enemies said his recovery was marvellous, and that his wound was miracu-
lously cured, so that no scar could be seen where the bullet entered and passed out of
his body, all of which was untrue. The morning after the nomination, Mr. Butterfield, who was as violent a whig as General Shields was a democrat, met one of the
judges in the Supreme Court room, who expressed his astonishment at the result, but
added the judge, "It was the war and that Mexican bullet that did the business."
"Yes," answered Mr. Butterfield, dryly, "and what an extraordinary, what a wonderful shot that was! The ball went clean through Shields without hurting him, or even
leaving a scar, and killed Breese a thousand miles away."
  "*Oyer*" *and* "*Terminer.*"—It was on one of the Northern Circuits, held by Judge
Jesse B. Thomas, that Mr. Butterfield, irritated by the delay of the judge in deciding
a case, which he had argued some time before, came in one morning and said with
great gravity: "I believe, if your Honor please, this Court is called the 'Oyer and
Terminer.' *I* think it ought to be called the 'Oyer *sans* Terminer,'" and sat down.
The next morning, when counsel were called for motions, Mr. Butterfield called up a
pending motion for new trial in an important case. "The motion is overruled," said
Judge Thomas, abruptly. "Yesterday you declared this Court ought to be called *Oyer
sans Terminer*, so," continued the judge, "as I had made up my mind in this case, I
thought I would decide it *promptly*." Mr. Butterfield seemed for a moment a little
disconcerted, but directly added: "May it please your Honor, yesterday this Court was
a Court of *Oyer sans Terminer*; to-day your Honor has reversed the order, it is now
Terminer sans Oyer. But I believe I should prefer the injustice of interminable
delay, rather than the swift and inevitable blunders your Honor is sure to make by
guessing without hearing argument."

few adjudicated cases could be found, so that the questions which arose had to be solved, not by finding a case in point, but by the application of principle. These men were therefore constantly trained to reason from analogy, and the result was a bar, which for ability, logic, and eloquence, had no occasion to fear comparison with any in the American Union. It was thus that Lincoln was educated and trained, and became one of the ablest lawyers and advocates in the United States. From 1839 to 1860 he was in constant practice before the State and Federal Courts of Illinois, and was often called on special retainers into other states.

There will be occasion to speak more fully of Lincoln as a lawyer and advocate by and by ; suffice it now to say that in his practice on the circuit and before the Supreme Court he was popular with the bench, bar, jury, and spectators. His wit and humor, his wonderful ability to illustrate by apt stories and anecdotes, was unrivaled.

This " circuit riding " involved all sorts of adventures. Hard fare at miserable country taverns, sleeping on the floor and fording swollen streams were every day occurrences. All such occurrences were met with good humor and often turned into sources of frolic and fun. In fording swollen streams, Lincoln was frequently sent forward as a scout, or pioneer. His extremely long legs enabled him, by taking off his boots and stockings, and by rolling up, or otherwise disposing of his trousers, to test the depth of the stream, find the most shallow water, and thus to pilot the party through the current without wetting his garments.

In 1840 he was again elected to the Legislature, and at this term he had as his colleague his old friend, John Calhoun. He was again a candidate for speaker. Having been elected four times to as many biennial terms of the Legislature, he declined again to be a candidate.

In looking over his eight years service in the General Assembly, there appears little indication of the great ability as a statesman, which he afterwards developed. It is true that his party was, at all times, in a minority, and that the population of the state was small. The legislation consisted largely of measures for opening roads, building bridges, and for other local purposes, and the bills for the construction of the Illinois and Michigan Canal, and other internal improvements. If he had died at the close of his service in the General Assembly, neither the nation nor his own state would have known very much of Abraham Lincoln. He had not yet fully developed those great qualities, nor rendered those great services, which have since made him known throughout the world. All who closely studied his history will observe that he continued to grow and expand in intellect and character to the day of his death.

CHAPTER IV.

MISCELLANEOUS SPEECHES AND MARRIAGE.

Speech of 1837 on Perpetuation of the Government.— Reply to Douglas in 1839.— Temperance Address.— Partnership with Judge Logan.— Campaign of 1840.— Protects Baker while Speaking.— Mary Todd.— Lincoln's Courtship.— Challenged by Shields.— His Marriage.— Entertains President Van Buren.— Elected to Congress.

During these years in the State Legislature, Lincoln had written and delivered various occasional addresses, which, in the light of his subsequent history, are curiously significant.

On the 27th of January, 1837, he read before the Young Men's Lyceum at Springfield, and at the request of that body, an address on the "Perpetuation of our Political Institutions." Also at the request of the young men composing the association he furnished a copy of this address for publication, and it may be found in the *Weekly Journal*, then published at Springfield. He was not at that time twenty-eight years old, and taking into consideration his early life and education, it is very remarkable as a literary effort. As such it would do credit to any college graduate. It is also the speech of a young statesman who has already reflected deeply upon our institutions and the dangers to which they are to be exposed. It is the speech of an ardent patriot, glowing with an enthusiastic love of liberty and of country. The language is impassioned and poetic, and as compared with the more sober and chastened efforts of later years, is especially interesting.   It begins as follows :

" In the great journal of things happening under the sun, we, the American people, find our account running under date of the nineteenth century of the Christian era.   We find ourselves in the peaceful posses- sion of the fairest portion of the earth, as regards extent of territory, fertility of soil, and salubrity of climate.   We find ourselves under the government of a system of political institutions, conducing more essen- tially to the ends of civil and religious liberty, than any of which the his- tory of former times tells us.   We, when mounting the stage of exist- ence, found ourselves the legal inheritors of these fundamental blessings. We toiled not in the acquirement or the establishment of them ; they are a legacy bequeathed to us by a once hardy, brave, and patriotic, but now lamented and departed race of ancestors.

" Theirs was the task (and nobly they performed it) to possess them- selves, and through themselves us, of this goodly land, and to rear upon its hills and valleys a political edifice of liberty and equal rights : 'tis ours only to transmit these, the former unprofaned by the foot of the invader ; the latter undecayed by the lapse of time.   This, our duty to ourselves and to our posterity, and love for our species in general, imper- atively require us to perform.

" How then shall we perform it ?   At what point shall we expect the approach of danger ?   By what means shall we fortify against it ? Shall we expect some trans-atlantic military giant to step across the ocean and crush us at a blow ?   Never.   All the armies of Europe, Asia and Africa combined, with all the treasure of the earth (our own excepted) in their military chest, with a Bonaparte for a commander, could not, by force, take a drink from the Ohio, or make a track on the Blue Ridge, in a trial of a thousand years.

" At what point then is the approach of danger to be expected ?   I answer, if it ever reaches us, it must spring up among us.   It can not come from abroad.   If destruction be our lot, we must ourselves be its author and finisher.   As a nation of freemen we must live through all time, or die by suicide.   *   *   *   *

" There is even now something of ill omen among us.   I mean the increasing disregard for law which pervades the country ; the growing disposition to substitute the wild and furious passions in lieu of the sober judgment of courts ; and the worse than savage mobs, for the executive ministers of justice.   This disposition is awfully fearful in any commu- nity, and that it now exists in ours, though grating to our feelings to admit, it would be a violation of truth, and an insult to our intelligence to deny."

He then proceeds to recite various instances of violation of law, and mob violence, and recalls the shocking case of negro burning at St. Louis, in these words :

"Turn then to that horror striking scene at St. Louis. A single victim only was sacrificed there. His story is very short, and is perhaps the most highly tragic of anything of its length, that has ever been witnessed in real life. A mulatto man, by the name of McIntosh, was seized in the street, dragged to the suburbs of the city, chained to a tree, and actually burned to death. And all within a single hour from the time he had been a free man, attending to his own business, and at peace with the world." * * * * * *

" I know the American people are *much* attached to their government. I know they would suffer *much* for its sake. I know they would endure evils long and patiently, before they would ever think of exchanging it for another. Yet notwithstanding all this, if the laws be continually despised and disregarded, if their rights to be secure in their persons and property, are held by no better tenure than the caprice of a mob, the alienation of their affection from the government is the natural consequence, and to that sooner or later it must come.

" Here, then, is one point at which danger may be expected. The question recurs, How shall we fortify against it ? The answer is simple. Let every American, every lover of liberty, every well wisher to his posterity, swear by the blood of the revolution, never to violate in the least particular the laws of the country, and never to tolerate their violation by others. As the patriots of ' seventy-six ' did to the support of the Declaration of Independence, so to the support of the Constitution and the Laws, let every American pledge his life, his property, and his sacred honor ;—let every man remember that to violate the law is to trample on the blood of his father, and to tear the charter of his own and his children's liberty. Let reverence for the laws be breathed by every American mother to the lisping babe that prattles on her lap. Let it be taught in schools, in seminaries, and in colleges. Let it be written in primers, spelling books and in almanacs. Let it be preached from the pulpit, proclaimed in legislative halls, and enforced in courts of justice. And in short, let it become the *political religion* of the nation."

" There is," says he, " no grievance that is a fit object of redress by mob-law." He then points out the dangers threatening our institutions, from military leaders and reckless ambition, and continues thus :

" Many great and good men, sufficiently qualified for any task they should undertake, may ever be found, whose ambition would aspire to nothing beyond a seat in Congress, a gubernatorial or a presidential chair. *But such belong not to the family of the lion, or the brood of the eagle.* What? Think you these places would satisfy an Alexander, a Cæsar, or a Napoleon? Never! Towering genius disdains a beaten path. It seeks regions hitherto unexplored. It sees no distinction in adding story to story, upon the monuments of fame, erected to the memory of others. It denies that it is glory enough to serve under any chief. It *scorns* to tread in the footsteps of any predecessor, however illustrious. It thirsts and burns for distinction, and if possible, it will have it, *whether at the expense of emancipating slaves,* or enslaving free men. Is it unreasonable, then, to expect that some men, possessed of the loftiest genius, coupled with ambition sufficient to push it to its utmost stretch, will at some time spring up among us? And when such a one does, it will require the people to be united with each other, attached to the government and laws, and generally intelligent, to successfully frustrate his design.

" Distinction will be his paramount object, and although he would as willingly, perhaps more so, acquire it by doing good as harm, yet that opportunity being passed, and nothing left to be done in the way of building up, he would sit down boldly to the task of pulling down. Here then is a probable case, highly dangerous, and such a one as could not have well existed heretofore."   *   *   *   *   *

Alluding to our revolutionary ancestors, he says :

" In history we hope they will be read of, and recounted, so long as the Bible shall be read. But even granting that they will, their influence *can not be* what it heretofore has been. Even then, they can not be so universally known, nor so vividly felt, as they were by the generation just gone to rest. At the close of that struggle, nearly every adult male had been a participator in some of its scenes. The consequence was, that those scenes, in the form of a husband, a father, a son, or a brother, a *living history* was to be found in every family—a history bearing the indubitable testimonies to its own authenticity, in the limbs mangled, in the scars of wounds received in the midst of the very scenes related ; a history, too, that could be read and understood alike by all, the wise and the ignorant, the learned and the unlearned. But *those* histories are gone. They *can* be read no more forever. They *were* a fortress of strength ; but what the invading foemen could *never do,* the silent artillery of time *has* done—the leveling of its walls. They are gone. They *were* a forest of giant oaks ; but the resistless hurricane has swept over them, and left only, here and there a lonely trunk, despoiled of its verdure, shorn of its foliage ; unshading and unshaded, to murmur in a few more gentle breezes, and to combat with its mutilated limbs a few more ruder storms, then to sink and be no more."

The figure of the "forest of giant oaks," and the effects upon it of time and tempest is a very striking one. That is also a curious passage in which he speaks of the ambitious man, who will seek glory and distinction, and who will have it by "*the emancipating of slaves*," or "enslaving freemen." Was that intense ambition of his, of which there exist so many evidences, and that mysterious presentiment that in some unknown way he was to be the deliverer of the slaves, the inspiration of the language quoted?

There is another very remarkable speech of his, made in the Hall of the House of Representatives, in December, 1839, in reply to Douglas, Lamborn, and Calhoun.[1] A joint discussion was arranged between the democratic and whig parties. Stephen A. Douglas, John Calhoun, Josiah Lamborn, and Jesse B. Thomas spoke for the democrats, and Stephen T. Logan, Edward D. Baker, Orville H. Browning, and Lincoln for the whigs. It was continued from evening to evening, an advocate of each party speaking alternately, until Lincoln's turn came to close the discussion. In reply to Mr. Lamborn, who taunted the opponents of Van Buren with the hopelessness of their struggle, Lincoln exclaimed:

"Address that argument to cowards, and knaves. With the free and the brave it will effect nothing. It may be true; if it must, let it. Many free countries have lost their liberties, and ours may lose hers, but if she shall, let it be my proudest plume, not that I was the last to desert, but that I never deserted her."

Alluding to the denunciation and persecution heaped upon those who opposed the administration, he says: "Bow to it I never will," and then in a prophetic spirit, with impassioned eloquence, he dedicated himself to the cause of his country:

"Here, before Heaven, and in the face of the world, I swear eternal fidelity to the just cause of the land of my life, my liberty, and my love." * * * "The cause approved of our judgment and our hearts, in disaster, in chains, in death, we never faltered in defending."

On the 22d of February, 1842, he delivered before the Washingtonian Temperance Society, at Springfield, an

1. See Weekly *Journal*, at Springfield.

5

address upon temperance. It is calm, earnest, judicious, and
it is difficult to find anywhere the subject treated with more
ability,[1] or with a finer spirit. "When," says he, " the victory
shall be complete, when there shall be neither a *slave* nor a
drunkard on the earth, how proud the title of that land
which may claim to be the birth-place and cradle of those
resolutions that shall have ended in that victory."   He was
already dreaming, it would seem, of the time when there
should be *no slave* in the republic.

Wishing to devote his time exclusively to his profession,
he did not, as has already been stated, seek in 1840 re-election to the Legislature.   He had been associated as partner
with one of the most prominent lawyers at the capital of the
state, and he himself was the leader of his party, and altogether the most popular man in Central Illinois. In August,
1837, Stuart, his partner, was elected to Congress over
Stephen A. Douglas, after one of the severest contests which
ever occurred in the state.   The district then extended from
Springfield to Chicago, and embraced nearly all the northern
part of Illinois. Stuart was re-elected in 1839. Their partnership terminated on the 14th day of April, 1841, and on
the same day Lincoln entered into a new partnership with
Judge Stephen T. Logan, one of the ablest and most successful lawyers of the state, and at that time universally
recognized as at the head of the bar at the capital.

In 1840, Lincoln was on the "Whig Electoral Ticket," as
candidate for state presidential elector. This was the presidential canvass known as the " Log Cabin " campaign, which
resulted in the election of General Harrison.   It was one of
the most exciting since the organization of the government.
Log cabins for political meetings, with the traditional gourd
in place of the mug for cider, hanging on one side of the
door, and the coon-skin nailed to the logs on the other,
sprang up like magic, not only on the frontier and over all
the West, but in every city, town, village and hamlet at the

---

1. Published in the Springfield *Journal*, and re-published in full in the Lincoln
Memorial Album, pp. 84-97.

East. Lincoln entered into the contest with great ardor, and " stumped " the state for his party, and in many parts of it he and Douglas held joint political discussions. In this way they traveled the large circuit of Judge Treat, speaking together at every county seat in the circuit.

A great whig meeting was held at the capital in June, to which the people came in throngs from every part of Illinois. Chicago sent a large delegation, which brought as a representative of the commercial capital, a full rigged ship on wheels. The delegation were supplied with tents and provisions, and plenty of cider, and at night, camped out like an army on the prairies. Their camp-fires illuminated the groves, and their campaign songs echoed and resounded all the way from Lake Michigan to the Illinois and the Sangamon. At this great meeting, all the leading whig orators spoke. Among them were Lincoln, Baker, and Logan, of Springfield; Hardin, of Morgan; Browning, of Quincy, and Butterfield and Lisle Smith, of Chicago. For argument and apt illustration, the palm was generally given to Lincoln, but he himself said that no one could be compared to a young lawyer from Chicago, whose name was Lisle Smith.[1]

It was during the canvass of 1840 that Lincoln protected Baker from a mob which threatened to drag him off the stand. Baker was speaking in a large room, rented and used for the court sessions, and Lincoln's office was in an apartment over the court room, and communicating with it by a trap-door. Lincoln was in his office, listening to Baker through the open trap-door, when Baker, becoming excited, abused the democrats, many of whom were present. A cry was raised, " Pull him off the stand ! " The instant Lincoln heard the cry, knowing a general fight was imminent, his athletic form was seen descending from above through the

1. This young man died in early life. I have heard the silver-tongued Baker, the vehement, passionate, and tempestuous Lovejoy, the great actor Clay, the majestic Webster, but within a certain narrow range, I never heard the equal of Smith. At a public dinner speech, a commemorative oration, or an eulogy, he was unequaled. For a union of music and poetry, beauty of language, and felicity of illustration, I have never heard his equal.

opening of the trap-door, and springing to the side of Baker, and waving his hand for silence, he said with dignity: " Gentlemen, let us not disgrace the age and country in which we live. This is a land where freedom of speech is guaranteed. Baker has a right to speak, and a right to be permitted to do so. I am here to protect him, and no man shall take him from this stand if I can prevent it." Quiet was restored, and Baker finished his speech without further interruption.

In 1839, Miss Mary Todd came from Lexington, Kentucky, to Springfield, on a visit to her sister, Mrs. Ninian W. Edwards, who was the daughter of the Hon. Robert S. Todd, of Kentucky. In 1778, John Todd, the great-uncle of Mary Todd, accompanied General George Rogers Clark to Illinois, and was present at the capture of Kaskaskia and Vincennes.[1] On the 12th of December, 1778, he was appointed by the Governor of Virginia, Patrick Henry, County Lieutenant, or commandant of the county of Illinois, in the state of Virginia. In 1779, John Todd arrived at Kaskaskia and organized civil government under the authority of Virginia.[2] It is a curious and interesting fact that the great-uncle of Mary Todd, afterwards wife of President Lincoln, should, in 1779, have been acting Governor of Illinois. He may be justly regarded as the founder of the state, a pioneer of progress, education, and liberty.[3] He was killed at the battle of Blue Licks, on the 18th of August, 1782. His two brothers, Levi and Robert, settled in Lexington, Kentucky. Levi was the grandfather of Mary Todd, afterwards Mrs. Lincoln, and he was the only field officer at the battle of Blue Licks who was not killed.[4] Such was the family

1. Manuscript Letter of Ninian W. Edwards, also "Illinois in the Eighteenth Century." by Edward G. Mason—a paper read before the Chicago Historical Society.

2. See the manuscript "Records of the County of Illinois," with Todd's appointment, in the Chicago Historical Society.

3. The original records of his administration, in manuscript, were presented to the Chicago Historical Society by Edward G. Mason.

4. Manuscript Letter of Ninian W. Edwards. Col. John Todd pre-empted a large tract of land in and near the present city of Lexington. While encamped on its site he heard of the battle of Lexington, in the far East, " and named his infant settlement in its honor."

and lineage of Mary Todd. When she came to visit her sister she was twenty-one years of age. Her mother died when she was a child, and she had been educated and well taught at a boarding school for young ladies at Lexington. She was intelligent and bright, full of life and animation, with ready wit, and quick at repartee and satire. Her eyes were a grayish blue, her hair abundant, and dark brown in color. She was a brunette, with a rosy tinge in her cheeks, of medium height, and form rather full and round.

The Edwards and the Stuarts were among the leading families in social life at the capital. Ninian W. Edwards was a lawyer of distinction. His father had been Chief Justice of Kentucky, and was the first Governor of the Territory of Illinois, holding the position from 1809 to 1818. He was the first senator from Illinois after its admission into the Union, and afterwards Governor of the State.

When Miss Todd came to Springfield, nearly all ambitious young men sought distinction at the bar and in public life. Young ladies sympathized with this ambition to an extent scarcely appreciated at the present day. This young Lexington belle was very ambitious, and is said to have declared on leaving Kentucky that she meant to marry some one who would be President. On her arrival at Springfield she met in Lincoln a man of bright political prospects, already popular, and the leader of his party; one who was regarded by her relations and connections as an intellectual prodigy.[1] Lincoln, who had had his fancies, and his romantic passion for Anne Rutledge, now became the suitor of Miss Todd. His courtship was distinguished with the somewhat novel incident of a challenge to fight a duel.

At this time there was living at Springfield, James Shields, a gallant hot-headed bachelor, from Tyrone County, Ireland.

1. It is noteworthy that those who heard Lincoln talk, even at that early day, were impressed with his ability. I have heard old settlers in Springfield say, " every lady wanted to get near Lincoln to hear him talk " An old gentleman told me that when dining one day at the same table with Miss Todd and Lincoln, he said to her after dinner, half in jest and half in earnest: " Mary, I have heard that you have said you want to marry a man who will be President. If so, Abe Lincoln is your man."

Like most of his countrymen, he was an ardent democrat, and he was also a great beau in society. He had been so fortunate as to be elected Auditor of the State. Miss Todd, full of spirit, very gay, and a little wild and mischievous, published in the "Sangamon Journal," under the name of "Aunt Rebecca, or the Lost Townships," some amusing satirical papers, ridiculing the susceptible and sensitive Irishman. Indeed Shields was so sensitive he could not bear ridicule, and would much rather die than be laughed at. On seeing the papers, he went at once to Francis, the editor, and furiously demanded the name of the author, declaring that unless the name of the writer was given he would hold the editor personally responsible. Francis was a large broad man, and Shields was very thin, and slim, and the editor realized that with his great bulk it would be very unsafe for him to stand in front of Shields' pistol. He had plenty of stomach, but none for such a fight. He was a warm personal and political friend of Lincoln, and knowing the relations between him and Miss Todd, in this dilemma he disclosed the facts to Lincoln, and asked his advice and counsel. He was not willing to expose the lady's name, and yet was extremely reluctant himself to meet the fiery Irishman on the field. Lincoln at once told Francis to tell Shields to regard him as the author.

The Tazewell Circuit Court, at which he had several cases of importance to try, being in session, Lincoln departed for Tremont, the county seat. As soon as Francis had notified Shields that Lincoln was the author of the papers, he and his second, General Whitesides, started in hot pursuit of Lincoln. Hearing of this, Dr. Merryman, and Lincoln's old friend Butler, started also for Tremont, "to prevent," as Merryman said, "any advantage being taken of Lincoln, either as to his honor, or his life." They passed the belligerent Shields and Whitesides in the night, and arrived at Tremont in advance. They told Lincoln what was coming, and he replied, that he was altogether opposed to duelling, and would do anything to avoid it that would not degrade him in the estimation of himself and of his friends, but if a *fight* were the only alternative of such degradation he would fight.

In the meanwhile, the young lady, having heard of the demand that Shields had made, wrote another letter in which she said: "I hear the way of these fire-eaters is to give the challenged party the choice of weapons, which being the case, I'll tell you in confidence, that I never fight with anything but broomsticks, or hot water, or a shovelful of coals, the former of which being somewhat like a shillala, may not be objectionable to him." This spirited and indiscreet young Kentucky girl, brought up where duelling was very common and popular, would undoubtedly have had the courage herself to meet the Irishman, with the usual weapon, the pistol, and, if public opinion had sanctioned it, would have enjoyed the excitement of the meeting.

While this *badinage* was going on, Shields had challenged Lincoln, and the challenge had been accepted. The weapons were to have been cavalry broad swords of the largest size, and the place of meeting was to have been on the west bank of the Mississippi, within three miles of Alton. The principals, and their seconds and surgeons, started for the place of meeting. As they approached the river, they were joined by Colonel Hardin and others, who sought to bring about a reconciliation. Hostilities were suspended. Shields was induced to withdraw the challenge, and satisfactory explanations were made. Lincoln declared that the obnoxious articles were written "solely for political effect," and with "no intention of injuring the personal or private character of Shields," and so the parties returned reconciled. It is quite clear that no tragedy was intended by Lincoln. With very heavy broad swords, under the conditions of this meeting, Shields, who was a comparatively weak man, could not have injured Lincoln, and Lincoln would not have injured Shields. If the meeting had taken place, however, nothing but a tragedy could have prevented its being a farce.

The romance of fighting for the lady to whom he was making love, probably deepened Lincoln's devotion, and the chivalry and courage of Lincoln in so promptly stepping forward as her champion, could not but increase Miss Todd's admiration for and attachment to him, and their union soon followed. The hostile correspondence took place late in September, 1842, and, on the 4th of November thereafter, Lincoln and Miss Todd were married. Neither before nor after the challenge, had Lincoln any unkind feelings towards Shields, and later, during the war of the rebellion, Shields having proved himself a brave soldier in the war against Mexico, the President gave him an important military command.

After their marriage, Lincoln and his wife went to live in pleasant rooms, in a very comfortable hotel, called the "Globe Tavern," kept by Mrs. Bede, and about two hundred yards southwest of the old "State House," paying four dollars a week only for board and rooms. On one occasion shortly after her marriage, Mrs. Lincoln, speaking of a friend who had married an old but very rich man, said : "I would rather marry a good man, a man of mind, with bright prospects for success, and power, and fame, than all the horses, and houses, and gold in the world." In 1844, Mr. Lincoln purchased of the Rev. Nathan Dresser, a small but comfortable house, in which he lived until his election as President, and his removal to Washington.

There are few Congressional districts in the republic which have been represented by such a succession of distinguished men, as those who represented the Sangamon district from 1839 to 1850 ; beginning with John T. Stuart, who was in 1839 elected over Stephen A. Douglas, and served until March, 1843. In 1842, three very prominent men were the whig candidates, Lincoln, Edward D. Baker, and John J. Hardin. Baker carried the delegation from Sangamon County, and Lincoln was one of the delegates to the Congressional Convention, and was instructed to vote for Baker. He took his defeat with good humor, saying, when he tried to nominate Baker : " I shall be fixed a good deal like the fellow who is made groomsman to the man who cut him out, and is marrying his own girl." [1] On this occasion Hardin, of Morgan County, was nominated and elected. In 1843, Baker was nominated and elected, and, in 1846, Lincoln was elected. Of these four members of Congress, Stuart alone survives, at the age of seventy-five years. The others all died by violence. Hardin was shot on the field of Buena Vista. Baker received a volley of bullets as he was leading his troops at Ball's Bluff, in Virginia, and Lincoln was assassinated.

Mr. Lincoln's opponent on the democratic ticket for Congress, was the celebrated Methodist circuit preacher, Peter Cartwright. The democrats supposed that the back-woods preacher would "run" far ahead of his ticket, and might beat Lincoln. But it fell otherwise ; the "Sangamon Chief," as he was sometimes called, receiving a majority of sixteen hundred and eleven, a vote considerably greater than his party strength.

In 1844, in the presidential contest between Clay and Polk, Lincoln, who had admired Clay from boyhood, was placed at the head of the electoral ticket, and canvassed with great zeal and ability, Illinois, and a part of Indiana for his favorite. In this campaign he again met the leaders of the democratic party, and especially Douglas, and added to his reputation as one of the ablest and most popular speakers of the Northwest. His chagrin and disappointment at the election of Polk was very great.

The partnership between Judge Logan and Lincoln was, on the 20th day of September, 1843, dissolved, and on the same day he formed a partnership with a young lawyer, William H. Herndon, a relative of one of his old Clary

---

1. Of Colonel Baker, the following incredible, but characteristic anecdote was current around the mess-table of the early circuit-riders and judges of Central Illinois. Soon after he settled in Springfield, a friend found him in the woods, seated on a fallen tree, weeping bitterly. On being pressed to tell the cause of his grief, he said : "I have been reading the Constitution of the United States, and I find a provision that none but *native* citizens can be President. I was born in England, and am ineligible."

Grove friends, which partnership continued until his election as President.

A very amusing illustration of Lincoln's power to entertain in conversation was given the author by the late Judge Peck.[1] In June, 1842, the year after Martin Van Buren had left the presidential office, he and the late Secretary of the Navy, Mr. Paulding, made a journey to the West, and visited Illinois. The party on their way to the capital were delayed by bad roads, and compelled to spend the night at Rochester, some miles from Springfield. The accommodations at this place were very poor, and a few of the ex-President's Springfield friends, taking some refreshments, went out to meet him, and try and aid in entertaining him. Knowing Lincoln's ability as a talker and narrator of anecdotes, they begged him to go with them, and aid in making their guest at the country inn pass the evening as pleasantly as possible. Lincoln, with his usual good nature, went with them, and, on their arrival, entertained the party for hours with graphic descriptions of Western life, bar anecdotes, and witty stories. Judge Peck, who was of the party, and then a democrat, and a warm friend of the ex-President, says that Lincoln was at his best, and adds: " I never passed a more joyous night." There was a constant succession of brilliant anecdotes and funny stories, accompanied by loud laughter in which Van Buren bore his full share. " He also," says the Judge, "gave us incidents and anecdotes of Elisha Williams, and other leading members of the New York Bar, and going back to the days of Hamilton and Burr—altogether there was a right merry time, and Mr. Van Buren said the only drawback upon his enjoyment was that his sides were sore from laughing at Lincoln's stories for a week thereafter."

1. See also to the same effect the statement of the Hon. Joseph Gillespie, in the Lincoln Memorial Album, p. 461. "As a boon companion," says Judge Gillespie, "Lincoln, though he never drank a drop of liquor, nor used tobacco in any form in his life, was without a rival."

During Lincoln's administration, John Van Buren, son of President Van Buren, and distinguished alike for his brilliant wit and his eloquence, visited Washington, and, dining with the President, the latter recalled and described to the son, the night which Van Buren and he had passed so pleasantly at the country inn on the prairies of Illinois.

CHAPTER V.

CONGRESS AND THE BAR.

LINCOLN TAKES HIS SEAT IN CONGRESS.— HIS COLLEAGUES AND
ASSOCIATES.— HOW HE IMPRESSED THEM.— HIS FIRST SPEECH.—
SPEECH ON THE MEXICAN WAR.— DELEGATE TO NATIONAL CON-
VENTION.— HIS CAMPAIGN SPEECH.— INTRODUCES BILL TO ABOL-
ISH SLAVERY IN DISTRICT OF COLUMBIA.— SEEKS APPOINTMENT AS
COMMISSIONER OF LAND OFFICE.— DECLINES TO BE GOVERNOR OF
OREGON.— AT THE BAR.— DEFENDS BILL ARMSTRONG.— LINCOLN
AS AN ADVOCATE, LAWYER AND ORATOR.

IN December, 1847, Lincoln took his seat in Congress
(the 30th) the only whig member from Illinois. His great
rival, Douglas, had already run a brilliant career in the
House, and now for the first time had become a member of
the United States Senate. These two had met at Vandalia,
and in the Illinois Legislature had always been rivals, and
each was now the acknowledged leader of his party. The
democratic party had, since the year 1836, been strongly in
the majority, and Douglas in his state, more than any other
man, directed and controlled it. Among Lincoln's colleagues
in Congress from Illinois, were John Wentworth, John A.
McClernand and William A. Richardson. This Congress
had among its members many very distinguished men.
Among them were ex-President John Quincy Adams ; George
Ashmun, who presided over the convention which nominated
Lincoln for President; Caleb B. Smith, a member of his cabinet ; John G. Palfrey, the historian of New England ; Robert C. Winthrop, speaker ; Jacob Collamer, postmaster-gen-

eral; Andrew Johnson, elected Vice-President with Lincoln on his second election ; Alexander H. Stephens, Vice-President of the Confederacy; besides Toombs, Rhett, Cobb, and other prominent leaders in the rebellion.

In the Senate were Daniel Webster, John P. Hale, John A. Dix, Simon Cameron, Lewis Cass, Thomas H. Benton, John J. Crittenden, Mason and Hunter from Virginia, John C. Calhoun, and Jefferson Davis. Lincoln entered Congress as the leader of the whig party in Illinois, and with the reputation of being an able and effective popular speaker. It is curious to learn the impression which this prairie orator, with no college culture, made upon his associates. Robert C. Winthrop, a scholarly and conservative man, representing the intelligence of Boston, says, when writing thirty-four years thereafter : " I recall vividly the impressions I then formed, both of his ability and amiability. We were old whigs together, and agreed entirely upon all questions of public interest. I could not always concur in the policy of the party which made him President, but I never lost my personal regard for him. For shrewdness and sagacity, and keen practical sense, he has had no superior in our day and generation." [1]

The vice-president of the Confederacy, Alexander H. Stephens, writing seventeen years after Lincoln's death, and recalling their service together in Congress, from 1847 to 1849, says :

"I knew Mr. Lincoln well and intimately, and we were both ardent supporters of General Taylor for President in 1848. Mr. Lincoln, Toombs, Preston, myself and others, formed the first Congressional Taylor club, known as ' The Young Indians,' and organized the Taylor movement, which resulted in his nomination." *   *   *

" Mr. Lincoln was careful as to his manners, awkward in his speech, but was possessed of a very strong, clear, vigorous mind." *   *   *   " He always attracted and riveted the attention of the House when he spoke. His manner of speech as well as thought was original. He had no model. He was a man of strong convictions, and what Carlyle would have called an earnest man. He abounded in anec-

1. The Lincoln Memorial Album, p. 165.

dote. He illustrated everything he was talking about by an anecdote, always exceedingly apt and pointed, and socially he always kept his company in a roar of laughter." [1]

From the time they parted as members of the Taylor Club, until the Hampton Roads Conference in 1865, of which hereafter, these two remarkable men did not again meet.

Lincoln took a more prominent part in the debates than is usual for new members. On the 8th of January, 1848, writing to his young partner, Herndon, he says: " By way of experiment, and of getting ' the hang of the house,' I made a little speech two or three days ago on a post-office question of no general interest." (He was second on the Committee of Post-offices and Post Roads.) "I find speaking here and elsewhere almost the same thing. I was about as badly scared, and no more than when I speak in court." Writing to his partner again soon after, he gave the young gentleman some very good advice. " The way for a young man to rise," said he, " is to improve himself every way he can, never suspecting anybody wishes to hinder him. Allow me to assure you that suspicions and jealousy never did help any man in any station." And it may be truthfully added, as will hereafter appear, that no man was ever more free from these faults than Lincoln.

On the 12th of January, 1848, he made an able and elaborate speech on the Mexican war, which established his reputation in Congress as an able debater. Douglas, long afterwards, in their joint debate at Ottawa, charged him with taking the side of the enemy against his own country in this Mexican war. To which Lincoln replied: " I was an old whig, and whenever the democratic party tried to get me to vote that the war had been righteously begun by the President, I would not do it. But when they asked money, or land warrants, or anything to pay the soldiers, I gave the same vote that Douglas did." [2]

1. Lincoln Memorial Album, p. 241.

2. Lincoln and Douglas debates.

He had offered resolutions calling on the President, Mr. Polk, for a statement of facts respecting the beginning of this war, and speaking to these resolutions said:

"Let him answer, fully, fairly, and candidly. Let him remember he sits where Washington sat, and so remembering let him answer as Washington would answer." * *

"But if the President," he said, "trusting to escape scrutiny by fixing the public gaze upon the exceeding brightness of military glory, that attractive rainbow that rises in showers of blood, that serpent's eye that charms to destroy, plunged into it (the war) and was swept on and on till disappointed in the ease with which Mexico might be enslaved, he now finds himself he knows not where."

On the 27th of July, after he had, as a delegate from Illinois, aided to nominate General Taylor for President, Lincoln made what is called a campaign speech to promote his election against Cass, the democratic candidate. For that purpose the speech was very effective. It is full of satire, sarcasm, and wit; some of it rather coarse, but it was designed to reach and influence a class of voters by whom coarse and keen illustrations would be appreciated. The following extract will exhibit its characteristics:

"But in my hurry I was very near closing on the subject of military coat-tails before I was done with it. There is one entire article of the sort I have not discussed yet; I mean the military tail you democrats are now engaged in dovetailing on to the great Michigander. Yes, sir, all his biographers (and they are legion) have him in hand, tying him to a military tail, like so many mischievous boys tying a dog to a bladder of beans. True, the material they have is very limited, but they drive at it might and main. He *in*vaded Canada without resistance, and he *out*-vaded it without pursuit. As he did both under orders, I suppose there was to him credit in neither of them; but they are made to constitute a large part of the tail. He was volunteer aid to General Harrison on the day of the battle of the Thames, and as you said in 1840 that Harrison was picking whortleberries, two miles off, while the battle was fought, I suppose it is a just conclusion with you to say Cass was aiding Harrison to pick whortleberries. This is about all, except the mooted question of the broken sword. Some authors say he broke it; some say he threw it away, and some others, who ought to know, say nothing about it. Perhaps it would be a fair historical compromise to say, if he did not break it, he did not do anything else with it."

Lincoln entered into this presidential canvass very zeal-
ously. Writing to Herndon to get up clubs and get the young
men to join, he says: "Let every one play the part he can play
the best. Some can speak, some sing, and all can hallo!"
He went to New York and New England, speaking often
and earnestly for Taylor. Returning, he spoke with great
effect in Illinois and other parts of the West during the canvass. General Taylor's election inspired hopes that the
extension of slavery might be stopped, and that the administration might be brought back to the policy of prohibiting
it in the territories.

The most important and significant act of Lincoln at this
Congress, was the introduction by him into the House, of a
bill to abolish slavery in the District of Columbia. The bill
provided that no person from without the District should be
held to slavery within it, and that no person born thereafter
within the District should be held to slavery. It provided
for the gradual emancipation of all the slaves in the District,
with compensation to their masters, and that the act should
be submitted to a vote of the people of the District. He
prepared the bill with reference to the condition of public
sentiment at that time, and what was possible to be accomplished. The bill represents what he hoped he could carry
through Congress, and into a law, rather than his own
abstract ideas of justice and right. He believed, as he had
declared many times, and emphatically in his protest to the
resolutions in the Illinois Legislature, that slavery was
"unjust to the slave, impolitic to the nation," and he meant
to do all in his power to restrict and get rid of it.

Even this bill, mild as it was, would not be tolerated by
the slave states, and their opposition was so decided and
unanimous that he was not able even to bring it to a vote.
He also at about this time voted against paying for slaves
lost by officers in the Seminole war. His term as member of
Congress expired March 4, 1849, and he was not a candidate for re-election.

He sought an appointment as Commissioner of the General Land Office from President Taylor, but, to the surprise of his friends, it was given to Justin Butterfield, a distinguished lawyer from Chicago. The offices of secretary and governor of Oregon Territory were offered to him, but were declined. When it is remembered how very active and influential he had been in securing the nomination and election of Taylor, the failure of the administration to appoint him to the office which his friends asked, is strange, and it was a great disappointment. He did not hesitate to decline the appointment to Oregon, conscious, perhaps, that there was a great work for him to do on this side of the Rocky Mountains.

After he became President, the member of Congress representing the Chicago district, in behalf of a son of Mr. Butterfield, asked for an appointment in the army. When the application was presented, the President paused, and after a moment's silence, said: " Mr. Justin Butterfield once obtained an appointment I very much wanted, and in which my friends believed I could have been useful, and to which they thought I was fairly entitled, and I have hardly ever felt so bad at any failure in my life, but I am glad of an opportunity of doing a service to his son." And he made an order for his commission. He then spoke of the offer made to him of the governorship of Oregon. To which the reply was made: " How fortunate that you declined. If you had gone to Oregon, you might have come back as senator, but you would never have been President." " Yes, you are probably right," said he, and then with a musing, dreamy look, he added: " I have all my life been a fatalist. What is to be will be, or rather, I have found all my life as Hamlet says:

> ' There's a divinity that shapes our ends,
> Rough-hew them how we will.' "

Mrs. Lincoln was not with him much of the time while he was in Congress. Robert Todd, their eldest son, was born on the 1st day of August, 1843; the second, Edward Baker,

6

on the 10th of March, 1846; the third, William Wallace, on December 21st, 1850; and the fourth, Thomas, on April 4th, 1853. The mother was too busily engaged with family cares and maternal duties while her husband was at Washington, to leave home for any considerable time. His term having expired, and he having failed to obtain the office his friends sought for him, he left the capital for his prairie home, not to return until he went back, amidst the throes and convulsions of the rebellion, clothed with the fearful responsibilities of the Executive. While at Washington as member of Congress, did any dim, mysterious vision of the future dawn upon his mind? Did he sometimes dream of the White House, of the Presidency, of emancipation? Did the prophecy of the Voudou negress ever recur to him? Whatever his dreams, he returned to Illinois to devote himself, with zeal and energy, to the practice of the law.

Before entering upon the history of the slavery conflict, let us pause and consider Mr. Lincoln as a lawyer, advocate, and orator. From his retirement from Congress in 1849, until the great Lincoln and Douglas debate in 1858, and, indeed, until his nomination for the Presidency in 1860, he was engaged in the laborious and successful practice of his profession. He rode the circuit, attended the terms of the Supreme Court of the state and United States circuit and district courts, and was frequently called on special retainers to other states. He had a very large, and it might have been a very lucrative practice, but his fees were, as his brethren of the bar declared, ridiculously small. He lived simply, comfortably, and respectably, with neither expensive tastes nor habits. His wants were few and simple. He occupied a small, unostentatious house in Springfield, and was in the habit of entertaining, in a very simple way, his friends and his brethren of the bar, during the terms of the Court and the sessions of the Legislature. Mrs. Lincoln often entertained small numbers of friends at dinner, and somewhat larger numbers at evening parties. In his modest and simple home, everything was orderly and refined, and there was always on the part of both Mr. and Mrs. Lincoln, a cordial, hearty, western welcome, which put every guest perfectly at ease. Her table was famed for the excellence of its rare Kentucky dishes, and in season was loaded with venison, wild turkeys, prairie chickens, quails, and other game, which in those early days was abundant. Yet it was the genial manner and ever kind welcome of the hostess, and the wit and humor, anecdote, and unrivalled conversation of the host, which formed the chief attraction, and made a dinner at Lincoln's cottage an event to be remembered.

Lincoln's income from his profession was from $2,000 to $3,000 per annum. His property at this time consisted of his house and lot in Springfield, a lot in the town of Lincoln, which had been given to him, and 160 acres of wild land in Iowa, which he had received for his services in the Black Hawk war. He owned a few law and miscellaneous books. All his property may have been of the value of $10,000 or $12,000.

When he returned from Washington in 1849, he would have been instantly recognized in any court room in the United States, as being a very tall specimen of that type of long, large-boned men produced in the northern part of the Mississippi valley, and exhibiting its most peculiar characteristics in the mountains of Virginia, Tennessee, Kentucky, and in Illinois. He would have been instantly recognized as a western man, and his stature, figure, dress, manner, voice, and accent indicated that he was from the Northwest. In manner he was cordial, frank, and friendly, and, although not without dignity, he put every one perfectly at ease. The first impression a stranger meeting him or hearing him speak would receive, was that of a kind, sincere and genuinely good man, of perfect truthfulness and integrity. He was one of those men whom everybody liked at first sight. If he spoke, before many words were uttered, the hearer would be impressed with his clear, direct good sense, his simple, homely, short Anglo-Saxon words, by his wonderful wit and humor.

Attention has already been called to the great number of short and simple words in his writings and speeches. Lincoln was, upon the whole, the strongest jury lawyer in the state. He had the ability to perceive with almost intuitive quickness the decisive point in the case. In the examination and cross-examination of a witness he had no equal. He could compel a witness to tell the truth when he meant to lie, and if a witness lied he rarely escaped exposure under Lincoln's cross-examination. He could always make a jury laugh, and often weep, at his pleasure. His legal arguments addressed to the judges were always clear, vigorous, and logical, seeking to convince rather by the application of principle than by the citation of cases. A stranger going into court when he was trying a cause would, after a few moments, find himself on Lincoln's side, and wishing him success. He seemed to magnetize every one. He was so straightforward, so direct, so candid, that every spectator was impressed with the idea that he was seeking only truth and justice. He excelled in the statement of his case. However complicated, he would disentangle it, and present the real issue in so simple and clear a way that all could understand. Indeed, his statement often rendered argument unnecessary, and frequently the court would stop him and say: " If that is the case, Brother Lincoln, we will hear the other side." His illustrations were often quaint and homely, but always apt and clear, and often decisive. He always met his opponent's case fairly and squarely, and never intentionally misstated law or evidence.[1]

Out of a multitude of causes a few are cited for illustration. One of the most interesting cases in which Lincoln was engaged early in his professional life, grew out of the sale of a negro girl named Nancy. It was the case of Bailey

1. Judge David Davis said of Lincoln: " In order to bring into activity his great powers, it was necessary he should be convinced of the right and justice of the case he advocated. When so convinced, whether the case was great or small, he was usually successful."

Judge Thomas Drummond says: " He had a clearness of statement which was itself an argument. * * He was one of the most successful lawyers we ever had in the state."

vs. Cromwell, argued and decided at the December term of the Supreme Court of Illinois, 1841.[1]

The girl was alleged to have been held as an indentured servant or slave, and had been sold by Cromwell to Bailey, and a promissory note taken in payment. Suit was brought in the Tazewell Circuit Court to recover the amount of the note, and judgment was recovered. The case was taken to the Supreme Court, and Mr. Lincoln made an elaborate argument in favor of reversing the judgment. Judge Logan represented the opposite side. Lincoln contended, among other positions, that the girl was free by virtue of the ordinance of 1787, prohibiting slavery in the Northwestern Territory, of which Illinois was a part, as well as by the constitution of the state, which prohibited slavery. He insisted that, as it appeared from the record that the consideration of the note was the sale of a human being in a free state, the note was void; that a human being in a free state could not be the subject of sale. The court, the opinion given by Judge Breese, reversed the judgment. The argument by Lincoln, a very brief and imperfect statement of which is given in the report, was most interesting, and the question of slavery under the constitution, the ordinance of 1787, and the law of nations, was very carefully considered. He was then thirty-two years of age, and it is probable that in preparing the argument of this case he gave the subject of slavery and the legal questions connected with it a more full and elaborate investigation than ever before.[2]

The suit of Case *vs.* Snow, tried at the spring term of tne Tazewell Circuit Court, illustrates both Mr. Lincoln's love of justice and his adroitness in managing an ordinary case. He had brought an action in behalf of an old man named Case, against the Snow boys, to recover the amount of a note given by them in payment for what was known as a

1. See 3d Scammon's Illinois Reports, p. 71, where an imperfect report of the case will be found.

2. Mr. Lincoln's private library was never large. There was a respectable law library at Springfield, and a fair miscellaneous library in the office of the Secretary of State, to which he always had access.

"prairie team." This consists of a breaking plow and two or three yoke of oxen, making up a team strong enough to break up the strong, tough, thick turf of the prairie. The defendants, the Snow boys, appeared by their counsel and plead that they were infants, or minors, when the note was given. On the trial Lincoln produced the note, and it was admitted that it was given for the oxen and plow. The defendants then offered to prove that they were under twenty-one years of age when they signed the note. "Yes," said Lincoln, "I guess that is true and we will admit it."

"Is there a count in the declaration for oxen and plow, sold and delivered?" inquired Judge Treat, the presiding judge.

"Yes," said Lincoln, "and I have only two or three questions to ask of the witness." This witness had been called to prove the age of the Snow boys.

"Where is that prairie team now?" said Lincoln.

"On the farm of the Snow boys."

"Have you seen any one breaking prairie with it lately?"

"Yes," replied the witness, "the Snow boys were breaking up with it last week."

"How old are the boys now?"

"One is a little over twenty-one, and the other near twenty-three."

"That is all," said Mr. Lincoln.

"Gentlemen," said Lincoln to the jury, "these boys never would have tried to cheat old farmer Case out of these oxen and that plow, but for the advice of counsel. It was bad advice, bad in morals and bad in law. The law never sanctions cheating, and a lawyer must be very smart indeed to twist it so that it will seem to do so. The judge will tell you what your own sense of justice has already told you, that these Snow boys, if they were mean enough to plead the baby act, when they came to be men should have taken the oxen and plow back. They can not go back on their contract, and also keep what the note was given for." The jury without leaving their seats gave a verdict for old farmer Case.[1]

One of the great triumphs of Lincoln at the bar was won in the trial of William D. Armstrong, indicted with one Norris, for murder. The crime had been committed in Mason County, near a camp-meeting. Norris was convicted and sent to the state prison. Armstrong took a change of venue to Cass County, on the ground that the prejudices of the people in Mason County were so strong against him that he could not have a trial. He was the son of Jack Armstrong, who had been so kind to Lincoln in early life. Jack was dead, but Hannah, who when Lincoln was roughing it at New Salem, had been so motherly; who had made his shirts, and mended his well worn clothes; who, when Lincoln was depressed and gloomy, had in her rude and motherly way tried to cheer him ; she now came to him and begged that he would save her son from the gallows. She had watched his rise to distinction with pride and exultation. In a certain way she looked upon him as her boy, and she believed in him. Lincoln, and Lincoln only, as she thought, could save Bill from disgrace and death ; he could do anything. She went to Springfield, and begged him to come and save her son. He at once relieved her by promising to do all he could.

The trial came on at Beardstown, in the spring of 1858. The evidence against Bill was very strong. Indeed, the case for the defence looked hopeless. Several witnesses swore positively to his guilt. The strongest evidence was that of a man who swore that at eleven o'clock at night he saw Armstrong strike the deceased on the head. That the moon was shining brightly and was nearly full, and that its position in the sky was just about that of the sun at ten o'clock in the morning, and that by it he saw Armstrong give the mortal blow. This was fatal, unless the effect could be broken by contradiction or impeachment. Lincoln quietly looked up an almanac, and found that, at the time this, the

1. See Lincoln Memorial Album, pp. 187-188.

principal witness, declared the moon to have been shining with full light, there was *no moon at all.* There were some contradictory statements made by other witnesses, but on the whole the case seemed almost hopeless. Mr. Lincoln made the closing argument. "At first," says Mr. Walker, one of the counsel associated with him, "he spoke slowly and carefully, reviewed the testimony, and pointed out its contradictions, discrepancies, and impossibilities. When he had thus prepared the way, he called for the almanac, and showed that, at the hour at which the principal witness swore he had seen, by the light of the full moon, the mortal blow given, there was no moon at all." [1]

This was the climax of the argument, and of course utterly disposed of the principal witness. But it was Lincoln's eloquence which saved Bill Armstrong. His closing appeal must have been irresistible. His associate says: "The last fifteen minutes of his speech was as eloquent as I ever heard." * * "The jury sat as if entranced, and when he was through, found relief in a gush of tears." One of the prosecuting attorneys says: "He took the jury by storm." * "There were tears in Lincoln's eyes while he spoke, but they were genuine." * * "I have said an hundred times that it was Lincoln's speech that saved that criminal from the gallows." He pictured to the jury the old Armstrong home, the log cabin at New Salem; the aged mother, her locks silvered with time, was sitting by his side, as he spoke; all the associations of those early days came thronging up, his own feelings were thoroughly roused, and when he was once thus roused, his personal magnetism was well nigh irresistible. None but men of the strongest will

---

1. The story has been widely circulated that Mr. Lincoln deceived the jury, by producing an almanac of a year other than the one in which the man was killed. Mr. Henry Shaw says (see Lamon's Lincoln, p. 330), " I have seen several of the jury, who sat in the case, who only recollect that the almanac *floored* the witness. * *

" My own opinion is that Lincoln was entirely innocent of any deception in the matter. Mr. Milton Logan, the foreman of the jury, says that he is willing to make an affidavit that the almanac was of the year of the murder." Shaw adds: " Armstrong was not cleared by want of testimony against him, but by the irresistible appeal of Mr. Lincoln " to the jury.

could stand against his appeals. The jury in this case knew and loved Lincoln, and they could not resist him. He told the anxious mother: " Your son will be cleared before sundown." When Lincoln closed, and while the state's attorney was attempting to reply, she left the court room and " went down to Thompson's pasture," where, all alone, she remained awaiting the result. Her anxiety may be imagined, but before the sun went down that day, Lincoln's messenger brought to her the joyful tidings : " Bill is free. Your son is cleared." For all of this Lincoln would accept nothing but thanks.

There was a latent power in him, which when roused was literally overwhelming. There were times, when fired by great injustice, fraud, or wrong, when his denunciation was so crushing that the object of it would be driven from the court room. A story is current around Springfield, that on one occasion his reply to an outrageous attack by a man named Thomas, was so severe, that Thomas was completely broken down, and ran out of the court room, weeping with rage and mortification.

The only instance known of his taking a fee regarded as large, was his charge of five thousand dollars to the Illinois Central Railroad, for very important services in the Supreme Court. This great corporation, extending with its road bed and branches, more than seven hundred miles in the state, was party in a case involving questions of difficulty ; in this case Lincoln appeared and obtained a decision of vast pecuniary importance to the road. His friends, knowing his custom of charging small fees, insisted that in this case, and against a client so abundantly able to pay, his charge should be liberal, and bear some relation to the great service he had rendered.

In 1855, he was retained by Manny, in the great patent case of McCormick *vs.* Manny, involving the question of the infringement of the McCormick reaping machine patents. It was argued at Cincinnati, before Justice McLean, of the Supreme Court of the United States.

Lincoln was associated with Edwin M. Stanton, afterwards his Secretary of War, and George Harding, of Philadelphia. On the side of McCormick were William H. Seward, Reverdy Johnson, and Edward N. Dickinson. [1]

The last case Mr. Lincoln ever tried, was that of Jones *vs.* Johnson, in April and May, 1860, in the United States Circuit Court, at Chicago. The case involved the title to land of very great value, the *accretion* on the shores of Lake Michigan. During the trial, Judge Drummond and all the counsel on both sides, including Mr. Lincoln, dined together at the house of the author. Douglas and Lincoln were at the time both candidates for the nomination for President. There were active and ardent political friends of each at the table, and when the sentiment was proposed, " May Illinois furnish the next President," it was drunk with enthusiasm by the friends of both Lincoln and Douglas.

Was Lincoln, then, an orator ? Yes, at times as great as the greatest of orators. He was always simple, earnest, and entirely sincere. At times he rose to the very highest eloquence—on rare occasions when greatly moved. When carried away by some great theme, with some vast audience before him, he seemed at times like one inspired. He would begin in a diffident and awkward manner, but, as he became absorbed in his subject, then there would come that wonderful transformation, of which so many have spoken. Self-consciousness, diffidence, and awkwardness disappeared. His attitude became dignified, his figure seemed to expand, his features were illuminated, his eyes blazed with excitement, and his action became bold and commanding. Then his voice and everything about him became electric, his cadence changed with every feeling, and his whole audience became completely magnetized. Every sentence called forth a responsive emotion. To see Lincoln, on such great occasions, on an open prairie, the central figure of ten thousand people, every sound but that of his voice hushed to perfect silence, every eye bent upon him, every ear open, eager to

---

1. See McCormick *vs.* Manny, 6 McLean's Rep. p. 539.

catch each word, his voice clear and powerful, and of a key that could be distinctly heard by all the vast multitude ; to hear him on such occasions, speaking on the great themes of liberty and slavery, was to hear Demosthenes thundering against Philip ; it was like hearing Patrick Henry plead for American liberty.

CHAPTER VI.

THE IRREPRESSIBLE CONFLICT.

SLAVERY AT THE ADOPTION OF THE CONSTITUTION.— EFFORTS FOR
ITS ABOLITION.— ORDINANCE OF 1787.— ITS GROWTH.— ITS
ACQUISITION OF TERRITORY.— FLORIDA.— LOUISIANA.— THE
MISSOURI COMPROMISE.— ANNEXATION OF TEXAS.— THE WILMOT
PROVISO.— MEXICAN PROVINCES SEIZED.— THE LIBERTY PARTY.
— ITS GROWTH.— THE BUFFALO CONVENTION.— THE COMPRO-
MISE OF 1850.

THE life of Lincoln had thus far been one of preparation. He had hardly begun his great work. He had become,
by study and experience, fitted and armed for the great
career upon which he was now about to enter. His life may be
considered as divided into three distinct periods, which may
be thus characterized. The first period, that of preparation,
embraces his life from his birth in 1809, to 1849–50; the
second covers the birth, growth, and triumph of the republican party from 1850 to 1860; the third includes his
administration and re-election, his triumph in the abolition
of slavery and the suppression of the rebellion, closing with
his death in 1865. When he entered upon his life-work, he
was, like Moses, the deliverer of the Jews, about forty years
of age.

Before entering upon the narrative of the second period
of his life, let us pause to consider his surroundings. To
understand and fully appreciate his work, we must first
sketch in brief outline, the history of African slavery in the
republic. The antagonism between freedom and slavery

has never been more strikingly exhibited than in the United States. From the beginning, slavery was the only serious cause of division in the republic. The people of our country were substantially one. They had to a great extent a common lineage, the same religion, literature, laws, and history. That portion of the earth known as the United States is adapted by its physical conformation to be the home of one great national family, and not of many. Without slavery the people would naturally have gravitated into one homogeneous nation. But the antagonism between free and slave labor produced a great conflict of ideas, growing more and more earnest and fierce, until it ended in a tremendous conflict of arms. Let us briefly sketch the history of this anomaly of slavery in a nation which, in the words of Lincoln, was "conceived in liberty and dedicated to the proposition that all men are created equal," and embodying in its Declaration of Independence, the great charter of human rights.

Slavery was introduced into the English Colonies in America, against the protests of the early settlers. As early as 1772, the Assembly of Virginia petitioned the British Government to stop the importation of slaves. To which petition the King replied that "upon pain of his highest displeasure, the importation of slaves should not be, in any respect, obstructed."

The fathers of the revolution tolerated slavery as a temporary evil, which they justly regarded as incompatible with the principles of liberty embraced in the Declaration of Independence, and the Constitution of the United States. They never intended that it should be a permanent institution, much less, that it should extend beyond the states in which it then existed. They confidently hoped that it would soon disappear before the moral agencies then operating against it. They believed that public opinion, finding expression through the press, public discussion, and religious organizations, would secure such state and national legislation, as would at an early day, secure liberty to all, throughout the republic.[1]

At the first general Congress of the colonies, held in Philadelphia, in 1774, Jefferson presented a bill of rights, in which it is declared that "the abolition of slavery is the greatest object of desire of these colonies." In October, 1774, Congress declared: "We will neither import, noɪ purchase any slave imported after the 1st of December next."

On the 14th of April, 1775, there was organized at the Sun Tavern, on Second Street, in Philadelphia, the first anti-slavery society ever formed.[2] Patrick Henry, in a letter dated January 18th, 1773, and addressed to Robert Pleasant, afterwards president of the Virginia Abolition Society, says: "I believe a time will come when an opportunity will be offered to abolish this lamentable evil." General Washington, in a letter to Robert Morris, speaking of slavery, says: "There is not a man living, who wishes more sincerely than I do, to see a plan adopted for the abolition of it." In 1787, Benjamin Franklin and Benjamin Rush, both signers of the Declaration of Independence, were president and secretary of the Pennsylvania Anti-Slavery Society. In 1787, a society was formed in New York, of which John Jay, who had presided over the Continental Congress, was president, "for promoting the manumission of slaves." Alexander Hamilton was a member, and afterwards president. The Maryland Society for the promotion of the abolition of slavery was formed in 1789, and in the same year, a society for the same purpose was organized in Rhode Island. The Connecticut Society was organized in 1790, and of this, Dr. Ezra Stiles, president of Yale College, was president. The Virginia Society was

1. There is nowhere to be found in American literature, an exposition of the opinions of the fathers on the subject of slavery, and the power of the Federal Gov‑ernment to control and prohibit its extension in the territories, as full as that con‑tained in Mr. Lincoln's Cooper Institute speech. It is thorough, exhaustive and accurate.

2. See a very carefully prepared and learned tract by William F. Poole, entitled "Anti-Slavery Opinions before 1800." P. 43.

formed in 1791, and that of New Jersey in 1792.[1] The officers of these anti-slavery societies were the most eminent men of the time.

In 1780, Pennsylvania passed a law for gradual emancipation, Rhode Island and Connecticut did the same in 1784, and New York in 1799. In 1784, Mr. Jefferson drew up an ordinance for the government of the western territories, prohibiting slavery after 1800. Had this been adopted, there would have been no slave state added to the original thirteen, for there would have been no slave territories out of which to form new slave states. The original thirteen were, state after state, abolishing slavery. The institution was thus, in the language of Lincoln, in "the way of ultimate extinction."

The ordinance of 1787, by which freedom was forever secured to the Northwest, to the territory out of which were formed the important states of Ohio, Indiana, Illinois, Michigan, and Wisconsin, was by far the most important anti-slavery measure from the organization of the government down to the proclamation of emancipation by Abraham Lincoln. Its influence has been decisive, both on the moral and martial conflict which was then a thing of the future. Without the votes and influence of the Northwest, slavery would probably have triumphed. It is true, that the love of freedom nurtured by the free schools and literature of New England, beginning like the source of her great rivers among her granite hills, expanded like those rivers, until it became a mighty stream, but it was the broad and majestic torrent from the Northwest, which, like its own Mississippi, gave to the current of freedom, volume and power and irresistible strength, until it broke down all opposition and swept away all resistance.

While the principles of the Revolution seemed likely by peaceful agencies to destroy slavery, new elements entered into the conflict. The most important of these was the

---

1. See "Anti-Slavery Opinions before 1800," by William F. Poole.

invention by Whitney of the cotton-gin, and the rapid increase in the production of cotton, thereby making slave labor far more profitable. This was followed soon after, by a vast addition to the domain of the Union of new territory, adapted to the cultivation by negro labor of the cotton plant. Then there soon arose also a gigantic pecuniary interest which found rapidly acquired wealth in slave labor. A powerful cotton and slave aristocracy was with consummate skill soon organized, and, with an immense property invested in lands and negroes, soon dominated over the cotton states, and by and by in its arrogance proclaimed "Cotton is King." In sympathy with this, there grew up in the more northern slave states a powerful interest which sought wealth in rearing negroes for sale. And simultaneously with these, there grew up in the North a strong cotton manufacturing interest hostile to any interference with slavery. Knowing their own weakness, feeling the insecurity of property founded upon wrong and injustice, the slaveholders, relatively few in numbers, combined and united into a compact, active, bold, unscrupulous, and determined political power. They became skillful politicians. They selected their ablest men for leaders, and kept them in office and power. They carefully educated their most talented young men for public life. In the free states they bought up, and subsidised, by the rewards of official position, many of the most talented and ambitious public men. The masses of the people in the free states, absorbed in material pursuits, engrossed with the labor of subduing the forests, and in opening their farms, in building towns, cities, schools, churches, colleges, canals, and railways, were skillfully kept divided, and were for many years ruled by the more adroit and experienced politicians of the slave states.

A great change in public sentiment soon became apparent. The abolition societies, which not long after the organization of the government were very generally formed, and embraced among their members the most prominent and influential citizens, gradually disappeared, while the religious organizations ceased to protest against slavery, and many of them went so far as to give the institution their sanction and support.

The vigilant and sagacious leaders of the slave power began carefully and systematically to strengthen and entrench. In 1790, Congress accepted from North Carolina the territory now constituting the state of Tennessee, upon condition that so much of the ordinance of 1787 as forbade slavery should not be applied to it, and that no regulation should be made by Congress for the emancipation of slaves. This was followed, in 1796, by the admission of Tennessee into the Union as a slave state.

In 1790, the capital was located at Washington, in the District of Columbia, upon territory ceded for that purpose to the United States by Maryland and Virginia. All the laws of these two states relating to slavery were continued over this territory. Thus slavery was legalized in the capital of the republic, and in a district over which Congress had exclusive jurisdiction and control. The capital, which had been on free soil in Philadelphia and New York, was removed to slave territory, and this was a most important step in strengthening the slave aristocracy. The public opinion of the capital to some extent gave tone to national sentiment. This change secured for slavery the great and active influence of fashionable society. The power of Washington society and public opinion over the executive, judicial, and legislative departments of the government, has always been felt, and down to the advent of Lincoln as President was an ever present ally of slavery.

In 1802, Georgia ceded to the United States the country lying between her present western boundary and the Mississippi, providing that the ordinance of 1787 should be extended over it, carefully excepting the clause which prohibited slavery. From the territory thus ceded came the slave state of Mississippi, admitted into the Union in 1817, and the state of Alabama, admitted in 1819. In 1803, the United States purchased from France, for fifteen millions of

7

dollars, the territory of Louisiana, where there were already forty thousand slaves. Louisiana territory was cut up into three states: Louisiana, admitted in 1812; Missouri, admitted in 1821, and Arkansas, admitted in 1836. In 1809, the United States purchased of Spain the territory of Florida, and Florida was admitted as a slave state in 1836.

Thus the slave aristocracy had secured four new slave states from the original territory of the United States, viz.: Kentucky, Tennessee, Alabama, and Mississippi, and from new territory purchased for its expansion it had secured four other states, to-wit: Louisiana, Missouri, Arkansas, and Florida. Not content with this, but eager for power and expansion, the slaveholders determined to extend the institution still further south, and as the first step, resolved to annex the immense territory of Texas. The leading slave-holding statesmen, shrewd and sagacious, now boldly declared that Texas would give them the control of the national government, and make slavery secure. "It will give a Gibraltar to slavery," said one of their leaders. This compact, well organized power now pursued its purpose with vigor and sagacity and relentless determination, striking down and politically sacrificing every statesman and every public man who dared to oppose its designs. Van Buren, Benton, and Wright, each of whom had been a trusted leader, were sacrificed because of their opposition to the annexation of Texas.

President Garfield, in Congress in 1865, speaking on the joint resolution to abolish and prohibit slavery forever throughout the republic, and alluding to the power of slavery, exclaimed: "Many mighty men have been slain by her, and many proud ones have humbled themselves at her feet. All along the coast of the political sea they lie like stranded wrecks, broken on the headlands of freedom."

Unable to accomplish the annexation by treaty, the leaders of the slavery party finally, in 1845, carried it by joint resolution of both houses of Congress. Thus slavery had secured nine slave states, and eighteen senators in the

United States Senate, thereafter appropriately called the citadel of its power. The free states saw with uneasiness these vast accessions of territory in the hands of imperious slave holders, and murmurs, deep if not loud, began to be heard, but the cotton growing and manufacturing interests rebuked these murmurs, tried to stifle discussion, and cried peace to those who agitated for freedom.

A most determined resistance was made to the admission of Missouri as a slave state. The conflict over this question continued from 1819 to 1821, and was finally settled by what is known as the Missouri Compromise, carried through Congress largely by the personal influence of Henry Clay. By this compromise, Missouri was admitted as a slave state, with a law providing that all the western territory, north of the parallel of latitude of 36° 30', should be forever free. It was the first great and direct conflict between the free and the slave states, and was terminated by a victory for the slaveholders in the form of this compromise, which all parties for a long time considered sacred, and which afterwards, the author of its repeal, Douglas, declared that " no ruthless hand would ever be reckless enough to disturb."

Although the admission of Missouri as a slave state was opposed with the utmost vigor, yet the importance of the question was not at the time fully appreciated by the free states. Had Missouri come in as a free state, it would probably have been decisive, and have given the balance of power to the North, and perhaps might have saved the republic from the great Civil War. As a free state, the route of free labor, of pioneer colonization, would have passed up the valleys of the Mississippi, the Missouri, and the Arkansas, to all the West, and to Northern Texas. As a slave state, free labor was crowded far to the North and West. By this success, the slave holders secured in the great state of Missouri, a most commanding position in the very center of the republic. From that time until 1860, the control of slavery over the National Government was substantially absolute. Whatever the slave power seriously determined should be done, was done.   It is true free labor triumphed in California and in Kansas, but it was over, and in spite of, the adverse influence of the Federal Government.   From the Missouri struggle down to, and after, the Mexican war, the predominating influence of the slave power was marked and decided.

That power had a great advantage in the provision of the Constitution which gave representation to slaves.   In the apportionment of members of Congress, and in the electoral college, a man owning five thousand slaves had a power equivalent to three thousand freemen, and practically far more, because the slaveholders, relatively few in number, and held together by a common interest, were a compact, vigilant, sagacious body.   They constituted an aristocratic class, carefully educated for affairs and public life.   Nearly all the brightest intellects of the South were absorbed in politics, while in the free states, they were engaged in all the varied pursuits of civilization.   They were inventing labor-saving machinery, producing the steam engine, the cotton gin, the telegraph, the reaping machine, opening canals and constructing railways, rivaling the world in ship building, creating a national literature and schools of art, and competing successfully with Europe in the products of skilled labor, in learning, in science, and in the fine arts.   During this period the slaveholders, though in a minority, largely monopolized the offices of power, profit, and influence under the government.   And it must be admitted, that they furnished able statesmen to govern the country.   They selected their best men, trained them for, and kept them permanently in public life, while in the North, a custom of rotation in office, kept many of the ablest men out of public life, and if elected, they did not remain long enough to acquire the practical skill and experience necessary to govern a great nation.   Thus the slave power, united, wise, and watchful, seized and held the reins of government.   The national capital became a slave mart.   The noble old commonwealth of Virginia, with her stern motto " *sic semper tyrannis*," sought wealth, but found poverty and barbarism, in breeding slaves for sale to the Gulf States.

We have already stated the fact that this power, desiring Texas for the extension of slavery, made war on Mexico, and seized and appropriated the coveted territory. Governor Wise, of Virginia, boldly announced the determination that "slavery should pour itself abroad, and have no limit but the southern ocean."

This grasping spirit, as will be seen directly, overreached itself. Texas, and Mexican territory, was needed for the extension of slavery, and Mexico refusing to sell or cede, the territory was seized by force. On the 7th of July, 1845, Commodore Sloat, of the United States Navy, issued a proclamation declaring that California (then a Mexican province) "now belongs to the United States." The gallant and adventurous Fremont scaled the Rocky Mountains, and took possession of that land of gold. Scott and Taylor marched their armies at will through Mexico, and took possession of its capital. Mexico, unable to resist, yielded all of Texas ; New Mexico and Upper and Lower California were also ceded, and now the slave power was more confident than ever of securing the ultimate control of the republic, and of the indefinite extension of the slave empire. But the end of the day of their supremacy was rapidly approaching.

When, in 1846, President Polk asked an appropriation of two millions, with which to negotiate peace, David Wilmot, member of Congress from Pennsylvania, moved what is known as the " Wilmot Proviso," which declared that it should be a condition to the acquisition of any territory from Mexico, " that neither slavery nor involuntary servitude should ever exist in any part thereof, except for crime, whereof the party should be duly convicted." This proviso was adopted by the House of Representatives, but was not at that session acted upon by the Senate. At the next session, President Polk asked an appropriation of three millions for the same purpose, and to that appropriation the same proviso was applied. It was adopted, after a fierce contest in the House, but rejected in the Senate, and the bill coming back to the House, was finally, after a long and passionate struggle, passed without the proviso. In the negotiations which followed, Mexico sought to make the prohibition of slavery a condition of cession, and this especially as slavery did not then exist in the territory in question. The United States minister peremptorily refused to treat on this basis, declaring that "if the whole territory was offered, increased ten fold in value, and covered a foot thick with pure gold, upon the single condition that slavery should be excluded therefrom, he would not entertain the idea, nor even think of communicating the proposition to Washington." Such was the animus of the Mexican war, and such the arrogance of the slave power. Mexico, weak and helpless, her capital and provinces held by the Federal troops, was compelled to accept such terms as were dictated to her. But these aggressions had at last aroused the free states, and brought on at last the " IRREPRESSIBLE CONFLICT."

An anti-slavery party, independent of all existing ones, was about to be organized, and thereafter rapidly to increase in power. In December, 1833, a few zealous and determined men met in Philadelphia, and formed the American Anti-Slavery Society. The convention was composed of sixty-two delegates from ten states.[1] John G. Whittier, the poet, was secretary. This, with other and similar local associations, formed the beginnings of the party which, twenty-seven years thereafter, elected the great statesman of Illinois to the presidency. These men planted the acorn of that oak which, in 1860, overshadowed the land. Garrison, Wendell Phillips, the Lovejoys, John Quincy Adams, Giddings, Gerrit Smith, Dr. Channing, Cassius M. Clay, and many others were pioneers in the great cause of freedom. Differing widely in opinions and as to means, yet in various ways they exerted a powerful influence in arousing the public mind to the wrongs of slavery, and the dangerous encroachments of the slave power.

1. See "Rise and Fall of the Slave Power," by Henry Wilson, pp. 254, 255. Whittier said thirty years thereafter, and after his fame as a poet had extended over the world: " I love perhaps too well the praise and good will of my fellow men, but I set a higher value on my name as appended to the anti-slavery declaration of 1833, than on the title page of any book."

The societies thus organized boldly declared their resolution to exterminate slavery from the republic, but declared
that this was to be done by moral influences.   They encountered mobs and personal violence.   Their printing presses
were destroyed.   The halls in which they met were burned,
and some of them were murdered for boldly expressing,
by voice and pen, their convictions.   While in the free states,
the outrages of mobs and the various persecutions to which
the anti-slavery men were subjected, served only rapidly to
add to their strength, in the slave states, liberty of the press
and freedom of speech were subject to every outrage, and
the laws furnished neither protection nor redress.   Neither
at the bar nor in the pulpit, neither from the newspaper nor
from the stump, not in courts nor in legislative halls, was the
voice of free debate permitted to be heard.   Free negroes
and fugitives from slavery were scourged, whipped, and tortured.   The literature of the vernacular in school books,
history, and poetry was expurgated, and the generous and
manly utterances of liberty stricken from their pages.   Such
was the dark despotism which settled over a republic which
had been constructed on the principles of the Declaration of
Independence.

It was against this despotic power, many of whose representatives were vulgar, gross, licentious, cruel, and treacherous men, that the free spirit of the North now rose.
The anti-slavery party, small in numbers, yet full of fiery
zeal and ardor, and counting in its ranks much of the culture and intellect of the nation, grappled with a power which
at that time controlled the national and nearly all the state
governments, which dominated both the great parties, ruled
the churches, the press, and the financial and business interests of the country ; a power whose social influence was
almost omnipotent.   It held the press and the sword of the
nation, and filled every office, from that of village postmaster to that of President.   This small anti-slavery party,
armed with truth and right, met this giant despotism, and
ultimately triumphed over it.   Although its first vote was so

small as to be almost counted among the "scattering," in 1840 it had increased more than ten fold. The ability, eloquence, and genius displayed by its advocates in their speeches and publications, largely aided by the encroachments, cruelties, and arrogance of the slave power, prepared the way for the free soil party of 1848.

In that year the whig party nominated as its candidate for President, General Zachary Taylor. The democratic party nominated General Lewis Cass over Mr. Van Buren, who had opposed the annexation of Texas. Both of these great parties refused to take position against the extension of slavery. Then the liberty, or anti-slavery democrats, with the anti-slavery men of all parties, called the convention which met at Buffalo in June, 1848, and organized the free soil party. It was largely attended, both by delegates from all the free states, and by representatives from Maryland, the District of Columbia, Delaware, Virginia, Kentucky, and Missouri. Many very distinguished and able men were there, who had hitherto acted with the whig and democratic parties, and their presence indicated the breaking up of old party organizations. Among its leading members were Salmon P. Chase, Charles Sumner, Preston King, Charles Francis Adams, Benjamin F. Butler of New York, Joshua R. Giddings, and many others scarcely less distinguished.

This memorable convention, made up of many thousands of active, intelligent, zealous men, exerted a great influence in advancing the cause of freedom. Its declaration of principles was bold and independent. Disclaiming any power to interfere with slavery in the states, it declared that Congress possessed and should exercise the right of prohibiting slavery in all the territories. To the demand of the South for more slave states and more slave territory, its answer was clear and categorical, "No more slave states and no slave territory."

The leaders of this free soil party were made up of ardent, enthusiastic democrats and whigs, active and zealous against the encroachments of slavery; and of the "Old

Guard." as they called themselves, who had organized and led the anti-slavery and liberty parties; and with these were many personal friends of Van Buren, indignant at, and determined to revenge his sacrifice by the slave power. They were determined by all means to defeat General Cass. The canvass against the old parties was conducted with a zeal, an eloquence, an ability of speech and of the pen, never surpassed. It was the romance and poetry of politics, the religion of patriotism.

John Van Buren, the son of the late President, then in the meridian of his power, canvassed most of the free states, and brought into the discussion an indignant personal feeling towards those who had "done his father to death." He possessed a fiery eloquence, a scathing wit and sarcasm, which rendered him a great popular favorite and secured for him a most brilliant national reputation. Each free state had its great popular leaders, and the people turned out in vast numbers to listen to eloquence, inspired by all the fervor and poetry of liberty, and the wrongs and cruelties of slavery. John P. Hale, Charles Sumner, Henry Wilson in New England, Benjamin F. Butler, William C. Bryant, Preston King and John A. Dix in New York, Salmon P. Chase and Joshua R. Giddings of Ohio, and David Wilmot of Pennsylvania, were among the most active and ardent in the contest. Although the ticket carried no electoral vote, it received a very large popular support, especially in New England, New York, Ohio, and the Northwest, and it defeated the election of Cass. General Taylor received the support of many earnest anti-slavery whigs. Among them were William H. Seward, Horace Greeley, and he who was, by and by, to lead the anti-slavery party to victory—Abraham Lincoln.

Meanwhile the whig and democratic leaders, alarmed by the rapid growth of this new and vigorous party, undertook again to settle the slavery question by compromise. When Congress met in December, 1849, the slavery issue confronted its members. The United States had acquired from Mexico, Upper and Lower California and New Mexico. The Wilmot proviso excluding slavery had twice passed the House of Representatives, but had been as often rejected by the Senate. The slave power had secured a cession of the territory, but the extension of slavery into it was not yet secure. Fourteen free states had adopted resolutions protesting against its extension. The slaveholders, fearing the result of a struggle in Congress, attempted to frustrate Congressional action by sending out emissaries to California to organize a slave state. After the inauguration of General Taylor, in March, 1849, Thomas Butler King, a whig, and a warm advocate of slavery, and Senator Gwin, of Mississippi, representing the democratic party, went to California and sought to get up a state constitution which should secure and protect slavery. Slaves were already there. Mr. King declared: "We can not settle this question on the other side of the Rocky Mountains. We look to you to settle it by becoming a state."

The friends of freedom on the eastern side of the continent had not much hope of success in the Constitutional Convention of California. They rather expected to be compelled to make the fight in Congress on the admission of that territory as a slave state. There was then no telegraph spanning the continent, and no railroad to the Pacific, and mails were slow and tedious. Few more thrilling messages from that distant shore were ever received than that which told that the new constitution excluded slavery. It was the prelude, heralding the death of the system. The miners and laborers of California, who had flocked there in great numbers, would not tolerate the competition of the slaveholder with his gang of slaves, and they, uniting with those who were opposed to slavery from conviction, secured by constitutional provision the exclusion of slavery, and now, with her free constitution, California presented herself at the capital for admission into the Union.

This was a surprise to the slaveholders, and they, who would have welcomed her as a slave state, now wheeled about and refused her admission.   Thus another issue was added to the grave questions growing out of slavery.   After long debate, Mr. Clay, who had carried through Congress the Missouri Compromise, reported a series of measures by which he and his associates hoped to settle the slavery agitation.   California was to be admitted as a free state. Territorial governments were to be established in New Mexico and Utah, without attaching to them the proviso excluding slavery.   The claim of Texas to nearly ninety thousand square miles of territory north of 36°, 30′, and thus made free by the Missouri Compromise, was to be recognized, and slavery extended over it.   Ten millions of dollars were to be paid to Texas for her relinquishment of New Mexico.   The slave trade was to be abolished at the national capital, but a new fugitive slave law, cruel and stringent in its provisions, was to be enacted.

These measures, by a combination of the leaders of both great parties, were finally forced through Congress.   Mr. Webster made them the occasion of his celebrated 7th of March speech, and now the leaders said: "There shall be no more agitation, these measures are a finality, and we will have peace," and they drew up and signed a paper declaring this, and pledging one another to oppose any man who should not so regard them.   But they soon learned that the conflict between slavery and freedom was irrepressible, inevitable, and must go on until one or the other should triumph.   In this Lincoln was wiser than Webster, and more sagacious than Clay, who in early life had been his great leader.

CHAPTER VII.

THE STRUGGLE FOR KANSAS.

STEPHEN ARNOLD DOUGLAS.— REPEAL OF THE MISSOURI COMPRO-
MISE.— THE NEBRASKA BILL.— CONDITION OF MATTERS IN KAN-
SAS.— LINCOLN COMES FORWARD AS THE CHAMPION OF FREE-
DOM.— SPEECHES AT SPRINGFIELD AND PEORIA.— ELECTION OF
TRUMBULL TO THE UNITED STATES SENATE.

THE 33d Congress convened December 5th, 1853. The
election of 1852 had resulted in the choice of Franklin
Pierce as President, General Scott, the whig candidate,
receiving the votes of only four states. The celebrated compromise measures of 1850, already described, were, it was
claimed, endorsed by the election of Pierce, and the leaders
of the slavery party boasted that the slavery question was
settled, and that the abolitionists and agitators were crushed
to rise no more. The territory out of which the great
states of Kansas and Nebraska were to grow, was then
becoming settled, and the people were asking for the organization of territorial governments. Throughout all this territory, slavery had been prohibited by the time-honored Missouri Compromise.

The great senatorial leaders, Webster, Clay, Calhoun, and
Benton, had left the theatre of their renown. In the Senate
there were three only, who were distinctly anti-slavery men,
or "free soilers," as they were called—Charles Sumner,
Salmon P. Chase and John P. Hale. Edward Everett occupied the seat of Webster, William H. Seward was the leader
of the anti-slavery whigs, but perhaps the most prominent

figure then in the Senate was the young and ambitious member from Illinois, Stephen Arnold Douglas.

Douglas was then not quite forty years old, but had already become the idol of his party, and was then in the zenith of his popularity. He had had a brilliant career in Illinois in the House of Representatives, and since his election to the Senate in 1847, had been constantly rising in influence and power. He was especially the favorite of the young democracy, who looked upon him as certain, and at no distant day, of the presidency. He had a frank, open, cordial, familiar manner; at the same time he was bold, decided, and magnetic, possessing the qualities which made a popular leader in a degree hardly surpassed by any other man in American history.

Possessed of a retentive memory, without being a scholar and without much study, by conversation and otherwise, his mind had become well stored with practical knowledge, and he was well informed in regard to the history and politics of the country. He did not forget anything he had ever read or seen or heard, and he had the happy faculty, so useful to the politician, of always remembering faces and names. His resources were fully at his command, so that he was always ready. Although he lacked humor and wit, yet as a speaker he had few equals, either in the Senate or on the stump. He had great fluency; he seized the strong points of his case, and enforced them with much vigor. His denunciation and invective were extremely powerful.

He was chairman of the Committee on Territories, and now had the audacity to introduce, in his bill organizing the territories of Kansas and Nebraska, a provision repealing the prohibition of slavery. The proposition startled the people of the free states like the fire-bell at midnight, and opened again the question of slavery, with a violence and bitterness never before equalled. The motives which led Douglas to introduce this measure were denounced with the greatest severity. He was accused of being bribed by the promise of the presidency to break down this barrier against

the extension of slavery. It was charged that the leaders of
the slavery party dazzled his eyes and bewildered his judgment by holding up to his eager ambition the White House.
But whatever his motives, the act was political suicide to him
and to slavery itself; it was the beginning of the end. From
that time on, the conflict raged with ever increasing force,
until slavery was destroyed in the flames which itself had
kindled. It must be conceded that Douglas carried on the
conflict with a nerve and vigor, a courage and ability, worthy
of a nobler cause.

Senators Seward, Chase, Sumner, and Hale led the opposition to the bill. The speech of Mr. Seward against it was
able, calm, and philosophic. After an historical review of
the whole question, he spoke of the uselessness of all efforts
to stifle the love of liberty and hatred of slavery. "You
may," said he, "drive the slavery question out of these halls
to-day, but it will revisit them to-morrow. You buried the
Wilmot proviso here in 1850, and here it is again to-day,
stalking through these halls in complete armor." * * *
"Slavery," he continued, "is an eternal struggle between
truth and error, right and wrong." * * * "You may
sooner, by act of Congress, compel the sea to suppress its
upheavings, and the earth to extinguish its internal fires, than
oblige the human mind to cease its inquiries, and the human
heart to desist from its throbbings." In its last maddened
throes, this early, able champion of liberty was struck down
by the hand of slavery, the same hand which assassinated
Lincoln, but not until he had lived as Secretary of State,
officially to proclaim, that "slavery no longer exists" in the
republic.

At five o'clock, on the 3d of March, 1854, the Nebraska
bill passed the Senate. On its passage, Senator Seward
said: "The shifting sands of compromise are passing from
under my feet." With characteristic hopefulness, he
exclaimed: "Through all the darkness and gloom of the
present hour, bright stars are breaking that inspire me with
hope, and excite me to persevere." Sam Houston, of Texas,

was one of the two senators from the slave states, who voted against the bill.[1] In concluding his speech against it, Houston said: "Yon proud symbol" (pointing to the eagle), "above your head remains enshrouded in black, as if deploring the misfortune that has fallen upon us, or as a fearful omen of the future calamities which await our nation in the event that this bill becomes a law."

In the House of Representatives, the struggle over the passage of the bill was renewed with still greater violence. During the struggle the House remained in continuous session for more than thirty-four hours. Colonel Benton, then a member of the House, and representing St. Louis, vigorously opposed the bill. Having gone out for refreshments, he was, on a call of the House, arrested and brought to the bar by the sergeant-at-arms, to offer an excuse for his absence. The venerable old man said: " It was neither on account of age nor infirmity that I was absent." * * * " I went away *animo revertandi*, intending to return, refreshed and invigorated, and take my share and sit it out; to tell the exact truth, to husband some strength for a pinch when it should come, for I did not think we had got to the tightest place."

Benton was indignant at the violation of the compact; he saw the danger which would follow, and resisted with all the ability and pluck of his best days.[2]

On the 8th of May, 1854, the bill finally passed the House. Salvos of artillery from Capitol Hill announced the triumph of the slave power, but the boom of these cannon awakened echoes and aroused the people, filling them with indignation, in every valley and on every hillside in the free states. The repeal of the Missouri Compromise shocked the moral sense, and was everywhere regarded in the free

---

1. John Bell, of Tennessee, was the other.

2. I am indebted to my late colleague in Congress, the Hon. E. B. Washburne, for much of the material and language of the account of the repeal of the Missouri Compromise. He was an able and fearless actor in these exciting scenes, and has written a most graphic sketch of them.

states, not only as a humiliation, but as a gross violation of faith. Thoughtful men realized that the days of concession, of mutual compromise and forbearance had passed, and that the struggle between freedom and slavery was irresistible and at hand.

The repeal of the Missouri Compromise removed the barrier against the extension of slavery over an area equal in extent to that of the entire thirteen original states. This territory was now open, and the leaders of the slaveholders determined to occupy and control it, and especially the southern portion, called Kansas. The people of the free states, betrayed and defeated at Washington, determined to prevent this. Douglas and a large portion of the democratic party defended the repeal, on the ground that the people of each territory should determine for themselves whether they would exclude or protect slavery. This doctrine, known as " popular sovereignty," or "squatter sovereignty," became a watchword of that party. Each section resolved to colonize and settle Kansas; the one to make it a free, and the other a slave state. The slave states had the immense advantage of proximity. Kansas was directly west of Missouri, and the only direct route to it was across Missouri, and up her great river to its border. Western Missouri was full of slaves, and their masters could not tolerate the idea of a free state just west of them.

Under the lead of General Atchison, then a senator, and formerly Vice-President of the United States, the slaveholders organized secret societies, known as " Blue Lodges," and by force of arms endeavored to seize and hold Kansas. With arms in their hands, their organized bands marched in military array into that territory, marked out their claims, and, taking their negroes with them, declared that slavery already existed there, and proclaimed " Lynch law " for all abolitionists. In New England and in the Northwest, and elsewhere in the free states, " Emigrant aid societies " were organized, with a view of aiding to settle Kansas with free labor. Settlers were furnished with mills, farming implements, domestic animals, seed, and cheap dwelling houses; school houses and churches were also supplied to the emigrants. This property soon began to be seized by the slave party in its passage up the Missouri river. Settlers and their families were arrested, maltreated, and their property plundered or destroyed, and they were compelled by force to turn back. But with pluck and persistence they turned aside, and with horses and ox teams, made the long, weary, overland journey through Iowa to the disputed territory. Each party was striving to found a state. The slaveholders had, as has been stated, the great advantage of close proximity, and, under the lead of Atchison and Stringfellow, sent their organized bands, armed with revolvers and bowie knives, to build up the new commonwealth with slaves and whiskey. In the long run it was found to be bad material.

The free state emigrant, starting often from a distance of hundreds of miles, took with him his family, his farming tools, school books for his children, his Bible, and often the farm house, school house, and little church framed at home, and by and by, he took also his Sharp's rifle, which he quickly learned to use with skill. Under the lead of John Brown, known in Kansas as Ossawatomie Brown, Charles Robinson, Generals Pomeroy and Lane, and others, farms were opened, and villages and settlements were located and built up. The negro in Kansas did not long remain a slave. The grog-shop, the bowie knife and the revolver could not permanently compete with the school house, free labor, order, and thrift. But the struggle was long, and for a time doubtful. On the side of slavery was all the influence of the United States officials, the state government of Missouri, its border militia, ever ready to make a raid into Kansas for plunder, violence, and destruction. The free state party had the aid of the northern press, Yankee enterprise and persistence, and the rough and rude sense of justice, which characterizes the pioneer of the West. The slave party, by the aid of votes imported from Missouri, the Missouri militia, and the Federal officers, held for a time the nominal government, and perpe-

8

trated a series of outrages, frauds, and ballot stuffings to secure a constitution establishing slavery. But the free state men soon outnumbered their wandering, plundering, whiskey drinking adversaries. The slaves ran away, and found security in the free state settlements or beyond the border.

Territorial governor after governor was appointed by Presidents Pierce and Buchanan, and resigned or was removed, finding the task of imposing slavery on Kansas too difficult. Governor Geary, one of these, became disgusted and indignant at the outrages of the slave party, and gives this picture of the situation. He says :

" I reached Kansas and entered upon the discharge of my official duties in the most gloomy hour of her history. Desolation and ruin reigned on every hand ; homes and firesides were deserted ; the smoke of burning dwellings darkened the atmosphere ; women and children, driven from their habitations, wandered over the prairies, and among the woodlands, or sought refuge and protection from the Indian tribes. The highways were infested with predatory bands, while the towns were fortified and garrisoned by armies of conflicting partisans, excited almost to frenzy, and determined on mutual extermination."

Such was the struggle in Kansas upon the slavery question. It was like the great civil war, of which it was the type and prophetic prelude, a contest between barbarism and civilization. Whenever anything like a fair vote of the actual settlers could be obtained, the free state men had large majorities. The story of this struggle between freedom and slavery ; between fraud, violence, and outrage on the one side, and heroic firmness, energy, and determination on the other, was carried all over the land, and made a profound impression upon the American people. It was amidst these scenes that John Brown of Ossawatomie was prepared, by the murder of his son, for his wild crusade against slavery in Virginia. It was here that the heroic Lyon and Hunter learned to hate that institution. The plains of Kansas were red with the blood of her martyrs to liberty ; her hills and valleys were black with the charred remains of her burned and devastated towns, villages, and cities, attesting alike the heroic constancy of her people to freedom, and the savage

barbarity of the slave power. When the convulsions of the
great national conflict began to shake the land, Kansas was
the rock which rolled back the tide of the slave conspirators.
All honor to Kansas. She successfully withstood the slave
power, backed by the Federal Government. The struggle
was watched by the people everywhere, with the most intense
solicitude, and it nerved them to a still firmer determination
to resist the encroachment of the slaveholders.

The repeal of the Missouri Compromise roused Lincoln
from retirement, and stimulated him to the utmost exertion
of his powers. He now prepared to enter the arena as the
great champion of freedom. He had bided his time. He
had waited until the harvest was ripe. With unerring sagacity he realized that the day for the triumph of freedom was
at hand. He entered upon the conflict with the deepest conviction that the perpetuity of the republic required the
extinction of slavery. So adopting as his motto, " A house
divided against itself cannot stand," he girded himself for
the contest. He sought to take with him, bodily, the old
whig party of Illinois, into the new organization called the
republican party. He was to build up and consolidate the
heterogeneous mass which composed the new party. The
years from 1854 to 1860, were, on his part, years of constant,
active, and unwearied effort. He had, in 1850, declared to
his old partner, Stuart, that the slavery question could not
be compromised. He was now to become the recognized
leader of the anti-slavery party in the Northwest, and in all
the valley of the Mississippi. His position in the state of
Illinois was central and commanding. He who could lead
the republican party of that state and the surrounding
states, would be pretty sure to lead that party in the Union.

Lincoln was a practical statesman, never attempting the
impossible—but seeking to do the best practicable under surrounding circumstances. If he was sagacious in selecting
the time, he was also skillful in the single issue he made. He
took his stand with the fathers of the republic, against the
extension of slavery. He knew that prohibition in the ter-

ritories would result in no more slave states, and no slave territory. And now, when the repeal of the Missouri Compromise shattered all parties into fragments, and he came forward to build up the free soil party, he threw into the conflict all his strength and vigor, and devoted his life to the struggle. From this time, Lincoln was to guide the whirlwind and direct the storm. He realized that the conflict was unavoidable and inevitable. The conviction of his duty was deep and sincere. Hence he plead the cause of liberty with an energy, ability, and power, which rapidly gained for him a national reputation. Conscious of the greatness of his cause, inspired by a genuine love of liberty, and animated and made strong by the moral sublimity of the conflict, he solemnly announced his determination to speak for freedom and against slavery, until, in his own words, wherever the Federal Government has power, "the sun shall shine, the rain shall fall, and the wind shall blow, upon no man who goes forth to unrequited toil."

It is difficult fully to realize or describe the gravity of the situation or the dignity of his topics. We can do so only by comparing them with great efforts of the orators of the past, and who, even of them, had a theme so grand? When Demosthenes sought to rouse the Athenians against Philip, the fate of his country hung on the issue, and the result was that great series of orations which are read with admiration to this day. When Cicero exposed and denounced the treason of Catiline, the Roman orator uttered words which yet echo through the Roman forum. When Edmund Burke and Sheridan plead the cause of the millions of India before the House of Lords, on the impeachment of Warren Hastings, the people of the world were spectators, and it taxed the graphic power of Macaulay to the utmost to picture the scene,[1] but when Lincoln plead the cause of liberty, not only the freedom of four millions of slaves, but the fate and perpetuity of the Union and the republic hung on the result. His speeches were great battles fought and won.

1. See Warren Hastings, by Macaulay.

Whole counties were sometimes revolutionized by one of his great arguments.

From 1854 to 1860 the conflict raged, and then the defeated party, beaten at the ballot-box, appealed from the forum of debate to the battlefield of arms. Let us try to tell the story of this prolonged debate. When, late in September, 1854, Douglas, after the passage of the Kansas and Nebraska bill, returned to Illinois, he was received with a storm of indignation which would have crushed a man of less power and will. A bold and courageous leader, conscious of his personal power over his party, he bravely met the storm and sought to allay it. In October, 1854, the State Fair being then in session at Springfield, and there being a great crowd of people from all parts of the state, Douglas went there and made an elaborate and able speech in defense of the repeal. Mr. Lincoln was called upon by all the opponents of this repeal to reply, and he did so with a power which he never surpassed, and which he had never before equalled. All other issues which had divided the people were as chaff, and were scattered to the winds by the intense agitation which arose on the question of extending slavery, not merely into free territory, but into territory which had been declared free by solemn compact.

Douglas had a hard and difficult task in attempting to defend his action in the repeal of this compact. But he spoke with his usual great ability. He had lately come from the discussions of the Senate Chamber, where he had carried the measure against the utmost efforts of Chase, Seward, Sumner, and others, and he was somewhat arrogant and overbearing. Lincoln was present and listened to this speech, and at its close it was announced that he would on the following day reply. This reply occupied more than three hours in delivery, and during all that time Lincoln held the vast crowd in the deepest attention. No report of this speech was made, but the arguments and topics were substantially the same as in the speech he delivered at Peoria on Monday, the 16th of October thereafter, and which Lincoln wrote out afterwards, it being published in the "Sangamon Journal." As printed it lacks the fire and vehemence of the extemporaneous speech, but as an argument against the extension of slavery it has no equal in the anti-slavery literature of the country. The effect of the Springfield speech upon his hearers was wonderful. Herndon, his partner, says: "The house (it was spoken in the State House) was as still as death. Lincoln's whole heart was in the subject. He quivered with feeling and emotion." Sometimes his emotions "came near stifling his utterance." Loud and long continued applause greeted his telling points. At the conclusion, every person who had heard Lincoln felt that the speech was unanswerable. The reader who peruses the Peoria speech to-day will so declare. Douglas himself felt that he was crushed. At the close of Lincoln's speech he attempted a reply, but he was excited, angry, loud, and furious, and after a short time closed by saying that he would continue his reply in the evening, but he did not return to the State House, and left the city without resuming his discourse.

Lincoln followed Douglas to Peoria. There Douglas spoke for three hours in the afternoon, and Lincoln again followed in the evening and spoke for three hours also. Here, as in Springfield, he carried the audience with him, and Douglas was more disconcerted by the vigor and ability of Lincoln's replies in these two great discussions than on any other occasion of his life. The consciousness of being in the wrong probably contributed to this result. There was something approaching the sublime in this intellectual conflict. Lincoln was then in the prime of life, of great physical and mental power, and perfectly master of his subject.

Douglas felt that he was beaten, and asked Lincoln not to follow or reply to him any more. He said: "Lincoln, you understand this question of prohibiting slavery in the territories better than all the opposition in the Senate of the United States. I cannot make anything by debating it with you. You, Lincoln, have here and at Springfield, given me more trouble than all the opposition in the Senate combined." Douglas then appealed to Lincoln's magnanimity and generosity, and proposed that each should go home, and that there should be no more joint discussions, to which Lincoln acceded.[1] There were then no more joint discussions, although Lincoln had started out with the purpose of following and replying to Douglas whenever he spoke, and a joint discussion had been arranged for at Lacon. Both went to Lacon, and neither spoke.

Lincoln, in the Peoria speech, gave a full history of the slavery question from the organization of the government, tracing the policy of prohibiting it in the territories to the author of the Declaration of Independence.

" Thus," said he, " with the author of the Declaration of Independence, the policy of prohibiting slavery in new territory originated. Thus, away back of the constitution, in the pure, fresh, free breath of the Revolution, the State of Virginia and the National Congress put that policy into practice. Thus, through sixty odd of the best years of the republic did that policy steadily work to its great and beneficent end. And thus in those five states, Ohio, Indiana, Illinois, Michigan, and Wisconsin, with their five millions of free, enterprising people, we have before us the rich fruits of this policy." * *

The speech is distinguished above all others by its full, accurate, and exhaustive knowledge of the history of the legislation relating to slavery. He demonstrates that under the policy of prohibition there had been peace, while the repeal of prohibition had brought agitation. He sums up:

" Slavery is founded in the selfishness of man's nature, opposition to it in his love of justice. These principles are in eternal antagonism; and when brought into collision so fiercely as slavery extension brings them, shocks and throes and convulsions must ceaselessly follow. Repeal the Missouri Compromise—repeal all compromise—repeal the Declaration of Independence—repeal all past history, you still cannot repeal human nature. It still will be out of the abundance of man's heart that he will declare slavery extension is wrong; and out of the abundance of his mouth he will continue to speak." * * *

1. Such is the statement, in substance, of W. H. Herndon. See Lamon's Life of Lincoln, p. 358, and the statement of B. F. Irwin. Lincoln's action seems strange, and I think there must have been other reasons not fully disclosed.

"Some Yankees in the East are sending emigrants to exclude slavery from it, and, so far as I can judge, they expect the question to be decided by voting in some way or other. But the Missourians are awake too. They are within a stone's throw of the contested ground. They hold meetings and pass resolutions, in which not the slightest allusion to voting is made. They resolve that slavery already exists in the territory; that more shall go there; that they remaining in Missouri will protect it, and that abolitionists shall be hung or driven away. Through all this, bowie-knives and six-shooters are seen plainly enough, but never a glimpse of the ballot-box, and really what is to be the result of this? Each party *within* having numerous and determined backers, *without*, is it not probable that the contest will come to blows and bloodshed? Could there be a more apt invention to bring about a collision and violence on the slavery question, than this Nebraska project?" * *

He urges the restoration of the Missouri Compromise. "But," says he, "restore the compromise, and what then? We thereby restore the national faith, the national confidence, the national feeling of brotherhood. We thereby re-instate the spirit of concession and compromise—that spirit which has never failed us in past perils, and which may be safely trusted for all the future. The South ought to join in doing this. The peace of the Nation is dear to them, as to us; in memories of the past, and hopes for the future, they share as largely as we."

But, says he, "they say if you do this you will be standing with the abolitionists. I say stand with anybody that stands *right*. Stand with him while he is *right*, and part with him when he goes *wrong*."

He contrasted the position of the founders of the republic towards slavery, with that now assumed, saying :

"Thus we see the plain, unmistakable spirit of that early age towards slavery was hostility to the principle, and toleration only by necessity. But now it is to be transformed into a 'sacred right.' Nebraska brings it forth, places it on the high road to extension and perpetuity, and with a pat on its back says to it: 'Go, and God speed you.' Henceforth it is to be the chief jewel of the nation, the very figure head of the ship of state. Little by little, but steadily as man's march to the grave, we have been giving the old for the new faith. Nearly eighty years ago we began by declaring that all men are created equal ; but now from that beginning we have run down to that other declaration, 'that for *some* men to enslave others is a sacred right of self government.'" *

* "In our greedy chase to make profit of the negro, let us beware lest we cancel and tear to pieces even the white man's charter of freedom."

On another occasion Mr. Lincoln said:[1] "Pharaoh's country was cursed with plagues, and his hosts were drowned in the Red Sea, for striving to retain in bondage a captive people who had already served them more than five hundred years. May like disaster never befall us." How like in sentiment to the paragraph in his second inaugural address, in which he said : "If God wills that it [the war] continues until all the wealth piled by the bondsman's two hundred and fifty years of unrequited toil shall be sunk, and until every drop of blood drawn with the lash, shall be paid by another drawn by the sword, as was said three thousand years ago, so still it must be said, that the judgments of the Lord are true, and righteous altogether."

When Lincoln made this Peoria speech he was an obscure man. Scarcely heard of out of Illinois, his audience was far inland, and away from the great cities, where reputation and fame are acquired. There were present no reporters of any great metropolitan papers, to take down the speech and spread it the next morning by the thousand, broadcast, on the breakfast tables of the voters. There were no admiring scholars, with wealth and appreciation, to put it in pamphlet form, and scatter it by the hundred thousand. There is a single copy of this speech in an obscure newspaper, and it would be difficult, if not impossible, to duplicate it. Had Charles Sumner made the speech in Faneuil Hall, all New England would, the next morning, have read and admired it. If it had been addressed to the United States Senate by Seward or Chase, it would have appeared the next day in the leading papers of Boston, New York, Philadelphia, Washington, Cincinnati, St. Louis, and Chicago. Nevertheless, from this time on, the fame of the prairie orator spread, and could be no longer hemmed in by state lines.

The Congressional election of that year, in Illinois, resulted in the election of four democrats, and five opposition members of Congress, and the State Legislature would

---

1. In his eulogy of Henry Clay, 1852.

have been completely revolutionized had there not been a large number of democrats in the State Senate, whose terms of office had not expired. The opponents of the Nebraska bill had in the House of Assembly forty, and the democrats thirty-five. In the Senate there were seventeen elected as democrats, and eight elected as opponents of the Nebraska bill. However, three of those elected two years before as democrats, now repudiated Douglas and his policy, and were ready to act with the opposition, at least so far as to aid in the election to the United States Senate of an anti-Nebraska senator. These were Norman B. Judd, of Chicago, Burton C. Cook, of Ottawa, and John M. Palmer, afterwards Governor of Illinois. These were all able men, and skillful politicians, and with their votes there would be on joint ballot a majority of two against Douglas.

James Shields, the colleague of Douglas in the Senate, and who had been induced by Douglas's great personal influence to vote for the Kansas and Nebraska bill, was a candidate for re-election. Lincoln had led the opposition, and to his efforts the great revolution in the state was largely to be attributed, and he was naturally selected as the candidate for United States senator. It is known that he especially desired the office of senator. In a letter to N. B. Judd, written some years thereafter, he said : "I would rather have a full term in the United States Senate than the Presidency." When the Legislature came together, it was generally expected that Lincoln would be elected senator in place of Shields. On the 8th of February, 1855, the Legislature met in joint session, and Palmer nominated Lyman Trumbull. Judge Logan nominated Abraham Lincoln. On the first ballot Lincoln received forty-five, Shields forty-one, and Trumbull five votes, and there were some scattering votes. Judd, Cook and Palmer steadily voted for Trumbull, who received other votes, varying in number, until the tenth ballot, when Lincoln urged his friends to vote for Trumbull, who received fifty-one votes, to forty-seven for Joel A. Matteson, and one for Archy Williams. [1]

1. House Journal, 1855, pp. 345–349.

This result was accomplished by the utmost personal efforts of Lincoln. When he saw that the friends of Trumbull were firm, and would not vote for any one else, and that there was danger that Matteson would be elected, he made an appeal to his personal and political friends so earnest that he carried them all, with one exception, over to Trumbull, and elected him. It was a most magnanimous and generous act, and exhibited such an unselfish devotion to principle as to call forth the admiration of all. It strengthened and consolidated the opposition, and contributed to their success in the following year. It is said that Judge Stephen T. Logan actually shed tears when, at Lincoln's earnest request, he gave up his friend Lincoln and voted for his life-long political opponent. Owen Lovejoy was a member of this Legislature, and voted for Lincoln as long as there was a probability of his election.

Trumbull was a brilliant and able lawyer, then residing in Belleville, in St. Clair County. He had been Secretary of State, and Judge of the Supreme Court of Illinois, and made a most able and distinguished senator. He was, during Lincoln's administration, chairman of the Committee on the Judiciary, and a very prominent member of the Senate.

CHAPTER VIII.

THE ORGANIZATION OF THE REPUBLICAN PARTY.

THE REPUBLICAN PARTY.—THE BLOOMINGTON CONVENTION.—PLAT-
FORM.— WILLIAM H. BISSELL.— REPUBLICAN CONVENTION AT
PITTSBURGH.—AT PHILADELPHIA.—NOMINATION OF FREMONT AND
DAYTON.—DOUGLAS OPPOSES THE LECOMPTON CONSTITUTION.—
THE DRED SCOTT DECISION.—LINCOLN NOMINATED FOR THE
SENATE.—HIS SPEECH AT SPRINGFIELD, JUNE, 1858.

LET us now turn back and notice some important events
which occurred at Washington. When Congress met in
December, 1855, the slavery conflict was raging with increasing violence. There was a long struggle for the election of
speaker. After sixty days spent in excited and fierce debate
and in balloting, Nathaniel P. Banks, of Massachusetts, was
elected over Governor Aiken, of South Carolina. In the
general breaking up of parties caused by the slavery agitation, a powerful section of the democratic party, having
strong convictions against slavery, was driven from its ranks.
The old whig party divided; a part, made up of the more
aged and conservative, went into a new organization, which
called itself the American party, the leading principle of
which was opposition to the influence of foreign-born citizens in American politics; a much larger portion became
"free soilers," and went into the republican party.

It was obvious that the time had come for the organization of a new party, on the basis of opposition to the extension of slavery. Into this party went the life, vigor,
enthusiasm, and genuine democratic principles of the old

democracy—the democracy of Jefferson. Among its representatives were Wilmot, the author of the Wilmot proviso, the Blairs, Fremont, Bryant, Bissell, and Trumbull. With them were the old liberty party, the abolitionists, and the anti-slavery whigs. Up to this time the democratic party, with its attractive name and professions, had secured nearly all the foreign-born vote of the country. But a large and intelligent class of Germans, Swedes, and Norwegians, and some Irish, were so hostile to slavery that they were now ready to join any party which should oppose it, and especially its leading principle, that of extension. It was apparent that, if these elements could be combined and consolidated, an organization would be formed having every element of success. Still there were difficulties, great difficulties, growing out of prejudice of race, former associations, and diversity of opinion, in the way of a cordial union. The new party needed a great leader, an organizer, and at length found such a leader in Abraham Lincoln. He was selected by the instincts of the people, and was, of all others, the representative man of this new organization. Perhaps the greatest difficulty was that of harmonizing the native American whigs with the foreign-born voters. Lincoln had the sagacity to make a simple and single issue, that of hostility to the extension of slavery, and prohibition in all the territories, and to fight the battle on that issue. A triumph upon this issue would be the triumph over slavery, and all else would follow.

The leaders called a convention to meet at Pittsburgh on the anniversary of Washington's birthday, the 22d of February, 1856. The venerable Francis P. Blair was an active member of the convention. It prepared the way for a national convention to nominate candidates for President and Vice-President.

On the 29th of May, 1856, a convention of the people of Illinois, who were opposed to the extension of slavery, met at Bloomington and organized the republican party. It was made up of elements which had never before acted together, and which stood for very conflicting opinions. The committee on resolutions found themselves, after hours of discussion, unable to agree, and at last they sent for Lincoln. He suggested that all could unite on the principles of the Declaration of Independence and hostility to the extension of slavery. " Let us," said he, " in building our new party, let us make our corner-stone the Declaration of Independence—let us build on this rock, and the gates of hell shall not prevail against us." The problem was mastered, and the convention adopted the following:

" *Resolved*, That we hold, in accordance with the opinions and practices of all the great statesmen of all parties for the first sixty years of the administration of the government, that, under the Constitution, Congress possesses full power to prohibit slavery in the territories; and that while we will maintain all constitutional rights of the South, we also hold that justice, humanity, the principles of freedom, as expressed in our Declaration of Independence and our National Constitution, and the purity and perpetuity of our government require that that power should be exerted, to prevent the extension of slavery into territories heretofore free."

Thus was organized the party which, against the potent influence of Douglas, revolutionized the state of Illinois, and elected Lincoln to the Presidency. Lincoln's speech to this convention has rarely been equalled. " Never," says one of the delegates, "was an audience more completely electrified by human eloquence. Again and again, during the delivery, the audience sprang to their feet, and by long-continued cheers, expressed how deeply the speaker had roused them." It fused the mass of incongruous elements into harmony and union.

Delegates were appointed to the national convention, which was to meet in Philadelphia, to nominate candidates for President and Vice-President. The convention then nominated as its candidate for Governor, the gallant soldier and eloquent statesman, Colonel William H. Bissell. He had distinguished himself for his courage on the field of Buena Vista, and elsewhere, in the war against Mexico. Returning to his home at Belleville, a grateful people elected him to Congress. At the session of 1850, the Illinois soldiers who had been in that battle, were assailed by a distinguished member of Congress from Virginia.[1] Bissell, on the 21st of July, 1850, replied in a speech in which he discussed the slavery question, and defended the Illinois soldiers with an eloquence and spirit which created a sensation throughout the Union, and which gave him a great personal popularity in the Northwest. For this manly defense he was challenged by Jefferson Davis, and promptly accepted the challenge. They were to fight with rifles. Intelligence of the challenge reached President Taylor, whose daughter Davis had married; he and other friends interfered, and the difficulty was adjusted.

In June, 1856, the national convention of the republican party met at Philadelphia, and nominated John C. Fremont for President, and William L. Dayton for Vice-President. The declaration of principles was substantially the same as that adopted at the Bloomington convention, and on which Lincoln and his friends had determined to fight the battle in Illinois. That Mr. Lincoln began to be appreciated as the leader of the new party in the Northwest was indicated by his receiving at this convention, on the informal ballot for Vice-President, one hundred and ten votes.

The democratic national convention met at Cincinnati, on the second of June, 1856, and on the sixteenth ballot for President, James Buchanan received one hundred and sixty-eight votes, and Douglas one hundred and twenty-one. Buchanan was finally nominated, Douglas being considered unavailable, because of his direct instrumentality in the repeal of the Missouri Compromise; and the incumbent, Pierce, being abandoned because he had been made unpopular by the outrages upon the free-state settlers in Kansas during his administration. John C. Breckenridge, of Kentucky, was nominated for Vice-President. The convention, although it dared not, or would not, nominate Douglas, indorsed the compromise measures of 1850, and the laws

1. Mr. Sedden.

organizing Kansas and Nebraska. The Southern whigs, and the "conservative " whigs of the North, sometimes called, in consideration of their wise and venerable looks, the "Silver Greys," nominated Millard Fillmore for President. This convention laid upon the table a resolution declaring that no man should be nominated who was not in favor of prohibiting slavery north of 36° 30', by Congressional action, whereupon a large number of delegates left the convention, and supported Fremont and Dayton.

Then followed one of the most animated, earnest, and, in the free states, most closely contested political campaigns since the organization of the government. Lincoln was constantly speaking. Up to the state elections in October it seemed quite probable that the republicans would succeed, but the democratic party managed to carry, by small majorities, the close and doubtful states of Pennsylvania and Indiana, and the contest was virtually ended. Buchanan received one hundred and seventy-two electoral votes, Fremont one hundred and fourteen, and Fillmore the vote of Maryland. The slaveholders were greatly elated by their triumph in the election of Buchanan, but the republicans, so far from being discouraged, became conscious of their power, nerved themselves for still greater efforts, and began at once to prepare for the campaign of 1860.

The contest between freedom and slavery in Kansas still went on. The pro-slavery men, by fraud and trickery, and by disfranchising the free-state voters, had formed a constitution at Lecompton, which established slavery. The voters in favor of a free state, after seeing the elections repeatedly carried by non-residents and armed intruders from Missouri, refused to take part in the mock elections, and, calling a convention of actual settlers, elected delegates to a convention, which met at Topeka, and adopted a free state constitution. This they submitted to the people, and it was almost unanimously adopted. They then proceeded to elect officers under it. This brought the contending parties into direct collision, and civil war menaced Kansas. In

1856, Congress appointed an investigating committee, which, after full investigation, reported that every election held under the auspices of the United States officials had been controlled, not by actual settlers, but by non-residents from Missouri, and that every officer in the territory owed his election to these non-residents. Meanwhile the persons elected by the *bona fide* settlers, under the Topeka constitution, had been arrested, and the Legislature dispersed, by the regular army of the United States, acting under orders of the President. It was thus that Kansas was to be brought into the Union as a slave state.

Douglas had the sagacity to see whither this extreme course of the administration was tending, and the courage and good faith to resist it. When President Buchanan, on the 9th of December, 1857, urged Congress to admit Kansas under the fraudulent Lecompton constitution into the Union, Douglas at once announced his opposition, and followed this announcement with an elaborate and able speech against the proposed measure. " Why," said he, " force this constitution down the throats of the people, in opposition to their wishes, and in violation of our pledges ? " * *
* " The people want a fair vote, and will never be satisfied without it." * * * " If it is to be forced upon the people, under a submission that is a mockery and an insult, I will resist to the last." Douglas never exhibited more commanding ability, than when he led the opposition, in the United States Senate, to the Lecompton constitution. His opposition so exasperated the slaveholders that they sought to degrade him, by taking from him the position he had long held as chairman of the Committee on Territories.

While the Kansas question was pending, the Illinois senator called at the White House on official business. Mr. Buchanan expostulated with him for opposing the administration in its Kansas policy. At length he went so far as to warn Douglas of the personal consequences. Recalling the fact that Douglas had always been a great admirer of General Jackson, the President said : "You are an ambitious man, Mr.

9

Douglas, and there is a brilliant future for you, if you retain the confidence of the democratic party ; if you oppose it, let me remind you of the fate of those who in former times rebelled against it. Remember the fate of Senators Rives and Talmadge, who opposed General Jackson, when he removed the government deposits from the United States Bank. Beware of their fate, Mr. Douglas."

" Mr. President," replied Douglas, " General Jackson is dead. Good morning, sir ! "

We have seen that the executive and legislative departments of the government had long been under the control of the slave party. The judiciary, over which, in the early days of the republic, had presided the pure and spotless abolitionist, John Jay, and the great constitutional lawyer and intellectual giant, John Marshall, had become an object of profound respect, even of reverence, to the people. It had been the forum before which the highest forensic discussions had been held, involving the most important questions of private rights and the gravest questions of constitutional power. The great lawyers and statesmen of the country, whose names are most prominent in forensic literature: Pinckney, Henry, Emmet, Ogden, Mason, Dexter, Webster, Wirt, Clay, Sargent, and others, had discussed before the Supreme Court, with matchless ability and learning, questions involving state rights and national sovereignty, as well as the law of nations, and of maritime and constitutional law. The people had learned to regard this court as the most dignified, learned, and august tribunal on earth. The period had now come when this great tribunal was to be prostituted, and our national jurisprudence disgraced, by its decision in the Dred Scott case.

Dred Scott, a negro, held as a slave in Missouri, had been voluntarily taken by his master into the free state of Illinois, and subsequently to Fort Snelling, in territory north of the line of 36° 30′, where slavery was prohibited by law. Up to the time of the decision in this case, it had been considered a well settled principle of law, that when a master voluntarily brought a slave from a slave state into a state or territory in which slavery was prohibited, that slave became free. The case was fully argued before the Supreme Court in May, 1854. It was for decision at the following term in 1855–6, but the decision was postponed until after the Presidential election of 1856. The intense excitement which the repeal of the Missouri Compromise and the outrages in Kansas had created, would have been greatly increased if the decision had been announced before the election, and it is quite probable that the result of the election would thereby have been changed. The court, through Chief Justice Taney, held that Dred Scott, being descended from an African slave, was not and could not be a citizen of the United States, and therefore could not maintain a suit in the Federal Court. This disposed of the case, but as the point had been made in the argument that Scott was free by the prohibition of the Missouri Compromise, the Chief Justice and a majority of the Court eagerly seized the opportunity, in the interest of slavery, to declare the prohibition unconstitutional and void, and the Court proceeded to say that, by virtue of the Constitution, slavery existed in all the territories, and that Congress had no power to prohibit it. Justices McLean and Curtis gave able dissenting opinions.

Thus the triumph of slavery was complete. The revolution on the subject was absolute. The government was organized on the basis that slavery was local, tolerated in the states, but prohibited in the territories, and on this principle "the government had been administered down to the Dred Scott decision." [1] It is difficult adequately to describe

1. George Bancroft, in his funeral oration on Lincoln, though a life-long democrat, thus characterizes this decision: "The Chief Justice of the United States, without any necessity or occasion, volunteered to come to the rescue of the theory of slavery; and from his court there lay no appeal but to the law of humanity and history. Against the Constitution, against the memory of the nation, against a previous decision, against a series of enactments, he decided that the slave is property; that slave property is entitled to no less protection than any other property; that the Constitution upholds it in every territory against any act of a local Legislature, and even against Congress itself; or, as the President for that term tersely promulgated the saying, 'Kansas is as much a slave state as South Carolina or Georgia; slavery, by virtue of the Constitution, exists in every territory.' "

the astonishment and indignation created by this decision. It everywhere roused the people to a sense of their danger. There was needed but one step further, and a much shorter step than the one taken in this case—namely, for the Court to say that the Constitution carried slavery as well into the states as into the territories, and the work would be done, for every state would thus become a slave state.

In June, 1858, the Illinois republican state convention met at Springfield, and nominated, with the greatest enthusiasm and with perfect unanimity, Lincoln as their candidate for senator.   The resolution nominating him was carried by acclamation, and that there should be no slip this time, the convention declared: " Abraham Lincoln is our first and only choice for United States Senator."

Lincoln's speech to this convention was the platform of the memorable debate between him and Douglas, and is one of the most remarkable in American history.   It was earnest and solemn, and gave so clear an exposition of the antagonism between liberty and slavery, that his words secured the immediate and universal attention of the nation.   " A house divided against itself cannot stand."   Governor Seward, on the 25th of October thereafter, at Rochester, expressed the same idea, and in language, some of which was identical with that used in June by Lincoln.   " It is," said he, " an irrepressible conflict between opposing and enduring forces, and it means that the United States will, sooner or later, become either a slaveholding nation, or an entirely free-labor nation."   This speech, whose great importance demands its insertion, was as follows:

MR. PRESIDENT AND GENTLEMEN OF THE CONVENTION : If we could first know where we are, and whither we are tending, we could better judge what to do, and how to do it.   We are now far into the fifth year since a policy was initiated with the avowed object and confident promise of putting an end to slavery agitation.   Under the operation of that policy, that agitation has not only not ceased, but has constantly augmented.   In my opinion, it will not cease until a crisis shall have been reached and passed.   " A house divided against itself cannot stand." I believe this government cannot endure permanently half slave and half free. I do not expect the Union to be dissolved, I do not expect the house to fall, but I do expect it will cease to be divided. It will become all one thing, or all the other. Either the opponents of slavery will arrest the further spread of it, and place it where the public mind shall rest in the belief that it is in the course of ultimate extinction, or its advocates will push it forward, till it shall become alike lawful in all the states, old as well as new—North as well as South.

Have we no tendency to the latter condition? Let any one who doubts, carefully contemplate that now almost complete legal combination—piece of machinery, so to speak—compounded of the Nebraska doctrine and the Dred Scott decision. Let him consider not only what work the machinery is adapted to do, and how well adapted, but also let him study the history of its construction, and trace, if he can, or rather fail, if he can, to trace, the evidences of design, and concert of action, among its chief architects from the beginning.

The new year of 1854 found slavery excluded from more than half the states by state constitutions, and from most of the national territory by Congressional prohibition. Four days later commenced the struggle which ended in repealing that Congressional prohibition. This opened all the national territory to slavery, and was the first point gained.

But so far Congress only had acted, and an indorsement by the people, real or apparent, was indispensable to save the point already gained and give chance for more.

This necessity had not been overlooked, but had been provided for, as well as might be, in the notable argument of "squatter sovereignty," otherwise called "sacred right of self-government," which latter phrase, though expressive of the only rightful basis of any government, was so perverted in this attempted use of it as to amount to just this: That if any *one* man choose to enslave *another* no *third* man shall be allowed to object. That article was incorporated into the Nebraska bill itself, in the language which follows: "It being the true intent and meaning of this act not to legislate slavery into any territory or state, nor to exclude it therefrom; but to leave the people thereof perfectly free to form and regulate their domestic institutions in their own way, subject only to the Constitution of the United States." Then opened the roar of loose declamation in favor of "squatter sovereignty," and "sacred right of self-government." "But," said the opposition members, "let us amend the bill so as to expressly declare that the people of the territory may exclude slavery." "Not we," said the friends of the measure, and down they voted the amendment.

While the Nebraska bill was passing through Congress, a *law case*, involving the question of a negro's freedom, by reason of his owner having voluntarily taken him first into a free state, and then into a free territory covered by the Congressional prohibition, and held him as a slave for a long time in each, was passing through the United States Circuit Court for the District of Missouri ; and both Nebraska bill, and law suit, were brought to a decision in the same month of May, 1854. The negro's name was "Dred Scott," which name now designates the decision finally rendered in the case. Before the then next presidential election, the law came to, and was argued in the Supreme Court of the United States ; but the decision of it was deferred until after the election. Still, before the election, Senator Trumbull, on the floor of the Senate, requested the leading advocate of the Nebraska bill to state *his opinion* whether the people of a territory can constitutionally exclude slavery from their limits, and the latter answers : " That is a question for the Supreme Court."

The election came. Mr. Buchanan was elected, and the endorsement, such as it was, secured. That was the second point gained. The endorsement, however, fell short of a clear popular majority, by nearly four hundred thousand votes, and so, perhaps, was not overwhelmingly reliable and satisfactory. The outgoing President, in his last annual message, as impressively as possible echoed back upon the people the weight and authority of the endorsement. The Supreme Court met again ; did not announce their decision, but ordered a re-argument. The presidential inauguration came, and still no decision of the Court ; but the incoming President, in his inaugural address, fervently exhorted the people to abide by the forthcoming decision, whatever it might be. Then in a few days, came the decision.

The reputed author of the Nebraska bill finds an early occasion to make a speech at this Capitol, indorsing the Dred Scott decision, and vehemently denouncing all opposition to it. The new President, too, seizes the early occasion of the Silliman letter to indorse and strongly construe that decision, and to express his astonishment that any different view had ever been entertained.

At length a squabble springs up between the President and the author of the Nebraska bill, on the mere question of *fact*, whether the Lecompton constitution was or was not, in any just sense, made by the people of Kansas ; and in that quarrel the latter declares that all he wants is a fair vote for the people, and that he cares not whether slavery be voted *down* or *up*. I do not understand his declaration, that he cares not whether slavery be voted down or voted up, to be intended by him other than as an apt definition of the policy he would impress upon the public mind—the principle for which he declares he has suffered so much, and is ready to suffer to the end. And well may he cling to that principle. If he has any parental feeling, well may he cling to it. That principle is the only shred left of his original Nebraska doctrine. Under the

Dred Scott decision, "squatter sovereignty" squatted out of existence, tumbled down like temporary scaffolding—like the mould at the foundry, it served through one blast and fell back into loose sand—helped to carry an election, and then was kicked to the winds. His late joint struggle with the republicans, against the Lecompton constitution, involves nothing of the original Nebraska doctrine. That struggle was made on a point—the right of the people to make their own constitution—upon which he and the republicans have never differed.

The several points of the Dred Scott decision, in connection with Senator Douglas's "care not" policy, constitute the piece of machinery, in its present state of advancement. This was the third point gained. The working points of that machinery are :

First, That no negro slave, imported as such from Africa, and no descendant of such slave, can ever be a citizen of any state, in the sense of that term as used in the Constitution of the United States. This point is made in order to deprive the negro, in every possible event, of the benefit of that provision of the United States Constitution, which declares that "citizens of each state shall be entitled to all privileges and immunities of citizens in the several states."

Secondly, That "subject to the Constitution of the United States," neither Congress nor a territorial legislature can exclude slavery from any United States territory. This point is made in order that individual men may fill up the territories with slaves, without danger of losing them as property, and thus to enhance the chances of permanency to the institution through all the future.

Thirdly, That whether the holding a negro in actual slavery, in a free state, makes him free, as against the holder, the United States Courts will not decide, but will leave to be decided by the courts of any slave state the negro may be forced into by the master. This point is made, not to be pressed immediately ; but, if acquiesced in for awhile, and apparently indorsed by the people at an election, then to sustain the logical conclusion that what Dred Scott's master might lawfully do with Dred Scott, in the free state of Illinois, every other master may lawfully do with any other one, or one thousand slaves, in Illinois, or in any other free state.

Auxiliary to all this, and working hand in hand with it, the Nebraska doctrine, or what is left of it, is to educate and mould public opinion not to care whether slavery is voted down or voted up. This shows exactly where we now are, and partially, also, whither we are tending.

It will throw additional light on the latter, to go back, and run the mind over the string of historical facts already stated. Several things will now appear less dark and mysterious than they did when they were transpiring. The people were to be left " perfectly free," " subject only to the Constitution." What the Constitution had to do with it, outsiders could not then see. Plainly enough now, it was an exactly fitted niche, for the Dred Scott decision to afterwards come in, and declare the perfect freedom of the people to be just no freedom at all. Why was the amendment expressly declaring the right of the people, voted down? Plainly enough now. The adoption of it would have spoiled the niche for the Dred Scott decision. Why was the court decision held up? Why even a senator's individual opinion withheld, till after the presidential election? Plainly enough now : the speaking out then would have damaged the perfectly free argument upon which the election was to be carried. Why the outgoing President's felicitation on the indorsement? Why the delay of a re-argument? Why the incoming President's advance exhortation in favor of the decision? These things look like the cautious patting and petting of a spirited horse preparatory to mounting him, when it is dreaded that he may give the rider a fall. And why the hasty after-indorsement of the decision by the President and others?

We cannot absolutely know that all these adaptations are the result of preconcert. But when we see a lot of framed timbers, different portions of which we know have been gotten out at different times and places, and by different workmen—Stephen, Franklin, Roger, and James, for instance, [1] and when we see these timbers joined together, and see they exactly make the frame of a house, or a mill, all the tenons and mortises exactly fitting, and all the lengths and proportions of the different pieces exactly adapted to their respective places, and not a piece too many or too few—not omitting even scaffolding—or, if a single piece be lacking, we see the place in the frame exactly fitted and prepared yet to bring such piece in, in such a case, we find it impossible not to believe that Stephen, and Franklin, and Roger, and James, all understood one another from the beginning, and all worked upon a common plan or draft, drawn up before the first blow was struck.

It should not be overlooked that, by the Nebraska bill, the people of a state as well as territory, were to be left " perfectly free," " subject only to the Constitution." Why mention a state? They were legislating for territories, and not for or about states. Certainly the people of a state are and ought to be subject to the Constitution of the United States; but why is mention of this lugged into this merely territorial law? Why are the people of a territory and the people of a state therein lumped together, and their relation to the Constitution therein treated as being precisely the same? While the opinion of the court, by Chief Justice Taney, in the Dred Scott case, and the separate opinions of all the

1. Stephen A. Douglas, Franklin Pierce, Roger B. Taney, and James Buchanan.

concurring judges, expressly declare that the Constitution of the United States neither permits Congress nor a territorial Legislature to exclude slavery from any United States territory, they all omit to declare whether or not the same Constitution permits a state, or the people of a state, to exclude it. *Possibly*, this is a mere omission; but who can be quite sure, if Mr. McLean or Curtis had sought to get into the opinion a declaration of unlimited power in the people of a state to exclude slavery from their limits, just as Chase and Mace sought to get such declaration, in behalf of the people of a territory, into the Nebraska bill;—I ask who can be quite sure that it would not have been voted down in the one case as it had been in the other? The nearest approach to the point of declaring the power of a state over slavery, is made by Judge Nelson. He approaches it more than once, using the precise idea, and almost the language, too, of the Nebraska act. On one occasion, his exact language is, "except in cases where the power is restrained by the Constitution of the United States, the law of the state is supreme over the subject of slavery within its jurisdiction." In what cases the power of the states is so restrained by the United States Constitution, is left an open question, precisely as the same question, as to the restraint on the power of the territories, was left open in the Nebraska act. Put this and that together, and we have another nice little niche, which we may, ere long, see filled with another Supreme Court decision, declaring that the Constitution of the United States does not permit a *state* to exclude slavery from its limits. And this may especially be expected if the doctrine of "care not whether slavery be voted down or voted up," shall gain upon the public mind sufficiently to give promise that such a decision can be maintained when made.

Such a decision is all that slavery now lacks of being alike lawful in all the states. Welcome, or unwelcome, such decision is probably coming, and will soon be upon us, unless the power of the present political dynasty shall be met and overthrown. We shall lie down, pleasantly dreaming that the people of Missouri are on the verge of making their state free, and we shall awake to the reality instead, that the Supreme Court has made Illinois a slave state. To meet and overthrow the power of that dynasty, is the work now before all those who would prevent that consummation. That is what we have to do. How can we best do it?

There are those who denounce us openly to their own friends, and yet whisper to us softly, that Senator Douglas is the aptest instrument there is with which to effect that object. They wish us to *infer* all, from the fact that he now has a little quarrel with the present head of the dynasty; and that he has regularly voted with us on a single point, upon which he and we have never differed. They remind us that he is a great man, and that the largest of us are very small ones. Let this be granted. But "a living dog is better than a dead lion." Judge Douglas, if not a dead lion for this work, is at least a caged and toothless one. How can he oppose the advances of slavery? He don't care anything about it. His avowed mission is impressing the "public heart" to *care nothing about it*. A leading Douglas democratic newspaper thinks Douglas's superior talent will be needed to resist the revival of the African slave trade. Does Douglas believe an effort to revive that trade is approaching? He has not said so. Does he really think so? But if it is, how can he resist it? For years he has labored to prove it a sacred right of white men to take negro slaves into the new territories. Can he possibly show that it is less a sacred right to buy them where they can be bought cheapest? And unquestionably they can be bought cheaper in Africa than in Virginia. He has done all in his power to reduce the whole question of slavery to one of a mere right of property; and as such, how can he oppose the foreign slave trade—how can he refuse that trade in that "property" shall be "perfectly free," unless he does it as a protection to the home production? And as the home producers will probably not ask the protection, he will be wholly without a ground of opposition.

Senator Douglas holds, we know, that a man may rightfully be wiser to-day than he was yesterday—that he may rightfully change when he finds himself wrong. But can we, for that reason, run ahead, and infer that he will make any particular change, of which he, himself, has given no intimation? Can we safely base our action upon any such vague inference? Now, as ever, I wish not to misrepresent Judge Douglas's position, question his motives, or do aught that can be personally offensive to him. Whenever, if ever, he and we can come together on principle, so that our cause may have assistance from his great ability, I hope to have interposed no adventitious obstacle. But clearly, he is not with us—he does not pretend to be—he does not promise ever to be.

Our cause, then, must be intrusted to, and conducted by, its own undoubted friends—those whose hands are free, whose hearts are in the work—who *do care* for the result. Two years ago the republicans of the nation mustered over thirteen hundred thousand strong. We did this under the single impulse of resistance to a common danger, with every external circumstance against us. Of strange, discordant, and even hostile elements, we gathered from the four winds, and formed and fought the battle through, under the constant hot fire of a disciplined, proud, and pampered enemy. Did we brave all then, to falter now?— now, when that same enemy is wavering, dissevered, and belligerent? The result is not doubtful. We shall not fail—if we stand firm, we *shall not fail*. Wise counsels may accelerate, or mistakes delay it, but, sooner or later, the victory is sure to come.

CHAPTER IX.

THE LINCOLN AND DOUGLAS DEBATE.

Douglas's Return to Illinois.—Speeches of Lincoln and Douglas at Chicago, Bloomington, and Springfield.—Lincoln and Douglas Compared.—The Joint Discussions at Charleston.—At Freeport.—At Alton.

The discussions between Lincoln and Douglas, in 1858, were unquestionably, with reference to the importance of the topics discussed, the ability of the speakers, and their influence upon events, the most important in American history.

There had been great debates in the old Continental Congress, on the subject of independence, and upon other vital questions; great debates in Congress in 1820-21, on the Missouri question. The discussion between Webster and Hayne, and Webster and Calhoun on nullification and the Constitution, were memorable; but the debates in 1858, between Lincoln and Douglas, in historic interest surpassed them all.

It is no injustice to others to say that these discussions, and especially the speeches of Lincoln, circulated and read throughout the Union, did more than any other agency to create the public opinion which prepared the way for the overthrow of slavery. The speeches of John Quincy Adams and of Charles Sumner were more learned and scholarly; those of Lovejoy and Wendell Phillips were more vehement and impassioned; Senators Seward, Hale, Trumbull, and Chase spoke from a more conspicuous forum; but Lincoln's were more philosophical, while as able and earnest as any, and his manner had a simplicity and directness, a clearness of statement and felicity of illustration, and his language a plainness and Anglo-Saxon strength, better adapted than any other to reach and influence the common people, the mass of the voters.

At the time of these discussions, both Lincoln and Douglas were in the full maturity of their powers. Douglas was forty-five, and Lincoln forty-nine years of age. Physically and mentally, they were as unlike as possible. Douglas was short, not much more than five feet high, with a large head, massive brain, broad shoulders, a wide, deep chest, and features strongly marked. He impressed every one at first sight, as a strong, sturdy, resolute, fearless man. Lincoln's herculean stature has been already described. A stranger who listened to him for five minutes would say: " This is a kind, genial, sincere, genuine man; a man you can trust, plain, straightforward, honest, and true." If this stranger were to hear him make a speech, he would be impressed with his clear good sense, by his wit and humor, by his general intelligence, and by the simple, homely, but pure and accurate language he used.

Douglas was, in his manners, cordial, frank, and hearty. The poorest and humblest found him friendly. In his younger days he had a certain familiarity of manner quite unusual. When he was at the bar, and even after he went on the bench, it was not unusual for him to come down from the bench, or leave his chair at the bar, and take his seat on the knee of a friend, and, with an arm thrown familiarly around the neck of his companion, have a social chat, or a legal or political consultation.[1]

Such familiarity had disappeared before 1858. In his long residence at Washington, Douglas had acquired the

1. Such familiarities were not general at the West, as is shown by an incident which illustrates the personal dignity of the great senator from Missouri, Mr. Benton. A distinguished member of Congress, who was a great admirer of Benton, but a man of brusque manners, one day approached and slapped Benton familiarly and rudely on the shoulder. The senator haughtily drew himself up and said: " That, sir, is a familiarity I never permit my friends, much less a comparative stranger. Sir, it must not be repeated."

bearing and manners of a perfect gentleman and man of the world. But he was always a fascinating and attractive man, and always and everywhere personally popular. He had been, for years, carefully and thoroughly trained ; on the stump, in Congress, and in the Senate, to meet in debate the ablest speakers in the state and nation. For years he had been accustomed to meet on the floor of the Capitol, the leaders of the old whig and free soil parties. Among them were Webster and Seward, Fessenden and Crittenden, Chase, Trumbull, Hale, and others of nearly equal eminence, and his enthusiastic friends insisted that never, either in single conflict, or when receiving the assault of the senatorial leaders of a whole party, had he been discomfited. His style was bold, vigorous, and aggressive, and at times even defiant. He was ready, fluent, fertile in resources, familiar with national and party history, severe in denunciation, and he handled with skill nearly all the weapons of debate. His iron will and restless energy, together with great personal magnetism, made him the idol of his friends and party. His long, brilliant, and almost universally successful career, gave him perfect confidence in himself, and at times he was arrogant and overbearing.

Lincoln was also a thoroughly trained speaker. He had met successfully, year after year, at the bar, and on the stump, the ablest men of Illinois and the Northwest, including Lamborn, Stephen T. Logan, John Calhoun, and many others. He had contended in generous emulation with Hardin, Baker, Logan, and Browning, and had very often met Douglas, a conflict with whom he always courted rather than shunned. He had at Peoria, and elsewhere, extorted from Douglas the statement, that in all his discussions at Washington, he had never met an opponent who had given him so much trouble as Lincoln. His speeches, as we read them to-day, show a more familiar knowledge of the slavery question, than those of any other statesman of our country. This is especially true of the Peoria speech, and the Cooper Institute speech. Lincoln was powerful in argument, always seizing the strong points, and demonstrating his propositions with a clearness and logic approaching the certainty of mathematics. He had, in wit and humor, a great advantage over Douglas. Douglas's friends loved to call him "the little giant;" Lincoln was physically and intellectually the big giant.

Such were the champions who, in 1858, were to discuss before the voters of Illinois, and with the whole nation as spectators and readers of the discussion, the vital questions relating to slavery. It was not a single debate, but, beginning at Chicago, in July, extended late into October, nearly to the time of the November elections. Reporters, representing the great daily newspapers of New York, Chicago, St. Louis, and Cincinnati, were present, and the speeches were reported, printed, and scattered broadcast over the nation : and were so widely read, that it is not too much to say that the whole American people paused to watch the progress of the debates, and hung with intense interest on the words and movements of the champions. [1]

It was indeed a grand spectacle. Each speaker, while addressing from five to ten thousand people, or as many as could hear any human voice in the open air, was also conscious that he spoke not to his hearers only, but to hundreds of thousands of readers; conscious that he was speaking, not for a day, or for a political campaign, but for all time—and thus stimulated, each rose to the gravity and dignity of the occasion. There was not then, nor is there now, any hall in Illinois large enough to receive the vast crowds which gathered. The groves and prairies alone could furnish adequate space, and so the people gathered under the locusts

1. As an illustration of this, I insert a paragraph from a letter of Henry W. Longfellow, to whom a sketch of this debate was sent a short time before his death. The letter is dated at Cambridge, Feb. 22d, 1881, and he says :

" I have read it (the sketch) with interest and pleasure, particularly that part of it which relates to Mr. Lincoln.

I well remember the impression made upon me by his speeches in this famous political canvass, in 1858, as reported in the papers at the time, and am glad to find it renewed and confirmed by your vivid sketches.

I am, my dear Sir,   Yours Very Truly,
                                        HENRY W. LONGFELLOW."

on the public square at Ottawa, on the oak and elm shaded banks of Rock River at Freeport, at Quincy near the Mississippi, and elsewhere, to hear these their leaders.

The first speech was made by Douglas, Lincoln being present, at Chicago, on the evening of the 9th of July, 1858, from the balcony of the old Tremont House; Dearborn and Lake Streets being completely packed with citizens, and the hotel parlors and rotunda filled with ladies and privileged guests. On the following evening Lincoln replied from the same place, to a crowd equally great. On the 16th of July, Douglas spoke again at Bloomington, Lincoln being present. On the 17th of July, Douglas spoke at the Capitol in Springfield, and on the evening of the same day Lincoln replied.

On the 24th of July, Lincoln addressed a note to Douglas, proposing arrangements for a series of joint discussions during the canvass.[1] After some correspondence it was agreed that there should be seven joint discussions, that the opening speech should occupy one hour, the reply one hour and a half, and the close a half hour, so that each discussion should occupy three hours. They were to speak at Ottawa, August 21st; at Freeport, August 27th; at Jonesborough, September 15th; at Charleston, September 18th; at Galesburg, October 7th; at Quincy, October 13th; and at Alton, October 15th. Douglas was to have the opening and the close of the debate at four of these seven meetings.

The disinterested spectator at one of these discussions would, when they began, probably find his sympathy with "the little giant," on the principle that one is apt to sympathize with the smaller man in a fight. If so, and he were to remain to the close, he would be likely to change sides before the end, seeing that Lincoln was so fair, so candid, so frank, so courteous, and answered every question so well,

1.   CHICAGO, ILL., July 24, 1858.
HON. S. A. DOUGLAS.—*My Dear Sir:* Will it be agreeable to you to make an arrangement for you and myself to divide time and address the same audiences the present canvass. Mr. Judd, who will hand you this, is authorized to receive your answer, and, if agreeable to you, to enter into the terms of such arrangement.
                    Your obedient servant,   A. LINCOLN.
—*Lincoln and Douglas Debates, p. 64.*

while Douglas was at times evasive, at others arrogant, and not always even courteous.

There is in one of Lincoln's speeches, made in 1856,[1] an allusion to Douglas, so beautiful, generous, and eloquent, that I quote it as an indication of the temper in which he carried on these discussions : " Twenty years ago," said he, " Douglas and I first became acquainted. We were both young then—he a trifle younger than I. Even then we were both ambitious—I, perhaps, quite as much as he. With me the race of ambition has been a failure—a flat failure. With him it has been one of splendid success. His name fills the nation, and is not unknown even in foreign lands. I affect no contempt for the high eminence he has reached. So reached, that the oppressed of my species might have shared with me in the elevation, I would rather stand on that eminence than wear the richest crown that ever pressed a monarch's brow." We know, the world knows, that Lincoln did reach that high, nay, far higher eminence, and that he did reach it in such a way that the "oppressed of his species" shared with him in the elevation.

There is no reason to doubt that each of these great men believed, at that time, that he was right. Douglas had that ardor of temperament which would make him believe while in the midst of such a conflict that he was right, and Lincoln's friends all know that he argued for freedom and against slavery with the most profound conviction that the fate of his country hung on the result. He said to a friend during the canvass: " Sometimes in the excitement of speaking I seem to see the end of slavery. I feel that the time is soon coming when the sun shall shine, the rain fall, on no man who shall go forth to unrequited toil." * * " How this will come, when it will come, by whom it will come, I cannot tell—but that time will surely come."

Lincoln had several advantages over Douglas in this conflict. He had the right side, the side of liberty, the side towards which the tide of popular feeling was setting with

1. See Holland's Life of Lincoln, p. 155.

tremendous force. Then he had the better temper, he was always good humored; while Douglas, when hard pressed, was sometimes irritable. Lincoln's wit and humor, his apt stories for illustration were an immense advantage, especially when addressing a popular assembly. Speaking then, for his country, for the principles of the fathers, and for freedom, his eloquence surpassed all his own previous efforts. His lips seemed at times touched by fire from off the very altar of liberty. Patrick Henry had always been his ideal orator, and both Henry and Lincoln were great men by nature, both country-bred and self-educated. Patrick Henry had little of Lincoln's humor, but Lincoln had at times the fire and enthusiasm of him who said : " Give me liberty or give me death." It was liberty that made Henry so eloquent; it was the same theme that made Lincoln so great.

Douglas, perhaps, carried away the more popular applause. Lincoln made the deeper, and more lasting impression. Douglas did not disdain an immediate, *ad captandum* triumph, while Lincoln aimed at permanent conviction. Sometimes, when Lincoln's friends urged him to raise a storm of applause, which he could always do by his happy illustrations and amusing stories, he refused, saying: " The occasion is too serious; the issues are too grave. I do not," said he, " seek applause, or to amuse the people, but to convince them." It was observed, in the canvass, that while Douglas was greeted with the loudest cheers, when Lincoln closed, the people seemed serious and thoughtful, and could be heard all through the crowds, gravely and anxiously discussing the subjects on which he had been speaking.

The echo and the prophecy of this great debate were heard, and inspired hope, in the far-off cotton and rice fields of the South. The toiling and superstitious negroes began to hope for freedom, and in a mysterious way (did the sibylline lips of the Voudou whisper it ?), faith was inspired in them that their deliverance was at hand, that their liberator was on the earth. In the words of Whittier, they lifted up their prayer:

10

" We pray de Lord.   He gib us signs
  Dat some day we be free;
  De Norf winds tell it to de pines,
  De wild duck to de sea.

" We tink it when de church bell ring;
  We dream it in de dream;
  De rice bird mean it when he sing;
  De eagle when he scream."

The friends of Douglas, who managed the machinery of
the campaign, did it well.   A special train of cars, a band of
music, a cannon to thunder forth his approach, and a party
of ardent and enthusiastic friends accompanied him to cheer
and encourage; so that his passage from place to place was
like that of a conquering hero.

The democratic party, so long dominant in Illinois, were
now, from Douglas down, confident, and his partisans full
of bluster and brag.   They everywhere boasted, and were
ready to bet, that their " little giant" would " use up and
utterly demolish ' old Abe '. "   They were so noisy and
demonstrative; they seemed so absolutely sure of success,
that many of the republicans, unconscious of the latent
power of Lincoln, became alarmed.   Douglas had so uni-
formly triumphed, and his power over the people was so
great, that many were disheartened, and feared the ordeal of
a joint discussion, which would certainly expose the weaker
man.   This feeling was apparent in the editorials of some
of the leading republican newspapers.

Just before the first joint discussion, which was to take
place at Ottawa, there was a large gathering at the Chenery
House, then the leading hotel at Springfield.   The house
was filled with politicians, and so great was the crowd, that
large numbers were out of doors, in the street, and on the
sidewalk.   Lincoln was there, surrounded by his friends,
but it is said [1] that he looked careworn and weary.   He had
become conscious that some of his party friends distrusted
his ability to meet successfully a man whom, as the demo-

1. By H. W. Beckwith, of Danville, Vermillion Co., Illinois.

crats declared and believed, had never had his equal on the stump. Seeing an old friend from Vermillion County, Lincoln came up, and, shaking hands, inquired the news. His friend replied: "All looks well, our friends are wide awake, but—," he continued, "they are looking forward with some anxiety to these approaching joint discussions with Douglas." A shade passed over Lincoln's face, a sad expression came and instantly passed, and then a blaze of light flashed from his eyes, and his lips quivered. "I saw," said his friend, "that he had penetrated my feelings and fears, and that he knew of the apprehensions of his friends. With his lips compressed, and with a manner peculiar to him, half jocular, he said : 'My friend, sit down a minute, and I will tell you a story.' We sat down on the door step leading into the hotel, and he then continued : 'You and I, as we have traveled the circuit together attending court, have often seen two men about to fight. One of them, the big, or the little giant, as the case may be, is noisy, and boastful ; he jumps high in the air, strikes his feet together, smites his fists, brags about what he is going to do, and tries hard to *skeer* the other man. The other says not a word.' Lincoln's manner became earnest, and his look firm and resolute. 'The other man says not a word, his arms are at his side, his fists are clenched, his teeth set, his head settled firmly on his shoulders, he saves his breath and strength for the struggle. This man will whip, just as sure as the fight comes off. Good-bye,' said he, 'and remember what I say.' From that moment, I felt as certain of Lincoln's triumph, as after it was won."

The joint discussion at Charleston, was on the 18th of September. This was in Lincoln's old circuit, where he was personally known, and popular, but a majority of the people were politically opposed to him. There was a vast throng, eager to witness the contest. Many were in wagons, having taken with them their provisions, and camping out in the groves at night. It was estimated that twenty thousand people were in attendance.

Lincoln, on that day, had the opening and the close.

This was the fourth joint discussion, and no one who witnessed it could ever after doubt Lincoln's ample ability to meet Douglas. The "little giant" and his friends, had learned that there were blows to be received, as well as to be given. The Senator, who had begun the canvass at Ottawa, aggressive and overbearing, had learned caution, and that he must husband his resources. Ugly questions had been propounded to him, which it was difficult for him to answer. His action in relation to the repeal of the Missouri Compromise, which he was trying to justify, enabled Lincoln to keep him on the defensive. In reply to Douglas's charge against Lincoln, of arousing sectional feeling, and leading a sectional party, the reply was always ready: "It was you, Douglas, that started the great conflagration; it was you that set the dry prairie on fire, by repealing the Missouri Compromise."

Douglas's reply to Lincoln at Charleston, was mainly a defense. Lincoln's close was intensely interesting and dramatic. His logic and arguments were crushing, and Douglas's evasions were exposed, with a power and clearness that left him utterly discomfited. Republicans saw it, democrats realized it, and "a sort of panic seized them, and ran through the crowd of up-turned faces." [1] Douglas realized his defeat, and, as Lincoln's blows fell fast and heavy, he lost his temper. He could not keep his seat, he rose and walked rapidly up and down the platform, behind Lincoln, holding his watch in his hand, and obviously impatient for the call of "time." A spectator says: "He was greatly agitated, his long grizzled hair waving in the wind, like the shaggy locks of an enraged lion."

It was while Douglas was thus exhibiting to the crowd his eager desire to stop Lincoln, that the latter, holding the audience entranced by his eloquence, was striking his heaviest blows. The instant the second hand of his watch reached the point at which Lincoln's time was up, Douglas, holding up the watch, called out: "Sit down, Lincoln, sit down. Your time is up."

1. The expression of a spectator.

Turning to Douglas, Lincoln said calmly : " I will.   I will *quit*.   I believe my time *is* up."   " Yes," said a man on the platform, " Douglas has had enough, it is time you let him up."   And this spectator expressed the feeling of friend and foe, concerning this battle of the giants.

Douglas had declared that certain telling charges made by Senator Trumbull, and indorsed by Lincoln, were false. He did not deny the facts stated by Trumbull, nor attempt by argument to disprove the conclusions which were drawn, but coarsely said that Trumbull had declared and Lincoln indorsed what was false.   In reply, Lincoln used this fine illustration, exposing the *ad captandum* argument :   " Why, sir," exclaimed Lincoln, " there is not a statement in Trumbull's speech that depends upon Trumbull's veracity.   Why does he not answer the facts ?"   *   *   *   *   " If," continued he, " you have ever studied geometry, you remember that by a course of reasoning Euclid proves that all the angles in a triangle are equal to two right angles.   Euclid has shown how to work it out.   Now, if you undertook to disprove that proposition, to show that it was erroneous, would you do it by calling Euclid a liar ?   That is the way Judge Douglas answers Trumbull." [1]   The result of this memorable campaign, so far as the voters were concerned, was a drawn battle.   Douglas was re-elected to the Senate, but the manly bearing, the vigorous logic, the great ability and love of liberty exhibited by Lincoln in these debates, secured, two years later, his nomination and election to the Presidency.

The debates and debaters have passed into history, and the world has pronounced Lincoln the victor ; but it should be remembered that Lincoln spoke for liberty and a young and enthusiastic party, and that Douglas, while a candidate for the Senate, was looking also to the White House, and that, while he kept one eye on Illinois, he had to keep the other on the slaveholders.   Thus he was hampered and embarrassed, but he made a brilliant canvass.   It should not be

---

1. Lincoln and Douglas Debates, p. 160.

forgotten that the whole power of Buchanan's administration was used to aid in his defeat. The patronage of the Federal Government, in the hands of the unscrupulous Slidell, was used against him.

There was something almost heroic in the gallantry with which Douglas threw himself into the contest, and dealt his blows right and left, against the republican party on the one hand, and the Buchanan administration on the other. Douglas's great power as a leader, and his personal popularity, are exhibited in the facts that every democratic member of Congress from Illinois stood by him faithfully, that the Democratic State Convention indorsed him, and that no considerable impression against him could be made by all the power and patronage of the administration.[1] There is, on the whole, hardly any greater personal triumph in the history of American politics, than his re-election.

No extracts from these debates can do anything like justice to their merits. They were entirely extemporaneous, and the reports which were made and widely circulated in book and pamphlet, while full of striking and beautiful passages, of strong arguments, and keen repartee, are disappointing and unsatisfactory to those who had the great pleasure of listening to them.

At the discussion at Freeport, Lincoln replied, with perfect fairness and frankness, to various questions of Douglas; questions skillfully framed to draw out unpopular opinions, and such as should be especially obnoxious to the extreme anti-slavery men. Lincoln answered all without evasion. He then in turn propounded certain questions to Douglas, and among others, questions designed to expose the inconsistency of the Senator, in upholding his doctrine of "popular sovereignty," and that part of the Dred Scott decision in which the court declared that the people—the "popular sovereigns," had no right to exclude slavery. His second

1. The popular vote stood thus: Lincoln, 126,084; Douglas, 121,940; Buchanan, 5,091. Douglas was elected by the party with a minority vote, because some democratic senators, representing republican districts, held over.

interrogatory was: " Can the people of a United States territory, in any lawful way, against the wish of any citizen of
the United States, exclude slavery from its limits, prior to the
formation of a state constitution." It was in reference to this
that a friend of Lincoln said: " If Douglas answers in such
a way as to give practical force and effect to the Dred Scott
decision, he inevitably loses the battle; but he will reply, by
declaring the decision an abstract proposition; he will adhere
to his doctrine of ' squatter sovereignty,' and declare that a
territory may exclude slavery." " If he does that," said Mr.
Lincoln, " he can never be President." " But," said the
friend, " he may be Senator." " Perhaps," replied Lincoln,
" but I am after larger game; the battle of 1860 is worth a
hundred of this."

It was obviously impossible to reconcile Douglas's position at Freeport, and elsewhere, that " the people could
exclude slavery if they pleased, and that their right to do so
was perfect and complete, under the Nebraska bill," with the
decision of the Court, that the people of the territory could
do nothing of the kind. The Court said that a master had
the right, under the Constitution, to take, and hold his slaves,
in all the territories. If so, slavery could not be excluded
by the people of the territory. Lincoln, in one of those
terse, clear sentences, into which he often condensed a whole
speech, exposed the absurdity of this. " Douglas holds,"
said he, " that a thing may lawfully be driven away from a
place where it has a lawful right to go." He thus describes
his appreciation of the momentous issue: " I do not claim
to be unselfish. I do not pretend that I would not like to go
to the United States Senate." * * * " But I say to you,
that in this mighty issue, it is nothing to the mass of the people of the nation, whether or not Judge Douglas or myself
shall ever be heard of after this night. It may be a trifle to
us, but in connection with this mighty issue, upon which, perhaps, hang the destinies of the nation, it is absolutely
nothing."

At their last joint discussion in October, at Alton, where

Lovejoy, twenty one years before, had been killed because of his fidelity to freedom, Lincoln, in closing the debate, said: " Is slavery wrong? That is the real issue. That is the issue that will continue in this country when these poor tongues of Judge Douglas and myself shall be silent. It is the eternal struggle between these two principles—right and wrong—throughout the world. They are two principles that have stood face to face from the beginning of time; and will ever continue to struggle. The one is the common right of humanity, and the other the divine right of kings. It is the same principle in whatever shape it developes itself. It is the same spirit that says: 'You work, and toil, and earn bread, and I'll eat it.' No matter in what shape it comes, whether from the mouth of a king who seeks to bestride the people of his own nation, and live by the fruit of their labor, or from one race of men, as an apology for enslaving another race, it is the same tyrannical principle." * * *

" On this subject of treating it (slavery) as a wrong, and limiting its spread, let me say a word. Has anything ever threatened the existence of the Union, save and except this very institution of slavery? What is it that we hold most dear among us? Our own liberty and prosperity. What has ever threatened our liberty and prosperity, save and except this institution of slavery? If this is true, how do you propose to improve the condition of things by enlarging slavery? By spreading it out and making it bigger? You may have a wen or cancer upon your person, and not be able to cut it out lest you bleed to death; but surely it is not the way to cure it, to engraft it and spread it over your whole body. That is no proper way of treating what you regard as wrong. You see this peaceful way of dealing with it as a wrong—restricting the spread of it, and not allowing it to go into new countries, where it has not already existed. That is the peaceful way, the old fashioned way, the way in which the fathers themselves set us the example."

CHAPTER X.

LINCOLN BECOMES PRESIDENT.

DOUGLAS RE-ELECTED TO THE SENATE.—LINCOLN ASSESSED FOR EX-
PENSES OF THE CANVASS.—VISIT TO KANSAS.—CALLED TO OHIO.
—SPEAKS AT COLUMBUS AND CINCINNATI.—IN THE NEW ENGLAND
STATES.—SHRINKS FROM THE CANDIDACY.—COOPER INSTITUTE
SPEECH.—NOMINATED FOR PRESIDENT.—HIS ELECTION.

THE great intellectual conflict was over. Lincoln, weary
but not exhausted, returned to his home at Springfield, and
when the returns came in, it appeared that he had won the
victory for his cause, his party, and his country. The republican state ticket was elected; he had carried a majority
of the popular vote, but he was again baffled in obtaining
the position of Senator, which he so much desired. A sufficient number of Douglas democrats elected two years before
from districts now republican, still held over, and inequali-
ties in the apportionment enabled Douglas to control a
small majority of the Legislature, although defeated in the
popular vote.

As soon as this became known, a perfect ovation was
given to that popular idol. After a little rest, the Senator
started for Washington, by way of the Mississippi river.
Popular receptions awaited him at St. Louis, at Memphis,
and at New Orleans. Taking a steamer to New York, on
his arrival in that city, he was welcomed by a great con-
course of people, and this welcome was repeated, with the
utmost enthusiasm, at Philadelphia, Baltimore, and Washington.

Lincoln was resting quietly at his little cottage in Springfield. He had been speaking constantly from July to November, for both he and Douglas, when not engaged in joint discussion, were speaking elsewhere. He was cheerful, and apparently so gratified with the result, that he almost forgot his personal disappointment. It does not appear that the honors lavished upon his rival disturbed his sleeping or waking hours. At the end of the canvass, both Douglas and Lincoln visited Chicago; Douglas was so hoarse that he could scarcely articulate, and it was painful to hear him attempt to speak. Lincoln's voice was clear and vigorous, and it really seemed in better tone than usual. His dark complexion was bronzed by the prairie sun and winds, but his eye was clear, his step firm, and he looked like a trained athlete, ready to enter, rather than one who had closed a conflict.

On the 16th of November, in reply to a letter of the Chairman of the State Committee relating to the expenditures of the canvass, he says:

" I have been on expense so long, without earning anything, that I am absolutely without money now to pay for even household expenses. Still, you can put in two hundred and fifty dollars for me towards discharging the debt of the committee. I will allow it when we settle the private matter between us." * *

" This, too, is exclusive of my ordinary expenses during the campaign, all of which, added to my loss of time and business, bears heavily on one no better off than I am." [1]

He owned at this time the little house and lot on which

---

1. The letter is as follows:

SPRINGFIELD, Nov. 16, 1858.

HON. N. B. JUDD—*My Dear Sir:* Yours of the 15th is just received. I wrote you the same day. As to the pecuniary matter, I am willing to pay according to my ability, but I am the poorest hand living to get others to pay. *I have been on expense* so long, without earning anything, that I am absolutely without money now for even household expenses. Still, if you can put in two hundred and fifty dollars for me towards discharging the debt of the committee, I will allow it when you and I settle the private matter between us. This, with what I have already paid with an outstanding note of mine, will exceed my subscription of five hundred dollars. This, too, is exclusive of my ordinary expenses during the campaign, all of which being added to my loss of time and business, bears pretty heavily upon one no better off than I am. But as I had the post of honor, it is not for me to be over-nice. You are feeling badly, ' *and this, too, shall pass away,*' never fear.

Yours as ever,   A. LINCOLN.

he lived, and a few law-books, and was earning not to exceed three thousand dollars per annum in his profession. He was not then worth over ten or fifteen thousand dollars altogether.

One would suppose that the sacrifice of time and money involved in paying his own expenses in the canvass, had fully met his share of the cost, and that the committee would have raised the money they had expended, from the wealthy members of the party in Chicago and elsewhere, rather than, under the circumstances, have called upon their candidate for the Senate. The close of his letter: "You are feeling badly," "and this too shall pass away, never fear," shows that so far from feeling chagrin or depression over his defeat, he had a word of cheer for his friends.

In the autumn of 1859 he visited Kansas, and the people of that young commonwealth received him as one who had so eloquently plead their cause should be received.

That Lincoln's friends began, during the debates of 1858, seriously to consider him as an available candidate for the Presidency, is well known. Late in the autumn of that year, after the close of the canvass, some of his friends proposed to begin an organization with the view of bringing him before the people for nomination in 1860. Mr. Fell, of Bloomington, Secretary of the Republican State Central Committee, had an interview with him on the subject.[1]

Lincoln discouraged the proposition, and said that he was not well enough known. "What," said he, "is the use of talking of me, whilst we have such men as Seward and Chase, and everybody knows them, and scarcely anybody, outside of Illinois, knows me? Besides," said he, "as a matter of justice, is it not due to them?" In reply, his friends urged his great availability, on the ground that he was not obnoxious as a radical, or otherwise. They reminded him that the party was in a minority; that defeated

---

1. See a full statement of this interview in the Lincoln Memorial Album, pp. 477-478.

in 1856, with Fremont, they would be beaten in 1860—unless a great many new votes could be obtained. These would be repelled by the extreme utterances and votes of Seward and Chase, but on the simple issue of opposing the extension of slavery, an issue with which Lincoln was distinctly identified, a majority could probably be obtained. That, by his debate with Douglas, he, more than any other man in the nation, represented that distinct issue, and that he had no embarrassing record ; that he was personally popular, and that with him for their candidate, the republican party had a fair chance of success. Nothing came of this conference at that time, but it was not forgotten.

In the autumn of 1859, Douglas visited Ohio, and made a canvass for the democratic party. On his appearance, the cry arose at once: "Where is Lincoln, the man who beat him in Illinois? Send for him!" Lincoln was sent for. He came, and spoke with great ability, at Columbus and at Cincinnati, and, at the latter place, addressed himself especially to Kentuckians. He said, among other things, that they ought to nominate for President "my distinguished friend, Judge Douglas." "In my opinion it is," says he, "for you to take him or be beaten."

A portion of this speech was as follows:

" I should not wonder that there are some Kentuckians about this audience; we are close to Kentucky; and whether that be so or not, we are on elevated ground, and by speaking distinctly, I should not wonder if some of the Kentuckians would hear me on the other side of the river. For that purpose I propose to address a portion of what I have to say to the Kentuckians. * * I have told you what we mean to do. I want to know now, when that thing takes place, what you mean to do. I often hear it intimated that you mean to divide the Union whenever a republican, or anything like it, is elected President of the United States. (A voice—' That is so.') ' That is so,' one of them says; I wonder if he is a Kentuckian? (A voice—' He is a Douglas man.') Well, then, I want to know what you are going to do with your half of it? Are you going to split the Ohio down through, and push your half off a piece? Or are you going to keep it right alongside of us outrageous fellows? Or are you going to build up a wall some way between your country and ours, by which that movable property of yours can't come over here any

more, to the danger of your losing it ? Do you think you can better yourselves on that subject, by leaving us here under no obligation whatever to
return those specimens of your movable property that come hither ? You
have divided the Union because we would not do right with you, as you
think, upon that subject; when we cease to be under obligations to do
anything for you, how much better off do you think you will be? Will
you make war upon us and kill us all ? Why, gentlemen, I think you
are as gallant and as brave men as live; that you can fight as bravely in
a good cause, man for man, as any other people living; that you have
shown yourselves capable of this upon various occasions; but man for man,
you are not better than we are, and there are not so many of you as there
are of us. You will never make much of a hand at whipping us. If we
were fewer in numbers than you, I think that you could whip us; if we
were equal it would likely be a drawn battle; but being inferior in numbers, you will make nothing by attempting to master us."

This speech showed how confident he was of success. It
defined his position, and added much to his popularity.

In December, 1859, the feeling in favor of his nomination for the Presidency had become so general, that he consented to permit his friends to take such steps as they deemed
expedient to bring him forward as a candidate for the nomination. On the 20th of December, he gave to Mr. Fell
that modest paper giving some details of his life, which has
already been set forth in the early part of this volume.

On Tuesday evening, February 27th, 1860, Mr. Lincoln
delivered, in the city of New York, the Cooper Institute
speech ; a speech that probably did more to secure his nomination, than any other act of his life. He had become
widely known as the successful stump-speaker against Douglas. It was known that he was an able, effective debater,
but many supposed that he was a mere declaimer, and successful stump-speaker only ; that with much coarse humor,
he was probably superficial. True, he had beaten Douglas,
and by beating Douglas, he had beaten the whole field ; but
exactly what manner of man he was, nobody outside of Illinois knew. Great curiosity was manifested to hear this Western prodigy, this prairie orator, this rough, uncouth, unlearned
backwoodsman. He realized all this, and his Cooper Institute speech, either designedly, or otherwise, was admirably

adapted to remove prejudice, and create confidence. It was the speech of a statesman.

Cooper Institute, an immense hall, was filled to its utmost capacity. Horace Greeley, who, in the New York Tribune, had advised the Illinois republicans not to oppose Douglas in his canvass for the Senate, and who had thus, by implication, opposed Lincoln, now said : " No man has been welcomed by such an audience of the intellect and mental culture of our city, since the days of Clay and Webster."

On the platform were the most distinguished scholars, jurists, and divines of the city. Bryant, the poet, presided, and introduced the speaker. Never was an audience more surprised, and never more delighted. It was a political argument ; brief, profound, and exhaustive. Instead of rant, declamation, striking and witty points, it was a calm, clear, learned, dignified, and complete exposition of the whole subject ; the speech of a scholar, and showed that he was an accurate and laborious student of history. There is compressed into it such an amount of historical learning, stated in the simplest language, as within such a compass, is perhaps unparalleled.

The argument demonstrating the right of Congress to prohibit slavery in the territories, and that such was the understanding of "our fathers," who framed the Constitution and organized the government, has never been surpassed; it never has been, nor can it be, successfully answered. The effort was so dignified, and exhibited so much learning, and such thorough mastery of the subject, that, coming from a source whence this kind of excellence was not expected, it was a surprise and revelation, and, therefore, made the greater impression. He awoke the next morning to find himself famous. He closed his great argument with these words : " Let us have faith that right makes might, and in that faith, let us to the end dare to do our duty as we understand it." The speech was published in full by the New York Tribune and other papers, and scattered all over the Union, and it perfectly satisfied the thoughtful and intellectual men of the republican party as to Lincoln's great intellectual power and wise moderation, and it prepared the way for his nomination Subsequently, he spoke in Connecticut, Rhode Island, and New Hampshire, everywhere making personal friends, and leaving a lasting impression of his great ability.

A clergyman of Norwich, Connecticut, who heard him in that city, met him the following day in the cars. Introducing himself, he said:

" Your speech last night was the most remarkable I ever heard." " I should like to know," said Lincoln, " what there was you thought so remarkable ? " The clergyman replied: " The clearness of your statements, the unanswerable style of your reasoning, and especially your illustrations, which were romance and pathos, fun and logic, all welded together." [1]

The presidential election of 1860 now approached. The storm of political excitement, North and South, was raging with intense violence. The democratic convention to nominate candidates was called to meet at Charleston, S. C., in April. Douglas was the popular candidate in the free states, with many strong personal friends in the slave states. The politicians of that party believed, as Lincoln had told them at Cincinnati, that they must take Douglas or be defeated. But the ultra slaveholders, as a class, were bitterly opposed to him, on account of his opposition to the Lecompton Constitution, and his replies to Lincoln at Freeport, Illinois. Hitherto the North had generally yielded to the more determined leaders among the slaveholders, and many supposed that the friends of Douglas, as those of Benton, Van Buren, and Wright had done in days gone by, would yield, and permit the nomination of some negative man, some compromise candidate. An Illinois republican, a short time before the Charleston convention, said to Colonel Richardson, one of Douglas's efficient friends, and one likely to lead his friends in that convention:

" Douglas will be sacrificed. As Van Buren was sacri-

1. The Rev. John Sullivan. New York Independent, September 1st, 1864.

ficed because of his opposition to Texas annexation, so the South will sacrifice Douglas because he opposed Lecompton."

"No," replied Richardson, "the South will find Douglas's friends as firm and determined as they are. We have the majority, and our leader shall not be sacrificed. The South will find they have now to deal with the West, with men as determined as themselves."

In the Charleston convention was a large party who were secessionists, disunionists, and who desired separation. They meant to push matters to extremes, to divide the democratic party, thereby rendering the success of the republican party certain, and then to make the election of a republican a pretext for the dissolution of the Union.

The first thing done after organization was the adoption of a platform. A majority reported resolutions declaring that neither Congress nor a territorial legislature had any power to abolish or prohibit slavery in the territories, "nor to impair or destroy the right of property in slaves by any legislation whatever." This was intended to be, and was, a direct repudiation of Douglas's doctrine of popular sovereignty, and his friends knew that they might as well give up the canvass as go before the people with this platform. A minority of the committee, but representing states which held a decided majority of the electoral votes, reported resolutions re-affirming the platform adopted by the national convention at Cincinnati four years before; declaring that "inasmuch as there were differences of opinion in the democratic party as to the powers of a territorial legislature, and as to the powers and duties of Congress under the Constitution over the institution of slavery in the territories, the democratic party would abide by the decrees of the Supreme Court on questions of constitutional law." Butler, of Massachusetts, reported the old Cincinnati platform. After voting down Mr. Butler's proposition, the convention adopted the minority report. This was supported by the friends of Douglas.

Thereupon L. P. Walker, subsequently the rebel Secretary of War, presented the protest of the delegates from Alabama, and these delegates withdrew from the convention. Among these delegates was William L. Yancey, long before a notorious secessionist. The delegates from Mississippi, Louisiana, Texas, South Carolina, Florida, Arkansas, Georgia, and Delaware thereupon also withdrew. The convention then resolved that it should require two-thirds of a full convention to nominate. After balloting several times, on each of which ballots Mr. Douglas had a large, but not the two-thirds majority required, the convention adjourned to meet at Baltimore on the 18th of June. The seceding delegates adjourned to meet at Richmond on the second Monday in June.

The Baltimore convention met and nominated Stephen A. Douglas for President, and Benjamin Fitzpatrick, of Alabama, for Vice-President; but on his declining, Herschel V. Johnson, of Georgia, was substituted. The convention of the seceders met at Richmond, and, adopting the resolutions of the majority of the committee, nominated John C. Breckenridge, of Kentucky, for President, and Colonel Joseph Lane, of Oregon, for Vice-President. The disruption of the democratic party was hailed with delight by the infatuated people of Charleston and other parts of the rebel states as the prelude to the breaking up of the Union.

The republican convention had been called to meet at Chicago on the 16th of May. On the 10th of May, the Illinois republican state convention was held at Decatur, in Macon County, to nominate state officers and appoint delegates to the national presidential convention. This was not very far from where Lincoln's father had settled and worked a farm in 1830, and where young Abraham Lincoln and Thomas Hanks had split the rails for enclosing the old pioneer's first corn field. On the 9th of February preceding, Lincoln had written a characteristic letter to Mr. Judd, the chairman of the state central committee, in which he said : " I am not in a position where it would hurt much for me not to be nominated on the national ticket, but I am where it would hurt some for me not to get the Illinois dele-gates." [1]

Lincoln was present at the Decatur convention, and as he entered the hall he was received with such demonstrations of attachment as left no doubt as to the wishes of Illinois on the question of his nomination. When he was seated, General Oglesby announced that an old democrat of Macon County desired to make a contribution to the convention. Immediately some farmers brought into the hall two old fence rails, bearing the inscription : *"Abraham Lincoln, the rail candidate for the Presidency in 1860. Two rails from a lot of three thousand, made in 1830, by Thomas Hanks and Abe Lincoln, whose father was the first pioneer of Macon County."*

The effect of this cannot be described. For fifteen minutes, cheer upon cheer went up from the crowd. Lincoln was called to the stand, but his rising was the signal for renewed cheering, and this continued until the audience had exhausted itself, and then Mr. Lincoln gave a history of these two rails, and of his life in Macon County. He told the story of his labor in helping to build his father's log cabin, and fencing in a field of corn. This dramatic scene was not planned by politicians, but was the spontaneous action of the old pioneers. The effect it had upon the people satisfied all present that it was a waste of words to talk in Illinois of any other man than Abraham Lincoln for President.

No public man had less of the demagogue than Mr. Lincoln. He never mentioned his humble life, or his manual labor, for the purpose of getting votes. He knew perfectly

---

1.   "SPRINGFIELD, ILL., February 9, 1860.

"HON. N. B. JUDD—*Dear Sir:* I am not in a position where it would hurt much for me not to be nominated on the national ticket; but I am where it would hurt some for me not to get the Illinois delegates. What I expected when I wrote the letter to Messrs. Dole and others is now happening. Your discomfited assailants are more bit-ter against me, and they will, for revenge upon me, lay to the Bates egg in the South and the Seward egg in the North, and go far towards squeezing me out in the middle with nothing. Can you not help me a little in this matter in your end of the vine-yard? (I mean this to be private.)   Yours as ever,   A. LINCOLN."

well that it did not follow because a man could split rails, that he would make a good statesman or President. So far from having any feeling of this kind, he realized painfully the defects of his education, and did his utmost to supply the deficiencies. When told that the people were talking of making him President, he said : " They ought to select some one who knows more than I do." But while he did not think any more of himself because he had in early life split rails, he had too much real dignity to lose any self-respect on that account.

The committee appointed to select delegates to the national convention, submitted the list of names to him. As illustrating how presidents are nominated, I will add that the committee, and other personal friends of Lincoln, among whom were Judd, David Davis, Swift, Cook, and others, retired from the convention, and, in a grove near by, lay down upon the grass and revised the list of delegates, which they reported to, and which were appointed by, the convention.

An immense building called the " *Wigwam,*" and capable of holding many thousands of people, had been erected especially for the meeting of the national convention. A full, eager, and enthusiastic representation was present from all the free states, together with representatives from Delaware, Maryland, Kentucky, Missouri, and Virginia, and some scattering representatives from some of the other slave states ; but the Gulf states were not represented. Indeed, few of the slave states were fully and perfectly represented. On motion of Governor Morgan, chairman of the national executive committee, David Wilmot, author of the Wilmot proviso, was made temporary chairman, and George Ashmun, of Massachusetts, permanent president.

There was not much difficulty about the platform. The convention resolved " that the new dogma that the Constitution carried slavery into all the territories, was a dangerous political heresy, revolutionary in tendency, and subversive of the peace and harmony of the country ; that the normal condition of all the territories is that of freedom ; that neither Congress, the territorial legislature, nor any individual, could give legal existence to slavery ; that Kansas ought to be immediately admitted as a free state ; that the opening of the slave trade would be a crime against humanity." It declared also in favor of a homestead law, harbor and river improvements, and the Pacific railroad.

The leading candidates for the nomination for President, were William H. Seward, of New York ; Abraham Lincoln, of Illinois ; Salmon P. Chase, of Ohio ; Simon Cameron, of Pennsylvania ; and Edward Bates, of Missouri ; but it early became apparent that the contest was between Seward and Lincoln. Mr. Seward had been for many years a leading statesman. Governor of New York, and long its most distinguished senator ; he had brought to the discussions of the great issue between liberty and slavery, a philosophic mind, broad and catholic views, great sagacity, and an elevated love of liberty and humanity. Few, if any, had done more to enlighten, create, and consolidate public opinion in the free states. His position had been far more conspicuous than that of Mr. Lincoln. Hence he had been supposed to be more in the way of rivals, and had become the object of more bitter personal and political hostility.

The Illinois candidate was principally known, outside of the Northwest, as the competitor of Douglas. Yet the *sobriquet* of " honest old Abe, the rail-splitter of Illinois," had extended throughout the free states ; he had no enemies, and was the second choice of nearly all those delegates of whom he was not the first. He was supposed by shrewd politicians to have, and he did possess, those qualities which make an available candidate. Although a resident of the state, he did not attend the convention, but was quietly at his home in Springfield.

Few men of that convention realized, or had the faintest foreshadowing of the terrible ordeal of civil war, which was before the candidate whom they should nominate and the people elect. Yet there seems to have been a peculiar propriety in Mr. Lincoln's nomination ; and there was here illustrated that instinctive sagacity, or more truly, *providential guidance*, which directs a people in a critical emergency to act wisely.

Looking back, we now see how wise the selection. The Union was to be assailed ; Lincoln was from the national Northwest, which would never surrender its great communications with the ocean, by the Mississippi, or the East. The great principles of the Declaration of Independence were to be assailed by vast armies ; his political platform had ever been that Declaration. Aristocratic power, with the sympathy of the kings and nobility of Europe, was to make a gigantic effort to crush liberty and democracy ; it was fit that the great champion of liberty, of a government " of the people, for the people, by the people," should be a man, born on the wild prairie, nurtured in the rude log cabin, and reared amidst the hardships and struggles of humble life.

On the first ballot, Mr. Seward received 173½ votes, to 102 for Lincoln ; the others being divided on Messrs. Cameron, Chase, Bates, and others. On the second ballot, Mr. Seward received 184, to 181 for Mr. Lincoln. On the third ballot Mr. Lincoln received a majority, and his nomination was then made unanimous.

An incident occurred, which, but for the tact and eloquence of George William Curtis, a delegate from New York, might have proved a serious blunder. Cartter, of Ohio, chairman of the committee, reported the resolutions constituting the platform, and endeavored to put them through under the previous question. Joshua R. Giddings, the old gray-haired veteran anti-slavery leader from the Western Reserve, Ohio, begged Cartter to withdraw the previous question, so that he might offer an amendment. Cartter refused but on a vote, the previous question was not sustained. The convention was not willing to treat the great Ohio abolitionist with rudeness, but was obviously afraid of his radicalism. He offered an amendment, embracing that part of the Declaration of Independence, which declares that "all men are created equal, and that they are endowed by their Creator with certain inalienable rights," etc. He accompanied his motion with a most earnest and eloquent speech, but the convention, by a large majority, rejected the amendment.

The venerable old man was grieved and disappointed, and, being the representative man of the abolitionists, it was feared the result would create coolness, or drive away these earnest men from supporting the ticket. Many members of the convention were still very much afraid of abolitionism. The party was far from homogeneous, and there was danger of a rupture. At this crisis, George William Curtis, one of the most scholarly, earnest, and enthusiastic young men in the republic, came forward, and renewed Giddings's amendment, slightly altered, and in a speech of ten or fifteen minutes, electrified, and carried with him the convention. "Is this convention prepared," cried he, "to vote down the Declaration of your fathers, the charter of American liberty?"

The speech was *impromptu*, but vehement and eloquent beyond description. It was received with deafening applause, and he carried with him the convention; the amendment was adopted by almost universal acclamation. No speaker ever achieved a more brilliant immediate triumph than young Curtis. It was touching to see old Mr. Giddings as he went up to Curtis, and throwing his arms around his neck, exclaimed: "God bless you, my boy. You have saved the republican party. God bless you." Curtis certainly did save the party from a great blunder, if from nothing worse.

On the first day of the convention, the friends of Lincoln discovered that there was an organized body of New Yorkers and others in the "Wigwam," who cheered vociferously whenever Seward's name was mentioned, or any allusion was made to him. The New Yorkers did the shouting, Lincoln's friends were modest and quiet.

At a meeting of the Illinois delegation at the Tremont, on the evening of the first day, at which Judd, Davis, Cook, and others were present, it was decided, that on the second day, Illinois and the West should be heard. There was then living in Chicago, a man whose voice could drown the roar of Lake Michigan in its wildest fury; nay, it was said that his shout could be heard on a calm day, across that lake; Cook, of Ottawa, knew another man, living on the Illinois River, a Dr. Ames, who had never found his equal in his ability to shout and huzza. He was, however, a democrat. Cook telegraphed to him to come to Chicago by the first train. These two men, with stentorian voices, met some of the Illinois delegation at the Tremont House, and were instructed to organize, each a body of men to cheer and shout, which they speedily did out of the crowds which were in attendance from the Northwest. They were placed on opposite sides of the "Wigwam," and instructed that when Cook took out his white handkerchief, they were to cheer, and not to cease until he returned it to his pocket. Cook was conspicuous on the platform, and, at the first utterance of the name of Lincoln, simultaneously with the wave of Cook's handkerchief, there went up such a cheer, such a shout as had never before been heard, and which startled the friends of Seward, as the cry of "Marmion" on Flodden Field "startled the Scottish foe." The New Yorkers tried to follow when the name of Seward was spoken, but, beaten at their own game, their voices were instantly and absolutely drowned by cheers for Lincoln. This was kept up until Lincoln was nominated, amidst a storm of applause never before equalled.

Ames was so carried away with his own enthusiasm for Lincoln, that he joined the republican party, and continued to shout for Lincoln during the whole campaign; he was afterwards rewarded with a country post-office. The New York delegation were greatly disappointed and chagrined, especially the immediate personal friends of Thurlow Weed and Mr. Seward.

Horace Greeley, while not especially pleased with Lincoln's nomination (his candidate having been Edward Bates, of Missouri), had telegraphed to his paper, the New York

Tribune, at 2 A. M. on the night preceding the day of Lincoln's nomination : " Seward will be nominated to-morrow." He now rejoiced at the defeat of Weed and Seward, but the New York delegation could not understand how it was done. On the second day Seward had lacked but a very few votes, and their confidence in Weed, who had long and successfully managed the politics and controlled the conventions of the Empire State, was so great, that he had acquired the title of the " Warwick of New York." He was the " King maker."

They wondered greatly how the Illinois boys had managed to beat the old veteran, and especially when, as many thought, he held the winning cards in his hands. The canvass for Lincoln had been skillfully conducted, and his personal friends, and especially Mr. Judd, the chairman of the delegation, together with David Davis and others, were entitled to great credit.

There was in the New York delegation, an eloquent and jovial member, James W. Nye, afterward Senator from Nevada. He was a great wag ; his wit and humor were well known, and the echo of the laughter caused by his jokes and stories had been heard from the Hudson to Lake Michigan. The Illinois delegation was in session, anxiously considering how the friends of Seward and Weed could be satisfied, so that they would give the ticket their cordial and hearty support. A knock at the door was heard, and the door-keeper announced : "General Nye, of New York. He says he has a message from New York to Illinois."

" Admit him instantly," said Judd, the chairman.

The General entered.

" What can Illinois do for New York?" enquired Judd. " Name it, and if in our power, consider it done."

" Well," said Nye, " if you sucker boys will please send an Illinois school-master to Albany to teach Thurlow Weed his political alphabet, we will be greatly obliged."

The Illinois delegation appreciated the compliment.

While the convention was in session, Lincoln was at his home in Springfield. The proceedings and the result of each ballot were immediately communicated to him by a telegraph wire extending from the "Wigwam." At the time of the second ballot, Lincoln was with some friends in the office of the "Sangamon Journal." Soon a gentleman hastily entered from the telegraph office, bearing a slip of paper, on which his nomination—the result of the third ballot—was written. He read the paper to himself, and then aloud, and then, without stopping to receive the congratulations of his friends, he said : " There is a little woman down at our house who will like to hear this. I'll go down and tell her." The incident speaks eloquently of the affectionate relations between him and his wife. She was far more anxious that he should be President than he himself was, and her early dream was now to be realized.

No words can adequately describe the enthusiasm with which this nomination was received in Chicago, in Illinois, and throughout the Northwest. A man who had been placed on top of the Wigwam to announce to the thousands outside the progress of the balloting, as soon as the secretary read the result of the third ballot shouted to those below: "*Fire the salute—Lincoln is nominated!*" The cannon was fired, and before its reverberations died away a hundred thousand voters of Illinois and the neighboring states were shouting, screaming, and rejoicing at the result. Hannibal Hamlin, of Maine, was nominated for Vice-President. The nomination of Lincoln was hailed with intense enthusiasm, not only by the crowds in attendance and the Northwest, but throughout the free states. Everywhere the people were full of zeal for the champion from the West. Never did a party enter upon a canvass with more earnest devotion to principle than the republican party of 1860. Love of country, devotion to liberty, hatred of slavery, pervaded all hearts. A keen sense of the wrongs and outrages inflicted upon the free state men of Kansas, the violence, and in many instances the savage cruelty, by which freedom of speech and liberty of the press had been suppressed in portions of the slave states, and strong indignation at the long catalogue of crimes of the slaveholders, fired all hearts. Confident of success, and determined to leave nothing undone to secure it, the republican party entered upon the canvass.

This Presidential campaign has had no parallel. The enthusiasm of the people was like a great conflagration, like a prairie fire before a wild tornado. A little more than twenty years had passed since Owen Lovejoy, brother of Elijah Lovejoy, on the bank of the Mississippi, kneeling on the turf not then green over the grave of the brother who had been killed for his fidelity to freedom, had sworn eternal war against slavery. From that time on, he and his associate abolitionists had gone forth preaching their crusade against oppression, with hearts of fire and tongues of lightning, and now the consummation was to be realized of a President elected on the distinct ground of opposition to the extension of slavery. For years the hatred of that institution had been growing and gathering force. Whittier, Bryant, Lowell, Longfellow, and others, had written the lyrics of liberty; the graphic pen of Mrs. Stowe, in "Uncle Tom's Cabin," had painted the cruelties of the overseer and the slaveholder, but the acts of slaveholders themselves did more to promote the growth of anti-slavery than all other causes. The persecutions of abolitionists in the South; the harshness and cruelty attending the execution of the fugitive slave laws; the brutality of Brooks in knocking down, on the floor of the Senate, Charles Sumner, for words spoken in debate; these and many other outrages had fired the hearts of the people of the free states against this barbarous institution. Beecher, Phillips, Channing, Sumner, and Seward, with their eloquence; Chase, with his logic; Lincoln, with his appeals to the principles of the Declaration of Independence, and to the opinions of the founders of the republic, his clear statements, his apt illustrations, above all, his wise moderation—all had swelled the voice of the people, which found expression through the ballot-box, and which declared that slavery should go no further. It was now proclaimed that " the further spread of slavery should be arrested, and it should be placed where the public mind should rest in the belief of its ultimate extinction."

A most remarkable feature of the campaign was the personal canvass made by Douglas.   This is almost the only instance in which a presidential candidate has taken the stump in his own behalf.   The division in the democratic party must have destroyed any hope on his part of success; yet he made a personal canvass, displaying all the vigor, and spirit, and eloquence, for which he was so distinguished. He spoke in most of the free, and in many of the slave states, and his appeals were against Breckenridge on one side, and Lincoln on the other, as representing sectionalism, while he assumed that he carried the banner of the Union. If the efforts of any one man could have changed the result, his would have changed it, but they were in vain.   Lincoln received 180 electoral votes, and a popular vote of 1,866,452. Douglas received 12 electoral votes, and 1,375,157 of the popular vote.   Breckenridge received 72 electoral, and a popular vote of 847,953; and Bell 39 electoral votes, and 590,631 of the popular vote.   By the success of Mr. Lincoln, the executive power of the country passed from the hands of the slaveholders.   They had controlled the government for much the larger portion of the time during which it had existed.

CHAPTER XI.

LINCOLN REACHES WASHINGTON.

BUCHANAN'S WEAKNESS.—TRAITORS IN HIS CABINET.—EFFORTS TO
COMPROMISE.—SEVEN STATES SECEDE AND ORGANIZE PROVISIONAL
GOVERNMENT.—COUNTING THE ELECTORAL VOTE.—LINCOLN
STARTS FOR WASHINGTON.—HIS JOURNEY.—ASSASSINATION PLOT.
—ARRIVAL AT THE CAPITAL.

ON the 7th of November, 1860, it was known throughout
the republic, that Lincoln had been elected. Not until the
4th of March could he be inaugurated. Meanwhile the
clouds, black and threatening, were gathering at the South.
It was evident that mischief was brewing. South Carolina
rejoiced over the election of Lincoln, with bonfires and pro-
cessions. His election furnished a pretext for rebellion. A
conspiracy had existed since the days of nullification, to
seize upon the first favorable opportunity to break up the
Union.[1]

For the four eventful months between Lincoln's election
and inauguration, conspirators against the Union would
still have control of the government. Buchanan, a weak,
old man, was influenced to a great extent by traitors in his
cabinet, and conspirators in Congress. A majority of his

1. In October, 1856, a meeting of the governors of slave states was held at Raleigh, North Carolina, convened at the instance of Governor Wise, who afterward
proclaimed that if Fremont had been elected, he would have marched to Washington at the head of twenty thousand men, and prevented his inauguration.

Mr. Keitt, member of Congress from South Carolina, said in the convention of
his state, which adopted the ordinance of secession: "I have been engaged in this
movement ever since I entered political life."

Mr. Rhett said: "The secession of South Carolina is not the event of a day. It
is not anything produced by Mr. Lincoln's election, or the non-enforcement of the
fugitive slave law. It is a matter that has been gathering head for thirty years."

Cabinet were open disunionists—secessionists, who retained their places, and used their power to disarm and dismantle the ship of state, that it might be surrendered an easy conquest to those preparing to seize it. Mr. Memminger, of South Carolina, who became the rebel Secretary of the Treasury, boasted that Buchanan being President, the Federal Government would be taken at great disadvantage, and it was necessary to prepare things, so that Lincoln would be for a while powerless.

On the 12th of December, Lewis Cass, Secretary of State, resigned, because the President refused to reinforce the forts in Charleston harbor. Jeremiah S. Black, who, as Attorney General of Buchanan, had given an opinion that the Federal Government had no power to coerce a seceding state, was his successor. Howell Cobb, of Georgia, the Secretary of the Treasury, and afterwards a general in the rebel army, managed to destroy the credit of the government, and when, December 10, he resigned, because his "duty to Georgia required it," he left the treasury empty.

John B. Floyd, soon to hold the rank of general in the rebel army, was Secretary of War. Before he resigned, he partly disarmed the free states, by transferring the arms in the northern arsenals to the slave states, and he sent the few soldiers belonging to the United States regular army so far away as not to be available, until the conspirators should have time to consummate the revolution. Isaac Toucey, of Connecticut, Secretary of the Navy, scattered the navy beyond seas, so that the naval force should be beyond the reach of the government. Such were the bold, unscrupulous acts of the conspirators. Some of them intended to prevent the inauguration of Lincoln, and to surrender the Capitol and the public archives to the insurgents, and it is probable that they would have carried out this design, but for the fact that General Winfield Scott was at the head of the army, and that with him was a small but reliable force, so that an overt act of treason might have been dangerous.

But the leaders of the conspiracy went forward in their

guilty preparations with impunity. If Buchanan had dismissed the traitors in his Cabinet, arrested the conspirators at the capital, called to his aid strong and loyal men, and declared like General Jackson: " The Union must be preserved," it is possible that the conspiracy might have been crushed in its inception. But he was weak, vacillating, and like clay in the hands of Jefferson Davis, Cobb, Toombs, and their associates. The strange spectacle was presented of a government in the hands of conspirators plotting to overthrow it. From the official desks and portfolios of its officers were sent forth their messages of treason. While in Congress, and in the Cabinet, the conspirators were boldly carrying on their schemes for the overthrow of the government, no attempt was made to interfere with, much less to arrest, open and avowed traitors.

I have said that nothing was done ; yet this is not strictly true. The feeble old man in the executive chair did appoint a day of fasting, humiliation, and prayer ; declaring that, though secession was wrong, he had no power to prevent it. Meanwhile the conspirators were laboring industriously to make the revolution an accomplished fact before the inauguration of Lincoln, or, if they could not accomplish this, then by plundering the government, securing the forts, ships, and munitions of war, they meant to leave Lincoln with no means at his command wherewith to protect and maintain the government, and put down the rebellion.

Some of the democratic party were indignant at the conduct of the Executive. General Cass, as has been stated, resigned because the President refused to reinforce Fort Moultrie, held by the gallant and faithful Major Anderson. Joseph Holt, of Kentucky, succeeded Floyd as Secretary of War. Edwin M. Stanton, bold, staunch, and true, succeeded Black as Attorney General, and General John A. Dix was appointed Secretary of the Treasury. Stanton, Dix, and Holt were unflinching Union men, and did all in their power to prevent the surrender of the government to the conspirators. They most efficiently aided General Scott in securing the peaceful inauguration of Lincoln.

The absence of any real grievance or excuse for rebellion was strongly expressed by Alexander H. Stephens, afterward Vice-President of the Confederate States, in a speech to the Legislature of Georgia, on the 14th of November, 1860. He said : " Mr. Lincoln can do nothing unless he is backed by the power of Congress. The House of Representatives is largely in majority against him. In the Senate he is power-less. There will be a majority of four against him." * * * " Many of us," said he, " have sworn to support the Constitution. Can we, for the mere election of a man to the Presidency, and that, too, in accordance with the forms of the Constitution, make a point of resistance without becoming the breakers of that same instrument ? " [1]

Lincoln remained at his home, a deeply anxious yet hopeful spectator. The whole country was eager to learn his views, and ascertain his intentions. He was reticent as to his policy, but expressed strong hopes of being able to quiet the storm and restore tranquillity. To an inquiry as to what kind of a man Lincoln was, an intimate friend replied : " He has the firmness and determination, without the temper, of Jackson." Those long days, from November, 1860, to March, 1861, were perhaps more gloomy than any during the war. Patriots saw conspirators plotting, and traitors plundering the treasury, dispersing the United States soldiers, sending armed ships abroad, stripping arsenals of arms, and with them arming the insurgents. They saw rebels preparing to scuttle the ship of state, and the very conspirators were the chief officers, and the people but passengers, with no power to interfere. The people watched, and earnestly prayed that the " ides of March " would come speedily, and bring Lincoln to the helm.

In the meanwhile, efforts at pacification and conciliation were made. Committees of the Senate and of the House

---

1. See McPherson's History of the Rebellion, pp. 20–25, for Stephens' speech in full.

were raised to consider measures of compromise. But all measures of this character were voted down by the conspirators themselves. They wished neither compromise nor guarantees, but separation. A so-called "Peace Convention" met at Washington, to see whether any terms could induce the disaffected to abandon their purposes. There were many who believed that the secession movement was all threat and bluster, made to secure additional guarantees for slavery. But when the most liberal concessions were made in the interests of peace, and were voted down by the most extreme slaveholders and disunionists, it became evident that those who controlled the slave power had deliberately resolved to force an issue, and go out of the Union.

Charles Francis Adams, from the House committee of thirty-three, reported "that no form of adjustment will be satisfactory to the recusant states, which does not incorporate into the Constitution of the United States, an obligation to protect and extend slavery. On this condition, and on this alone, will they consent to withdraw their opposition to the recognition of the constitutional election of the Chief Magistrate. Viewing the matter in this light, it seems unadvisable to attempt to proceed a step further in the way of offering unacceptable propositions." It was clear the conspirators had resolved on revolution.

During these gloomy days, Lincoln was firm and determined. On the question of slavery extension, he was as unyielding as adamant. On the 13th day of December, 1860, he wrote to his friend Washburne, member of Congress from Illinois, as follows:

"SPRINGFIELD, ILL., Dec. 13, 1860.

"HON. E. B. WASHBURNE—*My Dear Sir:* Your long letter received. Prevent as far as possible, any of our friends from demoralizing themselves and our cause, by entertaining propositions for compromise of any sort on the slavery extension. There is no possible compromise upon it, but which puts us under again, and leaves us all our work to do over again. Whether it be a Missouri line, or Eli Thayer's

Popular Sovereignty, it is all the same.   Let either be done, and immediately filibustering, and extending slavery recommences.   On that point
hold firm, as with a chain of steel.   Yours as ever,

                                                    " A. LINCOLN."

And again, on the 21st of December, he wrote as follows:

" *Confidential.*"
                                  "SPRINGFIELD, ILL., Dec. 21, 1860.
    " HON. E. B. WASHBURNE—*My Dear Sir:* Last night I received your
letter, giving an account of your interview with General Scott, and for
which I thank you.   Please present my respects to the General, and tell
him confidentially, I shall be obliged to him to be as well prepared as he
can to either *hold*, or retake, the forts, as the case may require, at and
after the inauguration.   Yours as ever,

                                              " A. LINCOLN." [1]

There was a meeting held at the capital on the night of
January 5th, at which Jefferson Davis, Senators Toombs,
Iverson, Slidell, Benjamin, Wigfall, and other leading conspirators were present.   They resolved in secret conclave to
precipitate secession and disunion as soon as possible, and
at the same time resolved that senators and members of the
House should remain in their seats at the Capitol as long as
possible, to watch and control the action of the Executive,
and thwart and defeat any hostile measures proposed.

In accordance with concerted plans, some of the senators and members, as the states they represented passed
ordinances of secession, retired from the Senate and House
of Representatives.   Some went forth, breathing war and
vengeance, others expressing deep feeling and regret.
Nearly all were careful to draw their pay, stationery, and
documents, and their mileage home from the treasury of the
government which they went forth avowedly to overthrow.
There were two honorable exceptions among the representatives from the Gulf states—Mr. Bouligny, representative
from New Orleans, and Andrew J. Hamilton, from Texas.
They remained true to the Union.   On the evening of the
3d of March, 1861, when the Thirty-sixth Congress was

1. The originals of these letters are in the Washburne MSS. in possession of the
Chicago Historical Society.

12

about to expire, Hamilton, upon bidding farewell to his associates, said: "*I am going home to Texas, and I shall stand by the old flag as long as there is a shred of it left as big as my hand.*"

In accordance with the programme of the conspirators, South Carolina had adopted the ordinance of secession on the 17th of November, 1860; Mississippi, January 9th, 1861; Georgia, January 19th; Florida, January 10th; Alabama, January 11th; Louisiana, January 25th, and Texas, February 1st.[1]

It is obvious that Lincoln had very clear and positive convictions of his duty. The Union and the integrity of the republic must be preserved at all hazards. Whether slavery would survive the impending struggle who could foretell? He feared immediate emancipation; he believed that gradual and compensated emancipation would be better, and how earnestly he urged this we shall by and by learn. But it would seem that slavery was one of those devils that could only be cast out by "fasting and prayer;" by bloodshed and war. Feeling deeply the responsibility, he asked earnestly and humbly the guidance of Providence, resolved "with malice toward none, and charity for all," to do his duty as God should give him to see his duty, and with this resolution to go forward.

While awaiting the course of events at Springfield, the religious—perhaps superstitious—character of Lincoln's mind was strongly manifested. Newton Bateman, a highly respectable and christian gentleman, was Superintendent of Public Instruction in Illinois, and his rooms were adjoining those of Lincoln in the Capitol at Springfield. They were associates and friends, and often conversed together in regard to the threatening condition of affairs. There was a remarkable interview between them shortly before the November election. It is quoted here in part, as detailed

1. McPherson's History of the Rebellion, pp. 2 and 3.

by Bateman,[1] not to prove Lincoln's belief or disbelief in any dogma, but as illustrating the tone and character of his mind. He said to Bateman: "I know there is a God, and he hates injustice and slavery. I see the storm coming. I know that his hand is in it. If he has a place and work for me—and I think he has—I believe I am ready. I am nothing, but truth is everything. I know I am right because I know that liberty is right, for Christ teaches it, and Christ is God. I have told them that a house divided against itself cannot stand, and Christ and reason say the same, and they will find it so."

"Douglas don't care whether slavery is voted up or down, but God cares, and humanity cares, and I care; and with God's help I shall not fail. I may not see the end; but it will come, and I shall be vindicated; and these men will find that they have not read their Bible right."

After a pause, he resumed. "Does it not appear strange that men can ignore the moral aspects of this contest? A revelation could not make it plainer to me that slavery or the government must be destroyed. The future would be something awful, as I look at it, but for this rock on which I stand" (alluding to the Testament, which he held in his hand).

The one who recounts this interview, continues thus: "He referred to his conviction that the day of wrath was at hand, and that he was to be an actor in the terrible struggle which would issue in the overthrow of slavery, though he might not live to see the end. He stated his belief in the duty and privilege, and efficacy of prayer."[2]

These passages are quoted, not to show, as before stated, his belief in any controverted question of theology, but to illustrate the religious character of his mind, his presenti-

---

1. Holland's Life of Lincoln, p. 237. Herndon says this interview was "colored." Bateman wrote to the author that, as reported by Holland, "it is substantially correct."

2. Holland's Life of Lincoln, p. 238.

ment of the part he was to act in the great drama, and that he placed his dependence for success on Divine assistance. Mr. Bateman may have made mistakes in the exact words used by Lincoln, but that the substance of what he said is given, there can be no reasonable doubt, and with these statements, his speeches, state-papers, and conduct, from this time to his death, are perfectly consistent. [1]

Time passed on, and the seceding states appointed delegates to meet in convention at Montgomery, Alabama. They met on the 4th of February, and organized a provisional government, similar in many respects to the Constitution of the United States, under which Jefferson Davis was made President, and Alexander H. Stephens, Vice-President.

The President of the Confederate States was a man of culture and large experience in public affairs. Born in Kentucky, educated at West Point, at the expense of the government he sought to overthrow, he entered public life as the follower of Calhoun. He was of an imperious temper,

---

1. To his friend, Judge Grant Goodrich, he made a statement in regard to his dependence on God, and his prayer, for assistance, of much the same purport.

In this connection I quote a paragraph from a paper written by John Hay, one of his private secretaries, and published in *Harper's Monthly Magazine*, for July, 1865. "It was just after my election, in 1860," said Mr. Lincoln, "when the news had been coming in thick and fast all day, and there had been a great ' hurrah, boys !' so that I was well tired out, and went home to rest, throwing myself upon a lounge in my chamber. Opposite to where I lay, was a bureau with a swinging glass upon it ; and looking in that glass, I saw myself reflected nearly at full length ; but my face, I noticed, had two separate and distinct images, the tip of the nose of one being about three inches from the tip of the other. I was a little bothered, perhaps startled, and got up and looked in the glass, but the illusion vanished. On lying down again, I saw it the second time, plainer, if possible, than before ; and then I noticed that one of the faces was a little paler—say five shades—than the other. I got up, and the thing melted away, and I went off, and, in the excitement of the hour, forgot all about it— nearly, but not quite—for the thing would once in a while come up, and give me a pang, as though something uncomfortable had happened. When I went home, I told my wife about it, and a few days after, I tried the experiment again, when, sure enough, the thing came back again ; but I never succeeded in bringing the ghost back after that, though I once tried very industriously to show it to my wife, who was worried about it somewhat. She thought it was a sign that I was to be elected to a second term of office, and that the paleness of one of the faces was an omen that I should not see life through the last term."

Mr. Lincoln regarded this as an optical illusion. Mrs. Lincoln's interpretation was a strange coincidence, to say the least, when compared with subsequent events.

and of a most intense personal ambition. He favored the repudiation by the state of Mississippi, of the bonds issued by that state, and thus brought deep disgrace upon the American character. He was called to the position of Secretary of War, by President Pierce, and in that position he deliberately conducted the affairs of the war department with a view to strengthen the slave states, preparatory to a separation, and even with a view to war, if it should be necessary to secure separation. As the head of the insurgents at Montgomery, he was guilty of opening the bloody tragedy of civil war, by ordering the fire upon Fort Sumter. The character of the man may be inferred from the language he used in a speech on his way from Mississippi to Montgomery, to assume the Presidency. "We will carry the war," said he, "where it is easy to advance, where food for the *sword* and *torch* awaits our armies in the densely populated cities." Such was the war this man inaugurated and carried on until his ignominious capture. How different this from the forbearing, dignified, christian spirit of magnanimity, which ever characterized the language of the Chief Magistrate of the Union during the war.

The Vice President, Alexander H. Stephens, was a very different character. Intellectually an abler, and morally a far better man, he had vigorously opposed secession, and never heartily approved of it. No man made sounder and stronger arguments than Stephens against secession. In the Georgia convention he said:

" Pause, I entreat you, and consider for a moment what reasons you can give that will even satisfy yourselves in calmer moments—what reasons you can give to your fellow-sufferers in the calamity that it will bring upon us. *What reasons can you give to the nations of the earth to justify it?* They will be calm and deliberate judges in the case; and what cause or one overt act can you name or point to, on which to rest the plea of justification. *What right has the North assailed?* What interest of the South has been invaded? What justice has been denied? And what claim, founded in justice and right, has been withheld? Can either of you name one governmental act of wrong, deliberately and purposely done by the government of Washington, of which the South has a right to complain." * * *

" When we of the South demanded the slave trade, or the importation of Africans for the cultivation of our lands, did they not yield the right for twenty years ? When we asked a three-fifth representation in Congress for our slaves, was it not granted ? When we asked and demanded the return of any fugitive from justice, or the recovery of those persons owing labor or allegiance, was it not incorporated in the Constitution, and again ratified and strengthened by the Fugitive Slave Law of 1850?" * * *

" Again, gentlemen, look at another act ; when we have asked that more territory should be added, that we might spread the institution of slavery, have they not yielded to our demands in giving us Louisiana, Florida, and Texas, out of which four states have been carved, and ample territory for four more to be added in due time, if you by this unwise and impolitic act do not destroy this hope, and perhaps by it lose all, and have your last slave wrenched from you, by stern military rule, as South America and Mexico were, *or by the vindictive decree of a universal emancipation, which may reasonably be expected to follow?*" * * *[1]

His prophetic declaration that "a decree of universal emancipation " might be reasonably expected, was most remarkable and sagacious.   He was by far the ablest of the Southern leaders.

On the 15th of February, 1861, the Houses of Congress met in joint session to count and declare the electoral vote. Fears were entertained that, by some fraud or violence, the ceremony might be interrupted, or not performed ; but the schemes of the conspirators were not yet ripe for violence. In accordance with the forms of the Constitution, both Houses of Congress met at 12 M., in the gorgeous hall of the House of Representatives ; the Vice-President, as President of the Senate, and the Speaker of the House, sitting side by side, and the Vice-President presiding.

The crowds of people who thronged to the Capitol, were impressed with the peculiarly solemn character of the proceedings.   The deep anxiety of the public mind found expression in the impressive prayer of the chaplain, who invoked the blessing and protection of Almighty God upon

1. McPherson's History of the Rebellion, p. 25.

the President elect ; prayed for his safe arrival at the capital and for his peaceful inauguration, and that threatened war might be averted. Vice-President Breckenridge and Senator Douglas, both unsuccessful candidates for the Presidency, were the most conspicuous personages present.

On the 11th of February, with his family and some personal friends, Lincoln left his home at Springfield for Washington. There is nothing in history more pathetic than the scene when he bade good-bye to his old friends and neighbors. Conscious of the difficulties and dangers before him ; difficulties which seemed almost insurmountable, but with a sadness, as though a presentiment that he should return no more was pressing upon him, and with a deep religious trust, which was very characteristic, he paused, as he stepped on the platform of the railroad carriage which was to bear him away, and uttered these beautiful and touching words :

" My Friends : No one, not in my position, can realize the sadness I feel at this parting. To this people I owe all that I am. Here I have lived more than a quarter of a century. Here my children were born, and here one of them lies buried. I know not how soon I shall see you again. I go to assume a task more difficult than that which has devolved upon any other man since the days of Washington. He never would have succeeded except for the aid of Divine Providence, upon which he at all times relied. I feel that I cannot succeed without the same Divine blessing which sustained him ; and on the same Almighty Being I place my reliance for support. And I hope you, my friends, will all pray that I may receive that Divine assistance, without which I cannot succeed, but with which success is certain. Again, I bid you an affectionate farewell."

As he grasped the hard hand of many an old friend and client, and bade farewell to the old home to which he was never to return, the responses came from many old neighbors : "God bless and keep you." "God save you from all traitors," his friends "sorrowing most of all," for the fear "that they should see his face no more."

The profound religious feeling which pervades this farewell speech, characterized him to the close of his life. He was sustained by his trust in God, and he earnestly solicited the prayers of the people. From the time of his departure from Springfield, until his remains were borne back from the capital of the republic he had saved, hallowed forever in the hearts of the people, and deified by the superstitious race he had emancipated—he was the object of constant and earnest prayer, at the family altar, and in the places of public worship. From the time when he started forth upon his great mission, and to fulfill his destiny and meet his martyrdom, the hearts of the people went with him.

On his way to Washington, he passed through the great states of Indiana, Ohio, New York, New Jersey, and Pennsylvania, and was everywhere received with demonstrations of loyalty, as the representative of the national government. He addressed the people at the capitals of these states, and at many of their chief towns and cities.

The city of Washington was surrounded by slave territory, and was really within the lines of the insurgents. Baltimore was not only a slaveholding city, but nowhere was the spirit of rebellion more hot and ferocious than among a large class of its people. The lower classes, the material of which mobs are made, were reckless, and ready for any outrage. From the date of his election to the time of his start for Washington, there had often appeared in the press and elsewhere, vulgar threats and menaces that he should never be inaugurated, nor reach the capital alive. Little attention was paid to these threats, yet some of the President's personal friends, without his knowledge, employed a detective,[1] who sent agents to Baltimore and Washington to investigate. Not only were the personal friends of Lincoln in Illinois uneasy, but the officers of the railroads from Philadelphia, Baltimore, and Washington, became apprehensive of a plot to destroy the roads, ferry-boats, and bridges, by which communication was carried on between Washington and Philadelphia. The detectives ascertained the existence of a plot to assassinate the President elect, as he passed through Baltimore.[2]

1. Allan Pinkerton.
2. See "The Spy of the Rebellion," by Allan Pinkerton, pp. 50-80.

The first intelligence of this conspiracy was communicated to Lincoln at Philadelphia. On the facts being laid before him, he was urged to take the train that night (the 21st of February), by which he would reach Washington the next morning, passing through Baltimore earlier than the conspirators expected, and thus avoid the danger. Having already made appointments to meet the citizens of Philadelphia at, and raise the United States flag over, Independence Hall, on Washington's birthday, the 22nd, and also to meet the Legislature of Pennsylvania at Harrisburg, he declined starting for Washington that night. Finally his friends persuaded him to allow the detectives and the officers of the railways to arrange for him to return from Harrisburg, and, by special train, to go to Washington the night following the ceremonies at Harrisburg.

On the 22nd of February, he visited old Independence Hall, where the Congress of the revolution had adopted the Declaration of Independence. This declaration of principles had always been the bible of his political faith. He honestly and thoroughly believed in it. His speech on that occasion was most eloquent and impressive. He said among other things :

"All the political sentiments I entertain have been drawn, so far as I have been able to draw them, from the sentiments which originated in, and were given to the world from, this hall. I never had a feeling, politically, that did not spring from the sentiments embodied in the Declaration of Independence." * * * * * *
" It was not the mere matter of the separation of the colonies from the mother-land, but that *sentiment* in the Declaration of Independence, which gave liberty not alone to the people of this country, but I hope to the world, for all future time. It was that which gave promise that, in due time, the weight would be lifted from the shoulders of men. This is the sentiment embodied in the Declaration of Independence. Now, my friends, can this country be saved upon that basis ? If it can, I will consider myself one of the happiest men in the world, if I can help to save it. If it cannot be saved upon that principle, it will be truly awful ! But if this country cannot be saved without giving up the principle, I was about to say : ' *I would rather be assassinated on the spot*, than surrender it.' " * * * * * * * *

" I have said nothing but what I am willing to live by, and if it be the pleasure of Almighty God, to die by."

The allusion to the assassination was not accidental. The subject had been brought to his attention in such a way that, although he did not feel that there was serious danger, yet he had been assured positively, by a detective, whose veracity his friends vouched for, that a secret conspiracy was organized at a neighboring city, to take his life on his way to the capital.

He went to Harrisburg, according to arrangement, met the Legislature, and retired to his room. In the meanwhile, General Scott and Mr. Seward had learned, through other sources, of the existence of the plot to assassinate him, and had despatched Mr. F. W. Seward, a son of Senator Seward, to apprise him of the danger. Information coming to him from both of these sources, each independent of the other, induced him to yield to the wishes of his friends, and anticipate his journey to Washington. Besides, there had reached him from Baltimore no committee, either of the municipal authorities or of citizens, to tender him the hospitalities, and to extend to him the courtesies of that city, as had been done by every other city through which he had passed. He was persuaded to permit the detective to arrange for his going to Washington that night.

The telegraph wires to Baltimore were cut, Harrisburg was isolated, and, taking a special train, he reached Philadelphia, and driving to the Baltimore depot, found the Washington train waiting his arrival, stepped on board, and passed on without interruption through Baltimore to the national capital. He found, on his arrival at Washington, Senator Seward, Mr. Washburne, and other friends awaiting him. Stepping into a carriage, he was taken to Willard's Hotel, and Washington was soon startled by the news of his arrival.

He afterwards declared: " I did not then, nor do I now believe I should have been assassinated, had I gone through Baltimore as first contemplated, but I thought it wise to run no risk where no risk was necessary." [1]   Such arrangements were made by General Scott and others, as secured his immediate personal safety. His family and personal friends followed and joined him, according to the programme of his journey.

1. See Lossing's Pictorial History of the Rebellion, Vol. 1, p. 279.

CHAPTER XII.

LINCOLN IN THE WHITE HOUSE.

LINCOLN'S INAUGURATION.—HIS CABINET.—DOUGLAS'S PROPHECY.—
BUTLER PREDICTS END OF SLAVERY.—SOUTH CAROLINA THE
PRODIGAL SON.—DOUGLAS'S RALLYING CRY FOR THE UNION.—HIS
DEATH.—DIFFICULTIES OF THE PRESIDENT.—REBELS BEGIN THE
WAR. — UPRISING OF THE PEOPLE. — DEATH OF ELLSWORTH.—
GREAT BRITAIN AND FRANCE RECOGNIZE THE CONFEDERATES AS
BELLIGERENTS.—NEGROES DECLARED "CONTRABAND."

MR. LINCOLN availed himself of the earliest opportunity after his arrival at the capital, and before his inauguration, to express his kindly feelings to the people of Washington and the Southern states. On the 27th of February, when waited upon by the Mayor and Common Council, he assured them, and through them the South, that he had no disposition to treat them in any other way than as neighbors, and that he had no disposition to withhold from them any constitutional right. He assured the people that they should have all their rights under the Constitution. "Not grudgingly, but fully and fairly."

On the 4th of March, 1861, he was inaugurated President of the United States. An inauguration so impressive and solemn had not occurred since that of Washington. The ceremonies took place, as usual, on the eastern colonnade of the Capitol. General Scott had gathered a few soldiers of the regular army, and had caused to be organized some militia, to preserve peace, order, and security.

Thousands of Northern voters thronged the streets of Washington, only a very few of them conscious of the volcano of treason and murder, thinly concealed, around and beneath them. The public offices and the departments were full of plotting traitors. Many of the rebel generals—Lee, Johnston, Ewell, Hill, Stewart, Magruder, Pemberton, and others, held commissions under the government they were about to abandon and betray. Rebel spies were everywhere. The people of Washington were, a large portion of them, in sympathy with the conspirators.

None who witnessed it, will ever forget the scene of that inauguration. There was the magnificent eastern front of the Capitol, looking towards the statue of Washington; and there were gathered together the Senate and House of Representatives, the Judges of the Supreme Court, the Diplomatic Corps, the high officers of the Army and the Navy, and, outside of the guards, a vast crowd of mingled patriots and traitors. Men looked searchingly into the eyes of every stranger, to discover whether he were a traitor or a friend. Standing in the most conspicuous position, amidst scowling traitors with murder and treason in their hearts, Lincoln was perfectly cool and self-possessed. Near him was President Buchanan, conspicuous with his white necktie, bowed as with the consciousness of duties unperformed; there were Chief Justice Taney and his associates, made notorious by the Dred Scott decision ; there was Chase, with his fine and imposing presence; and the venerable Scott, his towering form still unbroken by years; the ever hopeful and philosophic statesman, Seward ; the scholarly Sumner, and blunt Ben Wade, of Ohio. There were also distinguished governors of states, and throngs of eminent men from every section of the Union. But there was no man more observed than Douglas, the great rival of Lincoln. He had been most marked and thoughtful in his attentions to the President elect; and now his small but sturdy figure, in striking contrast to the towering form of Lincoln, was conspicuous; gracefully extending every courtesy to his successful competitor.[1] His bold eye, from which flashed energy

1. The author is here reminded of the following incident. As Mr. Lincoln removed his hat, before commencing the reading of his " Inaugural," from the

and determination, was eagerly scanning the crowd, not unconscious, it is believed, of the personal danger which encircled the President, and perfectly ready if need be to share it. Lincoln's calmness arose from an entire absence of self-consciousness; he was too fully absorbed in the gravity of the occasion and the importance of the events around and before him, to think of himself.

In the open air, and with a voice so clear and distinct that he could be heard by thrice ten thousand men, he read his inaugural address, and on the very verge of civil war, he made a most earnest appeal for peace. This address is so important, and shows so clearly the causelessness of the rebellion, that no apology is offered for the following quotations from it:

FELLOW CITIZENS OF THE UNITED STATES: In compliance with a custom as old as the government itself, I appear before you to address you briefly, and to take in your presence the oath prescribed by the Constitution of the United States, to be taken by the President " before he enters upon the execution of his office."   *   *   *   *   *

Apprehension seems to exist, among the people of the Southern states, that by the accession of a republican administration their property and their peace and personal security are to be endangered. There has never been any real cause for such apprehension. Indeed, the most ample evidence to the contrary has all the while existed and been open to their inspection. It is found in nearly all the published speeches of him who now addresses you. I do but quote from one of those speeches when I declare that " I have no purpose, directly or indirectly, to interfere with the institution of slavery, in the states where it now exists. I believe I have no lawful right to do so, and I have no inclination to do so." Those who nominated and elected me did so with a full knowledge that I had made this and many similar declarations, and have never recanted them.   *   *   *   *

I now reiterate those sentiments, and in so doing I only press upon the public attention the most conclusive evidence of which the case is susceptible, that the property, peace, and security of no section are to be in anywise endangered by the now incoming administration.   *   *   *

I hold, that in contemplation of universal law, and of the Constitu-

proximity of the crowd he saw nowhere to place it, and Senator Douglas, by his side, seeing this, instantly extended his hand and held the President's hat, while he was occupied in reading the address.

tion, *the Union of the states is perpetual.*   Perpetuity is implied, if not expressed, in the fundamental law of all national governments.   *   *

I therefore consider that, in view of the Constitution and the laws, the Union is unbroken, and to the extent of my ability *I shall take care,* as the Constitution itself expressly enjoins upon me, *that the laws of the Union be faithfully executed in all the states.*   *   *   *   *

As Mr. Lincoln pronounced the foregoing sentence, with clear, firm, and impressive emphasis, a visible sensation ran through the vast audience, and earnest, sober, but hearty cheers were heard.

In doing this there need be no bloodshed nor violence: and there shall be none, unless it be forced upon the national authority.   The power confided to me will be used to hold, and occupy, and possess the property and places belonging to the government, and to collect the duties and imposts; but beyond what may be necessary for these objects there will be no invasion, no using of force against or among the people anywhere.   *   *   *   *   *   *   *   *   *   *

Physically speaking, we cannot separate.   We cannot remove our respective sections from each other, nor build an impassable wall between them.   A husband and wife may be divorced, and go out of the presence, and beyond the reach of each other, but the different parts of our country cannot do this.   *   *   *   *   *   *   *   *   *

This country, with its institutions, belongs to the people who inhabit it.   Whenever they shall grow weary of the existing government, they can exercise the constitutional right of amending, or their revolutionary right to dismember or overthrow it.   I cannot be ignorant of the fact that many worthy and patriotic citizens are desirous of having the national Constitution amended.   *   *   *   *   *   *   *   *

My countrymen, one and all, think calmly and well upon this whole subject.   Nothing valuable can be lost by taking time.   If there be an object to hurry any of you in hot haste to a step which you would never take deliberately, that object will be frustrated by taking time; but no good object can be frustrated by it.   Such of you as are now dissatisfied, still have the old Constitution unimpaired, and on the sensitive point, the laws of your own framing under it.   The new administration will have no immediate power, if it would, to change either.   If it were admitted that you who are dissatisfied hold the right side in the dispute, there still is no single good reason for precipitate action.   Intelligence, patriotism, Christianity, and a firm reliance on Him, who has never yet forsaken this favored land, are still competent to adjust, in the best way, all our present difficulties.   *   *   *   *   *   *   *   *   *

No one can ever forget how solemn was his utterance of the following:

In your hands, my dissatisfied fellow-countrymen, and not in mine, are the momentous issues of civil war. The government will not assail you.

You can have no conflict without being yourselves the aggressors. You have no oath registered in heaven to destroy the government, while I have the most solemn one to " preserve, protect, and defend it."

I am loath to close. We are not enemies, but friends. We must not be enemies; though passion may have strained, it must not break, our bonds of affection.

The mystic chords of memory, stretching from every battle field and patriot grave to every living heart and hearthstone all over this broad land, will yet swell the chorus of the Union, when again touched, as surely they will be, by the better angels of our nature.

Alas! such appeals were received by the parties to whom they were addressed, with jeers, and ribaldry, and all the maddening passions which riot in blood and war. It was to *force* only, stern, unflinching, and severe, that the powers and passions of treason would yield.

With reverent look and impressive emphasis, he repeated the oath to preserve, protect, and defend the Constitution of his country. Douglas, who knew from his personal familiarity with the conspirators, better than Lincoln, the dangers that surrounded and were before him, who knew the conspirators and their plots, with patriotic magnanimity then grasped the hand of the President, gracefully extended his congratulations, and the assurance that in the dark future he would stand by him, and give to him his utmost aid in upholding the Constitution, and enforcing the laws of his country. Nobly did Douglas redeem that pledge.

Here the author pauses a moment, to relate a most singular prophecy in regard to the war, uttered by Douglas, January 1st, 1861. Senator Douglas, with his wife, one of the most beautiful and fascinating women in America, and a relative of Mrs. Madison, occupied one of the houses which formed the Minnesota block.

"On New Year's Day, 1861," says General Stewart, of New York, who tells the story, "I was making a New Year's call on Senator Douglas; after some conversation, I asked him :

"'What will be the result, Senator, of the efforts of Jefferson Davis and his associates, to divide the Union ?'

"We were," says Stewart, "sitting on the sofa together, when I asked the question. Douglas rose, walked rapidly up and down the room for a moment, and then pausing, he exclaimed, with deep feeling and excitement :

"'The cotton states are making an effort to draw in the border states to their schemes of secession, and I am but too fearful they will succeed. If they do, there will be the most fearful civil war the world has ever seen, lasting for years.'

"Pausing a moment, he looked like one inspired, while he proceeded : 'Virginia, over yonder across the Potomac,' pointing towards Arlington, 'will become a charnel-house ; but in the end the Union will triumph. They will try,' he continued, 'to get possession of this capital, to give them *prestige* abroad, but in that effort they will never succeed ; the North will rise *en masse* to defend it. But Washington will become a city of hospitals, the churches will be used for the sick and wounded. This house,' he continued, 'the *Minnesota block*, will be devoted to that purpose before the end of the war.'

"Every word of this prediction was literally fulfilled ; nearly all the churches were used for the wounded, and the Minnesota block, and the very room in which this declaration was made, became the 'Douglas Hospital.'"

"What justification is there for all this ?" asked Stewart.

"There is no justification," replied Douglas. "I will go as far as the Constitution will permit to maintain their just rights. But," said he, rising to his feet, and raising his arm, "if the Southern states attempt to secede, I am in favor of their having just so many slaves, and just so much slave territory, as they can hold at the point of the bayonet, and no more."

13

The President having been inaugurated, announced his
Cabinet as follows : William H. Seward, Secretary of State ;
Simon Cameron, Secretary of War ; Salmon P. Chase, Secretary of the Treasury ; Gideon Welles, Secretary of the
Navy ; Caleb B. Smith, Secretary of the Interior ; Montgomery Blair, Postmaster General ; and Edward Bates, Attorney General.

Seward, Chase, Cameron, and Bates had been his competitors for the nomination at the Chicago convention.   Disregarding the remonstrances of some of his friends, who
feared that such a Cabinet would lack harmony, and that
some of its members (as the fact turned out) would be seeking the Presidency, he is said to have replied :

" No, gentlemen, the times are too grave and perilous for
ambitious schemes, and personal rivalries.   I need the aid
of all of these men.   They enjoy the confidence of their several
states and sections, and they will strengthen the administration." To some of them he made an appeal, saying : "It will
require the utmost skill, influence, and sagacity of all of us to
save the republic ; let us forget ourselves, and join hands
like brothers to save the republic.   If we succeed, there
will be glory enough for all."

Mr. Seward, the Secretary of State, had been the President's most formidable competitor for the nomination.   He
was the recognized leader of the republican party in New
York, and he had been for many years a leading statesman in
the anti-slavery ranks.   His able speeches had done much
to create and consolidate the party which triumphed in 1860.
He was an accomplished scholar, a polished gentleman,
familiar with the history of his country, and its foreign policy ; a clear and able writer, familiar with international law,
and altogether well adapted to conduct its foreign correspondence.   He was hopeful and cheerful, an optimist, and
believed, or appeared to believe, the rebellion would be short.
He was a shrewd politician, and did not forget his friends in
the dispensation of patronage. [1]

1. In the early part of Lincoln's administration, a prominent editor of a German

Salmon P. Chase, Secretary of the Treasury, had been also a prominent candidate for the Presidency. He was a man of commanding person, fine manly presence, dignified, sedate, and earnest. His mind was comprehensive, logical, and judicial. He was an earnest, determined, consistent, radical abolitionist. His had been the master mind at the Buffalo Convention of 1848, and his pen had framed the Buffalo platform. By his writings, speeches, and forensic arguments, and as Governor of the State of Ohio, and in the United States Senate, acting with the accomplished free-soil senator from Massachusetts, Charles Sumner, he had contributed largely to the formation of the republican party. Up to the time when he became Secretary of the Treasury, he had developed no special adaptation to, or knowledge of finance ; but he brought to the duties of that most difficult position, a clear judgment and sound sense.

Simon Cameron had been a very successful Pennsylvania politician ; he was of Scotch descent, as his name indicates, with inherent Scotch fire, pluck, energy, and perseverance. He had a marked Scotch face, a keen gray eye, was tall and commanding in form, and had the faculty of never forgetting a friend or an enemy. He was accused of being unscrupulous, of giving good offices and fat contracts to his friends. He retired after a short time, to make room for the combative, rude, fearless, vigorous, and unflinching Stanton. A man who was justly said to have " *organized victory.*"

Montgomery Blair, the Postmaster General, represented the Blair family, one of large political influence, and long connected with national affairs. F. P. Blair, senior, as the editor of the *Globe* during General Jackson's administration,

newspaper published in the West, came to Washington to seek an appointment abroad. With the member of Congress from his district, he visited the "Executive Mansion," and his wishes were stated. The editor had supported Mr. Seward for the nomination as President. Mr. Lincoln immediately sent a messenger to the Secretary of State, asking him to come to the White House. Mr. Seward soon arrived, and Lincoln, after a cordial greeting, said : "Seward, here is a gentleman (introducing the editor) who had the good sense to prefer you to me for President. He wants to go abroad, and I want you to find a good place for him." This Mr. Seward did, and the President immediately appointed him.

was one of the ablest and strongest of the able men who surrounded that great man.   He had been associated with, and was the friend of, Benton, Van Buren, and Silas Wright ; he had seen those friends stricken down by the slave power, and he had learned to hate and distrust the oligarchy of slave-holders, and his counsels and advice, and his able pen, had efficiently aided in building up the party opposed to slavery. Montgomery Blair had argued against the Dred Scott decision.   F. P. Blair, Jr., and B. Gratz Brown, had led the anti-slavery men of Missouri, having, after a most gallant contest, carried the city of St. Louis, and the former was now its honored representative in Congress.

Edward Bates, the Attorney General, was a fine, dignified, scholarly, gentlemanly lawyer of the old school.   Gideon Welles had been a leading editor in New England, and conducted the affairs of the Navy with great ability. Caleb B. Smith was a prominent politician from Indiana, and had been a colleague of Mr. Lincoln in Congress.

On the evening of the 4th of March, when Mr. Lincoln entered the White House, he found a government in ruins. The conspiracy which had been preparing for thirty years, had culminated.   Seven states had passed ordinances of secession, and had already organized a rebel government at Montgomery.   The leaders in Congress and out of it, had fired the excitable Southern heart, and had infused into the young men a fiery, headlong zeal, and they hurried on, with the greatest rapidity, the work of revolution.

North Carolina still hesitated.   The people of that staunch old Union state, first voted down a call for a convention by a vote of 46,671 for, to 47,333 against, but a subsequent convention, on the 21st of May, passed an ordinance of secession.   Nearly all the Federal forts, arsenals, dock-yards, custom houses and post offices, within the territories of the seceded states, had been seized, and were held by the rebels.   Large numbers of the officers of the army and the navy deserted, entering the rebel service.   Among the most conspicuous in this infamy, was General David E.

Twiggs, the second officer in rank in the army of the United States, and in January, 1861, commanding the Department of Texas. He had been placed there by Secretary Floyd, because he was known to be in the conspiracy. Secretary Holt, on the 18th of January, ordered that he should turn over his command to Colonel Waite ; but before this order reached Colonel Waite, Twiggs had consummated his treason by surrendering to the rebel Ben. McCullough, all the national forces in Texas, numbering twenty-five hundred men, and a large amount of stores and munitions of war.

There was little or no struggle in the Gulf states, excepting in Northern Alabama, against the wild tornado of excitement in favor of rebellion, which carried everything before it. In the border states, in Maryland, Virginia, North Carolina, Tennessee, and Missouri, there was a contest, and the friends of the Union made a struggle to maintain their position. Ultimately the Union triumphed in Maryland, Kentucky, and Missouri ; and the rebels carried the state of Tennessee against a most gallant contest on the part of the Union men of East Tennessee, under the lead of Andrew Johnson, Governor Brownlow, Horace Maynard, and others. They also carried Virginia, which seceded April 17th, and North Carolina, which adopted secession on the 20th of May.

Some of the rebel leaders labored under the delusion, and they most industriously inculcated it among their followers, that there would be no war ; that the North was divided ; that the Northern people would not fight, and that if there was war, a large part of them would oppose coercion, and perhaps fight on the side of the rebellion. [1] There was in the tone of a portion of the Northern press, and in the speeches of some of the Northern democrats, much to encourage this

1. Ex-President Pierce, in a letter to Jefferson Davis, dated January 6th, 1860, among other things, said : "If through the madness of Northern abolitionists, that dire calamity (disruption of the Union), must come, the fighting will not be along Mason and Dixon's line merely. It will be *within our own borders, in our own streets*, between the two classes of citizens to whom I have referred. Those who defy law, and scout constitutional obligation, will, if we ever reach the arbitrament of arms, find occupation enough at home !" Such a letter is sufficiently significant.

idea, and some leading republican papers were at least ambiguous on the subject. There was, however, one prominent man from Massachusetts, who had united with the rebel leaders in the support of Breckenridge, and who sought to dispel this idea ; this was Benjamin F. Butler, who came to Washington, to know of his old political associates what it meant ? " It means," said his Southern friends, " separation, and a Southern Confederacy. We will have our independence, and establish a Southern government, with no discordant elements."

" Are you prepared for war?" said Butler.

" Oh ! there will be no war ; the North will not fight."

" The North will fight. The North will send the last man, and expend the last dollar to maintain the government," said Butler.

" But," said his Southern friends, "the North can't fight; we have too many allies there."

" You have friends," said Butler, " in the North, who will stand by you so long as you fight your battles in the Union ; but the moment you fire on the flag, the Northern people will be a unit against you. And," added Butler, " you may be assured if war comes, *slavery ends.*" Butler, sagacious and true, became satisfied that war was inevitable. With the boldness and directness which has marked his character, he went to Buchanan, and advised the arrest of the commissioners sent by the seceding states, and their trial for treason. This advice it was as characteristic of Butler to give, as it was of Buchanan to disregard.

As an illustration of the prejudice against Lincoln at the South, the following incident is related. Two or three days before the inauguration, on the 4th of March, 1861, and while Lincoln was staying at Willard's Hotel, a distinguished South Carolina lady—one of the Howards—the widow of a Northern scholar—called upon him out of curiosity. She was very proud, aristocratic, and quite conscious that she had in her veins the blood of " *all the Howards*," and she was curious to see a man who had been represented to her as a monster, a mixture of the ape and the tiger.

She was shown into the parlor where were Mr. Lincoln, and Senators Seward, Hale, Chase, and other prominent members of Congress. As Mr. Seward, whom she knew, presented her to the President elect, she hissed in his ear : "I am a South Carolinian." Instantly reading her character, he turned and addressed her with the greatest courtesy, and dignified and gentlemanly politeness. After listening a few moments, astonished to find him so different from what he had been described to her, she said :

"Why, Mr. Lincoln, you look, act, and speak like a kind, good-hearted, generous man."

"And did you expect to meet a savage?" said he.

"Certainly I did, or even something worse," replied she. "I am glad I have met you," she continued, "and now the best way to preserve peace, is for you to go to Charleston, and show the people what you are, and tell them you have no intention of injuring them."

Returning home, she found a party of secessionists, and on entering the room she exclaimed :

"I have seen him ! I have seen him !"

"Who ?" they inquired.

"That terrible monster, Lincoln, and I found him a gentleman, and I am going to his first levee after his inauguration."

At his first reception, this tall daughter of South Carolina, dressing herself in black velvet, with two long white plumes in her hair, repaired to the White House. She was nearly six feet high, with black eyes, and black hair, and, in her velvet and white feathers, she was a very striking and majestic figure. As she approached, the President recognized her immediately.

"Here I am again," said she, "that South Carolinian."

"I am glad to see you," replied he, "and I assure you that the first object of my heart is to preserve peace, and I wish that not only you, but every son and daughter of South Carolina was here, that I might tell them so."

Mr. Cameron, Secretary of War, came up, and after some remarks, he said : " South Carolina (which had already seceded), South Carolina is the prodigal son."

" Ah ! Mr. Secretary," said she, " if South Carolina is the prodigal son, ' Uncle Sam,' our father, ought to divide the inheritance, and let her go ; but they say you are going to make war upon us, is it so ? "

" Oh ! come back," said he, " tell South Carolina to come back now, and we will kill the fatted calf."

The conduct of Douglas towards the President was most magnanimous and patriotic. They who had been so long such keen and earnest competitors, became now close friends. Such friendship under such circumstances, shows that there was something fine, noble, and chivalrous in both. Conscious of the peril of the republic, Douglas did all in his power to strengthen the man who had beaten him in the race for the Presidency

On the 15th of April, the President issued his proclamation calling for seventy-five thousand soldiers. While he was considering the subject, Douglas called and expressed his approval, regretting only that it was not for two hundred thousand instead of seventy-five thousand, and, on the 18th of April, Douglas wrote the following dispatch, and placed it in the hands of the agents of the associated press, to be sent throughout the country:

"April 18th, 1861, Senator Douglas called on the President, and had an interesting conversation on the present condition of the country. The substance of it was, on the part of Mr. Douglas, that while he was unalterably opposed to the administration in all its political issues, he was prepared to fully sustain the President in the exercise of all his Constitutional functions, to preserve the Union, maintain the government, and defend the Federal capital. A firm policy and prompt action was necessary. The capital was in danger, and must be defended at all hazards, and at any expense of men and money. He spoke of the present and future without any reference to the past." [1]

1. The original of this dispatch in Douglas's handwriting was in possession of the late Hon. George Ashmun, of Massachusetts, who kindly furnished a copy to the author.

Douglas took this means to inform the country how he stood, and to exert all the weight of his influence in uniting the people to sustain the Executive in his efforts to suppress the rebellion by force.   Not only did he issue this dispatch, but he started for the Northwest, and everywhere, by his public speeches and conversation, sounded the alarm, and rallied the people to support the Government.   On the 23d of April, at Columbus, Ohio, he made a speech for the Union, in which he said that the chairman of a committee of secessionists had been instructed to tender the command of all the forces in Virginia to General Scott.   The reply of the General, said Douglas, was this: " I have served my country more than fifty years, and so long as I live, I shall stand by it, against all assailants, even though my native state, Virginia, be among them." [1]

Douglas made a speech at Wheeling, Virginia, of the same tenor, and passing on to Springfield, on the 25th of April, spoke to the Legislature and citizens of Illinois at the capital. In this great speech he said, among other things:

" So long as there was a hope of a peaceful solution, I prayed and implored for compromise.   I have spared no effort for a peaceful solution of these troubles; I have failed, and there is but one thing to do—to rally under the flag.   *   *   *   The South has no cause of complaint. *   *   *   Shall we obey the laws, or adopt the Mexican system of war on every election.   *   *   *   Forget party—all—remember only your country.   *   *   *   The shortest road to peace is the most tremendous preparation for war.   *   *   *   It is with a sad heart, and with a grief I have never before experienced, that I have to contemplate this fearful struggle.   *   *   *   But it is our duty to protect the government and the flag from every assailant, be he who he may." [2]

1. If General Lee, who had been chief-of-staff to General Scott, and his rebel associates, had followed the example of the Commander in Chief, how much bloodshed and misery might have been prevented.

2. Governor Shelby M. Cullom, then Speaker of the House, who presided at the meeting, says, in a letter to the author:

"Douglas spoke with great earnestness and power.   Never in all my experience in public life, before or since, have I been so impressed by a speaker.   While he was speaking, a man came into the hall bearing the American flag.   Its appearance caused the wildest excitement, and the great assemblage of legislators and citizens was wrought up to the highest enthusiasm of patriotism by the masterly speech "

Douglas told me that " the Union was in terrible peril, and he had come home to rouse the people in favor of the Union."

From Springfield, Douglas came to his home in Chicago, and, at the great "Wigwam," repeated his appeal for the Union. He said that we had gone to the very extreme to prevent war, and the return for all our efforts has been "armies marching on the national capital," a movement to blot the United States from the map of the world. "The election of Lincoln is a mere pretext," the secession movement is the result of an enormous conspiracy, existing before the election. "There can be no neutrals in this war—only patriots and traitors." Worn with excitement and fatigue, he went to the Tremont House in Chicago, was taken ill, and on the 3rd of June thereafter died, at the early age of forty-eight.

Senator McDougall, of California, his warm personal and political friend, said in the Senate, speaking of his last speeches: "Before I left home I heard the battle-cry of Douglas resounding over the mountains and valleys of California and far-off Oregon. His words have communicated faith and strength to millions. The last words of the dead Douglas, I have felt to be stronger than the words of multitudes of living men." [1]

The name of Douglas is familiar in Scottish history, as it is in Scottish poetry and romance, but among all the historic characters who have borne it, from him of " the bleeding heart " down, few, if any, have surpassed in interest Stephen Arnold Douglas.[2]

His death was a great loss to the country, and a severe blow to the President. It recalled the words which Mr. Van Buren, then Senator from New York, had spoken on the death of his great rival, De Witt Clinton: " I, who while Clinton lived, never envied him anything, am now almost

1. Congressional Globe, July 9th, 1861.

2, It fell to the author as the representative in Congress from Chicago, the home of Douglas, to make some remarks in the House of Representatives, on the occasion of his death. He attempted to compare Lincoln and Douglas, and to do justice to both. Neither Mrs. Lincoln nor Mrs. Douglas was pleased with the comparison. Each expressed to him afterwards her astonishment; the one that anybody could compare Douglas to *her husband*, and the other, that any one could think for a moment of comparing Lincoln to Douglas!

tempted to envy him his grave with its honors." [1] These words might have expressed in part the feelings of Lincoln on the death of Douglas.

The states in rebellion, having organized a hostile government, with Jefferson Davis as President, and Alexander H. Stephens as Vice-President, Lincoln anxiously surveyed the political horizon, that he might fully understand the difficulties and dangers by which he was surrounded. It should be remembered that although his electoral vote was large, his popular vote was in a minority of nearly one million.[2] The treasury was empty ; the national credit failing and broken ; the nucleus of a regular army scattered and disarmed ; the officers who had not deserted were strangers ; the old democratic party which had ruled for most of the time for half a century, was largely in sympathy with the insurgents. Lincoln's own party was made up of discordant elements ; neither he nor his party had acquired *prestige;* nor had the party yet learned to have confidence in its leaders. He had to create an army, to find military skill and leadership by experience. In this respect the rebels had great advantage. They had been for years preparing. The Southern people were the more used to firearms and to violence. They had in the beginning a great superiority in their military leaders. The national government had not at the beginning any officers known to the administration, who were equal in skill to Lee, Stonewall Jackson, and Johnston. Mr. Lincoln had to learn by costly experience who could win victories; he could not know by intuition, and in the beginning there were many and humiliating reverses, until merit and skill could be developed and placed at the head of the armies

In addition to all this, he entered upon his great work of restoring the integrity of the Union, without sympathy from any of the great powers of Western Europe. Those of

---

1. See address of William Allen Butler, on Martin Van Buren, p. 39.

2. The popular vote was: For Lincoln, 1,866,452; for Douglas, 1,375,157; for Breckenridge, 847,953; for Bell, 590,631. The three defeated candidates received a majority of 947,289 over Lincoln.

them who were not hostile, manifested a cold neutrality, exhibiting towards him and his government no cordial good will, nor extending to him any moral aid.

Let us trace the history of his administration, through these days of trial down to his final triumph. His first and great object was to encourage and strengthen the Union sentiment in the border states. If he could hold these states in the Union, the contest would be shortened. Therefore he had delayed his call for troops to the last moment, in the hope that by conciliation he might prevent the secession of the border states.

In the language of his inaugural, he left the "momentous issues of civil war" in the hands of the rebels. The war was "forced upon the national authority." On the 9th of April, the rebel commissioners, whom the government refused to receive or recognize, left Washington, declaring that "they accepted the gage of battle."[1] The Confederates had seized the "arsenals, forts, custom-houses, post-offices, ships, and materials of war of the United States," excepting the forts in Charleston Harbor, and were constructing fortifications and placing guns in position to attack even these. While some of the border states seemed to hesitate, the rebel government resolved, for the purpose of arousing sectional feeling and prejudice, to bring on at once a conflict of arms.

The attack on Fort Sumter was ordered by the rebel authorities on the 11th of April, Major Robert Anderson, in command, was summoned to surrender and refused. He had a feeble garrison of a handful of men, and was encircled with hostile cannon. A peremptory message was sent to him, that unless he surrendered within an hour, the rebel forts would open upon him. He still refused, and the bombardment began, and continued for thirty-six hours, when he and his seventy men surrendered.

The fall of Sumter and the President's call for troops were the signals for the rally to arms throughout the loyal states. Twenty millions of people, forgetting party divisions

1. McPherson's History of the Rebellion, p. 110.

and all past differences, rose with one voice of patriotic enthusiam, and laid their fortunes and their lives upon the altar of their country. The proclamation of the President calling for seventy-five thousand men and convening an extra session of Congress to meet on the 4th of July, was followed, in every free state, by the prompt action of the governors, calling for volunteers. In every city, town, village, and neighborhood, the people rushed to arms, and almost fought for the privilege of marching to the defense of the national capital. Forty-eight hours had not passed after the issue of the proclamation, when four regiments had reported to Governor Andrew, at Boston, ready for service. On the 17th, he commissioned B. F. Butler, of Lowell, as their commander.

Governor Sprague, of Rhode Island, calling the Legislature of that state together, on the 17th of July, tendered to the government a thousand infantry, and a battalion of artillery, and placing himself at the head of his troops, started for Washington.

The great state of New York, whose population was nearly four millions, through her Legislature, and the action of Governor Morgan, placed her immense resources in the hands of the national Executive. So did Pennsylvania, with its three millions of people, under the lead of Governor Curtin. And Pennsylvania has the honor of having furnished the troops that first arrived for the defense of the capital, reaching there on the 18th, just in time to prevent a seizure of the nearly defenceless city.

By the 20th of April, although the quota of Ohio, under the President's call, was only thirteen regiments, seventy-one thousand men had offered their services through Governor Dennison, the Executive of that state. It was the same everywhere. Half a million of men, citizen volunteers, at this call sprang to arms, and begged permission to fight for their country. The enthusiasm pervaded all ranks and classes. Prayers for the Union and the integrity of the nation were heard in every church throughout the free states. State legislatures, municipalities, banks, corporations, and capitalists everywhere offered their money to the government, and subscribed immense sums for the support of the volunteers and their families. Independent military organizations poured in their offers of service. Written pledges were widely circulated and signed, offering to the government the lives and property of the signers to maintain the Union. Great crowds marched through the principal cities, cheering the patriotic, singing national airs, and requiring all to show, from their residences and places of business, the stars and stripes, or "the red, white and blue." The people, through the press, by public meetings, and by resolutions, placed their property and lives at the disposal of the government.

Thus at this gloomy period, through the dark clouds of gathering war, uprose the mighty voice of the people to cheer the heart of the President. Onward it came, like the rush of many waters, shouting the words that became so familiar during the war—

"We are coming, Father Abraham,
Six hundred thousand strong."

The government was embarrassed by the number of men volunteering for its service. Hundreds of thousands more were offered than could be armed or received. Senators, members of Congress, and other prominent men, went to Washington to beg the government to accept the services of the eager regiments everywhere imploring permission to serve.

The volunteer soldier was the popular idol. He was everywhere welcome. Fair hands wove the banners which he carried, and knit the socks and shirts which protected him from the cold; and everywhere they lavished upon him luxuries and comforts to cheer and encourage him. Every one scorned to take pay from the soldier. Colonel Stetson, proprietor of the Astor House Hotel, in New York, replied to General Butler's offer to pay: "The Astor House makes no charge for Massachusetts soldiers." And while the best hotels were proud to entertain the soldier, whether private or officer, the latch-string of the cabin and farm-house was never drawn in upon him who wore the national blue. Such was the universal enthusiasm of the people for their country's defenders.

The feeling of fierce indignation towards those seeking to destroy the government, was greatly increased by the attack of a mob in the streets of Baltimore upon the Sixth Regiment of Massachusetts Volunteers, while passing from one depot to the other on their way to the capital. This attack, on the 19th of April, in which several soldiers were shot, roused the people to the highest pitch of excitement. The secessionists were so strong in that state as to induce the Mayor of Baltimore, and Governor Hicks, a Union man, to protest against troops marching over the soil of Maryland to the defense of the national capital. The rebels burned the bridges on the railroads leading to Washington, and for a time interrupted the passage of troops through Baltimore. The Governor so far humiliated himself, and forgot the dignity of his state and nation, as to suggest that the differences between the government and its rebellious citizens should be referred to Lord Lyons, the British Minister. The Secretary of State fittingly rebuked this unworthy suggestion; alluding to an incident in the late war with Great Britain, he reminded the Governor of Maryland "that there had been a time when a general of the American Union, with forces designed for the defense of its capital, was not unwelcome anywhere in Maryland;" and he added, "that if all the other nobler sentiments of Maryland had been obliterated, one, at least, it was hoped would remain, and that was, that no domestic contention should be referred to any foreign arbitrament, least of all to that of a European monarchy."

While such was the universal feeling of loyal enthusiasm throughout the free states, in the border slave states there was division and fierce conflict. Governor Magoffin, of Kentucky, in reply to the President's call, answered: "I say, emphatically, Kentucky will furnish no troops for the wicked purpose of subduing her sister Southern states." Governor Harris, of Tennessee, said: "Tennessee will not furnish a man for coercion, but fifty thousand for the defense of our Southern brothers." Governor Jackson, of Missouri, refused, saying: "Not one man will Missouri furnish to carry on such an unholy crusade;" and Virginia not only refused, through her governor, to respond, but her convention, then in session, immediately passed an ordinance of secession by a vote of eighty-eight to fifty-five.

The Northwest, the home of the President, and the home of Douglas, was, if possible, more emphatic, it could scarcely be more unanimous, than other sections of the free states, in the expression of its determination to maintain the Union at all hazards, and at any cost. The people of the vast country between the Alleghanies and the Rocky Mountains, and north of the Ohio, regarded the Mississippi as peculiarly *their* river, their great outlet to the sea. Proud and confident in their hardy strength, familiar with the use of arms, they never at any time, for a moment, hesitated in their determination not to permit the erection of a foreign territory between themselves and the Gulf of Mexico. Here were ten millions of the most energetic, determined, self-reliant people on earth; and the idea that anybody should dare to set up any flag other than theirs between them and the ocean, betrayed an audacity they would never tolerate. "Our great river," exclaimed Douglas, indignantly, "has been closed to the commerce of the Northwest." The seceding states, conscious of the strength of this feeling, early passed a law providing for the free navigation of the Mississippi. But the hardy Western pioneers were not disposed to accept paper guarantees for permission to "possess, occupy, and enjoy" their own. They would hold the Mississippi with their rifles. When closed upon them, they resolved to open it. They immediately seized upon the important strategic point of Cairo, and from Belmont to Vicksburg and Fort Hudson, round to Lookout Mountain, Chattanooga, and Atlanta, they never ceased to press the enemy, until the great central artery of the republic, and all its vast tributaries from its source to its mouth, were free; and then, marching to the sea, joined their gallant brethren on the Atlantic coast, to aid in the complete overthrow of the rebellion, and the final triumph of liberty and law.

It has been stated that the people of the border states had been divided in sentiment, and it was very doubtful for a time, which way they would go ; but the attack upon Fort Sumter, and the call by the President for troops, forced the issue, and the unscrupulous leaders were able to carry Virginia, North Carolina, Tennessee, and Arkansas, into the Confederate organization, against the will of a majority of the people of those states. Virginia, the leading state of the Revolution, the one which, under the leadership of Washington and Madison, had been the most influential in the formation of the national government, the " Old Dominion," as she was called, " the mother of states and of statesmen," had been for years descending from her high position. Her early and Revolutionary history had been one of unequaled brilliancy ; she had largely shaped the policy of the nation, and furnished its leaders. Her early statesmen were anti-slavery men, and if she had relieved herself of the burden of slavery, she would have held her position as the leading state of the Union ; but, with this heavy drag, the proud old commonwealth had seen her younger sisters of the republic rapidly overtaking and passing her in the race of progress, and the elements of national greatness. Indeed, she had fallen so low, that her principal source of wealth was from the men, women, and children she raised and sent South to supply the slave markets of the Gulf states. Her leading men had been advocating extreme state rights doctrines, fatal to national unity, and thus sowing the seeds of secession. Her politicians had threatened disunion, again and again. Still, when the crisis came, a majority of her people were true ; a large majority of their convention was opposed to secession, and when afterwards, by violence and fraud, the ordinance was passed, the people

14

of the Northwest, the mountain region of Virginia, resisted, and determined to stand by the Union. This portion of the state maintained its position with fidelity and heroism, and ultimately established the state of West Virginia.

The secession of Virginia added greatly to the danger of Washington, and a bold movement upon it then, in its defenceless condition, would have been successful. Alexander H. Stephens, Vice-President of the Confederacy, came to Richmond, and everywhere raised the cry of " on to Washington ! " The state authorities of Virginia did not wait the ratification of the secession ordinance by the people, to whom it was submitted for adoption or rejection, but immediately joined the Confederacy, commenced hostilities, and organized expeditions for the capture of Harper's Ferry and the Gosport Navy-yard. Senator Mason immediately issued an address to the people, declaring that those who could not vote for a separation of Virginia from the United States, " *must leave the state !* " Submission, banishment, or death was proclaimed to all Union men of the old commonwealth. Nowhere, except in West Virginia, and some small localities, was there resistance to this decree. In the Northwest, the mountain men rallied, organized, resolved to stand by the old flag, and protect themselves under its folds.

The secession of Virginia gave to the Confederates a moral and physical power, which imparted to the conflict the proportions of a tremendous civil war. She placed herself as a barrier between her weaker sisters and the Union, and she held her position with a heroic endurance and courage, worthy of a better cause and of her earlier days. Indeed, she kept the Union forces at bay for more than four long years, preserving her capital, and yielding only, when the hardy soldiers of the North had marched from the Ohio to the sea, cutting her off and making the struggle hopeless.

North Carolina naturally followed Virginia, and, on the 21st of May, adopted an ordinance of secession. Maryland, from her location between the free states and the national capital, occupied a position of the utmost importance. Could she be induced to join the Confederates, their design of seizing the national capital and its archives would be made comparatively easy. Emissaries from the conspirators were busy in her borders during the winter of 1861. But while there were many rebel sympathizers and traitors among her slaveholders, and while many leading families gave in their adhesion to the conspiracy, the mass of the people were loyal. The governor of the state, Thomas H. Hicks, though he yielded for a time to the apparent popular feeling in favor of the Confederates, and greatly embarrassed the government by his protests against troops marching over Maryland soil to the defense of the capital, was, at heart a loyal man and in the end became a decided and efficient Union leader. He refused, against inducements and threats of personal violence, to call the Legislature of the state together, a majority of whom were known to be secessionists, and who would have passed an ordinance of secession. But the man to whom the people of Maryland are most indebted, who was most influential in the maintenance of the Union cause at this crisis, and who proved the benefactor of the state in relieving her from the curse of slavery, was the bold, eloquent, and talented Henry Winter Davis. He took his position from the start, for the unconditional maintenance of the Union.

The officials of the city of Baltimore were, most of them, secessionists, and its chief of police was a traitor, and was implicated in the plot to assassinate Mr. Lincoln on his way to the capital. On the 19th of April, a mob in the city of Baltimore had attacked the Massachusetts Sixth Regiment, which was quietly passing through to the defense of the capital, and several soldiers and citizens were killed in the affray. The bridges connecting the railways from Pennsylvania and New York with Baltimore, were burned, and for a time, communication by railroad was interrupted. General B. F. Butler, leading the Massachusetts troops, together with the New York Seventh Regiment, was compelled to go around by Annapolis and to rebuild the railway to Washington. But one dark, stormy night, General Butler marched into Baltimore, encamped on Federal Hill, and reopened communication with the North. The Union men of Maryland rallied; the leading secessionists fled or were arrested, and from that time, Maryland was a loyal state, giving to the Union the aid of her moral influence, and furnishing many gallant soldiers to fight its battles.

What course would be taken by Missouri, the leading state west of the Mississippi ? With a population exceeding a million, she had only 115,000 slaves. Her interests were with the free states, yet she had a governor in direct sympathy with the traitors, as were the majority of her state officers. A state convention was called, but an overwhelming majority of Union men had been elected. The truth is, that although the slave power had succeeded in destroying the political power of her great senator, Thomas H. Benton, yet the seeds of opposition to slavery which he had scattered, were everywhere springing up in favor of union and liberty. The city of St. Louis, the commercial metropolis of the state, had become a free-soil city; it had elected Francis P. Blair, Jr., a disciple of Benton, to Congress. The large German population, under the lead of Franz Sigel and others, were for the Union, to a man.

To the President's call for troops, the rebel Governor, Claiborne F. Jackson, returned an insulting refusal, but the people, under the lead of Blair, responded. The United States Arsenal at St. Louis was, at this time, under a guard commanded by Captain Nathaniel Lyon, one of the boldest and most energetic officers of the army. He, in connection with Colonels Blair, Sigel, and others, organized volunteer regiments in St. Louis, preparing for a conflict, which they early saw to be inevitable. The arms of the St. Louis Arsenal were, during the night of the 25th of April, under the direction of Captains Stokes and Lyon, transferred to a steamer and taken to Alton, Illinois, for safety, and were soon placed in the hands of the volunteers from that state.

On the 19th of April, the President issued a proclamation, blockading the ports of the Gulf states, and on the 27th this was extended to North Carolina and Virginia, both of which states had been carried into the vortex of revolution. On the 3d of May, the President called into the service forty-two thousand volunteers and a large increase of the regular army. The navy was thus provided for. In the meanwhile, the insurgents had been active and enterprising. They had boldly seized Harper's Ferry, and the Gosport Navy-yard, near Norfolk, Virginia. Within twenty-four hours after the secession ordinance passed the Virginia Convention, they sent forces to capture those places, where were situated very important arsenals of arms and ordnance. Harper's Ferry had long been a national armory, and commanded the Baltimore and Ohio Railroad, one of the most important connections of the capital with the West. It was the gate of the beautiful valley of the Shenandoah, and of great importance as a military post. On the 18th of April, it was abandoned by its small garrison, and taken possession of by the insurgents. At about the same time, the Gosport Navy-yard, with two thousand pieces of heavy cannon and various material of war, and its large ships, including the Pennsylvania of one hundred and twenty guns, and the Merrimac, afterwards famous for its combat with the Monitor, fell into their hands. Owing to imbecility, or treachery, or both, this navy-yard, with its vast stores and property, estimated to be worth from eight to ten millions, was left exposed to seizure and destruction.

Meanwhile, troops gathered to the defense of the national capital. Among others, came Colonel Elmer E. Ellsworth, with a splendid regiment of picked men, which he had raised from the New York firemen. On the evening of the 23d of May, the Union forces crossed the Potomac and took possession of Arlington Heights, and the hills overlooking Washington and Alexandria. As Colonel Ellsworth was returning from pulling down a rebel flag from the Marshal House, in Alexandria, he was instantly killed by a shot fired by the keeper of the hotel over which the obnoxious symbol had floated.

This young man had accompanied Mr. Lincoln from Illinois to Washington, and was a *protégé* of the President. He had introduced the Zouave drill into the United States. He was among the first martyrs of the war, and his death was deeply mourned by the President. His body was taken to the Executive Mansion, and his funeral, being among the first of those who died in defense of the flag, was very impressive, touching, and solemn. A gold medal was taken from his body after his death, stained with his heart's blood, and bearing the inscription: "*non solum nobis sed pro patria*," "Not for ourselves alone, but for the country."

The secession of Virginia had been followed by the removal of the rebel government to Richmond. Virginia, North Carolina, Tennessee, and Arkansas had also joined the Confederacy. At last freedom and slavery confronted each other, face to face, in arms. The loyal states at this time, had a population of 22,046,472, and the eleven seceding states had a population of 9,103,333, of which 3,521,110 were slaves.

The rebel government having been established and its constitution adopted, Alexander H. Stephens, its Vice-President, boldly and frankly declared: "Our new government is founded, * * its foundations are laid, its corner-stone rests on the great truth that the negro is not equal to the white man, *that slavery, subordination to the superior race is the natural and normal condition.*[1]

The Confederate government being based on slavery, and the fact openly avowed that slavery was its corner-stone, how would it be received by Europe? and especially by those great nations England and France, both of which had so often reproached the United States for the existence of

1. McPherson's History of the Rebellion, p. 103.

slavery? These powers and the world were now to be spectators of a conflict between an established government, perfectly free, on one side, and a rebellion organized by a portion of its citizens with the avowed purpose to erect upon its
ruins a government based upon, and formed to protect and
extend, slavery. Surely there was every reason to expect
that these powers would rebuke with their indignation the
suggestion that they should recognize—even as belligerents
—a government with such a basis, and would, in the most
emphatic manner, express their opposition to a rebellion
begun and carried on, because the authority rebelled against
had opposed the further extension of slavery.

But far from doing this, Great Britain and France, acting in concert, even before the representatives of President
Lincoln's administration had arrived in London and Paris,
hastened to recognize the rebels as a belligerent power. This
eagerness to encourage rebellion ; this indecent haste to
accord belligerent rights to an insurgent power, based on
slavery, was justly attributed to a secret hostility on the part
of those governments towards the American republic. The
United States stood before the world as a long established
government, representing order, civilization, and freedom.
The Confederates, as a disorganizing rebellion, with no grievance, except opposition to the extension of slavery, with no
purpose, except to extend and perpetuate slavery; and yet the
powers of Western Europe, and especially the aristocracy of
England, made haste to hail them as belligerents, and extend
to them moral aid and sympathy.

The London Times, the organ of the English aristocracy, exultingly announced : " The great republic is no more !
Democracy is a rope of sand." The United States, it
said, lacked the cohesive power to maintain an empire of
such magnitude.

At the moment of extremest national peril, when the son
of the Western pioneer, whom the people had chosen for
their Chief Magistrate, was confronted by the dangers which
gathered around his country ; when his great and honest soul

bowed itself to God, and as a simple child, in deepest suppli-
cation asked his guidance and blessing ; at this hour, from
no crowned head, from no aristocratic ruler abroad, came any
word of sympathy ; but those proud rulers could coarsely jest
at his uncouth figure, his uncourtly bearing. " The bubble is
burst," said they. But the Almighty answered that prayer; he
joined the hearts and linked the hands of the American people and their President together ; and from that hour to his
death, the needle does not more quickly respond to the polar
influence, than did Lincoln to the highest and God-inspired
impulses of a great people—a people capable of the highest
heroism and the grandest destiny.

Very soon the work-shops of England and Scotland were
set in motion to prepare the means of sweeping American commerce from the ocean. The active sympathy of the masses of
European populations, and the cold and scarcely concealed
hostility of the aristocratic and privileged classes, were early
and constantly manifested during the entire struggle. This
was, perhaps, not unnatural. In addition to the uneasiness
which the rapid growth and commanding position of our
country had created, the whole world instinctively felt that
the contest was between freedom and slavery, democracy
and aristocracy. Could a government, for the people and by
the people, maintain itself through this fearful crisis ? It
was quite evident, from the beginning, that the privileged
classes abroad were more than willing to see the great republic broken up, to see it pronounced a failure. The conspirators had prepared the way, as far as possible, by their
scarcely veiled intrigues, for the recognition of the Confederacy. The rebels had a positive, vigorous organization,
with agents all over Europe, many of them in the diplomatic
service of the United States. They had created a
wide-spread prejudice against Mr. Lincoln, representing
him as merely an ignorant, vulgar " rail-splitter " of the
prairies.

Mr. Faulkner, of Virginia, represented our government
in France, and Mr. Preston, a slaveholder from Kentucky, in

Spain, both secessionists. It was not long, however, before Mr. Lincoln impressed the leading traits of his character upon our foreign policy. Frankness, straightforward integrity, patient forbearance, and unbroken faith in the triumph of the Union and liberty, based upon his trust and confidence in the Almighty and the American people, characterized his foreign policy. This policy was simple and thoroughly American ; our representatives were instructed to ask nothing but what was clearly right, to avoid difficulty, and to maintain peace, if it could be done consistently with national honor. The record of the diplomatic correspondence of the United States during the critical years of this administration, is one of which Americans may justly be proud. Time and events have vindicated the statesmanship by which it was conducted. Mr. Seward, in his instructions to Mr. Adams, on the eve of his departure for the Court of St. James, very clearly laid down the principles which should govern our relations with foreign nations. Mr. Adams was instructed not to listen to any suggestion of compromise between the United States and any of its citizens, under foreign auspices. He was directed firmly to announce that no foreign government could recognize the rebels as an independent power, and remain the friends of the United States. Recognition was war. If any foreign power recognized, they might prepare to enter into an alliance also, with the enemies of the republic. He was instructed to represent the whole country, and should he be asked to divide that duty with the representatives of the Confederates, he was directed to return home.

The action of the insurgent states was treated as a rebellion, purely domestic in its character, and no discussion on the subject with foreign nations would be tolerated. England did not recognize the Confederates as a nation. She did not choose war ; but short of recognition, alliance, and war, it is difficult to see how she could have done more to encourage and aid the insurgents than she did.

When the insurgents raised the flag of rebellion, the

army and navy were scandalized, and the nation disgraced, by large numbers of the officers deserting their flag. Nearly two hundred of the graduates of the military school at West Point deserted, and joined the rebel army.

Yet, among the officers born in the seceding states, were patriots and loyalists, faithful and true, and scorning all temptations addressed to their fidelity. Among others, in civil life, Andrew Johnson and Andrew J. Hamilton have been already named, and in the military and naval service were Scott and Thomas, Meade and Farragut, and many others. The names of Jefferson Davis and of his military associates grow dark, in contrast with those of the hero of Lundy's Lane, of the victors at Gettysburg and Nashville, and the blunt, honest, and chivalric sailor, who so gloriously triumphed over traitors at New Orleans and Mobile. Loyalty to a state may palliate, it cannot justify treachery and treason. Unless all moral distinctions are to cease, all good men who honor Scott and George H. Thomas must condemn Twiggs. Honoring David G. Farragut, they must condemn Raphael Semmes.

There were, at the time of the breaking out of the rebellion, and mostly in the rebel states, nearly four millions of slaves. How should they be treated? Should the government, by offering them freedom, make them its active friends, or alienate them by returning them to slavery? In the light of to-day it is difficult to understand why there should have been hesitation or vacillation in this matter. The transfer of four millions of people in the rebel states to the Union side would have been decisive.

In the beginning, the officers of the army, and especially those educated at West Point, were slow in availing themselves of the aid of the negroes. Some went so far as to return to the rebels their runaway slaves. General Butler did much towards ending this policy. In May, 1861, he was in command at Fortress Monroe. One evening three negroes came into camp, saying that " they had fled from their master, Colonel Mallory, who was about to set them to work on rebel fortifications." If they had been Colonel Mallory's horses or mules, there could be no question as to what should be done with them. But so strangely deluded were the army officers, that up to that time they had returned fugitive slaves to rebel masters, to work and fight for the rebel cause. Would Butler continue in this folly?

In reply, he said: "*These men are contraband of war.*" This sentence, expressing an obvious truth, was more important than a battle gained. It was a victory in the direction of emancipation, upon which the success of the Union cause was ultimately to depend. He, of course, refused to surrender them, but set them to work on his own defences. Up to this time the South had fought to maintain slavery, and the government, for fear of offending Kentucky and other border states, would not touch it. Strange as it may seem, a rebel officer had the presumption, under a flag of truce, to demand the return of these negroes under the alleged constitutional obligation to return fugitive slaves! General Butler, of course, refused, saying: "I shall retain the negroes *as contraband of war!* You were using them upon your batteries; it is merely a question whether they shall be used for or against us." Other generals of the Union army were very slow in recognizing this obvious truth. General McClellan, on the 26th of May, issued an address to the people of his military district, in which he said: "Not only will we abstain from all interference with your slaves, but we will, on the contrary, with an iron hand crush any attempt at insurrection on their part."

CHAPTER XIII.

EXTRA SESSION OF CONGRESS.

PROMINENT MEMBERS OF 37TH CONGRESS.— PRESIDENT'S MESSAGE.—
VACANT CHAIRS OF PROMINENT REBELS.— BAKER'S REPLY TO
BRECKENRIDGE.—ANDREW JOHNSON.—OWEN LOVEJOY.—LAW TO
FREE THE SLAVES OF REBELS.—BULL RUN.— FREMONT'S ORDER
FREEING SLAVES MODIFIED BY THE PRESIDENT.— CAPTURE AND
RELEASE OF MASON AND SLIDELL.

THE Thirty-seventh Congress convened in an extra and
called session, on the 4th of July, 1861. The Thirty-sixth
Congress had expired on the 4th of March, without making
any provision to meet the impending dangers. It devolved
upon this, the Thirty-seventh, to sanction what the President
had been compelled to do, and to clothe him with extraordinary war powers, and under his lead to call into the field,
and to provide for, those vast armies whose campaigns were
to extend over half the continent. It was for this Congress
to create and maintain that system of finance, which without
the aid of foreign loans, carried the republic triumphantly
through the most stupendous war of modern times, and
which, in the "green-back" currency, still survives.

Hannibal Hamlin, Vice-President, presided in the Senate;
Galusha A. Grow, of Pennsylvania, was elected Speaker, and
Emerson Etheridge, of Tennessee, Clerk of the House.
In the Senate, only twenty-three, and in the House
twenty-two states were represented. No representa-
tives in either appeared from North or South Caro-
lina, Georgia, Florida, Alabama, Mississippi, Louisiana,
Texas, or Arkansas. No senators, and only two members of

the House, appeared from Virginia. Andrew Johnson, from his mountain home in Tennessee, " faithful among the faithless," alone represented Tennessee in the Senate, and at the second session, Horace Maynard and Andrew J. Clements appeared, and took their seats in the House.

Among the more prominent senators of New England, and men who had already secured a national reputation, were Fessenden and Morrill, of Maine; Hale, of New Hampshire; Sumner and Wilson, of Massachusetts; Collamer and Foot, of Vermont, and Anthony, of Rhode Island. New York was represented by Preston King and Ira Harris.

Mr. Hale, from New Hampshire, had been the leader of the old " liberty party." " Solitary and alone " in the United States Senate, by his wit and humor, his readiness and ability, he had maintained his position against the whole senatorial delegation of the slave states, and their numerous allies from the free states.   From Vermont came the dignified, urbane, and somewhat formal Solomon Foot; his colleague, Jacob Collamer, was a gentleman of the old school, who had been a member of cabinets, and was one of the wisest jurists and statesmen of our country. Preston King had been the friend and confidant of Martin Van Buren, Silas Wright, and Thomas H. Benton, and a leader at the Buffalo convention; genial, true, and devoted to the principles of democracy. From Pennsylvania there was David Wilmot, who while a member of the House, had introduced the "Wilmot proviso," which connects his name forever with the anti-slavery contest.

The senators from Ohio were John Sherman, a brother of General Sherman, and late a distinguished member of the House of Representatives and Chairman of the Committee on Finance, and Benjamin Wade, staunch, rude, earnest, and true.   From Illinois, came Lyman Trumbull and Orville H. Browning, both distinguished lawyers and competitors at the bar with Douglas and Lincoln. From Iowa, Senators Grimes and Harlan ; from Wisconsin, Doolittle and Howe ; from Michigan, Bingham and Chandler ; from Indiana,

Jesse D. Bright and Henry S. Lane, the latter of whom had presided over the Philadelphia convention of 1856.

The House of Representatives of this memorable Congress was composed in the main of men of good sense, respectable abilities, and earnest patriotism. It well represented the intelligence, integrity, and devotion to their country of the American people. The leader of the House, as Chairman of the Committee of Ways and Means, was Thaddeus Stevens, of Pennsylvania; although a man of nearly three score years and ten, he combined with large experience, the vigor and the energy of thirty-five. He was the most sarcastic and witty, as well as the most eccentric member of the House. Respected, and somewhat feared, alike by friend and foe, few desired a second encounter with him in the forensic war of debate. If he did not demolish with an argument or crush with his logic, he could silence with an epigram or a sarcasm. Ready, adroit, and sagacious, as well as bold and frank, he exerted a large influence upon legislation. He was a bitter and uncompromising party chief, and better adapted to lead an opposition, than to conduct and control a majority.

In the New York delegation was Roscoe Conkling, already distinguished for his eloquence and ability, Charles B. Sedgwick, Chairman of the Committee on Naval Affairs, and E. G. Spaulding and Erastus Corning, leading members of the Committee of Ways and Means. From Ohio were Pendleton, Vallandigham, and Cox, leaders of the remnant of the democratic party, and among the republicans was John A. Bingham, one of the most ready and effective debaters on the floor. Schuyler Colfax, from Indiana, a rising member, was then serving his fourth term. He was industrious and genial, with great tact and good sense. Differing from his political opponents, he did not rouse their anger by strong statements, or harsh language, and he was popular on both sides of the House. Illinois was represented by Washburne, Lovejoy, Kellogg, and Arnold, republicans; while among the friends of Douglas were

Richardson, McClernand, Fouke, and Logan, and these generally supported the war measures of the administration. They had followed the lead of Douglas ; and McClernand, Fouke, and Logan entered the Union army, and, especially Logan, did good service as soldiers during the war.

But many vacant chairs in the House and the Senate, indicated the extent of the defection, the gravity of the situation, and the magnitude of the impending struggle. The old pro-slavery leaders were absent, some in the rebel government set up at Richmond, and others in the field, marshalling their troops in arms against their country. The chair of the late senator, now the rebel President, Jefferson Davis, those of the blustering and fiery Bob Toombs, of the accomplished Hunter, of the polished and learned Jew from Louisiana, Judah P. Benjamin, of the haughty and pretentious Mason, of the crafty and unscrupulous Slidell, and of their compeers, who had been accustomed to domineer over the Senate, were all vacant.

The seat of Douglas, the ambitious and able senator from Illinois, had been vacated, not by treason, but by death. Life-long opponents, recalling his last patriotic words spoken at Springfield, and in Chicago, gazed sadly on that unoccupied seat, now draped in black. Well had it been for John C. Breckenridge, lately the competitor of Douglas, if his chair also had been made vacant by his early death. But still conspicuous among the senators was the late Vice-President, now the senator from Kentucky. His fellow traitors from the slave-states had all gone. He alone lingered, shunned, and distrusted by all loyal men, and treated with the most freezing and formal courtesy, by his associates. Dark and lowering, he could be daily seen in his carriage—always alone—driving to the Senate chamber, where his voice and his votes were always given to thwart the war measures of the government. It was obvious that his heart was with his old associates at Richmond. As soon as the session closed, he threw off all disguise, and joined the army of the insurgents. While at Washington, gloomy, and it may be sorrowful, he said : " We can only look with sadness on the melancholy drama that is being enacted."

Hostile armies were gathering and confronting each other, and from the dome of the Capitol, on the distant hills beyond Arlington, and on towards Fairfax Court House, could be seen the rebel flag. President Lincoln, in his message to this Congress, calmly reviewed the situation. He called attention to the fact that at his inauguartion the functions of the Federal Government had been suspended in the states of Georgia, South Carolina, Alabama, Mississippi, Louisiana, Texas, and Florida. All the national property in these states had been appropriated by the insurgents. They had seized all the forts, arsenals, etc., excepting those on the Florida coast, and Fort Sumter, in Charleston harbor, and these were then in a state of siege by the rebel forces. The national arms had been seized, and were in the hands of the hostile armies. A large number of the officers of the United States army and navy, had resigned and taken up arms against their government. He reviewed the facts in relation to Fort Sumter, and showed that by the attack upon it, the insurgents began the conflict of arms, thus forcing upon the country immediate dissolution, or war. No choice remained but to call into action the *war powers of the government*, and to resist the force employed for its destruction, by force, for its preservation. The call for troops was made, and the response was most gratifying. Yet no slave state, except Delaware, had given a regiment through state organization. He then reviewed the action of Virginia, including the seizure of the national armory at Harper's Ferry, and the navy-yard at Gosport, near Norfolk. The people of Virginia had permitted the insurrection to make its nest within her borders, and left the government no choice but to deal with it where it found it. He then reviewed the action of the government, the calls for troops, the blockade of the ports in the rebellious states, and the suspension of the *habeas corpus*. He asked Congress to confer upon him the power to make the conflict short and decisive. He asked to have placed at his disposal four hundred thousand men, and four hundred millions of money. Congress responded promptly to the message of the President, and voted five hundred thousand men, and five hundred millions of dollars, to suppress the rebellion.

As an illustration of those days and debates, let us recall an incident which occurred in the Senate, on the first of August, a few days after the battle of Bull Run. Senator Baker, of Oregon, Lincoln's old friend and competitor, and his successor in Congress from the Springfield district, was making a brilliant and impassioned reply to a speech of Breckenridge. Charles Sumner, speaking of this, and alluding to Breckenridge, said : " A senator with treason in his heart, if not on his lips, has just taken his seat." Baker, who had entered the chamber direct from his camp, rose at once to reply. [1] His rebuke of the disloyal sentiments of Breckenridge was severe, and in the highest degree dramatic, and worthy of the best days of that Roman eloquence to which he alluded.

" What," said he, " would the senator from Kentucky have? These speeches of his, sown broadcast over the land ; what clear, distinct meaning have they ? Are they not intended for disorganization in our very midst ? Are they not intended to destroy our zeal ? Are they not intended to animate our enemies? Sir, are they not words of brilliant, polished *treason ;* even in the very Capitol of the republic ? What would have been thought, if, in another Capitol, in another republic, in a yet more martial age, a senator as grave, not more eloquent or dignified than the senator from Kentucky, yet with the Roman purple flowing over his shoulders, had risen in his place, surrounded by all the emblems of Roman glory, and declared that the cause of the advancing Hannibal was just, and that Carthage ought to be dealt with in terms of peace? What would have been thought, if after the battle of Cannæ, a senator there had risen in his place, and denounced every levy of the Roman people, every expenditure of its treasure, and every appeal to the old recollections, and the old glories ? "

There was a silence so profound throughout the Senate and galleries, that a pinfall could have been heard; while every eye was fixed upon Breckenridge. Fessenden ex-

1. Congressional Globe, Dec. 11, 1861.

claimed, in deep, low tones: " He would have been hurled from the Tarpeian rock." Baker then resumed:

" Sir, a senator, himself learned far more than myself in such lore (Mr. Fessenden), tells me, in a voice I am glad is audible, that ' he would have been hurled from the Tarpeian rock.' It is a grand commentary upon the American Constitution, that we permit these words of the senator from Kentucky to be uttered. I ask the senator to recollect, too, what, save to send aid and comfort to the enemy, do these predictions amount to ? Every word thus uttered falls as a note of inspiration upon every Confederate ear."

Baker was the man, brilliant alike as an orator and a soldier, of whom Sumner happily said: " He was the Prince Rupert of debate, and if he had lived, would have become the Prince Rupert of battle." It was he who, on the prairies of Illinois, had contested the palm of eloquence with Lincoln and Douglas, who had gone to California and pronounced the memorable oration over Senator Broderick, and who, going thence to Oregon, came to Washington as senator from that state.

Andrew Johnson, in reply to Breckenridge, on the 27th of July, quoted the remark: " When traitors become numerous enough, treason becomes respectable. Yet," said he, " God willing, whether traitors be many or few, as I have heretofore waged war against traitors and treason, I intend to continue to the end." [1] His denunciation of Jefferson Davis was vehement and impassioned. He said: " Davis, a man educated and nurtured by the government, who sucked its pap, who received from it all his military instruction, a man who got all his distinction, civil and military, in the service of the government, beneath its flag, and then without cause, without being deprived of a single right or privilege, the sword he unsheathed in vindication of the stars and stripes in a foreign land, given to him by the hand of a cherishing mother, he stands this day prepared to plunge into her bosom." [2]

Senator Fessenden, Chairman of the Committee on Finance,

1. Congressional Globe, July 27, 1861, p. 291.
2. See Congressional Globe.

and the successor of Mr. Chase as Secretary of the Treasury, was a very able and learned New England senator. Ever ready, well informed, keen, witty, and sarcastic, as a general debater he had no superior.

At this its first session, Congress inaugurated that series of measures against slavery, which, in connection with the action of the President and the victories of the Union soldiers, resulted in its destruction. Among its members, known distinctly as an abolitionist, was Owen Lovejoy; a man, as has been stated, of powerful frame, strong feelings, and great personal magnetism as a speaker. In February, 1859, during his first term in Congress, in reply to the furious denunciations of the slaveholders, which charged among other things, that he was a "nigger stealer," he indignantly and defiantly exclaimed :

"Yes, I do assist fugitives to escape. Proclaim it upon the housetops; write it upon every leaf that trembles in the forest; make it blaze from the sun at high noon, and shine forth in the radiance of every star that bedecks the firmament of God. Let it echo through all the arches of heaven, and reverberate and bellow through all the deep gorges of hell, where slavecatchers will be very likely to hear it. Owen Lovejoy lives at Princeton, Illinois, and he aids every fugitive that comes to his door and asks it. Thou invisible demon of slavery! Dost thou think to cross my humble threshold, and forbid me to give bread to the hungry and shelter to the homeless? I bid you defiance in the name of God."[1]

1. At the May term, 1842, of the Bureau County Circuit Court, Richard M. Young, presiding ; Norman H. Purple, Prosecuting Attorney *pro tem.;* the grand jury returned a "true bill" against Owen Lovejoy (then lately a preacher of the Gospel), for that "a certain negro girl named Agnes, then and there being a fugitive slave, he, the said Lovejoy, knowing her to be such, did harbor, feed, secrete, and clothe," contrary to the statute, etc., and the grand jurors did further present, "that the said Lovejoy, a certain fugitive slave called Nance, did harbor, feed, and aid," contrary to the statute, etc. At the October term, 1842, the Hon. John Dean Caton, a Justice of the Supreme Court, presiding, the case came up for trial, on the plea of *not guilty.* Judge Purple, and B. F. Fridley, State's Attorney for the people, and James H. Collins, and Lovejoy in person, for the defense. The trial lasted nearly a week, and Lovejoy and Collins fought the case with a vigor and boldness almost without a parallel. The prosecution was urged by the enemies of Lovejoy, with an energy and vindictiveness with which Purple and Fridley could have had little sympathy. When the case was called for trial, a strong pro-slavery man, one of those by whom the indictment had been procured, said to the State's Attorney :

"Fridley, we want you to be sure and convict this preacher, and send him to prison."

On the 6th of August, a bill introduced by Senator Trumbull, giving freedom to all slaves used by the rebels in carrying on the war became a law. It was vehemently opposed by Breckenridge and other democratic members, as an interference with the rights of the slaveholders, but those who voted for the bill, justified their votes on the ground that in the battle of Bull Run and other engagements, the rebels used their negroes and slaves, not only in constructing fortifications, but in battle against the Union forces. Burnett, of Kentucky, declared that the bill would result in a wholesale emancipation of slaves in the states in rebellion, and some one replied: " If it does, so much the better." Thaddeus Stevens then said : " I warn Southern gentlemen, that if this war continues, there will be a time when it will be declared by this free nation, that every bondman in the South, belonging to a rebel (recollect, I confine it to them), shall be called upon to aid us in war against their masters, and to restore the Union."

From the beginning of the contest, the slaves flocked to the Union army, as to a haven of refuge. They believed freedom was to be found within its picket lines and under the shelter of its flag. They were ready to act as guides, to dig, to work, to fight for liberty. The Yankees, as their masters called the Union troops, were believed by them to come as their deliverers from long and cruel bondage. And yet, almost incredible as it may now seem, many officers permitted masters and agents to enter their lines, and carry away by force these fugitive slaves. Many cruelties and outrages were perpetrated by these masters, and in many instances, the colored men who had rendered valuable service to the Union cause, were permitted to be carried from beneath the flag of the Union back to bondage.

Lovejoy was most indignant at this stupid and inhuman

"Prison ! Lovejoy to prison !" replied Fridley," your persecutions will be a damned sight more likely to send him to Congress."

Fridley was right. Lovejoy was acquitted, and very soon after elected to the State Legislature, and then to Congress, where, as all know, he was soon heard by the whole country.

treatment, and early in the special session, introduced a resolution declaring that it was no part of the duty of the soldiers of the United States, to capture and return fugitive
slaves. This passed the House by a very large majority, the
vote being ninety-three to fifty-nine.

While the President, by his moderation, was seeking to
hold the border states, and while his measures were severely
criticized by many extreme abolitionists, he enjoyed, to
the fullest extent, the confidence of Lovejoy and other radical members from Illinois. This old and *ultra* abolitionist
perfectly understood and appreciated the motives of the
Executive. On the death of Lovejoy, in 1864, Lincoln said:
"Throughout my heavy and perplexing responsibilities
here (at Washington), to the day of his death, it would
scarcely wrong any other to say: he was my most generous
friend." [1]

There were, in the border states, many Union men who
desired to maintain the Union, and who wished also, that
there should be no interference with slavery. These, with
the small band of anti-slavery men in Maryland, Kentucky,
and Missouri, had rendered efficient aid in preventing those
states from seceding. Their representative man in Congress was the aged, venerable, and eloquent John J. Crittenden, of Kentucky. He had been the confidential friend and
colleague of Clay, and had never faltered in his loyalty to
the Union. He had been conspicuous in the Thirty-sixth
Congress, in attempting to bring about terms of compromise
to prevent the threatened war.

On the 15th of July, on motion of General John A.
McClernand, the House, by a vote of one hundred and
twenty-one to five, adopted a resolution pledging itself to vote
any amount of money and any number of men which might be
necessary, to ensure a speedy and effectual suppression of
the rebellion.

On the 22d of July, 1861, Mr. Crittenden offered the following resolution, defining the object of the war:

1. Letter from Lincoln to John H. Bryant, dated May 30, 1864.

Resolved, That the present deplorable civil war has been forced upon the country by the disunionists of the Southern states, now in revolt against the constitutional government, and in arms around the capital; that, in this national emergency, Congress, banishing all feeling of mere passion or resentment, will recollect only its duty to the whole country; that this war is not waged, upon our part, in any spirit of oppression, nor for any purpose of conquest, or subjugation, nor purpose of over‐throwing or interfering with the rights or established institutions of those states; but to defend and maintain the supremacy of the Constitution, and to preserve the Union, with all the dignity, equality, and rights of the several states unimpaired; that as soon as these objects are accomplished, the war ought to cease." [1]

This resolution was adopted by the House, there being only two dissenting votes. It served to allay the apprehension of the border states, whose sensitiveness had been excited by the agents and abettors of the rebellion.

Congress, after long debate, sanctioned the acts of the President, and, as has been stated, voted more men and money than he had in his message called for. Among the speeches made at this special session, one of the ablest was that of Senator Baker, whose effective reply to Breckenridge has already been noticed. His speech on the resolutions approving the acts of the President, was distinguished for its eloquence, its boldness, and its almost prophetic sagacity. He said:

" I am one of those who believe that there may be reverses. I am not quite confident that we shall overrun the Southern states, as we shall have to overrun them, without severe trials of our courage and patience. I believe they are a brave, determined people filled with enthusiasm, false in its purpose as I think, but still one which animates almost all classes of their population. But however that may be, it may be that instead of finding within a year loyal states sending members to Congress, and replacing their senators upon this floor, we may have to reduce them to the condition of territories, and send from Massachusetts, or from Illinois, governors to control them." [2]

The military situation was substantially as follows: The Union troops held Fortress Monroe and vicinity, and thus guarded Baltimore and the approaches to Washington; a

1. See Congressional Globe, July 22, 1861, p. 223.

2. Congressional Globe, July 10th, 1861, pp. 44-45.

force under command of George B. McClellan, was driving the rebels out of West Virginia. The Confederates, under Beauregard, confronted the Union army near Washington, holding a position along Bull Run creek, their right at Manassas, and left at Winchester, under Johnston. The people of the North, confident, sanguine, and impatient of delay, through an excited press, urged an immediate attack by the Union troops, and the army, under General McDowell, started on the 16th of July, and on the 21st attacked the enemy. The attack seemed well planned and was at first successful, but re-enforcements under the rebel General Johnston reaching the field at the crisis of the battle, General Patterson, of the Union army, neither holding Johnston in check, nor coming up in time, the Union troops were repulsed, a panic seized them, and they fled towards Washington in great confusion.

The disaster of Bull Run mortified the national pride, but aroused also the national spirit and courage. The morning following the defeat witnessed dispatches flashing over the wires to every part of the North, authorizing the reception of the eager regiments ready to enter the service and retrieve the results of the battle. The administration and the people, immediately upon learning of this defeat, set themselves vigorously to increase and reorganize the army. Grave and thoughtful men left their private pursuits, organized regiments, and offered them to the government. None were now refused. The popular feeling throughout the loyal states again rose to a height even greater than it did at the time of the attack upon Fort Sumter.

Expeditions were organized and sent to the South, and Fort Hatteras was surrendered to the Union troops on the 28th of August. On the 31st of October, Port Royal came into the possession of the Union army. The rebels were driven out of West Virginia, and General George B. McClellan, who had been in command there, and who was believed at the time to possess military ability of a high order, was called to command the armies, again gathering in vast numbers around the capital. In October, General Scott retired on account of age and infirmity, and General McClellan was appointed to the command.

When the war began, John C. Fremont was in Paris. He immediately returned home, was appointed a Major General, and given command of the Western Department, embracing Missouri and a part of Kentucky. On the 30th of August, he issued an order declaring martial law throughout Missouri, confiscating the property of rebels, and saying: " Their slaves, if any they have, are hereby declared free men." [1]

This grave act was done without consulting the President, and severely embarrassed the Executive in the efforts he was making to retain Maryland, Kentucky, and other border states, in the Union. It was received with the greatest alarm and consternation by the Union men of these states.[2] The President, on the 2d of September, wrote to Fremont, saying: " There is great danger. * * The confiscation of property and liberating slaves will alarm our Southern Union friends, and turn them against us, perhaps ruin our fair prospect for Kentucky." [3]

He asked Fremont to modify his order so as to conform to the act of Congress lately passed on that subject. General Fremont replied, excusing and justifying his acts, and requesting the President himself to modify the order, which the President did, issuing an order himself, altering that of Fremont so that it should conform to and not " transcend " the act of Congress.

The reason for this modification, and also for his action with reference to the suggestions of the Secretary of War, Cameron, as to arming the negroes, and with reference to the emancipation order of General David Hunter, appear in a letter dated April 4th, 1864, in which he says:

" When, early in the war, General Fremont attempted military emancipation, I forbade it, because I did not then think it an indispensable

1. McPherson's History of the Rebellion, p. 246.

2. See Protest of Joseph Holt and other Union men of Kentucky.

3. See McPherson's History of the Rebellion, pp. 246–247.

necessity. When, a little later, General Cameron, then Secretary of War, suggested the arming of the blacks, I objected, because I did not yet think it an indispensable necessity. When, still later, General Hunter attempted military emancipation, I again forbade it, because I did not yet think the indispensable necessity had come. When, in March, and May, and July, 1862, I made earnest and successive appeals to the border states, to favor compensated emancipation, I believed the indispensable necessity for military emancipation and arming the blacks would come, unless averted by that measure. They declined the proposition, and I was, in my best judgment, driven to the alternative of either surrendering the Union, and with it, the Constitution, or of laying strong hands upon the colored element. I chose the latter. In choosing it, I hoped for greater gain than loss, but of this I was not entirely confident. More than a year of trial now shows no loss by it in our foreign relations, none in our home popular sentiment, none in our white military force, no loss by it anyhow, or anywhere. On the contrary, it shows a gain of quite a hundred and thirty thousand soldiers, seamen, and laborers. These are palpable facts, about which, as facts, there can be no cavilling. We have the men; and we could not have had them without the measure." [1]

The President for a time adhered firmly, and against the earnest remonstrance of many friends, to what was called the border state policy.

Military preparations on a large scale were going on. McClellan, who had, on the resignation of General Scott, been appointed commander in chief, had organized an immense army, which was encamped around Washington. On the 21st of October occurred the fight at Ball's Bluff, at which Colonel Baker, the senator from Oregon, fell, pierced by a volley of bullets. In September, 1861, information was communicated to the government that the Legislature of Maryland was to meet, with a view of passing an act of secession. General McClellan was directed to prevent this by the arrest of the members. His order to General Banks, dated September 12th, 1861, says, among other things : " When they meet on the 17th, you will please have everything prepared to arrest the whole party, and be sure that none escape." * * "If successfully carried out, it will go far towards breaking the backbone of the

1. McPherson's History of the Rebellion (letter to Col. Hodges), p. 336.

rebellion."   *   *   " I have but one thing to impress upon you, the absolute necessity of secresy and success." [1]

This act has been censured as an arbitrary arrest. However arbitrary, it was a military measure of great importance, and in the propriety of which General McClellan fully coincided. Governor Hicks said in the Senate of the United States : " I believe that arrests, and arrests alone, saved the state of Maryland from destruction. I approved them then, and I approve them now."

On the 8th of November, 1861, Captain Wilkes, in the *San Jacinto*, intercepted the *Trent*, a British mail steamer from Havana, with Messrs. Mason and Slidell, late senators, and then rebel agents, on their way to represent the Confederacy at the courts of St. James and St. Cloud. He took them prisoners, and bringing them to the United States, they were confined at Fort Warren, in Boston harbor. There were few acts in the life of Lincoln more characteristic, indicating a higher and firmer courage and independence, together with the exercise of a cool, dispassionate judgment, than the release of Mason and Slidell. No act of the British Government, since the days of the Revolution, ever excited such an intense feeling of hostility, as her haughty demand for the release of these rebels. The people had already been exasperated by her hasty recognition of the Confederates as belligerents, and the seizure by Captain Wilkes of these emissaries, gratified popular passion and pride. On the first day of the session of Congress, after intelligence of the seizure reached Washington, Lovejoy, by unanimous consent, introduced a resolution of thanks to Captain Wilkes, which, with blind impetuosity, was rushed through under the call of the previous question.

The position of the President was rendered still more embarrassing by the hasty and ill-considered action of members of his Cabinet. The Secretary of the Navy wrote to Wilkes a letter of congratulation on the " great public service" he had rendered in " capturing the rebel emissaries

1. McPherson's History of the Rebellion, p. 153.

Mason and Slidell." [1] Stanton cheered and applauded the act. The Secretary of State was at first opposed to any concession or the surrender of the prisoners. [2] The people were ready to rush " pell mell" into a war with England. The Confederates were rejoicing at the capture, as the means of bringing the English navy and armies to their aid. But Lincoln, cool, sagacious, and far-seeing, uninfluenced by resentment, with courage and a confidence in the deliberate judgment of the country never exceeded, stepped in front of an exasperated people, told them to pause and "to forbear." "We fought Great Britain," said he, "for doing just what Captain Wilkes has done. If Great Britain protests against this act and demands their release, we must adhere to our principles of 1812. We must give up these prisoners. Besides," said he significantly, "one war at a time." It is scarcely too much to say that his firmness and courage saved the republic from a war with England.

Had the President, yielding to popular clamor, accepted the challenge of Great Britain and gone to war, he would have done exactly what the rebels desired, and would have thus made Mason and Slidell incomparably more useful to the Confederates than they were after their surrender, and while hanging around the back doors of the Courts to which they were sent, but at which they were never received. No one can calculate the results which would have followed upon a refusal to surrender these men. The sober second thought of the people recognized the wise statesmanship of the President. The Secretary of State, with his facile pen, made an able argument sustaining the views of the President. No instance in which Lincoln ever

1. Benson J. Lossing, in Lincoln Album, p. 328.

2. See Lincoln and Seward, by Gideon Welles, p. 188.
Secretary Welles distinctly says :
" Mr. Seward was at the beginning opposed to any idea of concession, which involved giving up the emissaries, but yielded at once, and with dexterity, to the peremptory demand of Great Britain."
" The President expressed his doubts of the legality of the capture * * * * and from the first was willing to make the concession."
Lincoln and Seward, by Gideon Welles, pp. 186–188.

acted from private resentment towards any individual, or nation, can be found.   Towards individuals who had injured him, he was ever magnanimous, and often more than just ; and towards nations, no more striking illustration of his dignified disregard of personal insult and injustice could be found than that furnished by his conduct towards England at this time.   He was not insensible of the personal insults and injuries heaped upon him in England, but he was too great to be to any extent influenced by them.   It required nerve and moral courage to stem the tide of popular feeling, but he did not for a moment hesitate.   And when the excitement of the hour had passed, his conduct was universally approved.   Lovejoy's speech in Congress illustrates the hatred and excitement which the conduct of Great Britain produced.[1]

* 1. Congressional Globe, Second Session Thirty-seventh Congress, p. 333. Lovejoy said: "Every time this Trent affair comes up; every time that an allusion is made to it.   *   *   *   *   I am made to renew the horrible grief which I suffered when the news of the surrender of Mason and Slidell came. I acknowledge it, I literally wept tears of vexation. I hate it; and I hate the British government. I have never shared in the traditional hostility of many of my countrymen against England. But I now here publicly avow and record my inextinguishable hatred of that government. I mean to cherish it while I live, and to bequeath it as a legacy to my children when I die. And if I am alive when war with England comes, as sooner or later it must, for we shall never forget this humiliation, and if I can carry a musket in that war, I will carry it. I have three sons, and I mean to charge them, and I do now publicly and solemnly charge them, that if they shall have, at that time, reached the years of manhood and strength, they shall enter into that war."

Senator Hale, of New Hampshire, went so far as to threaten the administration of Mr. Lincoln.

"If," said he, "this administration will not listen to the voice of the people, they will find themselves engulphed in a fire that will consume them like stubble: they will be helpless before a power that will hurl them from their places."

See Congressional Globe, 2d Session 37th Congress, January 7, 1862, p. 177.

CHAPTER XIV.

EFFORTS FOR PEACEFUL EMANCIPATION.

PRESIDENT'S MESSAGE. — CONDITION OF THE COUNTRY. — DEATH OF
BAKER.—EULOGIES UPON HIM.—STANTON, SECRETARY OF WAR.—
ABOLITION OF SLAVERY IN THE DISTRICT OF COLUMBIA.—PROHIBI-
TION IN THE TERRITORIES.—EMPLOYMENT OF NEGROES AS SOL-
DIERS.—EMANCIPATION IN THE BORDER STATES.

WHEN Congress met, December 2, 1861, no decisive military events had occurred, but the great drama of civil war
was at hand. Thus far the work had been one of preparation. Nearly two hundred thousand Union troops, under
General George B. McClellan, on the banks of the Potomac,
confronted a rebel army, then supposed to number about the
same, but now known to have been much smaller. The
President in his message, congratulated Congress that the
patriotism of the people had proved more than equal to the
demands made upon it, and that the number of troops tendered to the government greatly exceeded the force called
for. He had not only been successful in holding Maryland,
Kentucky, and Missouri in the Union, but those three states,
neither of which had in the beginning given, or promised
through state organization, a single soldier, had now forty
thousand men in the field under the Union flag. In West
Virginia, after a severe struggle, the Union had triumphed,
and there was no armed rebel force north of the Potomac
or east of the Chesapeake, while the cause of the Union
was steadily advancing southward.

On the slavery question, he said : "I have adhered to
the act of Congress freeing persons held to service, used for

insurrectionary purposes." In relation to the emancipation, and arming the negroes, he said : "The maintenance of the integrity of the Union is the primary object of the contest."

*   *   *   *   *   *

"The Union must be preserved, and all *indispensable means must be employed.* We should not be in haste to determine that radical and extreme measures, which may reach the loyal, as well as the disloyal, are indispensable."

Before proceeding to view in detail the action, during this session, of Congress and the President on the slavery question, let us pause a moment to notice the honors paid in the Senate to the memory of Senator Baker. It will be remembered that he was killed at Ball's Bluff, on the 21st of October, while leading his troops against the enemy.

When Congress assembled in regular session, the 11th of December was fixed as the day on which the funeral orations in his honor should be pronounced in the Senate. The chamber of the Senate was draped in black; the brilliant colors of the national flag, which the war made all worship, were now mingled with the dark, in honor of the dead soldier and senator. The floor was crowded with senators, members of the House, governors of states, and distinguished civil and military officers, among whom Seward and Chase, and the Blairs and Stanton were conspicuous. The galleries were filled by members of the diplomatic corps, ladies, and prominent citizens from all parts of the republic. As soon as Vice-President Hamlin had called the Senate to order, President Lincoln, in deep mourning, slowly entered from the marble room, supported by the senators from Illinois: Trumbull and Browning. Not very long before he had been present among the chief mourners at the funeral in the White House of his *protégé*, young Ellsworth, shot down in the bloom of youth, and now it was Baker, his old comrade at the bar of Sangamon County; his successor in Congress; he for whom the President's second son, Edward Baker Lincoln, had been named, and to whom he was very warmly attached.

Senator Nesmith, of Oregon, sorrowfully announced the death of Baker, and was followed by McDougall of California, in one of the most touching and beautiful speeches ever heard in the Senate. Turning towards Lincoln, aud alluding to the dead senator's enthusiastic love of poetry, he said: " Many years since, on the wild plains of the West, in the midst of a starlight night, as we journeyed together, I heard from him the chant of that noble song, ' The Battle of Ivry.'

" He loved freedom, if you please, Anglo-Saxon freedom, for he was of that grand old race."

As descriptive of the warlike scenes of every-day occurrence when Baker left the senatorial forum for the field, McDougall repeated in a voice which created a sensation throughout the Senate:

> " Hurrah ! the foes are moving. Hark to the mingled din
> Of fife, and steed, and trump, and drum, and roaring culverin!
> The fiery duke is pricking fast across St. André's plain,
> With all the hireling chivalry of Guelders and Almayne.
> Now by the lips of those ye love, fair gentlemen of France,
> Charge for the golden lilies! upon them with the lance!"

And then comparing Baker at Ball's Bluffs with Henry of Navarre, McDougall quoted the words:

> " And if my standard-bearer fall, as fall full well he may,
> For never saw I promise yet of such a bloody fray—
> Press where ye see my white plume shine, amidst the ranks of war,
> And be your oriflamme to-day the helmet of Navarre!"

It was a most eloquent speech, and as McDougall recalled the old comradeship of Lincoln and Baker, and Browning, and himself in early days as circuit riders in Central Illinois, every heart was touched, and few eyes were dry.

Sumner's speech was among the best he ever made. It was perhaps the only occasion upon which he ever cut loose from his manuscript, and gave free scope to the inspiration of the scene and the moment.

Senator Browning, the successor of Douglas, followed,

and his speech was as good as the best. " Baker," said he,. " to a greater extent than most men, combined the force and severity of logic, with grace, fancy, and eloquence, filling at the bar, at the same time the character of the astute and profound lawyer, and of the able, eloquent, and successful advocate; and in the Senate, the wise, prudent, and discreet statesman was combined with the chaste, classic, brilliant, and persuasive orator. He was not only a lawyer, an orator, a statesman, and a soldier, but he was also a poet, and at times spoke and acted under high poetic inspiration."

The remains of Baker were taken across the continent to California, and he was buried by the side of his friend Broderick,[1] in " The Lone Mountain Cemetery." There on that rocky cliff, by the Bay of San Francisco, looking out upon the Golden Gate and the Pacific, lies the dust of the gallant soldier and eloquent senator. At this session of Congress, three of Lincoln's old associates at the bar in Illinois (if Baker had been alive, there would have been four), occupied seats in the Senate: Trumbull and Browning from Illinois, and McDougall from California.[2]

There was something very beautiful and touching in the attachment and fidelity of these his old Illinois comrades to Lincoln. They had all been pioneers, frontiersmen, circuit-riders together. They were never so happy as when talking over old times, and recalling the rough experiences of their early lives. Had they met at Washington in calm and peaceful weather, on sunny days, they would have kept up their party differences as they did at home, but coming together in the midst of the fierce storms of civil war, and in the hour

1. Late a senator from California, and killed in a duel. Baker had pronounced in San Francisco, a funeral oration over his remains.

2. One evening in the summer of 1863, when the President was living in a cottage at the " Soldier's Home," on the heights north of the capital, some one spoke to him of Baker's burial place in the " *Lone Mountain Cemetery*." The name seemed to kindle his imagination and touch his heart. He spoke of this " Lone Mountain " on the shore of the Pacific, as a place of repose, and seemed almost to envy Baker his place of rest. Lincoln then gave a warm and glowing sketch of Baker's eloquence, full of generous admiration, and showing how he had loved this old friend.

of supreme peril, they stood together like a band of brothers. Not one of them would see an old comrade in difficulty or danger, and not help him out.   The memory of these old Illinois lawyers and statesmen: Baker, McDougall, Trumbull, Lovejoy, Washburne, Browning, and others, recalls a passage in Webster's reply to Hayne.   Speaking of Massachusetts and South Carolina, the great New England orator said: "Shoulder to shoulder they went through the Revolution together; hand in hand they stood around the administration of Washington, and felt his own great arm lean on them for support."

So, in the far more difficult administration of Lincoln, these old and trusty comrades of his, whatever their former differences, stood shoulder to shoulder, and hand in hand, around the administration of Lincoln; his strong arm leaned on them for support, and that support was given vigorously and with unwavering loyalty. [1]

On the 14th of January, 1862, Simon Cameron resigned the position of Secretary of War, accepting the place of Minister to Russia.   Edwin M. Stanton was appointed his successor.   The new secretary soon gave evidence of his great energy, industry, and efficiency as an organizer.   In accomplishing great objects he was not very scrupulous about the means of removing obstacles, and was somewhat

---

1. McDougall, before going to California, had been a prominent lawyer at Jacksonville and Chicago, and Attorney-General of Illinois.   He was the bitter enemy of the Secretary of State, Mr. Seward having caused some of his California friends to be arrested, and confined in Fort LaFayette. I shall state what was universally known and deeply mourned by all of McDougall's friends, when I mention that habits of intemperance overclouded the last years of his life.   But it could not be said of him that " when the wine was *in*, the wit was *out*."   Poor McDougall's wit was always ready, drunk or sober.

Coming down from the Senate chamber, after a late executive session in which he had been opposing one of Seward's nominations, he found the rain falling in torrents, the night dark and dismal, and his own steps unsteady.   As he passed from the Capitol gate towards Pennsylvania Avenue, the senator had to cross a ditch full of filth and water.   McDougall, in the darkness, made a misstep, and tumbled in.   A policeman ran to his aid, and helping him out, enquired gruffly :   " Who are you, anyhow ? "   " I, I was," said poor Mac, " I, I was Senator McDougall, when I fell in, now I think," looking at his filthy garments with disgust, "now, I think I, I am *Seward*."

16

careless of the forms and restraints of law. Honest and true, and intensely in earnest if he believed a thing was right, he was not likely to be thwarted by any formal obstacles which might stand in the way. He was irritable, but placable in temper; sometimes doing acts of injustice, which the more patient and considerate President was obliged to correct, but he himself was ready to repair a wrong when satisfied that one had been committed.

At this session, Congress entered upon that series of anti-slavery measures which were to end in the emancipation proclamation, and the amendment of the Constitution prohibiting slavery throughout the republic. The forbearance towards slavery and slaveholders, so conspicuous at the beginning of the war, disappeared rapidly before the fierce necessities of the conflict.

The House had scarcely completed its organization, when Lovejoy, indignant that loyal negroes should still be sent back to slavery from the camps of the Union army, on the 4th of December introduced a bill making it a penal offence for any officer to return a fugitive slave. Senator Wilson gave early notice of a bill in the Senate for the same purpose. The various propositions on the subject finally resulted in the enactment of an additional article of war, forbidding, on pain of dismissal from the service, the arrest of any fugitive, by any officer or person in the military or naval service of the United States.

The location of the capital on slave territory had proved one of the most important triumphs ever achieved by the slaveholders. The powerful influence of society, local public sentiment, fashion, and the local press, in favor of the institution, was ever felt; and its power, from 1800 to 1860, could scarcely be overestimated. Our country had long been reproached and stigmatized by the world, and the character of a pro-slavery despotism over the colored race fixed upon it, by reason of the existence of slavery at the national capital. The friends of liberty had for years chafed and struggled in vain against this malign influence.

Congress had supreme power to legislate for the District of Columbia, and was exclusively responsible for the continued existence of slavery there. Mr. Lincoln, it will be remembered, when serving his single term in Congress, had, in December, 1849, introduced a bill for its· gradual abolition. The President and his friends thought it quite time this relic of barbarism at the national capital should be destroyed.

Senator Wilson, of Massachusetts, the confidential friend of the President, on the 15th of December introduced a bill for the immediate emancipation of slaves in the District of Columbia, and the payment to their loyal masters of an average sum of three hundred dollars for each slave thus set free; providing for the appointment of commissioners to assess the sums to be paid each claimant, and appropriating one million of dollars for the purpose. The debates upon this bill involved the whole subject of slavery, the rebellion, the past, present, and future of the country. The bill passed the Senate by yeas twenty nine, nays six.

When the bill came up for action in the House, containing as it did an appropriation of money, under the rules, it was necessarily referred to the committee of the whole House. As there was a large number of bills in advance of it on the calendar, its enemies, although in a minority, had hopes of delaying action or defeating it. The struggle to take up the bill came on the 10th of April, under the lead of that accomplished, adroit, and bold parliamentarian, Thaddeus Stevens. He moved that the House go into committee, which motion was agreed to, Mr. Dawes of Massachusetts in the chair. The chairman called the calendar in its order, and on motion of Mr. Stevens every bill was laid aside until the bill for the abolition of slavery in the District was reached. An unsuccessful effort to lay the bill on the table was made by a member from Maryland.

F. P. Blair, Jr., in an able speech, advocated colonization in connection with abolition. He said: " It is in the gorgeous region of the American tropics, that our freedmen will find their homes ; among a people without prejudice against their color, and to whom they will carry and impart new energy and vigor, in return for the welcome which will greet them, as the pledge of the future protection and friendship of our great republic; I look with confidence to this movement, as the true and only solution of this question of slavery."[1] Mr. Bingham closed an eloquent speech by saying: "One year ago (11th April, 1861) slavery opened its batteries of treason upon Fort Sumter at Charleston; let the anniversary of the crime be signalized by the banishment of slavery from the national capital."

The bill passed the House by ninety-two ayes to thirty-eight noes, and, on the 16th of April, was approved by the President. Lincoln said: "Little did I dream in 1849, when I proposed to abolish slavery at this capital, and could scarcely get a hearing for the proposition, that it would be so soon accomplished." Still less did he anticipate that he as President would be called upon to approve the measure.

The territories had long been the battle-fields on which free labor and slavery had struggled for supremacy. The early policy of the government, that of the fathers, was prohibition. The proposition of Jefferson, that slavery should never exist in any territory in the United States, failed only by one vote, caused by the absence of a delegate from New Jersey. The Ordinance of 1787 inaugurated the policy. Slavery was strong enough in 1820 to secure a division by the line of 36° 30' of latitude, in what was called the Missouri Compromise. In 1854, that compromise was repealed, with the avowed purpose on the part of the slaveholders of carrying slavery into all the territories. Then came the Dred Scott decision, that Congress could not prohibit slavery in the territories, and then followed the hand-to-hand struggle in Kansas. The distinct issue of the exclusion of slavery by Congressional enactment was, in 1860, submitted to the people, and Mr. Lincoln was elected upon the distinct and unequivocal pledge of prohibition.

On the 24th of March, 1862, Mr. Arnold, of Illinois,

---

1. Congressional Globe, 2d Session 37th Congress, pp. 1634–1635.

introduced "a bill to render freedom national, and slavery sectional," and which, after reciting: "To the end that freedom may be and remain forever the fundamental law of the land in all places whatsoever, so far as it lies in the power, or depends upon the action of the government of the United States to make it so," enacted that slavery, except as a punishment for crime, whereof the party had been duly convicted, should henceforth cease and be prohibited forever, in all the following places, viz.: First, in all the territories of the United States then existing, or thereafter to be formed or acquired in any way. Second, In all places purchased or acquired with the consent of the United States for forts, magazines, dock-yards, and other needful buildings, and over which the United States have or shall have exclusive legislative jurisdiction. Third, In all vessels on the high seas. Fourth, In all places whatsoever where the national government has exclusive jurisdiction." [1]

Mr. Cox opposed the bill vehemently, declaring that, in his judgment, it was a bill for the benefit of secession. Mr. Fisher, in an able speech, also opposed the passage of the bill. In conclusion, he appealed to the majority to "let this cup pass from our lips." He said: "We have done nobly; we have done much in behalf of liberty and humanity at this session of Congress. Let us then here call a halt and take our bearings." Finally, as a concession to the more conservative members, Mr. Lovejoy offered an amendment striking out all except the prohibition of slavery in the territories, which amendment Mr. Arnold accepted, and on which he demanded the previous question.

The bill passed the House, ayes, eighty-five, noes, fifty, was slightly modified in the Senate, and finally passed the House on the 19th of June, prohibiting slavery forever in all the territories of the United States then existing, or that might thereafter be acquired. Thus, the second great step towards the destruction of slavery was taken ; and thus was terminated the great struggle over its existence in the terri-

1. Congressional Globe, 2d Session 37th Congress, p. 2042.

tories, which had agitated the country, with short intervals, from the organization of the republic. Had this act been passed in 1784, when Jefferson substantially proposed it, the terrible war of the slaveholders might not have come. The institution would never have grown to such vast power. Missouri would have had the wealth of Ohio, and slavery, driven by moral and economical influences towards the Gulf, would have gradually and peacefully disappeared.[1]

Slavery having been abolished at the capital, and prohibited in all the territories, the question of arming the freedmen, and of freeing the slaves and organizing and arming them as soldiers that they might fight for their liberty and that of their race, pressed more and more upon the government.

The first regiment of negro troops raised during the war was organized by General David Hunter, in the spring of 1862, while in command of the Department of the South. Finding himself charged with the duty of holding the coasts of Florida, South Carolina, and Georgia, with inadequate force, and these three states swarming with able bodied negroes, ready to fight for their liberty, he saw no reason why they should not be organized and used as soldiers.

On the 9th of July, 1862, Senator Grimes, of Iowa, proposed that "there should be no exemption from military service on account of color," and authorized the President to organize negro soldiers. The proposition was vehemently opposed by the border states, and by some of the democratic members of Congress. Senator Garret Davis, of Kentucky, said : " You propose to place arms in the hands of the slaves, or such. of them as are able to handle arms, and manumit the whole mass, men, women, and children, and leave them among us. Do you expect us to give our sanction and approval to these things ? No ! No ! We would regard their authors as our worst enemies, and there

1. The New York Tribune of June 20, 1862, speaking of the law, said : " It is not often that so much of that 'righteousness that exalteth a nation,' is embodied in a legislative act. Had this act been passed in 1784, when Jefferson proposed something similar, the war in which we are now engaged would never have existed."

is no foreign despotism, that could come to our rescue, that we would not joyfully embrace before we would submit.[1]

The proposition authorizing the employment of negroes as soldiers, and conferring freedom on all who should render military service, and on the families of all such as belonged to rebel owners, became a law on the 17th of July, 1862. On this subject Lincoln said : " Negroes, like other people, act from motives. Why should they do anything for us, if we do nothing for them ?   If they stake their lives for us, they must be prompted by the strongest of motives, even the promise of freedom. And the promise being made must be kept."

The opposition to the employment of the negroes as soldiers, seems now almost inexplicable. That the master's claim to the negro should be set up in the way of the government's superior claim to the service of the negro as a soldier, seems to us very strange. The government could, forsooth, take the son from his father for a soldier, but not the slave from the master ! If the slave be considered as property, the plea of the master is equally absurd. It is conceded by all that the government, in case of necessity, could take the horses and animals of loyal or disloyal, and press them into service. And if animals, why not persons held as property? If the negroes were property, they could be taken as such for public use, and if considered as persons, they were like others subject to call for military service.

In discussing the many and grave questions growing out of the war, confiscation, and emancipation, wide differences appeared among the friends of the administration. The discussions of these questions in Congress, were earnest, and often intemperate and violent, and the opinions and conduct of the President were often criticised by his own political friends, with a degree of passion rarely paralleled by the attacks of even political opponents upon the Executive. The President bore these unjust and often unfair attacks with patience, and without resentment. Senator Trumbull,

1. Congressional Globe, 2d Session 37th Congress, 4th Part, p. 3205, July 9, 1862.

from Illinois, on the 27th of June, 1862, made some remarks in relation to him, so just and so appropriate that they will help us to understand his character. He said :

"I know enough of honest Abraham Lincoln to know that he will not regard as his truest friends men who play the courtier, and swear that everything he does is right. He, sir, is honest enough, and great enough, and talented enough, to know that he is not perfect, and to thank his friends who rally around him in this hour of trial, and honestly suggest to him, when they believe such to be the fact, that some measures that he has adopted may not be the wisest. He will think better of a man who has the candor and the honesty to do it, than he will of the sycophant who tells him 'all is right that you do, and you cannot do wrong.' Sir, he is no believer in 'the divine right of kings,' or that a chief magistrate can never do wrong. He is a believer in the intelligence of the people, and knowing his own fallibility, is not above listening to their voice." [1]

There was a very large and earnest party among the President's friends, who urged immediate and universal emancipation. Regarding slavery as the cause of the war, and believing that freedom would bring the negroes to the Union cause, they were impatient of any delay, or consideration of the rights of the owners, even when the owners were loyal. Up to this period, as has been observed, Lincoln had carefully considered the rights, under the Constitution, of the loyal slaveholders of the border states. Naturally conservative, he hesitated before adopting the extreme measure of emancipation. But the question was every day becoming more and more pressing.

On the 6th of March, 1862, in a special message to Congress, he said : "In my judgment, gradual, and not sudden, emancipation, is better for all." [2] In this message he suggested the adoption of a joint resolution, declaring "that the United States ought to coöperate with any state which may adopt a gradual abolition of slavery, giving to such state pecuniary aid to compensate for the inconvenience, public and private, produced by such change of system." [3]

1. Congressional Globe, 2d Session 37th Congress, part 4th., p. 2973.

2. President's Message. McPherson's History of the Rebellion, p. 209.

3. Congressional Globe, 2d Session 37th Congress, part 2d, p. 1102.

He strongly urged this policy as a means of shortening the war, with all its expenses and evils. He concluded his message by saying :   " In full view of my great responsibility to my God, and to my country, I earnestly beg the attention of Congress and the people to the subject." [1]

On the 10th of March, Roscoe Conkling, of New York, moved the adoption by the House, of the resolution which the President had sent to the House with his message.[2] Thaddeus Stevens said :   " I think it (the President's proposition) about the most diluted milk and water gruel proposition that was ever given to the American people." [3]   Mr. Olin, of New York, on the contrary, said :   " It is the magnanimous, the great, the god-like policy of the administration." [4]   It was vehemently opposed by the members from the border states, the very states it was intended especially to aid. Hickman, of Pennsylvania, said : " I regard this message as an awful note of warning to those residing in the border states, and as an act of justice and magnanimity to them, which I am sorry to see some of their representatives on this floor fail to appreciate." [5]   The resolution was adopted.

On the 10th of March, 1862, there was a conference between the President and the representatives of the border states, at which the subject was discussed, and the President earnestly urged his plan upon their consideration, but no action followed.   On the 12th of July, the President invited the members of Congress from the border states to meet him at the Executive Mansion, and submitted to them an appeal in writing, in which he said :

" Believing that you, in the border states, hold more power for good than any other equal number of members, I feel it a duty which I cannot justifiably waive, to make this appeal to you." * * *

1. Congressional Globe, 2d Session 37th Congress, part 2d, p. 1103.
2. Congressional Globe, 2d Session 37th Congress, part 2d, p. 1154.
3. Congressional Globe, 2d Session 37th Congress, part 2d, p. 1154.
4. Congressional Globe, 2d Session 37th Congress, part 2d, p. 1170.
5. Congressional Globe, 2d Session 37th Congress, part 2d, p. 1176.

" I intend no reproach or complaint when I assure you that in my opinion, if you all had voted for the resolution in the gradual emancipation message of last March, the war would now be substantially ended. And the plan therein proposed is yet one of the most potent and swift means of ending it. Let the states which are in rebellion see definitely and certainly that in no event will the states you represent ever join their proposed confederacy, and they cannot much longer maintain the contest." * * *

" If the war continues long, as it must, if the object be not sooner attained, the institution in your states will be extinguished by mere friction and abrasion, by the mere incidents of the war. It will be gone, and you will have nothing valuable in lieu of it. Much of its value is gone already. How much better for you and for your people to take the step which at once shortens the war and secures substantial compensation for that which is sure to be wholly lost in any other event ! How much better to thus save the money which else we sink forever in the war ! How much better to do it while we can, lest the war ere long render us pecuniarily unable to do it ! How much better for you as seller, and the nation as buyer, to sell out and buy out that without which the war could never have been, than to sink both the thing to be sold and the price of it in cutting one another's throats !"

" I do not speak of emancipation *at once*, but of a *decision* to emancipate *gradually*." * * *

" Upon these considerations I have again begged your attention to the message of March last. Before leaving the Capitol, consider and discuss it among yourselves. You are patriots and statesmen, and as such I pray you consider this proposition, and at the least commend it to the consideration of your states and people. As you would perpetuate popular government for the best people in the world, I beseech you that you do in nowise omit this. Our common country is in great peril, demanding the loftiest views and boldest action to bring a speedy relief. Once relieved, its form of government is saved to the world, its beloved history and cherished memories are vindicated, and its happy future fully assured and rendered inconceivably grand. To you, more than to any others, the privilege is given to assure that happiness and swell that grandeur, and to link your own names therewith forever." [1]

In his proclamation of the 19th of May, 1862, relating to the proclamation of General Hunter, declaring the slaves in the states of Georgia, Florida, and South Carolina free, the President alludes to his proposition to aid the states which should inaugurate emancipation, and says:

1. McPherson's History of the Rebellion, pp. 213, 214.

" To the people of those states I now earnestly appeal.   I do not argue—I beseech you to make the argument for yourselves—you cannot if you would, be blind to the signs of the times.   I beg of you a calm and enlarged consideration of them, ranging, if it may be, far above personal and partisan politics.   This proposal makes common cause for a common object, casting no reproach upon any.   It acts not the Pharisee.   The change it contemplates would come gently as the dews of heaven, not rending or wrecking anything.   Will you not embrace it ? So much good has not been done by one effort, in all past time, as, in the providence of God, it is now your high privilege to do.   May the vast future not have to lament that you have neglected it." [1]

It will be remembered that the interview between the President and the members of Congress from the border states, took place on Saturday, the 12th of July.   On Sunday, July 13th, two members of Congress from Illinois called upon him at his summer residence at the " Soldier's Home."   He conversed freely of his late interview with the border state members, and expressed the deep anxiety he felt that his proposition should be acted upon and accepted by these states.   Rarely, if ever, was he known to manifest such great solicitude.   In conclusion, addressing Lovejoy, one of his visitors, he said :   " Oh, how I wish the border states would accept my proposition.   Then," said he, " you, Lovejoy, and you, Arnold, and all of us, would not have lived in vain !   The labor of your life, Lovejoy, would be crowned with success.   You would live to see the end of slavery."

In his second annual message, the President again urged the proposition of gradual and compensated emancipation, with an earnestness which can scarcely be over-stated.   He presented a most able and impressive argument to show that the plan proposed would shorten the war and lessen the expenditure of money and of blood.   He concluded a most eloquent appeal to Congress in these words :

" The dogmas of the quiet past are inadequate to the stormy present.   The occasion is piled high with difficulty, and we must rise with

1. McPherson's History of the Rebellion, p. 251.

the occasion. As our case is new, so we must think anew, and act anew. We must disenthrall ourselves, and then we shall save our country."

"Fellow citizens, we cannot escape history. We, of this Congress and this administration, will be remembered in spite of ourselves. No personal significance or insignificance can spare one or another of us. The fiery trial through which we pass will light us down, in honor or dishonor, to the latest generation. We *say* we are for the Union. The world will not forget that we say this. We know how to save the Union. The world knows we do know how to save it. We—even we *here*,—hold the power, and bear the responsibility. In *giving* freedom to the *slave* we *assure* freedom to the *free*—honorable alike in what we give and what we preserve. We shall nobly save, or meanly lose, the last, best hope of earth. Other means may succeed; this could not fail. The way is plain, peaceful, generous, just—a way which, if followed, the world will forever applaud, and God must forever bless."

The plan so earnestly and repeatedly pressed by the President resulted in no action. He realized that the time was rapidly approaching, when it would become his duty as Commander in Chief to issue a military proclamation of immediate and unconditional emancipation.

CHAPTER XV.

THE EMANCIPATION PROCLAMATION.

LINCOLN AND EMANCIPATION.— GREELEY DEMANDS IT.— THE PEO-
PLE PRAY FOR IT.— MCCLELLAN'S WARNING.— CRITTENDEN'S
APPEAL.— LOVEJOY'S RESPONSE.— THE PROCLAMATION ISSUED.—
ITS RECEPTION.— THE QUESTION OF ITS VALIDITY.

THE bestowal of freedom upon the negro race, by military edict, had long been considered, and was now to be
decided upon by the President.   The dream of his youth,
the aspiration of his life, was to be the liberator of the negro
race. [1]   But in his wish to promote alike the happiness of
white and black, he hesitated before the stupendous decree
of immediate emancipation.   He wished the change to be
gradual, as he said in his appeal to the border states, "he
wished it to come gently as the dews of heaven, not rending or wrecking anything."

The people were watching his action with the most
intense solicitude.   Every means was used to influence him,
alike by those who favored, and those who opposed, emancipation.   Thousands of earnest men believed that the fate,
not only of slavery, but of the republic, depended upon his
decision.   The anxiety of many found expression in daily
prayers, sent up from church, farm-house, and cabin, that
God would guide the President to a right conclusion.   The
friends of freedom across the Atlantic sent messages urging the destruction of slavery.   Many of the President's

---

1. See his Lyceum speech of January 27th, 1837, in which he said : "Towering
genius disdains a beaten path.   *   *   *   It thirsts and burns for distinction, and will seek it by *emancipating slaves*, or in regions hitherto unexplored," etc.

friends believed that there could be no permanent peace while slavery existed. " Seize," cried they, " seize the opportunity, and hurl the thunderbolt of emancipation, and shatter slavery to atoms, and then the republic will live. Make the issue distinctly between liberty and slavery, and no foreign nation will dare to intervene in behalf of slavery."

It was thus that the friends of liberty impeached slavery before the President, and demanded that he should pass sentence of death upon it. They declared it the implacable enemy of the republic. "A rebel and a traitor from the beginning, it should be declared an outlaw." " The institution now," said they, " reels and totters to its fall. It has by its own crime placed itself in your power as Commander in Chief. You cannot, if you would, and you ought not, if you could, make with it any terms of compromise. You have abolished it at the national capital, prohibited it in all the territories. You have cut off and made free West Virginia. You have enlisted, and are enlisting, negro soldiers, who have bravely shed their blood for the Union on many a hard fought battle-field. You have pledged your own honor and the national faith, that they and their families shall be forever free. That pledge you will sacredly keep. Here then you stand on the threshold of universal emancipation. You will not go back, do not halt, nor hesitate, but strike, and slavery dies."

On the 19th of August, Horace Greeley published, under his own name, in the New York Tribune, a letter addressed to the President, urging emancipation. With characteristic exaggeration, he headed his long letter of complaint: " The Prayer of Twenty Millions of People !" It was full of errors and mistaken inferences, and written in ignorance of many facts which it was the duty of the President to consider.

On the 22d of August, the President replied. He made no response to its " erroneous statements of facts," its " false inferences," nor to its " impatient and dictatorial tone," but in a calm, dignified, and kindly spirit, as to " an

old friend, whose heart he had always supposed to be right,"
he availed himself of the opportunity to set himself right
before the people.

The letter was as follows

EXECUTIVE MANSION,
Washington, *Friday, Aug.* 22, 1862.

Hon. Horace Greeley :

DEAR SIR : I have just read yours of the 19th instant, addressed to
myself, through the New York Tribune.

If there be in it any statements or assumptions of fact, which I may
know to be erroneous, I do not now and here controvert them.

If there be any inferences which I believe to be falsely drawn, I do
not now and here argue against them.

If there be perceptible in it, an impatient and dictatorial tone, I
waive it in deference to an old friend, whose heart I have always supposed to be right.

As to the policy "I seem to be pursuing," as you say, I have not
meant to leave any one in doubt. I would save the Union. I would save
it in the shortest way under the Constitution.

The sooner the national authority can be restored, the nearer the
Union will be—the Union as it was.

If there be those who would not save the Union, unless they could
at the same time save slavery, I do not agree with them.

If there be those who would not save the Union, unless they could
at the same time destroy slavery, I do not agree with them.

*My paramount object is to save the Union, and not either to save or
destroy slavery.*

If I could save the Union without freeing any slave, I would do it.
And if I could save it by freeing all the slaves, I would do it. And
if I could save it by freeing some, and leaving others alone, I would
also do that.

What I do about slavery, and the colored race, I do because I believe
it helps to save the Union, and what I forbear, I forbear because I do
not believe it would help to save the Union.

I shall do less whenever I believe what I am doing hurts the cause,
and shall do more, whenever I believe doing more will help the cause.

I shall try to correct errors, when shown to be errors, and I shall
adopt new views, so fast as they shall appear to be true views.

I have here stated my purpose, according to my view of official duty,
and I intend no modification of my oft-expressed personal wish, that all
men everywhere could be free.   Yours,

A. LINCOLN.

To this letter Mr. Greeley, on the 24th of July, replied

through the Tribune, and his tone and spirit may be inferred from a single paragraph: "Do you," said the editor of the paper to the President of the United States, "Do you propose to do this (save the Union) by recognizing, obeying, and enforcing the laws, or by ignoring, disregarding, and, in fact, defying them?" Such was the insolent language of this "old friend."

On the other hand, the Union men of the border states were urging the President not to interfere with slavery, and from the headquarters of the army on the Potomac, General McClellan wrote to him, under date of July 7th, warning him by saying that a "declaration of radical views, especially upon slavery, will rapidly disintegrate our present armies." To be thus menaced by the general commanding, and notified that the measure he had under consideration would "rapidly destroy the armies in the field," was a very grave matter.

There were at this time in Congress two distinguished men, who well represented the two contending parties into which the friends of the Union were divided—John J. Crittenden, of Kentucky, and Owen Lovejoy, of Illinois. Both were sincere and devoted personal friends of the President. Each enjoyed his confidence, each was honest in his convictions, and each, it is believed, would have cheerfully given his life to save the republic. Lovejoy, the ultra-abolitionist, was one of Lincoln's confidential advisers. Crittenden had been in his earlier days—in those days when the President was a Henry Clay whig—his ideal of a statesman. Lincoln and Crittenden were both natives of Kentucky, old party associates, and life long personal friends. Crittenden —a man whom every one loved—now old, his locks whitened by more than seventy years, yet still retaining all his physical and mental vigor, had been a distinguished Senator, Governor of his state, and Attorney General of the United States. Now, in his extreme old age, he had accepted a seat in Congress that he might aid in preserving the Union. His tall and venerable form, his white head, which a member[1] said " was like a Pharos on the sea to guide our storm-tossed and storm-tattered vessel to its haven," made him a conspicuous figure on the floor of the House.   He was a courtly, fascinating, genial gentleman of the old school. He would often relieve the tedium of routine business by stories and anecdotes of western life, and characteristic incidents of Clay, Webster, Calhoun, Benton, and Jackson, with whom he had served many years in public life.   Of Lovejoy and his relations to the President we have already spoken.

When the question of emancipation became the engrossing topic, the border state members of Congress, with wise sagacity, selected Mr. Crittenden to make on the floor of the House a public appeal to the President that he withhold the proclamation, which they believed would lead to disaster and ruin.   None who witnessed can ever forget the eloquent and touching appeal which this venerable statesman and great orator made.   He said:

" I voted against Mr. Lincoln, and opposed him honestly and sincerely; but Mr. Lincoln has won me to his side.   There is a niche in the temple of fame, a niche near to Washington, which should be occupied by the statue of him who shall save his country.   Mr. Lincoln has a mighty destiny.   It is for him, if he will, to step into that niche.   It is for him to be but a President of the people of the United States, and there will his statue be.   But if he chooses to be in these times, a mere sectarian and a party man, that niche will be reserved for some future and better patriot.   It is in his power to occupy a place next to Washington—the *founder* and the *preserver*, side by side.   Sir, Mr. Lincoln is no coward.   His not doing what the Constitution forbade him to do, and what all our institutions forbade him to do, is no proof of cowardice."[2]

Lovejoy made an impassioned impromptu reply to Crittenden.   He said: " There can be no union until slavery is destroyed.   *   *   We may bind with iron bands, but there will be no permanent, substantial Union, and this nation will not be homogeneous, and be one in truth as well as in form, until slavery is destroyed."

1. Cox, of Ohio.

2. Congressional Globe, 2d Session 37th Congress, Part 2, p. 1805.

17

" The gentleman from Kentucky says he has a niche for Abraham Lincoln. Where is it ?" and Lovejoy turned to Crittenden, who raised his hand and pointed upwards, whereupon Lovejoy resuming said:

" He points towards Heaven. But, sir, should the President follow the counsels of that gentleman, and become the defender and perpetuator of human slavery, he should point downward to some dungeon in the temple of Moloch, who feeds on human blood, and is surrounded with fires, where are forged manacles and chains for human limbs; in the crypts and recesses of whose temple woman is scourged, and man tortured, and outside the walls are lying dogs gorged with human flesh, as Byron describes them, stretched around Stamboul. That is a suitable place for the statue of one who would defend and perpetuate human slavery.[1]   *   *   *

" I, too, have a niche for Abraham Lincoln, but it is in freedom's holy fane, and not in the blood-besmeared temple of human bondage; not surrounded by slaves, fetters, and chains, but with the symbols of freedom; not dark with bondage, but radiant with the light of liberty. In that niche he shall stand proudly, nobly, gloriously, with shattered fetters, and broken chains, and slave whips at his feet. If Abraham Lincoln pursues the path evidently pointed out for him in the providence of God, as I believe he will, then he will occupy the proud position I have indicated. That is a fame worth living for; ay, more, that is a fame worth dying for, though that death led through the blood of Gethsemane, and the agony of the accursed tree. That is a fame which has glory, and honor, and immortality, and eternal life. Let Abraham Lincoln make himself, as I trust he will, the emancipator, the liberator, as he has the opportunity of doing, and his name shall not only be enrolled in this earthly temple, but it will be traced on the living stones of the temple which rears itself amidst the thrones and hierarchies of heaven, whose top-stone is to be brought in with shouting of ' Grace, grace unto it.' "[2]

Such were the appeals addressed to the President. One party promised him a niche beside Washington, if he would not issue the proclamation, and the other that " his name should be enrolled in heaven," among the benefactors of the world, if he would issue it.

To his personal friends of the Illinois delegation in Congress, who conferred with him on the subject, he said that

1. Congressional Globe, 2d Session 37th Congress, Part 2, p. 1818.

2. Congressional Globe, 2d Session 37th Congress, Part 2, p. 1818.

in his letter to Greeley, he meant that he would proclaim freedom to the slaves, just as soon as he felt assured he could do it effectively and that the people would sustain him, and when he felt sure that he would strengthen the Union cause thereby.

On the 13th of September, a delegation of the clergy of nearly all the religious organizations of Chicago waited upon him at the Executive Mansion, and presented a memorial urging immediate and universal emancipation. For the purpose of drawing out their views, in accordance with his old practice as a lawyer, he started various objections to the policy they urged, he himself stating the arguments against emancipation by proclamation, a rough draft of which he had already made. This he did to see what answer they would make to these objections. After a free and full discussion, he said:

" I am approached with the most opposite opinions and advice, and by religious men who are certain they represent the Divine Will. * * * I hope it will not be irreverent in me to say, that if it be probable that God would reveal his will to others, on a point so connected with my duty, it might be supposed he would reveal it directly to me. * * * If I can learn His will, I will do it. These, however, are not the days of miracles, and I suppose I am not to expect a direct revelation. I must study the plain physical facts of the case, and learn what appears to be wise and right. * * * Do not misunderstand me, because I have mentioned these objections. They indicate the difficulties which have thus far prevented my action in some such way as you desire. I have not decided against a proclamation of emancipation, but hold the matter in advisement. The subject is in my mind by day and by night. Whatever shall appear to be God's will I will do." [1]

What were the feelings of the negroes during these days of suspense ? They knew, many of them, and this knowledge was most widely and mysteriously spread about, that their case was being tried in the mind of the President. Long had they prayed and hoped for freedom. The north star had often guided the panting fugitive to liberty. They saw armies come forth from the North and fight their masters.

1. McPherson's History of the Rebellion, p. 231.

The starry flag they now hoped was to be the emblem of their freedom as well as that of the white man. They had welcomed the Union soldiers with joy, and given them food, and guidance, and aid, to the extent of their limited and humble means. The hundreds of thousands of these slaves, from the Shenandoah and the Arkansas, to the rice swamps of the Carolinas and the cane brakes of Louisiana, believed their day of deliverance was at hand. In the corn and sugar fields, in their cabins, and the fastnesses of swamps and forests, the negro prayed that " Massa Linkum and liberty " would come. Their hopes and prayers were happily expressed by the poet Whittier :

" We pray de Lord ; he gib us signs
   Dat some day we be free ;
 De Norf wind tell it to de pines,
   De wild duck to de sea.

" We tink it when de church bell ring,
   We dream it in de dream ;
 De rice bird mean it when he sing,
   De eagle when he scream.

" De yam will grow, de cotton blow,
   We'll hab de rice and corn ;
 Oh nebber you fear if nebber you hear
 De driver blow his horn !
     *   *   *
" Sing on, poor heart ! your chant shall be
   Our sign of blight or bloom—
 The vala-song of liberty,
   Or death-rune of our doom."

With these considerations and under these influences, as early as July, the President, without consulting the Cabinet, made a draft of the proclamation. In August, he called a special meeting of his Cabinet, and said to them that he had resolved to issue the proclamation, that he had called them together, not to ask their advice, but to lay the matter before them, and he would be glad of any suggestions after they had heard the paper read. After it had been read, there was some discussion. Mr. Blair deprecated the policy, fearing it would cause the loss of the approaching fall elections.   But this had been considered by the President, and it did not at all shake his purpose.   Mr. Seward then said: " Mr. President, I approve of the proclamation, but I question the expediency of its issue at this juncture.   The depression of the public mind consequent upon our repeated reverses is so great, that I fear the effect of so important a step.   It may be viewed as the last measure of an exhausted government—a cry for help ; the government stretching forth its hands to Ethiopia, instead of Ethiopia stretching forth her hands to the government.   Now, while I approve the measure, I suggest, sir, that you postpone its issue until you can give it to the country supported by military success, instead of issuing it, as would be the case now, upon the great disasters of war."   Mr. Lincoln was impressed by these considerations, and resolved to delay the issuing of the proclamation for the time.   These events had been occurring in the darkest days of the summer of 1862, made gloomy by the disastrous campaigns of McClellan and Pope.

Meanwhile General Lee was marching northwards towards Pennsylvania, and now the President, with that tinge of superstition which ran through his character, " made," as he said, " a solemn vow to God that if Lee was driven back he would issue the proclamation." [1]   Then came

1. The following interesting account of the proclamation is from Carpenter's " Six Months in the White House."   "It had got to be," said he, " midsummer, 1862. Things had gone on from bad to worse, until I felt that we had reached the end of our rope on the plan of operations we had been pursuing ; that we had about played our last card, and must change our tactics, or lose the game!   I now determined upon the adoption of the emancipation policy; and, without consultation with, or the knowledge of the Cabinet, I prepared the original draft of the proclamation, and, after much anxious thought, called a Cabinet meeting upon the subject.   This was the last of July, or the first part of the month of August, 1862."   (The exact date he did not remember.)   " This Cabinet meeting took place, I think, upon a Saturday.   All were present, excepting Mr. Blair, the Postmaster-General, who was absent at the opening of the discussion, but came in subsequently.   I said to the Cabinet that I had resolved upon this step, and had not called them together to ask their advice, but to lay the subject-matter of a proclamation before them; suggestions as to which would be in order, after they had heard it read.   Mr. Lovejoy," said he, " was in error when he informed you that it excited no comment, excepting on the part of Secretary Seward.   Various suggestions were offered.   Secretary Chase wished the language stronger in reference to the arming of the blacks.   Mr. Blair, after he came in, dep-

news of the battle of Antietam, fought on the 17th of September. "I was," said Lincoln, "when news of the battle came, staying at the Soldiers' Home. Here I finished writing the second draft. I came to Washington on Saturday, called the Cabinet together to hear it, and it was published on the following Monday, the 22d of September, 1862." [1]   It

recated the policy, on the ground that it would cost the administration the fall elections. Nothing, however, was offered that I had not already fully anticipated and settled in my own mind, until Secretary Seward spoke. He said in substance: 'Mr. President, I approve of the proclamation, but I question the expediency of its issue at this juncture. The depression of the public mind, consequent upon our repeated reverses, is so great that I fear the effect of so important a step. It may be viewed as the last measure of an exhausted government, a cry for help; the government stretching forth its hands to Ethiopia, instead of Ethiopia stretching forth her hands to the government.' His idea,' said the President, "was that it would be considered our last *shriek*, on the retreat." (This was his *precise* expression.) "'Now,' continued Mr. Seward, 'while I approve the measure, I suggest, sir, that you postpone its issue, until you can give it to the country supported by military success, instead of issuing it, as would be the case now, upon the greatest disasters of the war!'" Mr. Lincoln continued : "The wisdom of the view of the Secretary of State struck me with very great force. It was an aspect of the case that, in all my thought upon the subject, I had entirely overlooked. The result was that I put the draft of the proclamation aside, as you do your sketch for a picture, waiting for a victory. From time to time I added or changed a line, touching it up here and there, anxiously waiting the progress of events. Well, the next news we had was of Pope's disaster at Bull Run. Things looked darker than ever. Finally, came the week of the battle of Antietam. I determined to wait no longer. The news came, I think, on Wednesday, that the advantage was on our side. I was then staying at the Soldiers' Home (three miles out of Washington). Here I finished writing the second draft of the preliminary proclamation; came up on Saturday; called the Cabinet together to hear it, and it was published the following Monday."

At the final meeting of September 20th, another interesting incident occurred in connection with Secretary Seward. The President had written the important part of the proclamation in these words :—

"That on the first day of January, in the year of our Lord one thousand eight hundred and sixty-three, all persons held as slaves within any state or designated part of a state, the people whereof shall then be in rebellion against the United States, shall be then, thenceforward, and forever FREE; and the Executive Government of the United States, including the military and naval authority thereof, will *recognize* the freedom of such persons, and will do no act or acts to repress such persons, or any of them, in any efforts they may make for their actual freedom." "When I finished reading this paragraph," resumed Mr. Lincoln, "Mr. Seward stopped me, and said, 'I think, Mr. President, that you should insert after the word "*recognize*," "*and maintain*."' I replied that I had already fully considered the import of that expression in this connection, but I had not introduced it, because it was not my way to promise what I was not entirely *sure* that I could perform, and I was not prepared to say that I thought we were exactly able to 'maintain' this."

"But," said he, " Seward insisted that we ought to take this ground; and the words finally went in!"

1. Carpenter's Six Months in the White House, pp. 21–23.

was the act of the President alone.   It exhibited far-seeing sagacity, courage, independence, and statesmanship.   The words "and maintain," after "recognize," were added at the suggestion of Mr. Seward, and Secretary Chase wrote the concluding paragraph in the final proclamation :   "And upon this act, sincerely believed to be an act of justice, warranted by the Constitution upon military necessity, I invoke the considerate judgment of mankind, and the gracious favor of Almighty God."   In this paragraph the words "upon military necessity," were inserted by the President.[1]

1. The proclamation of September 22, 1862, is in these words:

I, Abraham Lincoln, President of the United States of America, and Commander-in-Chief of the army and navy thereof, do hereby proclaim and declare that hereafter, as heretofore, the war will be prosecuted for the object of practically restoring the constitutional relations between the United States and each of the states and the people thereof, in which states that relation is or may be suspended or disturbed.

That it is my purpose, upon the next meeting of Congress, to again recommend the adoption of a practical measure tendering pecuniary aid to the free acceptance or rejection of all slave states, so called, the people whereof may not then be in rebellion against the United States, and which states may then have voluntarily adopted, or thereafter may voluntarily adopt, immediate or gradual abolishment of slavery within their respective limits; and that the effort to colonize persons of African descent with their consent upon this continent or elsewhere, with the previously obtained consent of the governments existing there, will be continued.

That on the first day of January, in the year of our Lord one thousand eight hundred and sixty-three, all persons held as slaves within any state or designated part of a state, the people whereof shall then be in rebellion against the United States, shall be then, thenceforward, and forever free; and the Executive government of the United States, including the military and naval authority thereof, will recognize and maintain the freedom of such persons, and will do no act or acts to repress such persons, or any of them, in any efforts they may make for their actual freedom.

That the Executive will, on the first day of January aforesaid, by proclamation, designate the states and parts of states, if any, in which the people thereof respectively, shall then be in rebellion against the United States; and the fact that any state, or the people thereof, shall on that day be, in good faith, represented in the Congress of the United States by members chosen thereto at elections wherein a majority of the qualified voters of such state shall have participated, shall, in the absence of strong countervailing testimony, be deemed conclusive evidence that such state, and the people thereof, are not in rebellion against the United States.

That attention is hereby called to an act of Congress entitled "An act to make an additional article of war," approved March 13, 1862, and which act is in the words and figures following:

"*Be it enacted by the Senate and House of Representatives of the United States of America in Congress assembled*, That hereafter the following shall be promulgated as an additional article of war, for the government of the army of the United States, and shall be obeyed and observed as such.

"ARTICLE —. All officers or persons in the military or naval service of the United States are prohibited from employing any of the forces under their respective commands for the purpose of returning fugitives from service or labor who may have

The final proclamation was issued on the 1st of January, 1863. In obedience to an American custom, the President had been receiving calls on that New Year's day, and for

escaped from any persons to whom such service or labor is claimed to be due, and any officer who shall be found guilty by a court-martial of violating this article shall be dismissed from the service.

"SEC. 2. *And be it further enacted*, That this act shall take effect from and after its passage."

Also to the ninth and tenth sections of an act entitled "An act to suppress insurrection, to punish treason and rebellion, to seize and confiscate property of rebels, and for other purposes," approved July 17, 1862, and which sections are in the words and figures following:

"SEC. 9. *And be it further enacted*, That all slaves of persons who shall hereafter be engaged in rebellion against the government of the United States or who shall in any way give aid or comfort thereto, escaping from such persons and taking refuge within the lines of the army; and all slaves captured from such persons or deserted by them, and coming under the control of the government of the United States; and all slaves of such persons found *on* [or] being within any place occupied by rebel forces, and afterwards occupied by the forces of the United States, shall be deemed captives of war, and shall be forever free of their servitude, and not again held as slaves.

"SEC. 10. *And be it further enacted*, That no slave, escaping into any state, territory, or the District of Columbia, from any other state, shall be delivered up, or in any way impeded or hindered of his liberty, except for crime, or some offence against the laws, unless the person claiming said fugitive shall first make oath that the person to whom the labor or service of such fugitive is alleged to be due is his lawful owner, and has not borne arms against the United States in the present rebellion, nor in any way given aid and comfort thereto; and no person engaged in the military or naval service of the United States shall, under any pretence whatever, assume to decide on the validity of the claim of any person to the service or labor of any other person, or surrender up any such person to the claimant, on pain of being dismissed from the service."

And I do hereby enjoin upon and order all persons engaged in the military and naval service of the United States to observe, obey, and enforce, within their respective spheres of service, the act and sections above recited.

And the Executive will in due time recommend that all the citizens of the United States who shall have remained loyal thereto throughout the rebellion, shall (upon the restoration of the constitutional relation between the United States and their respective states and people, if that relation shall have been suspended or disturbed) be compensated for all losses by acts of the United States, including the loss of slaves.

In witness whereof, I have hereunto set my hand, and caused the seal of the United States to be affixed.

Done at the city of Washington this twenty-second day of September, in the year of our Lord one thousand eight hundred and sixty-two, and of the Independence of the United States the eighty-seventh.   ABRAHAM LINCOLN.

By the President: WILLIAM H. SEWARD, *Secretary of State.*

The final proclamation of January 1, 1863, is as follows :

WHEREAS, on the twenty-second day of September, in the year of our Lord one thousand eight hundred and sixty-two, a proclamation was issued by the President of the United States, containing, among other things, the following, to-wit:

"That on the first day of January, in the year of our Lord one thousand eight hundred and sixty-three, all persons held as slaves within any state or designated part of a state, the people whereof shall then be in rebellion against the United States, shall be then, thenceforward, and forever, free; and the Executive government of the United States, including the military and naval authority thereof, will recognize and maintain the freedom of such persons, and will do no act or acts to repress such persons, or any of them, in any efforts they may make for their actual freedom.

"That the Executive will, on the first day of January aforesaid, by proclamation, hours shaking hands. As the paper was brought to him by the Secretary of State to be signed, he said : " Mr. Seward, I have been shaking hands all day, and my right hand is almost paralyzed. If my name ever gets into history, it will be for this act, and my whole soul is in it. If my hand trembles when I sign the proclamation those who examine

designate the states and parts of states, if any, in which the people thereof, respectively, shall then be in rebellion against the United States; and the fact that any state, or the people thereof, shall on that day be in good faith represented in the Congress of the United States, by members chosen thereto at elections wherein a majority of the qualified voters of such states shall have participated, shall, in the absence of strong countervailing testimony, be deemed conclusive evidence that such state, and the people thereof, are not then in rebellion against the United States."

Now, therefore, I, ABRAHAM LINCOLN, President of the United States, by virtue of the power in me vested as Commander-in-Chief of the Army and Navy of the United States, in time of actual armed rebellion against the authority and government of the United States, and as a fit and necessary war measure for suppressing said rebellion, do, on this first day of January, in the year of our Lord one thousand eight hundred and sixty-three, and in accordance with my purpose so to do, publicly proclaimed for the full period of one hundred days from the day first above mentioned, order and designate as the states and parts of states wherein the people thereof, respectively, are this day in rebellion against the United States, the following, to-wit:

Arkansas, Texas, Louisiana, (except the parishes of St. Bernard, Plaquemine, Jefferson, St. John, St. Charles, St. James, Ascension, Assumption, Terre Bonne, Lafourche, St. Mary, St. Martin, and Orleans, including the city of New Orleans,) Mississippi, Alabama, Florida, Georgia, South Carolina, North Carolina, and Virginia, (except the forty-eight counties designated as West Virginia, and also the counties of Berkeley, Accomac, Northampton, Elizabeth City, York, Princess Anne, and Norfolk, including the cities of Norfolk and Portsmouth,) and which excepted parts are for the present left precisely as if this proclamation were not issued.

And by virtue of the power and for the purpose aforesaid, I do order and declare that all persons held as slaves within said designated states and parts of states are, and henceforward shall be, free; and that the Executive government of the United States, including the military and naval authorities thereof, will recognize and maintain the freedom of said persons.

And I hereby enjoin upon the people so declared to be free to abstain from all violence, unless in necessary self-defence; and I recommend to them that, in all cases when allowed, they labor faithfully for reasonable wages.

And I further declare and make known that such persons, of suitable condition, will be received into the armed service of the United States to garrison forts, positions, stations, and other places, and to man vessels of all sorts in said service.

And upon this act, sincerely believed to be an act of justice, warranted by the Constitution upon military necessity, I invoke the considerate judgment of mankind and the gracious favor of Almighty God.

In witness whereof, I have hereunto set my hand and caused the seal of the United States to be affixed.

Done at the city of Washington this first day of January, in the year of our Lord one thousand eight hundred and sixty-three, and of the independence of the United States of America the eighty-seventh.   ABRAHAM LINCOLN.

By the President:

WILLIAM H. SEWARD, *Secretary of State.*

the document hereafter, will say : ' He hesitated.' " Then resting his arm a moment, he turned to the table, took up the pen, and slowly and firmly wrote, *Abraham Lincoln.* He smiled as, handing the paper to Mr. Seward, he said : " That will do."

This edict was the pivotal act of his administration, and may be justly regarded as the great event of the century. Before the sun went down on the memorable 22d of September, the contents of this edict had been flashed by the telegraph to every part of the republic. By a large majority of the loyal people of the nation, it was received with thanks to its author, and gratitude to God. Bells rang out their joyous peals over all New England and over New York, over the mountains of Pennsylvania, across the prairies of the West, even to the infant settlements skirting the base of the Rocky Mountains. Great public meetings were held in the cities and towns ; resolutions of approval were passed, and in thousands of churches thanksgiving was rendered. In many places the soldiers received the news with cheers, and salvos of artillery ; in others, and especially in some parts of the army commanded by General McClellan, some murmurs of dissatisfaction were heard,[1] but generally the intelligence gave gladness, and an energy and earnestness before unknown. The governors of the loyal states held a meeting at Altoona, on the 24th of September, and sent an address to the President, saying: " We hail with heartfelt gratitude and encouraged hope the proclamation " [2]

When the words of liberty and emancipation reached the negroes, their manhood was roused and many thousands joined the Union army, so that before the close of the war, nearly two hundred thousand were mustered into the service of the United States.[3]

1. See General McClellan's orders.

2. McPherson's History of the Rebellion, p. 232.

3. The original draft of the proclamation was offered for sale at the Sanitary Fair held at Chicago, in the autumn of 1863. It was purchased by Thomas B. Bryan, Esq., and by him presented to the Chicago Historical Society, in whose hall it was burned at the time of the great fire of October, 1871. The following letters will show its history :

It will be observed that the state of Tennessee was not included in the proclamation. It was omitted in deference to the opinions and wishes of Andrew Johnson, and other Union men of that state.[1] The Union men of Tennessee themselves changed the constitution of that state, abolishing and prohibiting slavery.

Congress, on the 15th of December, 1862, by a very large majority, adopted a resolution sanctioning the edict.[2] A bill was also, on the 14th of December, 1863, introduced into the House, by a member from Illinois, prohibiting the holding, or attempting to hold, as slaves, any persons declared free by the proclamation, or their descendants.[3]

Along the path of the once feeble, obscure, and persecuted abolitionists, to this their crowning victory, are to be found the wrecks of many parties, and the names of great

WASHINGTON, October 13, 1863.

To THE PRESIDENT—*My Dear Sir :* I take the liberty of inclosing to you the circular of the *Northwestern Fair* for the Sanitary Commission, for the benefit and aid of the brave and patriotic soldiers of the Northwest. The ladies engaged in this enterprise will feel honored by your countenance, and grateful for any aid it may be convenient for you to give them.

At their suggestion, I ask, that you would send them the original of your proclamation of freedom, to be disposed of for the benefit of the soldiers, and then deposited in the Historical Society of Chicago, where it would ever be regarded as a relic of great interest. This, or any other aid it may be convenient for you to render, would have peculiar interest as coming from one whom the Northwest holds in the highest honor and respect.

Very respectfully yours,

ISAAC N. ARNOLD.

EXECUTIVE MANSION, WASHINGTON, October 26, 1863.

Ladies having in charge the Northwestern Fair for the Sanitary Commission, Chicago, Illinois :

According to the request made in your behalf, the original draft of the emancipation proclamation is here inclosed. The formal words at the top, and the conclusion, except the signature you perceive, are not in my handwriting. They were written at the State Department, by whom I know not. The printed part was cut from a copy of the preliminary proclamation, and pasted on merely to save writing. *I had some desire to retain the paper ; but if it shall contribute to the relief or comfort of the soldiers, that will be better.*

Your ob't serv't,   A. LINCOLN.

1. Such was the statement of the President to the author.

2. Congressional Globe, December 15, 1862. Also McPherson's History of the Rebellion, p. 229.

3. Congressional Globe, 1st Session 38th Congress, part 1, p. 20. Also McPherson's History of the Rebellion, pp. 229, 230.

men who had fallen by placing themselves in the way of this great reform. Liberty and justice are mighty things to conjure with, and vain is the power of man when he tries to stay their advance. The timid and over-cautious were startled by the boldness and courage of this act of the President, and his opponents, and especially those who sympathized with the rebels, hoped to make it the means of the defeat and overthrow of his administration. They did not realize or appreciate the strength of a good cause, and the power of courage in behalf of a great principle. From the day of its promulgation to the final triumph of the Union cause, Lincoln grew stronger and stronger in the confidence of the people, and the tide of victory in the field set more and more in favor of the republic.

While congratulations came pouring in upon the President from the people of Great Britain, Lincoln rather expected that now the government of good old Mother England would pat him on the head and express its approval. Senator Sumner, whose social relations with many English members of Parliament had been most friendly and cordial, said to the President: " The British government cannot fail to hail your proclamation with fraternal congratulations. Great Britain, whose poets and whose orators have long boasted that

'Slaves cannot breathe in England,'

will welcome the edict of freedom with expressions of approval and good will ; " yet, when the proclamation reached London, Lord John Russell, in a dispatch to the British minister at Washington, sneered at the paper " as a measure of a very questionable kind," " an act of vengeance on the slave owner." " It professes," said he, with cynical ill-nature, " it does no more than profess, to emancipate slaves, where the United States authorities cannot make emancipation a reality, but emancipates no one where the decree can be carried into effect."[1] Yet, without the good

1. Memorial Address of George Bancroft, on Lincoln, pp. 30, 31.

wishes of his lordship, or encouragement from the English government, the United States did make emancipation eventually a reality, and Lord Russell lived to see the decree of Mr. Lincoln carried into effect to the extent of freeing every slave in the republic. But for this result no thanks to him or to the government of which he was the organ.

Was this proclamation valid, and effectual in law to free the negroes? This question is not now, since the amendments to the Constitution of the United States and of the states, abolishing and prohibiting slavery, of very great practical importance. It did result, practically, in the destruction of slavery, and under its operation, as carried into effect by the President and military and naval authorities of the United States, slavery ceased. Was it a legal and valid edict under the Constitution and laws of war?

The government of the United States possessed all the powers with reference to the Confederates in rebellion, and who were making war upon the republic, which any nation has with relation to its enemies in war. It had the clear right to treat them as public enemies, according to the laws of war. The emancipation of an enemy's slaves is a belligerent right, and it belongs exclusively to the President, as Commander in Chief, to judge whether he will exercise this right. The exercise of the tremendous power of enfranchising the slaves, and thereby weakening the public enemy and strengthening the government, is in accordance with the law of nations, and with the practice of civilized belligerents in modern times.

The able and learned lawyer and publicist, Alexander H. Stephens, in the passage already quoted, took it for granted that this power would be exercised by the Federal Government, and before hostilities commenced he warned the people of Georgia against it. He knew that in May, 1836, that learned jurist and statesman, John Quincy Adams, had declared on the floor of Congress that the President could legally exercise this power. Mr. Adams had concluded an exhaustive discussion of the question, by saying: "I lay this down as the law of nations, that in case of war, the President of the United States and the commander of the army *has power to order* the universal emancipation of the slaves." [1]

The right was claimed and exercised by Great Britain, both in the war of the revolution and the war of 1812. Sir Henry Clinton, Lord Dunmore, and Lord Cornwallis all issued proclamations promising liberty to the slaves of the colonies. Jefferson says, in a letter to Dr. Gordon, that under Lord Cornwallis [2] Virginia lost about thirty thousand slaves. Speaking of the injury to himself, he says: "He (Cornwallis) carried off about thirty slaves." "Had this been done to give them freedom, he would have done right." The English commanders in the war of 1812 invited, by proclamation, the slaves to join them, promising them freedom. The slaves who joined them were liberated and carried away. The United States, when peace was declared, demanded indemnity. The question was referred to the Emperor of Russia as umpire, who decided that indemnity should be paid to the extent to which payment had been stipulated *in the treaty of peace*, but for such as were not included in the treaty no payment should be made.

Justice Miller, of the Supreme Court of the United States, says: " In that struggle (to subdue the rebellion) slavery as a legalized social institution perished." [3] * *
" The proclamation of President Lincoln expressed an accomplished fact as to a large portion of the insurrectionary districts, when he declared slavery abolished." In the state of Louisiana it has been judicially decided that the sale of a slave after the proclamation of emancipation was void.[4] In the state of Texas it was held by the Supreme Court, in 1868, that the effect of the President's proclama-

---

1. See Whiting's War Powers. Mr. Adams's speech, pp. 77-79. In that able work of Mr. Whiting will be found a full discussion of the subject.

2. Whiting's War Powers, p. 69.

3. The Slaughter House Cases, 16 Wallace Reports, p. 68.

4. See 20th Louisiana Rep., p. 199.

tion of January 1, 1863, was to liberate the slaves under the national control, that all slaves became free as fast as the nation obtained control, and that, on the final surrender, all slaves embraced in the terms of the edict became free.[1] Judge Lindsey says: " The legal effect of the proclamation was *eo instanti* to liberate all slaves under control of the federal forces." " It was a proper measure, and made effectual by force of arms." Chief Justice Chase says: "Emancipation was confirmed rather than ordained by the amendment prohibiting slavery throughout the Union."[2]

The proclamation of emancipation did not change the local law in the insurgent states, it operated on the persons held as slaves; " all persons held as slaves are and henceforth shall be free." The law sanctioning slavery was not necessarily abrogated, hence the necessity for the amendment of the Constitution.[3] The Supreme Court of the United States declared that: " When the armies of freedom found themselves upon the soil of slavery, they (and the President their commander) could do nothing less than free the poor victims whose enforced servitude was the foundation of the quarrel."[4] Let then no impious hand seek to tear from the brow of Lincoln the crown so justly his due, as the emancipator of the negro race in America.

1. See 31st Texas Rep., p. 504–531, 551, for able opinions of the judges. See also 44th Alabama Rep., p. 71.

2. Chief Justice Chase, in 7 Wall. Rep. 728.

3. See also North American Review, for December, 1880, A. A. Ferris, and cases cited.

4. Wallace Rep. 16, p. 68.

CHAPTER XVI.

MILITARY OPERATIONS IN 1861–1862.

BATTLES IN THE WEST.— FROM BELMONT TO CORINTH.— SUCCESSES
IN THE SOUTH.— FARRAGUT CAPTURES NEW ORLEANS.— THE
MONITOR.— McCLELLAN AND THE PRESIDENT.— POPE'S CAM-
PAIGN.— McCLELLAN RE-INSTATED IN COMMAND.

THAT a consecutive narrative might be given of the action
of Congress and of the Executive, on the all-important
question of slavery, up to the period of emancipation, military movements have been neglected. Everything depended
upon the success of the Union armies. Laws and proclamations, without victories, would amount to little. The
President realized this, and on the threshold of the war, his
most anxious thought, and most difficult problem, was to find
officers who could lead the Union troops to victory. The
republic had few soldiers of experience. Scott and Wool
had won reputation in the war of 1812, and in Mexico, but
were old for active service. Military skill must be developed
by costly experience. In his appointments to high command,
the President, without regard to party or personal considerations, sought for skill and ability. None realized more
fully than he, that the success of his administration depended
upon the triumph of his armies. Hence, while he
appointed Fremont, and Hunter, and McDowell, Banks, and
others, from among his political and personal friends, he did
not hesitate to give to those who had hitherto acted with
the democratic party, such as McClellan, Halleck, Buell,
Grant, and others, the very highest positions. The question

with him was—who will lead our troops to the most speedy and decisive victories ?

The general plan of the war seemed to be : *first*, to blockade the entire coast of the insurgent states ; *second*, the military occupation of the border slave states, so as to protect and sustain the Union men resident therein ; *third*, the recovery of the Mississippi River to the Gulf, by which the Confederacy would be divided, and the great outlet of the Northwest to New Orleans and the ocean would be secured; *fourth*, the destruction of the rebel army in Virginia, and the capture of Richmond, the rebel capital. To accomplish these purposes, and to resist their accomplishment, stupendous preparations were made on both sides.

In the autumn of 1861, General George B. McClellan had under his command, at Washington and its vicinity, on the line of the Baltimore and Ohio, and at Fortress Monroe, more than two hundred thousand well armed men. General Halleck, who was in command in the West, had a very large army. McClellan was a skillful organizer, and had the power of making himself personally popular, but was slow, very cautious, and was never ready. With his magnificent army, greatly exceeding that which confronted him—he lay inactive all the fall of 1861, and the winter of 1861-2, into February, permitting the Potomac to be closed by batteries on the western shore, above and below his army, and the rebel flag to be flaunted in his face, and in that of the government, from the Virginia hills overlooking the capital. [1]

It was the era of brilliant reviews and magnificent military displays, of parade, festive parties, and junketings. The President was impatient at this inactivity, and again and again urged action on the part of the General. But McClellan, having in August, 1861, offended General Scott, by whom he was styled " an ambitious Junior," and caused the

---

1. " During all this time the Confederate army lay at Centerville, insolently menacing Washington.   *   *   It never presented an effective strength of over 50,-000 men." Webb's Peninsular Campaign, p. 26.

18

old veteran to ask to be placed on the retired list, [1] was left in command. When urged to action by the President, he always had some plausible excuse for delay. At length the patience of the Executive was exhausted, and, on the 27th of January, 1862, he issued an order that a general movement of the land and naval forces should be made, on the 22d of February, against the insurgents. This order has been much criticised. It was addressed to the army and navy generally, but was intended especially for General McClellan and his army.

A brief recital of what had been done at the West and elsewhere, will show that, with the exception of the great army of the Potomac, the forces of the republic had been active, energetic, and generally successful. On the 6th of November, 1861, General U. S. Grant, moving from Cairo, attacked Belmont, and destroyed the military stores of the enemy at that place. On the 10th of January, 1862, Colonel James A. Garfield attacked and defeated Humphrey Marshall, at Middle Creek, Kentucky. On the 18th of January, General George H. Thomas, a true and loyal Virginian, who, like Scott, was faithful to his flag, gained a brilliant victory over the rebel Generals Zollicoffer and Crittenden, at Mill Spring.

The Cumberland and Tennessee rivers, having their sources far within the rebel lines, and running to the north and west, empty into the Ohio. To secure these rivers from Union gun-boats, the insurgents had constructed and garrisoned Fort Henry, on the Tennessee, and Fort Donelson, on the Cumberland. Flag-officer Foote, one of the most skillful and energetic officers of the navy, commanded the Union fleet on the Western rivers. Co-operating with General Grant, they planned an attack on Fort Henry. On the 6th of February, Foote, with his gun-boats, attacked and captured that Fort—not waiting for the arrival of Grant, who was approaching. Grant and Foote then moved to the attack of Fort

---

1. The Records of the War of the Rebellion, Series 1, Vol. II, Part 3d, Correspondence, etc , pp, 4, 5. 6, etc.

Donelson.   On the 16th of February, they invested the fort. After several days hard fighting, the rebel General Buckner sent a flag of truce to General Grant, asking a cessation of hostilities, to settle terms of surrender.   Grant replied: " No terms except unconditional surrender can be accepted.   I propose to move immediately on your works." Buckner did not wait the assault, but surrendered at discretion.   This victory, and the note of Grant, gave to him the sobriquet of " Unconditional Surrender Grant."   Arms, stores, and more than twelve thousand prisoners were captured.   This brilliant victory electrified the country, and the President, impatient, and careworn over the long and mysterious delay of the army of the Potomac, looked ten years younger upon the evening of the reception of the inspiring news.

General Floyd, late the treacherous Secretary of War under Buchanan, and who had been in command, was conscious that a man who had plotted treason against the national government while in the Cabinet, deserved punishment as a traitor, and fled at night before the surrender. These substantial victories compelled the evacuation by the rebels of Kentucky, and opened Tennessee to the Union forces.   Bowling Green, called by the insurgents the Gibraltar of Kentucky, was, on the 15th of February, occupied by General Mitchell of the Union army.

On the 24th of February, the Union troops occupied Nashville, the capital of the great state of Tennessee, and, in March thereafter, Andrew Johnson, having been appointed provisional governor, arrived, and the persecuted Unionists of the state gladly rallied around him.   In East Tennessee —his old home—loyalty was general, and the Union flag was hailed with exclamations of joy and gratitude.

On the 6th, 7th, and 8th of March, was fought the battle of Pea Ridge, and General Halleck telegraphed with exultation: " The Union flag is floating in Arkansas."   On the 13th of March, General John Pope, of Illinois, moving down the west bank of the Mississippi, compelled the evacuation of New Madrid, and then laid siege to Island No. 10, in the

Mississippi, which, on the 7th of April, he captured, with provisions, arms, and military stores.

Thus the Union forces had been steadily advancing in the valley of the Mississippi. Buell's army was at Nashville, and the Confederates saw with dismay Missouri, Kentucky, Arkansas, and Tennessee, wrenched from them, and realized that unless the armies of Grant and Buell could be driven back, the whole valley of the Mississippi would be lost.

Lee seemed to calculate, with confidence, that all would remain "quiet on the Potomac" as usual, for he sent Beauregard from his army in Virginia to the West, while the rebel forces west of the Alleghanies were placed under the command of their ablest general, Albert Sidney Johnston. He realized the vast, perhaps decisive importance of the impending conflict in the valley of the Mississippi. In his address to his army, before the battle of Shiloh, he said: " Remember, soldiers, the fair, broad, abounding lands, the happy homes, that will be desolated by your defeat. The eyes and hopes of eight millions of people rest upon you."

On the 6th of April, the great armies met on the bank of the Tennessee and fought the terrible and bloody battle of Shiloh, or Pittsburgh Landing. General Grant occupied the southern bank of the river. Buell was approaching from the north. It was the intention of the Confederates to surprise and whip Grant before Buell could come to his support. Before six o'clock, on the morning of April 6th, the rebel columns attacked furiously, and rushing on like a whirlwind, threatened to drive the Union troops into the river. Grant arrived on the field at 8 A. M., and, rallying and re-forming his lines, with unflinching determination, continued the fight. Charge after charge was made by the impetuous and confident Confederates, but they were met with dogged and persistent courage. Thus the fight went on during the long day, but the Union troops were gradually forced back towards the river, into a semi-circle, with the river in the rear. The Union General Wallace, and the rebel commander Johnston, with many other brave and distinguished officers on both sides, were killed. The long dreary day closed, with the advantage all on the side of the rebels, and Beauregard at evening announced a complete victory. But with the night Buell arrived with his gallant army, and the morrow brought victory to the Union arms. Grant had exhibited those stubborn, resolute, persistent qualities, which would not know defeat. With the fresh troops of Buell and Lew Wallace, he early the next morning attacked the rebels, drove them from the field, and pursued them towards their intrenchments at Corinth.

This, one of the most bloody battles of the war, was fought by troops not many months in the service, but many of whom had been already often in battle. It was a long, terrible fight, but when the sun went down on the second day, it went down on an army of flying rebels, who had gained an experience of the courage, persistence, and efficiency of the soldiers of the West, which they never forgot.

On the 30th of May, the batteries of General Halleck, commanding in the West, opened on the rebel fortifications at Corinth, in the state of Mississippi, and the rebels were driven out, abandoning their fortifications with a vast quantity of military stores. Such, in brief, is the eventful story of the armies of the West, during the year 1861 and the earlier part of 1862. Nor were the national forces idle at the extreme South.

On the 8th of February, 1862, Roanoke Island, on the coast of North Carolina, was captured by General Burnside and Admiral Goldsborough, with prisoners, arms, and military stores. On the 14th of March, General Burnside captured Newbern. On the 11th of April, General David Hunter captured Fort Pulaski, and on the 25th of April, 1862, Fort Macon was taken.

New Orleans, at the mouth of the Mississippi, was early in the war an object of anxious consideration on the part of the President. Having passed his life in the West, knowing this great river as one who in early manhood had urged a boat over its majestic waters, he had seen its thousands of miles of navigable tributary streams, and itself from the Gulf to the far North, covered with steamers, carrying to salt water the vast products of a delta and territory more productive than that of the Nile. From the beginning, he felt perfectly certain that the hardy Western pioneers would "hew their way to the sea." New Orleans had long been the object of national pride. The victory of General Jackson at that place had always been regarded as one of the most brilliant military achievements on record. This interesting city, over which had floated the lilies of France; this metropolis of the Southwest had fallen by the treason of General Twiggs, an unresisting victim, into the toils of the conspirators.

In the autumn of 1861, an expedition under the command of Captain David G. Farragut, and General B. F. Butler, was organized for its capture. Farragut was a native of Tennessee, a hearty, bluff, honest, downright sailor, full of energy, determination, and ability; with a courage and fertility of resources never surpassed. He was one of those men who dare everything, and rarely fail. There is no brighter name than his among the naval heroes of the world. On the 25th of March, 1862, Butler landed his troops on Ship Island, in the Gulf of Mexico, between New Orleans and Mobile. On the 17th of April, Farragut with his fleet arrived in the vicinity of the forts which guarded the approach to the city. After bombarding these forts for several days without reducing them, with the inspiration of genius he determined to run past their guns. The hazard was fearful. Forts St. Philip and Jackson, on opposite sides of the river, mounted over an hundred heavy cannon; besides this, the river was blocked up by sunken hulks, piles, and every obstruction which could be devised. In addition, he would have to encounter thirteen gunboats, the floating ironclad Louisiana, and the ram Manassas. The authorities at New Orleans were confident. "Our only fear," said the city press, "is that the Northern invaders will not appear." Farragut soon dissipated these fears. On the night of the 24th of April, amidst a storm of shot and shell, the darkness illuminated by the mingled fires of ships, forts, and burning vessels, he passed Forts Jackson and St. Philip; he crushed through all obstructions; he destroyed the ram and gunboats which opposed him; he steamed past the batteries; he ascended the great river, and laid his broadsides to the proud city of the Southwest.

The town of one hundred and fifty thousand people surrendered, and the flag of the Union floated once more over the Crescent City, never again to be removed. For, as was grimly said by a rebel officer on the fall of Richmond, "It has never been the policy of the Confederates to retake the cities and posts captured by the Union forces." Baton Rouge, the capital of Louisiana, was taken without resistance on the 7th of May, Natchez on the 12th, and for a time the Mississippi was opened as far up as Vicksburg.

As the President read the report of these various successes, he could not fail to compare and to contrast them with the inaction of the grand army of the Potomac. Of that army great and sanguine expectations had been formed. It was commanded, as has been stated, by George B. McClellan, who at the time of his appointment, in November, 1861, as General in Chief of the armies of the United States, was less than thirty-six years of age. Popular feeling, eager to welcome victories and to reward him with honor, had already called him the " Young Napoleon."

The army of the Potomac was regarded as the main army; it was encamped in and around Washington, the source of supplies; when there were not arms for all, this army was first supplied, and if there was a choice, this body of troops had the preference. It is not intended to question the patriotism or the courage of the General in Chief, nor to suggest a doubt of his loyalty, but he did not disguise his hostility to the radicals. He had no sympathy for the abolitionists, and he let them know it. While condemning secession, he had more sympathy for slaveholders than for slaves. He criticised freely the radical acts of Congress and the administration, and he very soon became the center around which gathered all who opposed the radical measures of the President and of Congress. They flattered the young general, and suggested to him that he could become the great pacificator. This may aid in explaining his strange and mysterious inactivity.

It will be remembered that on the 27th of January the President issued an order for active operations. This order contemplated a general advance in concert by all the forces in the field. On the 31st of January, the President ordered an expedition, the immediate object of which was to seize and occupy a position on the railway southwest of Manassas Junction. McClellan did not move until early in March, and then reached Centreville with his immense army, to find it abandoned, and wooden guns in position on the works behind which the rebels, in far inferior numbers, had remained all the autumn and winter unassailed. But his words, addressed to his army at Fairfax Court House, led the country to hope that he would now make up in energy and celerity his long delay. He said : " The army of the Potomac is now a real army. Magnificent in material, admirable in discipline, excellently equipped and armed. Your commanders are all that I could wish."

Such being the case, and with a force more than one hundred and fifty thousand strong, carrying three hundred and fifty pieces of artillery, a brilliant and triumphant campaign was confidently looked for. Lincoln had given McClellan his confidence, and was very slow to withdraw it, for he was always noted for the unflinching fidelity with which he stood by those whom he trusted. He had sustained this general against a very large majority of the earnest Union men of the nation. The committee on the conduct of the war appointed by Congress, the fiery Secretary of War, and many others, had chafed and complained during all the winter of 1861–62 at McClellan's inactivity. He had done a great work in organizing this splendid army, but he could not be made to lead a bold, aggressive campaign. Could this army, on the day it struck its tents around Washington, have been transferred to the command of a rapid, indefatigable, and energetic officer like Sheridan, or to the hero of Atlanta and the "Grand March," or to Thomas, or to the unflinching iron will of Grant, it would have marched into Richmond long before McClellan reached the Chickahominy.

Celerity of movement, quick and rapid blows, were impossible with the amount of *impedimenta* which hampered McClellan's movements. Washington was an attractive place to the gay young officers of this army. Members of Congress were curious to learn what was the camp equipage which required six immense four-horse wagons drawn up before the door of the general, each wagon marked: "Headquarters of the Army of the Potomac;" and when it was reported that Grant had taken the field with only a spare shirt, a hair brush, and a tooth brush, comparisons were made between Eastern luxury and Western hardihood.

During this long inaction on the Potomac, while the forces of the West were capturing Forts Donelson and Henry, and driving the rebels out of Kentucky, Missouri, and Tennessee, the impatience of the President was not always suppressed. On one occasion he said : " If General McClellan does not want to use the army for some days, I should like to borrow it and see if it cannot be made to do something."

On the 8th of March, the President directed that, Washington being left entirely secure, a movement should begin not later than the 18th of March, and that the General in Chief should be responsible for its commencement as early as that day. Also that the army and navy should coöperate in an immediate effort to capture the rebel batteries on the Potomac. [1] The army did not coöperate, and the batteries were not captured.

1 President's War Order No. 3. *See* Official Records of the War of the Rebellion, Series 1, Vol II., p. III, p. 58.

On the 12th of March, at a council of war held at Fairfax Court House, a majority decided to proceed against Richmond by Fortress Monroe. The President acquiesced, although his opinion had been decidedly in favor of a direct march upon Richmond. His acquiescence was upon the condition that Washington should be left entirely secure, and the remainder of the force move down the Potomac to Fortress Monroe, or anywhere between Washington and Fortress Monroe, "or at all events to move at once in pursuit of the enemy by some route."

While impatiently following the slow movements of McClellan, the nation was electrified by news of a conflict upon the water, between the iron clad "Virginia" and the "Monitor," which took place on the 9th of March, 1862. When Norfolk was shamefully abandoned in the spring of 1861 by the federal officers, among other vessels left in the hands of the enemy was the "Merrimac." Sheathing her sides with iron armor, and changing her name to the "Virginia," on the 9th of March she steamed down the James, and attacked and destroyed the United States frigates, "Cumberland" and "Congress." The officers of the "Cumberland" fought until the ship went down with her flags still flying. The "Minnesota," coming to the aid of the "Cumberland," ran aground and lay at the mercy of this terrible iron-clad battery. But just at the time when it seemed that the James, and the Potomac, and Washington itself, was at the mercy of this apparently invulnerable ship, there was seen approaching in the distance, a low, turtle-like looking nondescript, which, as she came nearer, was made out to be the iron-clad "Monitor," just built as an experiment by the distinguished engineer, Ericsson. She mounted two eleven inch Dahlgren guns, carrying one hundred and sixty-eight pound shot. As compared with the "Virginia," she was a David to a Goliath. She boldly and successfully attacked her gigantic enemy, thereby saving the fleet, and perhaps the capital. Whole broadsides were fired at the little "Monitor," with no more effect than volleys of stones would have had.

On the 3rd of April, the President ordered the Secretary of War to direct General McClellan "to commence his forward movement from his new base at once."[1] On the 5th of April, General McClellan, when near Yorktown, said to the President: "The enemy are in large force along our front, * * * their works formidable,"[2] and adds: "I am of opinion I shall have to fight all the available force of the rebels not far from here." On the other hand, the rebel General Magruder, in his report of July 3rd, says that the whole force with which Yorktown was held, was eleven thousand, and that a portion of his line was held by five thousand men. "That with five thousand men exclusive of the garrisons, we stopped and held in check over one hundred thousand of the enemy. * * * The men slept in the trenches, and under arms, but to my great surprise, he (McClellan) permitted day after day to elapse without any assault."[3]

This force detained McClellan from April 1st to May 4th. With an army of nearly or quite one hundred thousand men, he set down to a regular siege, and when he was fully ready to open with his great guns, the enemy had left. A vigorous and active commander would not have permitted this handful of men to delay his march. On the 11th of April, the President telegraphed to McClellan: "You now have one hundred thousand troops with you, independent of General Wool's command. I think that you had better break the enemy's line at once."[4]

In reply to McClellan's constant applications for re-enforcements, the President, on the 9th of April, wrote him a

1. Official Records of the Rebellion, Series I. VII. p. 3d, p. 65.

2. Official Reports of the Rebellion, S. I. VII. p. 3d, p. 71.

3. This report of Magruder is corroborated by a letter from General Raines to General Hill, in which he says that when McClellan approached Yorktown, Magruder had but 9,300 effective men. See Official Records of the War of the Rebellion, S. I. VII. p. 3d, p. 516.

4. Report of the Committee on the Conduct of the War, pp. 319-320.

very kind and frank letter, in which, among other things, he says: " I suppose the whole force which has gone forward to you, is with you by this time, and if so, I think that it is the precise time for you to strike a blow. By delay, the enemy will relatively gain upon you—that is, he will gain faster by fortifications and re-enforcements than you can by re-enforcements alone; and once more let me tell you, it is indispensable to you that you strike a blow. I am powerless to help this. You will do me the justice to remember I always insisted that going down the bay in search of a field, instead of fighting near Manassas, was only shifting, not surmounting the difficulty. * * * The country will not fail to note—and it is now noting—that the present hesitation to move upon an intrenched enemy, is but the story of Manassas repeated. I beg to assure you I have never written * * * in greater kindness, nor with a fuller purpose to sustain you, so far as in my most anxious judgment I consistently can. *But you must act.*" [1]

Yet McClellan, disregarding these urgent and repeated appeals and orders, still remained in front of the works at Yorktown. His "long delay," as Johnston called it, was as inexplicable to the Confederates, as to the administration at Washington. [2] On the 22d of April, General Joseph E. Johnston, writing to Lee, says, "No one but McClellan could have hesitated to attack." [3]

No one can read the official records of the war, as published by the government, without being impressed by the patience and forbearance of the President. Earnestly, and frequently, and vainly, he urged, entreated, and directed McClellan, again and again, " to strike a blow." The impartial judgment of the future will be that Lincoln's forbear-

---

1. Report on Conduct of War, p. 1. pp. 321-322.

2. General Johnston, writing to General Robert E. Lee, April 29th, says :"I suspect McClellan is waiting for iron-clad war vessels for James River. They would enable him to reach Richmond three days before us. I cannot account otherwise for this long delay here." * * " Yorktown cannot hold out." See Official Records of the War of the Rebellion, Sec. 1, Vol. VII, Pt. 3d, p. 473.

3. The same, p. 454.

ance was continued long after it had "ceased to be a virtue."

On the 6th of April, the President telegraphed to McClellan : "I think you had better break the enemy's line from Yorktown at once." On the 9th of April, he said : " I think it the precise time for you to *strike a blow*. It is indispensable for you to strike a blow. You must act." On the 1st of May, he asked : "Is anything to be done ?" On the 25th of May, Mr. Lincoln telegraphed McClellan : "I think the time is near at hand when you must either attack Richmond, or give up the job, and come to the defense of Washington."

On the 21st of June, McClellan, from his camp on the Chickahominy, addressing the President, asked permission "to lay before your Excellency my views as to the present state of military affairs throughout the whole country." The President replied, with great good nature and some sarcasm : " If it would not divert your time and attention from the army under your command, I should be glad to hear your views on the present state of military affairs throughout the whole country."

On the 27th of June, McClellan announced his intention to retreat to the James River, and he had the indiscretion to send to the Secretary of War an insubordinate and insulting dispatch, in which he says : " If I save this army, I tell you plainly, I owe no thanks to you, nor to any one at Washington. You have done your best to destroy this army." Such a dispatch addressed to any government, the head of which was less patient and forbearing than Lincoln, would have resulted in his removal, arrest, and trial. The great army, with its spirit unbroken, at times turning at bay, retreated to Malvern Hill.

On the 7th of July, while at Harrison's Landing, McClellan had the presumption to send to the President a long letter of advice upon the general conduct of the administration. This letter is important, as it illustrates the character of the man, and the relations between him and the Executive.

Unfortunately for his usefulness as a soldier, he had permitted himself to become the head of a party, and was looking to the Presidency, at the hands of those in opposition to the President, and whose nominee he became at the next Presidential election.

The high command which Mr. Lincoln had given him ; the crowd of staff-officers and subordinates, by which he was surrounded and flattered ; his personal popularity with his soldiers ; all these had turned his head, and his failures as a leader did not restore his judgment. This young captain of engineers, not thirty-seven years old, who had never seen a day's service in public life, whose studies had been those of a civil and military engineer, and who, by the grace and favor of the President was in command of the army, undertook to enlighten the Executive on the most grave, and novel, and complex questions involved in the civil war. Questions which taxed to the utmost the ablest and most experienced statesmen of the world. This young engineer and railroad president had the presumption to advise and seek to instruct the President and his Cabinet.

The tone of the letter was immodest and dictatorial. McClellan said to his commander: " Let neither military disaster, political faction, nor foreign war shake your settled purpose to enforce the equal operation of the laws upon the people of every state." Then he tells the Executive how the war must be carried on. " Neither confiscation of property, political executions of persons, territorial organization of states, or forcible abolition of slavery should be contemplated for one moment." And he then intimates, that unless his views as presented, " should be made known and approved, the effort to obtain the requisite forces will be almost hopeless. A declaration of radical views, especially upon slavery, will rapidly disintegrate our present armies." [1]

The President had a right to expect from the commander of his armies personal fidelity and sympathy, if not loyalty

---

1. McPherson's History of the Rebellion, pp. 385-386.

to his administration. General McClellan gave him neither.
He was in the hands, and he was the instrument, of those
who wished to overthrow the administration, and to go into
power upon its ruins. Knowing this, Mr. Lincoln continued
him at the head of the armies, and urged him again and
again " to strike a blow," to achieve those victories which
might have made him President. General McClellan had
done nothing then—he has done nothing since—to justify
or excuse the presumption of his conduct.

On the 8th of July, 1862, the President visited the camp
of General McClellan, and was depressed upon finding that,
of the magnificent army with which that general had started
to capture Richmond, and with all the re-enforcements which
had been sent to it, there were now remaining only eighty-
five thousand effective men. There is a touching story in
Roman history of the Emperor Augustus calling in vain
upon Varus to give him back his legions. The President
might well have said to McClellan, at Harrison Landing :
" Where are my soldiers, where the patriotic young volunteers, vainly sacrificed in fruitless battles from Yorktown to
Malvern Hill, and the still larger numbers who have perished in hospitals, and in the swamps of the Chickahominy ?"
" What has been gained by this costly sacrifice ? "

The records of the Confederates make it perfectly clear
that there were several occasions when the army of the
Potomac could have broken through their thin lines and
gone into Richmond, but McClellan had not the sagacity to
discover it, and if he had known of their weakness, he would
probably have hesitated until it was too late. The disasters and failures of the great army of McClellan, contrasted with the brilliant successes at the West, naturally
suggested the transfer to the East of some of the officers
under whom these successes had been achieved. On the
11th of July, 1862, Halleck had been appointed General in
Chief, and on the 23d he entered upon his duties as such.

General John Pope, son of Nathaniel Pope, United
States District Judge of Illinois, in whose courts the Presi-

dent had for many years practised law, was believed to be one of the most brilliant and rising young officers of the West. He had been successful at Island No. 10, and at New Madrid on the Mississippi. Lincoln knew him and his family well. They had been neighbors, and the President rejoiced in his fame. On the 27th of June he issued an order, creating the army of Virginia, under the command of General Pope, to consist of the three army corps of Generals Fremont, Banks, and McDowell. Fremont resigned on the ground that Pope was his junior.

On the 14th of July, Pope assumed command, and issued an address to his army in which he said:

" I have come to you from the West, where we have always seen the backs of our enemies ; from an army whose business it has been to seek an adversary, and beat him when found ; whose policy has been attack and not defense. In but one instance has the enemy been able to place our Western armies in a defensive attitude. I presume I have been called here to pursue the same system, and to lead you against the enemy. It is my purpose to do so, and that speedily. I am sure you long for an opportunity to win the distinction you are capable of achieving; that opportunity I shall endeavor to give you. In the meantime, I desire you to dismiss certain phrases I am sorry to find in vogue amongst you."

" I hear constantly of taking strong positions and holding them—of lines of retreat and bases of supplies. Let us discard such ideas. The strongest position a soldier should desire to occupy is one from which he can most easily advance against the enemy. Let us study the probable line of retreat of our opponents, and leave our own to take care of itself. Let us look before us and not behind. Success and glory are in the advance—disaster and shame lurk in the rear. Let us act on this understanding, and it is safe to predict that your banners shall be inscribed with many a glorious deed, and that your names will be dear to your countrymen forever."

This indiscreet address, though so full of the ardor of a young, successful, and sanguine soldier, was as bad in taste as mistaken in policy. While it indicated a vigorous policy and a spirited campaign, it naturally created an intense feeling of hostility against him among the officers of the army of the Potomac. It aroused local jealousy, and increased the prejudice which resulted in the sacrifice of Pope and others. At the close of a brilliant and successful campaign it would have been more excusable.

The failure of McClellan's campaign did not in the least dishearten the North, nor shake the determination of the people to crush the rebellion. It created the necessity for still greater efforts. The governors of seventeen states met at Altoona, in Pennsylvania, on the 28th of June, and united in an address to the President, announcing the readiness of the people of their respective states to respond to a call for more soldiers, and their desire for the most vigorous meas- ures for carrying on the war. The President issued a call for three hundred thousand additional volunteers.

Pope had but about thirty-eight thousand men. With this small force he was to defend Washington, hold the valley of the Shenandoah, and repel the expected approach of Lee. He was early aware that he had incurred the hos- tility of McClellan, and that he could not rely on the hearty coöperation of that general and his subordinates. Conscious of this, and seeing the fearful odds he was to encounter, he asked to be relieved. This was declined, and there was nothing left for him but to do all that was possible with the force under his command. Lee and the army of Virginia were nearer Washington than McClellan. General Burn- side had brought his army to Fortress Monroe, ready to coöperate with McClellan. A bold move upon Richmond would keep Lee on the defensive, but such a movement under McClellan—judging from the past—could scarcely be expected. It was determined to withdraw McClellan's army from the James, and concentrate it with the command of Pope. Pope was active and vigilant, and did all that could be done with the force under his control. On the 14th of August, he was reinforced by General Reno's division of Burnside's army. On the 16th, he captured a letter of General Lee to Stuart, showing that Lee was preparing to mass an overwhelming force in his front, and crush him before he could be re-enforced from the army of the Poto-

mac. He retired on the night of the 18th behind the Rappahannock. The presence of the army of McClellan was
now imperatively needed, and its absence made Pope's position critical.

Where was it, and why did it not coöperate with Pope?
It made no movement towards Richmond nor towards Pope.
Why was this, and who was responsible for Pope's defeat?
Let us examine the orders which were sent to McClellan,
and try to determine whether he honestly and in good faith
obeyed these orders, or whether he sullenly disregarded
them, and left Pope to be crushed. As early as the 30th of
July, McClellan had been ordered to send away his sick and
wounded, and to clear his hospitals, preparatory to moving.
This order was repeated August 2d. On the 3d, he was
directed to prepare to withdraw his army to Acquia Creek, a
stream that empties into the Potomac, and within supporting distance of Pope. He remonstrated, delayed obedience,
and remained where he was until the 6th. He was then
advised that "the order to withdraw would not be
rescinded," and it was said to him, with emphasis: "You
will be expected to obey it with all *possible promptness*." On
the 6th, he was ordered to send a regiment of cavalry and
several batteries to Burnside, who was at Acquia Creek.
Instead of obeying promptly, he sent reasons for still further delay, and said he would "obey as soon as circumstances would permit it."

McClellan did not arrive at Alexandria until August
26th. On the 9th, General Halleck telegraphed as follows :
" I am of the opinion that the enemy is massing his forces
in front of Generals Pope and Burnside, and that he expects
to crush them, and move forward to the Potomac. You
must send re-enforcements instantly to Acquia Creek. Considering the amount of transportation at your disposal, your
delay is not satisfactory. You must move with all possible
celerity ! " This was August 9th, and· yet re-enforcements
did not leave Fortress Monroe for Acquia, until the 23d
of August ! On the 10th, a week after the order was

first given, Halleck again telegraphed : " The enemy is crossing the Rapidan in large force. They are fighting General Pope to-day. There *must be* no *further delay* in your movements. That which has already occurred was entirely unexpected, and must be satisfactorily explained."

Pope was gallantly fighting against an overwhelming force. Lee was massing troops to crush him and reach Washington, and yet McClellan did not move. On the 12th of August, General Halleck telegraphed :

" The Quartermaster General informs me that nearly every available steam vessel in the country is now under your control. Burnside moved nearly thirteen thousand troops to Acquia Creek in less than two days, and his transports were immediately sent back to you. All the vessels in the James River and the Chesapeake Bay were placed at your disposal, and it was supposed that eight or ten thousand of your men could be transported daily. There has been, and is, the most urgent necessity for dispatch, and not a single moment must be lost in getting additional troops in front of Washington."

On the 21st, Halleck again telegraphed to McClellan at Fortress Monroe :

" The forces of Burnside and Pope are hard pushed, and require aid as rapidly as you can send it. By all means see that the troops sent have plenty of ammunition," etc.

On the evening of August 23d, the reluctant and tardy McClellan at last sailed from Fortress Monroe, arriving at Acquia Creek on the morning of the 24th, and at Alexandria on the 27th of August !

It would seem that no candid mind can read the correspondence between Halleck and McClellan and the President, from early August until September, without being convinced that McClellan neglected to obey orders, and that he did so with a knowledge of the dangerous position of Pope. If Porter, or any of McClellan's lieutenants had been in the position of Pope, would he have been left to fight, with the force at his command, the battles of the 27th, 28th, and 29th of August ?

It may be asked—as it often has been—why was not

McClellan removed? He was popular with his army. His subordinates were generally his friends. He was the head, and expected candidate of the democratic party for the Presidency. It had been the earnest endeavor of Mr. Lincoln to unite and combine with the republican party all of the democrats who were loyal to the Union; the removal of McClellan would be regarded by many as a political movement, and for these and other political reasons, his removal was considered unwise.

Meanwhile Pope was being driven towards Washington, by Jackson, Longstreet, and Lee himself, and neither Porter, nor Franklin, nor any of McClellan's subordinates, came to his aid. Porter, although within the sound of Pope's artillery and the rebel guns, and conscious of his critical position, did not go to his support. He was tried for his disobedience to orders, found guilty, and dismissed from the army. This judgment the President approved.

It is not intended to review the trial of Porter. [1] His

---

1. At 12 o'clock, on the 27th of August, Halleck telegraphed to McClellan: "Telegrams from Porter to Burnside." "Porter is marching on Warrenton to re-enforce Pope." * * "Porter reports a general battle imminent. Franklin's corps should move out by forced marches," etc.

On the 25th Halleck telegraphed to McClellan:

"Not a moment must be lost in pushing as large a force as possible towards Manassas, so as to communicate with Pope before the enemy is re-enforced." See Report on the Conduct of War, Pt. 1, pp. 459, 461.

On the same day he telegraphed again:

"There must be no further delay in moving Franklin's corps towards Manassas; they must go to-morrow morning, ready or not ready. If we delay too long to get ready, there will be no necessity to go at all, for Pope will either be defeated or victorious, without our aid. If there is a want of wagons, the men must carry provisions with them till the wagons can come to their relief."

At 3 P. M., on the 29th, Halleck telegraphed to McClellan, in reply to his dispatch of 12 M.:

"I want Franklin's corps to go far enough to find out something about the enemy. Perhaps he may get such information at Anandale as to prevent his going further, otherwise he will push on towards Fairfax. Try to get something from direction of Manassas, either by telegram or through Franklin's scouts. Our people *must* move more actively, and find out where the enemy is. I am tired of guesses."

At 2:40, the President, in his intense anxiety to know the fate of the army fighting against odds, telegraphed to McClellan to know: "What news from direction of Manassas Junction? What generally?"

At 2:45, General McClellan replied:

"The last news I received from the direction of Manassas, was from stragglers, to the effect that the enemy were evacuating Centreville, and retiring towards Thor-

conduct has been much discussed.   He was found guilty by
a court of general officers, composed of men of the highest
character.   There does not seem to be any room for doubt
that he did not give Pope his loyal and hearty support.
Some of his apologists have said that this ought not to
have been expected ; that it was not in human nature.
This depends on the sort of human nature.   A true
patriot and soldier would have forgotten his grievances, and
those of his chief ; would have been at the front in the battle.   His duty clearly was to do his utmost to relieve Pope.
Few candid men will believe he did this.   Suppose McClellan had been in the position of Pope—are there any who
believe Fitz-John Porter would have left him alone " to get
out of his scrape ? "   Or suppose Porter had been fighting
Lee and his whole army, as Pope was, would it have taken
McClellan an entire month to come up the Potomac to his
relief ?   No, McClellan would have joined his favorite lieutenant long before the arrival of Longstreet, and Lee would
have had to meet the combined armies.   If McClellan had
been exposed as Pope was, the guns of Porter would have
been playing upon the enemy, and not at rest in sullen
silence in his camp.

On the 2d of September, Pope fell back to the fortifications of Washington.   The situation was critical.   As Pope
retired to Washington, Lee advanced towards Maryland,

oughfare Gap. This is by no means reliable. I am clear that one of two courses
should be adopted : *First,* To concentrate all our available forces to open communication with Pope.   *Second, To leave Pope to get out of his scrape,* and at once use all
means to make the capital perfectly safe.   No middle course will now answer.   Tell
me what you wish me to do, and I will do all in my power to accomplish it.   I wish
to know what my orders and authority are.   I ask for nothing, but will obey whatever orders you give.   I only ask a prompt decision, that I may at once give the necessary orders.   It will not do to delay longer "

General Halleck telegraphed the following peremptory order, at 7:30, on the
29th :

" You will immediately send construction train and guards to repair the railroad
to Manassas.   Let there be no delay in this.   I have just been told that Franklin's
corps stopped at Anandale, and that he was this evening at Alexandria.   This is all
contrary to my orders.   Investigate and report the fact of this disobedience.   That
corps *must* push forward as I directed, to protect the railroad, and open communication with Manassas."

threatening the capital. The defeat of Pope might have been prevented by the union and co-operation with him of McClellan. Two courses of action were discussed in the Cabinet of Mr. Lincoln. One, urged by the friends of McClellan, was to place him in command of all the forces, including the remnants of the army of Virginia; the other, to arrest him and some of his subordinates, and try them for disobedience and insubordination. General Halleck, the Secretary of War, and others, charged him with being responsible for the defeat of Pope, and many in high positions declared that he ought to be shot for his military offences. It was one of the most critical periods of the war. Party spirit was a violent faction in Congress, and as represented by the press, was intemperate. The army was split by cabals, jealousies, and quarrels. This, with defeat and disaster in the field, made the prospect gloomy and perilous, but the President's fortitude and courage did not desert him. Unselfish and firm, he trusted in the people and in God. That firm belief in an overruling Providence, which some called superstition, sustained him in this the darkest hour.

McClellan was the representative man of the so-called war democrats. He had the confidence of his officers, and was personally popular with the soldiers. The President yielded to the military necessity, or supposed military necessity, and placed him again in command of all the troops, and McClellan assumed the responsibility of defending the capital, and defeating Lee. Indeed, it seems the wisest thing he could have done. The army of the Potomac was demoralized, some of it on the verge of mutiny, and the conduct of Franklin and Fitz-John Porter indicates the spirit in which McClellan's lieutenants would have supported any other chief. With Lee and his victorious troops menacing Washington, it was a military necessity; Lincoln, with his usual good sense, saw and yielded to it.

CHAPTER XVII.

ANTIETAM AND CHANCELLORSVILLE.

HARPER'S FERRY CAPTURED.—ANTIETAM.—McCLELLAN'S DELAY.—
RELIEVED OF COMMAND.—BURNSIDE APPOINTED HIS SUCCESSOR.
—FREDERICKSBURG.—BURNSIDE RESIGNS.—HOOKER SUCCEEDS
HIM.—LINCOLN'S LETTER TO HOOKER.—CHANCELLORSVILLE.

LINCOLN now magnanimously gave General McClellan
another and a splendid opportunity to achieve success. His
command embraced the army of the Potomac, the remains
of the army of Pope, and the troops of Burnside, while to
these were added the large number of recruits and volunteers which poured in from the loyal states, so that he had,
before November, more than two hundred thousand soldiers
under his command.

If he had possessed to any extent the elements of a hero,
if he could have led a rapid and brilliant campaign, he had
now the opportunity, and the people would have eagerly
crowned him with the laurels of victory. But as soon as he
was settled in his command, he continued to make the old
complaints and calls for more troops. He wished those
engaged in the defense of Washington sent to him, even if
the capital should fall into the hands of the enemy.[1]

Colonel Miles and General Julius White, in September,
1862, occupied the picturesque village of Harper's Ferry,
with some twelve thousand soldiers. On the 11th, McClellan asked that these troops be directed to join his army.
That order was not given, but it was suggested to him that

---

1. He wished the troops sent to him, "even if Washington should be taken."
 *   *   "That would not bear comparison with a single defeat of this
army." Report on Conduct of the War, Pt. 1, p. 39.

he open communication with Harper's Ferry, and that then these troops would be under his command. On the 13th, he knew that Lee's army was divided, and that Jackson had been detached from the main army for the purpose of capturing Harper's Ferry. McClellan by promptness could have saved Harper's Ferry. Swinton, who excuses him when he can, says: "If he had thrown forward his army with the vigor used by Jackson * * * he could have relieved Harper's Ferry, which did not surrender until the 15th." [1] Palfrey, in his "Antietam and Fredericksburg," says: "He was not equal to the occasion. He threw away his chance, and a precious opportunity of making a great name passed away." [2]

On the 17th, was fought the bloody battle of Antietam. Of this battle, alluding to McClellan's delay in attacking while Lee's forces were divided, Palfrey says : " He fought his battle *one day too late, if not two.*" "He did very little in the way of compelling the execution of his orders." [3] A very large portion of his army did not participate in the battle, and Palfrey adds: "It is probable, almost to a point of certainty, that if a great part of the Second and Fifth corps, and all the Sixth, animated by the personal presence of McClellan, had attacked vigorously in the center, and Burnside on the Federal left, * * * the result would have been the *practical annihilation of Lee's army!*" [4]

McClellan, against the advice of Burnside and others, decided not to renew the attack on the 18th. "It is," says Palfrey, "hardly worth while to state his reasons." Two divisions had joined him. "The fault was in the man. There was force enough at his command either day had he seen fit to use it." [5] By the time that McClellan got ready to renew the attack Lee was gone. On the 18th, the enemy

1. Swinton's Army of the Potomac, p. 202.

2. Palfrey's " Antietam and Fredericksburg," p. 41.

3. Palfrey's " Antietam and Fredericksburg," p. 119.

4. Palfrey's "Antietam and Fredericksburg," pp. 121-122.

5. Palfrey's " Antietam and Fredericksburg," p. 127.

were permitted to retire across the Potomac. The Union army slowly followed, occupying Maryland Heights on the 20th, and Harper's Ferry on the 23d of September. On the 7th of October, Halleck telegraphed to McClellan that "the army *must* move. The country is becoming very impatient at the want of activity of your army, and we must push it on."

The President was also impatient at these slow movements of McClellan, and to a friend of the General's who called at the White House, he said, doubtless with the expectation that it would be repeated : " McClellan's tardiness reminds me of a man in Illinois, whose attorney was not sufficiently aggressive. The client knew a few law phrases, and finally, after waiting until his patience was exhausted by the non-action of his counsel, he sprang to his feet and exclaimed: 'Why don't you go at him with a *fi. fa.*, *demurrer*, a *capias*, a *surrebutter*, or a *ne exeat*, or something; and not stand there like a *nudum pactum*, or a *non est ?* ' "

By the 6th of October, the President's impatience of McClellan's long delay induced him to telegraph the General: " The President directs that you cross the Potomac and give battle to the enemy or drive him South." McClellan did not obey. On the 10th, Stuart, a rebel cavalry officer, crossed the Potomac, went as far as Chambersburg in Pennsylvania, made the circuit of the Federal army, and re-crossed the Potomac without serious loss. This was the second time Confederate cavalry had been permitted to ride entirely around McClellan's army. On the 13th of October, the President made one more effort to induce McClellan to act, by writing him a long and kindly personal letter.[1]

1. The letter was as follows :

" *My Dear Sir:*—You remember my speaking to you of what I called your over-cautiousness. Are you not over-cautious when you assume that you cannot do what the enemy is constantly doing? Should you not claim to be at least his equal in prowess, and act upon the claim?

"As I understand, you telegraphed General Halleck that you cannot subsist your army at Winchester, unless the railroad from Harper's Ferry to that point be put in working order. But the enemy does now subsist his army at Winchester, at a distance nearly twice as great from railroad transportation, as you would have to do without the railroad last named. He now wagons from Culpepper Court House, which is just

Near the end of October McClellan started, and on the
2d of November his army crossed the Potomac. Thus
the autumn had gone by, from the battle of Antietam on the
17th of September until the 2d of November, before
McClellan crossed the Potomac. The President had written, begged, and entreated McClellan to act. In his letter of
October 13th, he says: " I say *try*. If we never try, we
shall never succeed." "We should not operate so as to

about twice as far as you would have to do from Harper's Ferry. He is certainly not
more than half as well provided with wagons as you are. I certainly should be pleased
for you to have the advantage of the railroad from Harper's Ferry to Winchester; but
it wastes all the remainder of autumn to give it to you, and, in fact, ignores the
question of *time* which cannot and must not be ignored.

"Again, one of the standard maxims of war, as you know, is, 'to operate upon
the enemy's communications as much as possible without exposing your own.' You
seem to act as if this applies *against* you, but cannot apply in your *favor*. Change
positions with the enemy, and think you not he would break your communication with
Richmond within the next twenty-four hours? You dread his going into Pennsylvania.
But if he does so in full force, he gives up his communication to you absolutely, and
you have nothing to do, but to follow and ruin him; if he does so with less than full
force, fall upon and beat what is left behind, all the easier.

" Exclusive of the water line, you are now nearer Richmond than the enemy is,
by the route that you *can*, and he *must* take. Why can you not reach there before him,
unless you admit that he is more than your equal on a march. His route is the arc of
a circle, while yours is the chord. The roads are as good on yours as on his.

" You know I desired, but did not order you, to cross the Potomac below, instead
of above the Shenandoah and Blue Ridge. The idea was that this would at once
menace the enemy's communications, which I would seize, if he would permit. If he
should move northward, I would follow him closely, holding his communications. If
he should prevent our seizing his communications, and move towards Richmond, I
would press closely to him, fight him if a favorable opportunity should present, and
at least try to beat him to Richmond on the inside track. I say try; if we never try,
we shall never succeed. If he makes a stand at Winchester, moving neither north
nor south, I would fight him there, on the idea that if we cannot beat him when he
bears the wastage of coming to us, we never can when we bear the wastage of going
to him. This proposition is a simple truth, and is too important to be lost sight of for
a moment. In coming to us, he tenders us an advantage which we should not waive.
We should not so operate as to merely drive him away. As we must beat him some-
where, or fail finally, we can do it, if at all, easier near to us than far away. If we
cannot beat the enemy where he now is, we never can, he again being within the
intrenchments of Richmond.

" Recurring to the idea of going to Richmond on the inside track, the facility for
supplying from the side away from the enemy, is remarkable, as it were by the different spokes of a wheel extending from the hub towards the rim, and this, whether you
move directly by the chord or on the inside arc, hugging the Blue Ridge more closely.
The chord line, as you see, carries you by Aldie, Haymarket, and Fredericksburg, and
you see how turnpikes, railroads, and finally the Potomac, by Acquia Creek, meet you
at all points from Washington. The same, only the lines lengthened a little, if you
press closer to the Blue Ridge part of the way. The gaps through the Blue Ridge, I

merely to drive him (the enemy) away." In a dispatch on the 27th day of October, the President says: "I now ask a distinct answer to the question: "Is it your purpose not to go into action again until the men now being drafted are incorporated in the old regiments?"[1] The patience of Mr. Lincoln was finally exhausted, and, on the 5th of November, he issued an order relieving McClellan, and directing him to turn over the command to General Burnside. Thus ends the military career of George B. McClellan.

The judgment of General Palfrey, who served under him, is certainly not too severe. He sums up his military history in these words: "His interminable and inexcusable delays upon the Peninsula afforded great ground for dissatisfaction, and they seemed—to say no more—to be followed by similar delays upon the Potomac." "He never made his personal presence felt on a battle-field."[2]

McClellan retired to New Jersey, to emerge no more except as the candidate for the Presidency, in 1864, of the party who declared "the war a failure." He contributed to this failure, in so far as it was one—considering the means at his command to make it a success—more than almost any other man. But he himself was the most conspicuous failure of the war. After all his disasters and delays upon the Peninsula, the President generously re-instated him in command, and at Antietam and afterwards, he had golden opportunities to redeem his failure. He was retained long after

understand to be about the following distances from Harper's Ferry, to-wit: Vestala, five miles; Gregory's, thirteen; Snicker's, eighteen; Ashby's, twenty-eight; Manassas, thirty-eight; Chester, forty-five; and Thornton's, fifty-three. I should think it preferable to take the route nearest the enemy, disabling him to make an important move without your knowledge, and compelling him to keep his forces together for dread of you. The gaps would enable you to attack if you should wish. For a great part of the way you would be practically between the enemy and both Washington and Richmond, enabling us to spare you the greatest number of troops from here. When at length, running for Richmond ahead of him, enable him to move his way; if he does so, turn and attack him in rear. But I think he should be engaged long before such point is reached. It is all easy if our troops march as well as the enemy, and it is unmanly to say they cannot do it. This letter is in no sense an order.

"Yours truly,   A. Lincoln."

1. Report on Conduct of the War, pt. 1, p. 525.

2. Palfrey's "Antietam and Fredericksburg," p. 133–134.

his removal had been demanded by the friends of the President. The patience, fidelity, and forbearance of the President in his treatment of McClellan, are strikingly illustrated by his correspondence. History will censure him for adhering to the General too long rather than for any failure to support him. But McClellan was a courteous gentleman, whose personal character was amiable and respectable. Mr. Lincoln respected his private virtues, and said of him: "With all his failings as a soldier, McClellan is a pleasant and scholarly gentleman. He is an admirable engineer, but," he added, "he seems to have a special talent for a *stationary engine.*"

On the 9th of November General Burnside assumed command of the great army. He was a frank and manly soldier, of fine person, and everywhere respected as a gentleman and an unselfish patriot. He accepted the high position with diffidence, and with the consciousness that he would scarcely receive the earnest coöperation of the favorite generals of McClellan. On the 12th of this month, Generals Halleck and Meigs visited him in his camp, and held a conference on the movements to be made. Halleck and Burnside failed to agree, and the subject was referred to the President. Burnside's plan was to make a feint on Gordonsville, but to concentrate rapidly and attack Fredericksburg. The President, in assenting to Burnside's plan as reported by Halleck, said to the General: "He thinks it (the plan) will succeed if you move rapidly; otherwise not."

The absolute necessity of rapid movement, and the crossing of the Rappahannock before Lee could concentrate his army and fortify Fredericksburg, were obvious. By some misunderstanding or gross neglect, the pontoons with which to cross the river were not sent forward in time. This delay was fatal in its consequences. Burnside arrived at Falmouth, on the banks of the Rappahannock, on the 19th of November, but the pontoons did not arrive until the 25th. By this delay, all the advantages of surprise were lost; the enemy had time to concentrate his army on the heights overlooking Fredericksburg, to intrench and prepare to meet the attack.   There has been much discussion as to who was responsible for this delay in the arrival of the pontoons. Considering the importance of their being there in time, and that the fate of the movement depended on their presence when needed, it would seem that all were negligent—Halleck, and Meigs, and Burnside.   Each should have known personally that the pontoons were there in time.   When, on the 13th of December, Burnside attacked Fredericksburg, he found Lee with his army concentrated and occupying a strong position which had been well and skillfully fortified. The assault on these works was gallantly made, but, as might have been anticipated, was repulsed with terrible slaughter.   Lee occupied a fortified ridge, the approach to which was swept by artillery.   It is difficult to understand why this army should have been ordered across a river like the Rappahannock, and to assault a fortified position so well covered by breast-works and rifle-pits ; or why, when the delay of the pontoons and failure to surprise the enemy rendered success impossible, some flank movement, such as was repeatedly made by Sherman and Grant, should not have been made, thus forcing the enemy to battle on more equal ground.

After a fearful loss of life, the troops were withdrawn to Falmouth, and there the two armies confronted each other from the opposite banks of the river.[1]

In the campaign of 1862, in the East, the results were on the whole favorable to the rebels.   With a much smaller force, they kept the Union army during all the autumn of 1861 and the winter of 1862 in the defences of Washington. They blockaded the Potomac.   They had, by the blunders and want of vigor of McClellan, repulsed him from Richmond.   They had sent Stonewall Jackson like an eagle swooping down through the valley of the Shenandoah, driving Banks across the Potomac, and escaping from Fremont

---

1. It is no more than justice to McClellan to say, that he never sacrificed his soldiers by a blunder like this.

and McDowell.   They had frightened McClellan from Richmond without ever decidedly defeating his combined army. On the contrary, his troops often gained great advantages over the rebels, yet he would never follow up these successes and seize the fruits of victory; but always, after knocking the enemy down, would stop, call for re-enforcements, or run away from them.

Then came the hard fought campaign of Pope, when, if McClellan and Porter had loyally obeyed and heartily coöperated with Pope, the armies of McClellan, Pope, and Burnside would have been consolidated on the field of Manassas, and would have crushed the much smaller force of Lee. Then came the rebel march into Maryland, the battle of Antietam, a repulse of Lee which ought to have been a crushing defeat, followed again by the long delays of McClellan—a dreary waste of time, and of inactive complaint. Then came McClellan's removal, Burnside's campaign, and the slaughter of Fredericksburg. Such is the sad story of the brave but badly commanded army of the Potomac to the close of 1862.

Burnside survived his terrible defeat; survived to render good but subordinate service on the field, and died a useful and respected senator in Congress from Rhode Island.

The progress of the Union armies was also checked in the West. Buell was forced back, and the rebel General Bragg entered Kentucky, and occupied Frankfort, Lexington, and other important positions. A provisional government was organized by the rebels at Frankfort. Louisville and Cincinnati were threatened and fortified. On the 8th of October, the battle of Perryville was fought. On the 25th, Buell was superseded by General Rosecrans.

Vicksburg, on the Mississippi, a strong position by nature, and fortified with skill, was still an insurmountable obstacle to the complete recovery by the Union troops of the Mississippi. Generals Sherman and McClernand, on the 29th of December, 1862, made a gallant assault upon the defences in the rear of this stronghold, but were repulsed with serious loss. On the 31st of December, the Union army under Rosecrans fought the battle of Stone River, where there was great loss on both sides, but the rebels, under their able leader, Johnston, retreated to Murfreesboro.

The year 1862 closed in gloom. There had been vast expenditures of blood and treasure by the government, and great successes, yet the Union cause had suffered still greater defeats and many grievous disasters, and the hopes of the insurgents rose high.

The President was greatly depressed by the terrible defeat at Fredericksburg, and especially by the great and useless sacrifice of the lives of his gallant soldiers. The leading generals of the army of the Potomac were quarreling and abusing each other. Burnside demanded the peremptory removal of several of them, and among others that of Hooker, making this the condition of his retaining his own command. The Cabinet was divided, and its members denouncing each other. Faction ran high in Congress, and the committee on the conduct of war became censorious and abusive. The press grew bitter, arrogant, and denunciatory, Mr. Greeley in the New York Tribune demanding foreign intervention, and declaring to Raymond that he would drive Lincoln into it.[1]

Leading officers of the army went so far as to say that " both the army and the government needed a dictator." [2] During these gloomy days, in which it seemed that many of the leading men in civil and military life lost their heads, and were ready for almost any change, however wild, the President was calm, patient, tolerant of those who differed from him, and hopeful. At this crisis, when his generals were denouncing each other, his Cabinet quarreling and making combinations against him, Congress factious, foreign nations hostile and ready to recognize the Confederacy, and some in high position calling for a dictator, it is not too

1. Private Journal of Henry J. Raymond, printed in Scribner's Magazine, March, 1880.

2. *See* Letter of Lincoln to Hooker, dated January 26, 1863, quoted hereafter.

much to say that Lincoln bore on his Atlantean shoulders the fate of the republic, that his firm, vigorous hand saved the country from anarchy and ruin.

On the 26th of January, the President sent the following letter to General Hooker :

EXECUTIVE MANSION, WASHINGTON, D. C.,
January 26, 1863.

MAJOR GENERAL HOOKER.—*General :* I have placed you at the head of the army of the Potomac. Of course I have done this upon what appear to me to be sufficient reasons ; and yet I think it best for you to know that there are some things in regard to which I am not satisfied with you. I believe you to be a brave and skillful soldier, which of course I like. I also believe that you do not mix politics with your profession, in which you are right. You have confidence in yourself, which is a valuable if not indispensable quality. You are ambitious, which, within reasonable bounds, does good rather than harm ; but I think that, during General Burnside's command of the army, you have taken counsel of your ambition, and thwarted him as much as you could, in which you did a great wrong to the country, and to a most meritorious and honorable brother officer. I have heard, in such a way as to believe it, of your recently saying that both the army and the government needed a dictator. Of course, it was not for this, but in spite of it, that I have given you the command. Only those generals who gain success can be dictators. What I now ask of you is military success, and I will risk the dictatorship. The government will support you to the utmost of its ability, which is neither more nor less than it has done and will do for all commanders. I much fear that the spirit which you have aided to infuse into the army, of criticizing their commander and withholding confidence from him, will now turn upon you. I shall assist you as far as I can to put it down. Neither you nor Napoleon, if he were alive again, could get any good out of an army while such a spirit prevails in it. And now, beware of rashness. Beware of rashness, but, with energy and sleepless vigilance, go forward and give us victories.

Yours, very truly,   A. LINCOLN.

Hooker passed three months in preparation, and then suffered the terrible defeat of Chancellorsville, and again was the brave army of the Potomac beaten by superior generalship. Among the misfortunes of the rebels in this battle was the death of their most brilliant soldier, Stonewall Jackson. It was the nature of Mr. Lincoln to do full justice to his enemies. His heart was touched by the death of Jackson, and he said to a friend [1] who praised the dead : " I honor you for your generosity to one who, though contending against us in a guilty cause, was a gallant man. Let us forget his sins over his fresh made grave."

1. Col. J. W. Forney, editor.

CHAPTER XVIII.

THE TIDE TURNS.

The Conscription.— West Virginia Admitted.— The War Powers.— Suspension of Habeas Corpus.— Case of Vallandigham.— Grant's Capture of Vicksburg.— Gettysburg.— Lincoln's Speech.

We now approach the turning point in this great civil war. Up to 1863, the fortunes of the conflict had been so varied ; victory and defeat had so alternated, that neither party to the struggle could point to anything absolutely decisive. After the Union defeats at Fredericksburg and Chancellorsville, the world of spectators seemed to think the probabilities of success were with the rebels. But in the summer of 1863, the tide turned, and a series of successes followed the national armies, which rendered their triumph only a question of time. Before entering upon a narration of these successes, we must turn for a brief space from the camp and battle field to the halls of Congress.

During this entire conflict, public opinion was guided, and largely controlled, by the pen and the tongue of the President. No voice was so potent as his, either in Congress or elsewhere, to create and guide public opinion. His administration was continually assailed by the democratic party, and criticised, often with asperity and injustice, by the leading members of his own party. The great leaders of the press were fault-finding, unjust, and often unfriendly. This threw upon him, in addition to all his other great difficulties and cares, the burden of explaining and defending the measures of his administration. He made many speeches, and wrote many letters, in addition to his messages and state papers. His frankness and sincerity, his unselfish patriotism, and his great ability as a speaker and writer, were never more strikingly illustrated than in those speeches and writings.

When Congress convened, in December, 1862, the President communicated the fact of his proclamation of the 22d of September. The absolute necessity of national union was never presented in a more statesmanlike manner than in this message. He says :

" A nation may be said to consist of its territory, its people, and its laws. The territory is the only part which is of certain duration. ' One generation passeth away, and another generation cometh, but the earth abideth forever.' That portion of the earth's surface which is owned and inhabited by the people of the United States, is well adapted to be the home of one national family ; and it is not well adapted for two, or more. Its vast extent, and its variety of climate and productions, are of advantage, in this age, for one people, whatever they might have been in former ages. Steam, telegraphs, and intelligence, have brought these to be an advantageous combination for one united people. * * *

* There is no line, straight or crooked, suitable for a national boundary, upon which to divide. Trace through, from East to West, upon the line between the free and slave country, and we shall find a little more than one-third of its length are rivers, easy to be crossed, and populated, or soon to be populated thickly upon both sides ; while nearly all its remaining length are merely surveyor's lines, over which people may walk back and forth, without any consciousness of their presence. No part of this line can be made any more difficult to pass by writing it down on paper or parchment as a national boundary. The fact of separation, if it comes, gives up on the part of the seceding section the fugitive slave clause, along with all other constitutional obligations upon the section seceded from, while I should expect no treaty stipulations would ever be made to take its place.

" But there is another difficulty. The great interior region, bounded east by the Alleghanies, north by the British dominions, west by the Rocky Mountains, and south by the line along which the culture of corn and cotton meets, and which includes part of Virginia, part of Tennessee, all of Kentucky, Ohio, Indiana, Michigan, Wisconsin, Illinois, Missouri, Kansas, Iowa, Minnesota, and the territories of Dakota, Nebraska, and part of Colorado, already has above ten million people, and will have fifty millions within fifty years, if not prevented by any political folly or mistake. It contains more than one-third of the country owned by the United States, certainly more than one million square miles. Once half as populous as Massachusetts already is, it would have more than seventy-five million people. A glance at the map shows that, territorially speaking, it is the great body of the republic. The other parts are but marginal borders to it, the magnificent region sloping west from the Rocky Mountains to the Pacific, being the deepest, and also the richest in undeveloped resources. In the production of provisions, grains, grasses, and all which proceed from them, this great interior region is naturally one of the most important in the world. Ascertain from statistics the small proportion of the region which has, as yet, been brought into cultivation, and also the large and rapidly increasing amount of its products, and we shall be overwhelmed with the magnitude of the prospect presented. And yet this region has no sea-coast, touches no ocean anywhere. As part of one nation, its people may find, and may forever find their way to Europe by New York, to South America and Africa by New Orleans, and to Asia by San Francisco. But separate our common country into two nations, as designed by the present rebellion, and every man of this great interior region is thereby cut off from some one or more of these outlets, not, perhaps, by a physical barrier, but by embarrassing and onerous trade regulations."

Lincoln uttered the convictions, the sentiments, and the unwavering determination of a vast majority of the people of the West, when he declared that the " portion of the earth's surface called the United States is adapted to be the home of *one national* family, and not for two or more."

Lincoln had come to be recognized as not only the leading mind of the Mississippi Valley, but of the republic, and he declared with authority that there could be " no peace except on the basis of national unity." He closes this most statesmanlike paper with these words:

" I do not forget the gravity which should characterize a paper addressed to the Congress of the nation by the Chief Magistrate of the nation. Nor do I forget that some of you are my seniors, nor that many of you have more experience than I in the conduct of public affairs. Yet I trust that in view of the great responsibility resting upon me, you will perceive no want of respect to yourselves in any undue earnestness I may seem to display. * * * The dogmas of the quiet past are inadequate to the stormy present. The occasion is piled high with difficulty, and we must rise with the occasion. As our case is new, so we must think anew and act anew. We must disenthrall ourselves, and then we shall save our country.

" Fellow citizens, we cannot escape history. We, of this Congress and this administration, will be remembered in spite of ourselves. No personal significance, or insignificance, can spare one or another of us. The fiery trial through which we pass will light us down, in honor or dishonor, to the latest generation. We say we are for the Union. The world will not forget that we say this. We know how to save the Union. The world knows we do know how to save it. We—even *we here*—hold the power and bear the responsibility. In *giving* freedom to the *slave* we *assure* freedom to the *free*—honorable alike in what we give and what we preserve. We shall nobly save, or meanly lose, the last, best hope of earth. Other means may succeed, this could not fail. The way is plain, peaceful, generous, just—a way which, if followed, the world will forever applaud, and God must forever bless."

At this session of Congress an enrollment bill providing that all able bodied citizens, black as well as white, should be liable to military duty, and subject to be drafted into service, was passed. The Confederates had nearly a year before passed a much more stringent conscription law. The democratic party opposed vehemently the bill. Senator Kennedy, of Maryland, said : " I stand in the midst of the ruins of the republic. I deplore that I can see no hope from the black gloomy cloud of convulsion and ruin by which we are surrounded." [1]

A law was also passed at this session admitting West Virginia into the Union, upon condition of the abolition of slavery. The great civil war called into exercise, by the Executive and Congress, a class of powers called war powers ; powers dormant until the exigencies arose demanding their exercise, and of the existence of which many of the statesmen of the republic had been unconscious. The people, educated to an appreciation of the full value of the quiet securities of liberty embraced in Magna Charta, and still more perfectly in the Constitution of the United States, were always jealous of the exercise of extraordinary powers. Those safeguards of liberty: freedom of the press, liberty of speech, personal security protected by the writ of

1. Congressional Globe, 37th Congress, p. 1374.

habeas corpus, an independent judiciary, a speedy and fair trial by jury, the old, time-honored principles of the common law that no person should be deprived of life, liberty, or property but by due and impartial process of law and judgment of his peers ; these great principles were the foundations of our government. They were revered as sacred, and no people were ever more jealous or watchful of every encroachment upon them. In these principles the President, as a lawyer, had been educated, and he was slow and reluctant to assume the exercise of the vast and novel and ill-defined powers growing out of insurrection and war. Imperative necessity forced him to the exercise of such powers. The rebels, and those who sympathized with them, claimed all the rights of citizens. They claimed that even while waging war against the Constitution, they should enjoy all the rights of citizenship under it ; that while they made war on the government, they could claim its protection as citizens. Mr. Lincoln was reluctant to proclaim martial law, even where conspirators were plotting treason and organizing rebellion. He suffered the rebels, Breckenridge and others, to talk rebellion and organize treason at the national capital without arrest, and then to leave and join the rebel armies. But the public safety finally compelled him to exercise the powers necessary to preserve the life of the republic. He saved Maryland to the Union, and prevented a bloody civil war among its citizens, by causing General McClellan to arrest the Maryland Legislature, when it was about to pass an act of secession. He proclaimed martial law, suspended the writ of habeas corpus, and caused persons to be summarily arrested who held criminal intercourse with the enemy. The suspension of the writ of habeas corpus is authorized by the Federal Constitution, " when in cases of rebellion or invasion the public safety may require it." But who is to judge when the public safety does require it? Congress may authorize the Executive to exercise this power. But the exigency and necessity for its exercise may arise when Congress is not in session. If so, may the President, or a military commander, do it when and where public safety demands it ? These, and cognate questions, were most earnestly discussed by the public press, in Congress, and before judicial tribunals ; and these discussions may be regarded as settling the question that the President may rightfully exercise this power when and where such necessity exists, and that of this necessity he must in the first instance judge. [1]

The case of Vallandigham, who was arrested, tried by court martial, found guilty of expressing in public speeches disloyal sentiments, and sentenced to confinement during the war, was very much discussed. Public meetings were held at Albany, New York, and in Ohio, by the democratic friends of Vallandigham, and memorials were drawn up and presented to the President, asking him to restore Vallandigham to liberty. To these memorials the President made full and careful replies, in which, with the clearness, earnestness, and great ability for which his papers were distinguished, he discussed the questions involved. These papers of the President went far towards satisfying the public mind that such arrests were but the proper exercise of the legal powers of the Executive. In these papers there is exhibited that clear, simple statement and argument, by which Mr. Lincoln always made himself perfectly understood by the mass of the people, and by which he rarely failed to carry conviction. He said:

"Of how little value the constitutional provisions I have quoted will be rendered, if arrests shall never be made until defined crimes shall have been committed, may be illustrated by a few notable examples. General John C. Breckenridge, General Robert E. Lee, General Joseph E. Johnston, General John B. Magruder, General William B. Preston, General Simon B. Buckner, and Commodore Franklin Buchanan, now occupying the very highest places in the rebel war service, were all within the power of the government since the rebellion began, and were nearly as well-known to be traitors then as now. Unquestionably if we had seized and held them, the insurgent cause would be much weaker. But no one of

1. See opinion of Chief Justice Parsons. Reprinted in McPherson's " History of the Rebellion," pp. 162-163.

them had then committed any crime defined in the law. Every one of them, if arrested, would have been discharged on habeas corpus were the writ allowed to operate. In view of these and similar cases, I think the time not unlikely to come, when I shall be blamed for having made too few arrests rather than too many. * * * * Long experience has shown that armies cannot be maintained unless desertion shall be punished by the severe penalty of death. The case requires, and the law and the Constitution sanctions, this punishment. Must I shoot a simple-minded soldier-boy who deserts, while I must not touch a hair of a wily agitator who induces him to desert? This is none the less injurious when effected by getting a father, or brother, or friend into a public meeting, and there working upon his feelings till he is persuaded to write the soldier-boy that he is fighting in a bad cause, for a wicked administration of a contemptible government, too weak to arrest and punish him if he shall desert. I think that, in such a case, to silence the agitator and save the boy is not only constitutional, but withal a great mercy."

This correspondence satisfied all the loyal people that these war powers would be used by the President only to the extent of maintaining the government, that the rights of no individual would be wantonly violated, and that the liberties of the people were entirely safe in the hands of Abraham Lincoln.[1]

After a very full and able discussion in the Senate and in the House, a law was passed on the 3d of March, 1863, authorizing the President, whenever during the existence of the rebellion the public safety might require, to suspend the writ of habeas corpus throughout the United States, or any part thereof.

The President often spoke upon the absolute necessity that our country should be the home of " one national family, and no more." His convictions on this subject so ably presented to Congress in December, 1862, were often expressed. To restore this so necessary union, the President and his military advisers planned the campaign of 1863. To open the Mississippi by capturing Vicksburg was the great objective point of the campaign in the West. The President

---

1. See McPherson's History of the Rebellion, pp. 163-167, for this correspondence in full.

was unquestionably the best informed person in the republic concerning its military condition. His rooms at the White House were full of maps and plans, every movement was carefully traced on these maps, and no subordinate was so completely advised of, and master of the military situation as the Commander in Chief. To open the Mississippi, as has been stated, by the capture of the stronghold of Vicksburg, was the great objective point of the campaign in the West, and in the East to destroy the army of Lee, and seize the rebel capital.

Lincoln selected General Grant to lead the difficult enterprise against Vicksburg. There were those high in position, who at that time charged Grant with habits of intoxication, and sought to shake the confidence of the President in him. To such Lincoln replied: "If Grant is a drunkard I wish some of my other generals would give the same evidence of intoxication."

On the 2nd of February, 1863, Grant arrived in the vicinity of Vicksburg, and assumed command. After various fruitless expedients, in April, he finally resolved to send his army by land from Milliken's Bend to a point below Vicksburg, and to run his transports and gunboats past and below the menacing batteries of that city. A large fleet of ironclad gunboats and transports were prepared, protected as far as possible by cotton bales, hay, railroad iron, timber, and chains. The night of the 16th of April was selected for the attempt. Everything was in readiness before dark. The plan was that the iron-clads should pass down in single file —with intervals between them, and when opposite the batteries, should engage them, and that then, under cover of smoke, the transports should endeavor to pass.

The country had been growing impatient of the long delays at Vicksburg. The cutting of the canals and the opening of the bayous had proved failures. All the attempts thus far to flank the stronghold, seemed likely to prove abortive, and great anxiety existed in the public mind. After all these failures, Grant, with a persistence which has marked his whole career, conceived a plan without parallel in military history for its boldness and daring. This was to march his army and send his transportation by land on the Louisiana side of the Mississippi, from Milliken's Bend to a point below Vicksburg; then to run the bristling batteries of that rebel Gibraltar, exposed to its hundreds of heavy guns, with his transports; then to cross the Mississippi below Vicksburg, and returning, attack that city in the rear.

The crews of the frail Mississippi steamers used as transports, conscious of the hazardous service, with one exception refused to go. Volunteers were called for by General Grant, and no sooner was the call made, than from the noble army of the West, pilots, engineers, firemen, and deck-hands offered themselves for the dangerous adventure in such numbers, that it became necessary to select those needed from the crowd of volunteers by lot. Such was the generous emulation among the soldiers to participate in the dangerous service, that one Illinois boy who had drawn the coveted privilege of exposing his life, was offered one hundred dollars in greenbacks for his chance; but he refused to take it, and held his post of honor.

Ten o'clock at night was the hour at which the fleet was to start. At that hour the camps of the Union army were hushed into silence, watching with intense anxiety the result. All was obscurity and silence in front of the city. Soon an indistinct, shadowy mass was seen, dimly, noiselessly floating down the river. It was the flag-ship, the iron-clad Benton. It passed on into the darkness, and another and another followed, until ten black masses, looking like spectral steamers, came out of the darkness, passed by, and disappeared down the river. No sound disturbed the stillness. Every eye was fixed on the space in front of the city; every ear intent, expecting each moment to see the gleam and flash of powder and fire, and hear the thunders of cannon. For three-quarters of an hour the silence was unbroken, when first came a sharp line of light from the extreme right of the batteries, and in an instant after, the whole length of the bluffs was one blaze of fire and roll of crashing thunder. The light exhibited the fleet squarely in front of the city; and immediately its heavy guns were heard in reply, firing directly upon the city. Clouds of smoke enveloped the gunboats, and then the transports, putting on full steam, plunged down the river. The batteries were passed in an hour and a quarter; and although some of the transports were injured and one set on fire, no person on either of them was killed; and General Grant immediately prepared and sent the remaining transports. Meanwhile, the army marched around and struck the river below Vicksburg, nearly opposite Grand Gulf. This was a strong position on the east bank of the Mississippi, below the mouth of the Big Black. It was hoped that Admiral Porter with the gunboats could reduce the batteries at Grand Gulf, after which the troops would be taken over in the transports, and carry the place by assault. But, after nearly five hours bombardment, Admiral Porter drew off his fleet. Grant, after consulting with Porter, adopted a new expedient; this was to march his troops three miles below Grand Gulf, and after night the transports were to run these batteries, as they had done those of Vicksburg. When darkness came, Porter renewed the attack with his gunboats; and amidst the thunder and smoke of this attack, the transports went safely by, and reaching the camps below, cheered the soldiers as they approached, by responding " all's well " to their anxious inquiries. In the morning they were in readiness to transfer the army to the long coveted position below Vicksburg.

Early the next morning, General Grant, on the Benton, led the way to a landing for his eager army. Going ashore at Bruinsburg, he found faithful and intelligent negroes to guide him in the important movements which were now to be made. Instantly the debarkation of the troops commenced, and the line of march was taken up towards Port Gibson. Before two o'clock the next morning, May 1, 1863, the enemy was encountered, and the battle of Port Gibson was fought, the first of the series of battles and victories resulting in the investment and capture of Vicksburg. The attitude of Grant was certainly a bold one. He was in the enemy's country, a fortified city above him, a fortified city below him, a large army gathering under Johnston to assail him and relieve Vicksburg, with another large army to protect and garrison its fortifications. Celerity was of the highest importance. No better troops ever met an enemy than those he commanded; and he was most ably seconded by Sherman, McClernand, McPherson, Logan, Blair, Oster-haus, and others.

To the indomitable will, energy, and activity of Grant, striking the enemy in detail, beating him in every field, giv-ing him no time for concentration, the country is indebted for these wonderful successes, not surpassed by any other achievements in military history. General Grant seemed fully conscious that success in this, the boldest movement of the war, depended upon striking quick and rapid blows, and hence he himself set the example of taking no baggage. He took neither horse nor servant, nor camp chest, nor overcoat, nor blanket; his entire personal bag-gage, according to Washburne, who accompanied him during the six eventful and decisive days from his landing, was a *tooth brush*. During this time, his fare was the common soldier's rations, and his bed the ground, with no covering but the sky.

The victory at Port Gibson was so important that General Grant issued a general order thanking his soldiers, and in a few spirited words advised them that more difficulties and privations were before them, but called upon them to endure these manfully. " Other battles," said he, " are to be fought ; let us fight them bravely. A grateful country will rejoice at our success, and history will record it with immortal honor." Moving rapidly to the north, General Grant interposed his forces between the army of Johnston, seeking to relieve Vicksburg, and the garrison under Pem-berton, seeking a junction with Johnston. Then followed the rapid marches, brilliant with gallant charges and deeds of heroic valor, the victories won in quick succession at Raymond, on the 12th; at Jackson, the capital of Mississippi, on the 14th; at Baker's Creek and Champion Hills on the 16th, and at the Big Black River on the 17th, and finally closing with driving the enemy into his works at Vicksburg, and with the aid of Admiral Porter and the gunboats, completely investing the city. And now, on the 19th of May, Grant and his army were before the stronghold. Jefferson Davis, conscious of the importance of this position, had implored every man who could do so to march to Vicksburg. General Grant now determined to take the city by assault. On the 22d of May, the attack was most gallantly made. The assaulting columns moved promptly and steadily upon the rebel works, and stood for hours under a withering fire, failing only because the position could not possibly be taken by storm.

Then, with tireless energy, with sleepless vigilance night and day, with battery and rifle, with trench and mine, the army made its approaches, until the enemy, worn out with fatigue, exhausted of food and ammunition, and driven to despair, finally laid down their arms.

On the 3d of July, General Grant received a communication from Lieutenant-General Pemberton, commanding the rebel forces, proposing an armistice and commissioners to arrange terms of capitulation. This correspondence resulted in the surrender of the city and garrison of Vicksburg on the 4th of July, 1863. This capture and the preceding battles resulted in a loss to the rebels of thirty-seven thousand taken prisoners, including fifteen general officers; ten thousand killed and wounded, and ammunition for sixty thousand men.

Thus perseverance, skill, and valor triumphed. The stronghold of the Mississippi was taken. No language can describe the tumultuous joy which thrilled the hearts of the gallant men who had won this great prize. The exultation of the army is illustrated in the glowing language of the young and brave McPherson, in his congratulatory address issued on the 4th of July.

"The achievements of this hour," said he, "will give a new meaning to this memorable day: and Vicksburg will heighten the glow in the patriot's heart which kindles at the mention of Bunker Hill and Yorktown. The dawn of a conquered peace is breaking before you. The plaudits of an admiring world will hail you wherever you go."

President Lincoln fully comprehended what he termed "the almost unappreciable services" of Grant in the capture of Vicksburg. He wrote to him the following letter, which illustrates the generous feelings of his heart:

"*My dear General:* I do not remember that you and I ever met personally. I write this now as a grateful acknowledgment for the almost inestimable service you have done the country. I wish to say a word further. When you first reached the vicinity of Vicksburg, I thought you should do what you finally did, march the troops across the neck, run the batteries with the transports, and thus go below; and I never had any faith except a general hope that you knew better than I, that the Yazoo Pass expedition and the like could succeed. When you got below and took Port Gibson, Grand Gulf, and vicinity, I thought you should go down the river and join General Banks; and when you turned northward, east of the Big Black, I thought it was a mistake. I now wish to make the personal acknowledgment that you were right and I was wrong."

No military enterprise recorded in history presented greater difficulties to be overcome, none the success of which was ever more fatal to an enemy, nor is there any which exhibits in a higher degree, courage, endurance, military skill, bold conception, fertility of resource, and rapidity of execution, than that which triumphed in the fall of Vicksburg. Take it altogether it was perhaps the most brilliant operation of the war, and establishes the reputation of Grant as one of the greatest military leaders of any age.

Let us now return to the armies near Washington. After the defeat of the Union army at Chancellorsville, Lee assumed the offensive, and advanced again into Maryland. He now made the greatest preparations for striking a decisive blow, and hoped to carry the war into Pennsylvania and the North. Hooker, marching on an interior line, covered Washington.

On the 28th of June, General Lee, having entered Pennsylvania, occupied Chambersburg. Learning that Hooker's army had crossed the Potomac and was advancing northward, he gave orders for the concentration of his forces at Gettysburg. On the 27th, General Hooker, in consequence of a refusal by Halleck to order the troops at Harper's Ferry to join him, asked to be relieved, and Halleck gladly issued the order by which he was relieved, and the command of the army transferred to General Meade. On that day, the headquarters of the Union army were at Frederick City, and those of the slaveholder's army were at Hagerstown. The Union force was thus interposed between the rebels, and Baltimore and Washington. On the 30th, General Meade issued an address to his army, in which he pointed out the important issue involved in the approaching conflict. " Homes, firesides, and domestic altars are involved. The army has fought well heretofore; it is believed it will fight more desperately and bravely than ever."

On Wednesday, General Reynolds of the First Corps, marching directly through the town of Gettysburg, came unexpectedly upon the enemy. The heroic General Wadsworth, who had left his princely estate on the banks of the Genessee, in Western New York, to offer himself as a volunteer for liberty and union, led the advance, the division of General Doubleday, one of the subordinates of Anderson at Fort Sumter, followed and formed on the left, with Robinson on the right. On discovering the enemy in force, Reynolds sent word to Howard to hasten up the Eleventh; that Eleventh, that since Chancellorsville had been in disgrace; a disgrace that must now be wiped out.

The advance encountered a heavy force of the enemy, and was forced back, but retired in good order. The enemy rashly pressing too far on the center, the left closed in upon them, and took many prisoners. As General Reynolds was pressing up to the front, he was killed by a sharpshooter. At 1 P. M., the gallant Howard, riding in advance of his corps, reached the field and assumed command, leaving his corps in charge of the gallant young soldier and eloquent German orator, Carl Schurz. The death of Reynolds left Doubleday in command of the First Corps. At half-past two, from the heights of Cemetery Hill, could be seen the long line of rebel gray-backs under Ewell, the famous brigade which Stonewall Jackson had so often led to victory. As they advanced they were met by a fire so sharp as to cause them to fall back. Twice the rebels were repulsed, but being re-enforced, the remnants of the First Corps were ordered back to the town. In moving, the left of the Eleventh was exposed, and a heavy rebel advance compelled it to fall back in some confusion. The enemy pursued and took possession of the town, while the two corps took possession of the western slope of the hill.

While the Union troops were being driven by superior numbers through the town, a rapid and general charge might possibly have destroyed these two corps; but it was not made, and their commander, the one-armed hero Howard, posted them on a commanding eminence south of the town, called Cemetery Hill, and prepared for the shock. When the line of gray again advanced, it met a shower of balls and shells which arrested its progress. It had been a fearful and bloody fight; one single brigade, which under Wadsworth held the left, going into battle with one thousand, eight hundred and twenty men, came out with only seven hundred.

Thus ended the first day's conflict. Each army was being concentrated as rapidly as possible. Howard had seized and occupied Cemetery Hill, south and a little east of the village. To the right of it, the hills extended to Rock Creek, and across this was Wolf Hill; while to the left, the hills extended south, and bent a little westward to the Round Top. The Union army was posted on these hills, in shape like a crescent, with its center on Cemetery Hill, its left extending to Round Top, and its right to Rock Creek. It had the advantage of position, and was so placed that the wings and center could readily support each other.

At dark on Wednesday evening, the Third and Twelfth Corps came in and were posted, the former on the ridge extending south and to the left of Cemetery Hill, and the latter on the same ridge as it curved to the right. The Third came up during Wednesday night, and the Fifth at 10 o'clock Thursday morning. At 11 o'clock at night, General Meade arrived upon the field and placed the troops in order of battle. Howard with the Eleventh, and what was left of the First and the Second under the gallant Hancock, constituted the center. The Twelfth under Slocum held the right. The Third under Sickles, and the Fifth, after its arrival, were placed on the extreme left. The Union army was so compact, that troops could be readily removed from either wing to the other, or to the center, as they might be needed. General Meade had his headquarters on the ridge, in the rear of the cemetery, and more than one hundred guns bristled along the crest of these hills fronting the enemy, and were confronted by one hundred and fifty guns of the rebels. An effort was made to induce Meade to assume the offensive and attack on Thursday morning, pouring his whole army on the rebel center, and smashing through, dividing it into two parts; but Meade wisely preferred to await the attack in his strong position. Thus the bright July morning wore away, and no movement of importance was made until near the middle of the afternoon.

Lee had ordered a general attack by Longstreet on the Union left and center, to be followed by Hill. While preparations were being made in the rebel army for this movement, Sickles sent Berdan's regiment of sharp-shooters into the woods in his front, and they, advancing a mile, descried the gray-backs moving large masses to turn the Union left. Longstreet was bringing his whole corps, nearly a third of the slaveholder's army, to precipitate it upon the Union left. Sickles immediately moved out and occupied another ridge, which he thought a more commanding position than the one

in which he had been placed, but which did not connect with
the main force. His left rested upon Round Top hill. On
came the rebels, and both armies opened with artillery. Then
came the wild yell, and the charge of the gray-backs was
met by a storm of grape and canister, and their line shattered and sent whirling back; immediately another line came
from the forest, and another and weightier charge was
approaching. General Warren, who as chief of staff was
watching the fight, sent for re-enforcements. Sedgwick and
the fighting Sixth were not yet available. Sickles held on
desperately; aid after aid was dispatched for help; but from
the clouds of smoke and flame it was seen that Sickles
was being pushed back. He finally yielded so far as to
occupy his first position, and the Fifth Corps came to his
support, while the brigades, winding down among the rocks
to the front, braced up his lines, and like a rock turned back
the assaulting columns. Longstreet was repulsed, and then
Anderson moved upon the Union center. With massed
columns, and the well known yell with which the rebels ever
charged, they come swarming on. Hancock repelled the
assault. Sickles, severely wounded, was borne from the
front, and Birney, the abolitionist, assumed command.

The conflict in the center raged fiercely. Hancock was
wounded in the thigh, and Gibbon in the shoulder. The
First and Second wavered; the rebels pressed to the muzzle
of the batteries, shot down the artillery horses, and the fight
was hand to hand, when the banners of the welcome Sixth
Corps, under the brave Sedgwick, came up. Although wearied
with a march of thirty-two miles in seventeen hours, they
hurried forward with shouts to the rescue, and the enemy
were hurled back, repulsed—destroyed. The right had been
weakened to sustain the left and center; and now Ewell made
a dash upon Slocum on the extreme right. For a short time
the attack was most ferocious; but a part of the Sixth and
some of the First came again at the critical moment, and the
enemy, although they had succeeded in taking some positions held by Slocum, were finally driven back, and the day

closed with the rebels repulsed from every part of the field.
It had been a bloody day. Sickles's and Hancock's corps
had been badly shattered, both these commanders wounded,
and Sickles had a leg shot off. For miles, every house and
barn was filled with the wounded and the dying. Thursday
had gone and yet the result was not decided. Friday came,
and Northern persistence was to crown with victory the three
days struggle.

Early in the morning a file of soldiers marched slowly to
the rear, bearing tenderly upon a stretcher the heroic Sickles;
yesterday leading his corps with the dash and spirit for
which he was ever distinguished; to-day, with his right leg
amputated, grave and stoical, his cap drawn over his face,
and a cigar in his mouth. The enemy opened at daylight
with artillery. At dawn, General Slocum made an attack on
Ewell, who commanded, it will be remembered, Stonewall
Jackson's men, and the fight was maintained with equal spirit
on both sides, Slocum being aided by Sykes's and Hum-
phreys's divisions of the Third Corps. Ewell's forces were
at length driven back, and at eleven o'clock, A. M., there
was quiet on the bloody field.

It has been stated that the key to the Union position
was Cemetery Hill. Lee determined to make a desperate
effort to get possession of this hill. With this purpose he
directed upon it the concentric fire of more than one hundred guns, ranged in a half circle. The lull had continued
until nearly 1 P. M. Meade, Howard, and other leaders
were watching for the attack, when at one o'clock, the thunder of a hundred heavy guns burst upon the position. It was
held by the Eleventh and Twelfth Corps. The storm came
suddenly. Soldiers and officers worn with battle and seeking
rest were scattered upon the grass. Many were struck as they
lay; some died with cigars in their mouths; some at their dinners on the crest of the hill, and some with letters and photographs of friends in their hands; taking a last fond look
before the battle which all knew was to be decisive, and fatal
to many. Horses were shot down as they stood quietly wait-

ing for their riders to mount. The air in an instant was filled with missiles and splinters; the earth and rocks torn up and shattered; the air filled with clouds of dust; the branches of trees were torn off, and the grave stones and monuments scattered in wild confusion. Within five minutes after the terrific rain of death began, the hill was cleared in all its unsheltered places of every living thing. All but the dead sought shelter. For an hour and a half, this terrible concentrated fire on Cemetery Hill was continued, and was replied to with equal vigor by the batteries on the ridge and range of hills. After the cannonade had continued about three hours, General Howard slackened his fire to allow his guns to cool. It was supposed by the enemy that our batteries were silenced, and that the time for an irresistible charge had come. The divisions of Virginians under General Pickett led the advance, supported by large bodies of other troops. As the leading columns of the advance emerged from the woods and became fully exposed to the Union fire, they wavered. But Pickett's brigades did not falter; although they were exposed to the terrific fire of grape, canister, and shell from at least forty guns, with a bravery worthy of old Virginia, they still held on their way steady and firm, closing up their ranks as their comrades were cut down. They crossed the Emmittsburg road, and approached the masses of infantry. General Gibbon, then in command of the Second Corps, walked along his line bare-headed, shouting: "Hold your fire, boys, they are not near enough yet." Still they came on, and with fixed bayonets swept up to the rifle pits. "Now fire!" thundered Gibbon. A blaze of death all along the line of the Second Corps followed; down fell the rebels, but the survivors did not yet falter; they charged on the pits, pressing up to the very muzzles of the artillery; but here they were met with such storms of grape and canister, that the survivors threw down their arms and surrendered, rather than run the gauntlet of the retreat. Three thousand prisoners were taken. The result is thus stated by General Meade in a dispatch dated at 8:30 P. M.:

" The enemy opened at one o'clock, P. M., from about one hundred and fifty guns. They concentrated upon my left center, continuing without intermission for about three hours, at the expiration of which time they assaulted my left center twice, being upon both occasions handsomely repulsed with severe loss to them, leaving in our hands nearly three thousand prisoners." [1]

When the repulse was complete, whole companies and regiments threw down their arms and surrendered, to avoid the terrific fire to which they were exposed. The battle was over. The army of the Potomac had again vindicated its bravery and its endurance. As General Meade rode proudly yet sadly over the bloody field, a band passing, struck up, " Hail to the Chief."

The next morning was as sweet, fresh, and balmy, as though the storm of death had not been sweeping for three long days over these quiet, pastoral Pennsylvania hills and valleys. Alas ! must the historian forever, to the last period of recorded time, recount these terrible scenes of slaughter, suffering, and death !

Lee was in no condition to renew the attack. His ammunition was short, the spirit of his army broken, and yet Meade made no vigorous pursuit. The rebel loss was fourteen thousand prisoners, and probably twenty-five thousand in killed, wounded, and missing. The Union loss was about twenty-three thousand in all. Few battles in ancient or modern times have been more severely contested; there have been few where greater numbers were engaged, and where there was a greater loss of life; none where more heroic valor was displayed on both sides. Had Sheridan, or Grant, or McPherson, commanded in place of Meade, it is believed Lee's army would never have recrossed the Potomac.

We have seen with how grateful a heart Lincoln returned thanks to Grant and his brave officers and soldiers in the West. He received the intelligence of the victory of the army of the Potomac with emotions not less warm. On the 4th of July, he issued the following announcement:

1. Military and Naval History of the Rebellion, p. 404. *See* Meade's Report.

" The President of the United States announces to the country, that the news from the army of the Potomac, up to 10 o'clock P. M. of the 3d, is such as to cover the army with the highest honor—to promise great success to the cause of the Union—and to claim the condolence of all for the many gallant fallen; and that for this, he especially desires that on this day, ' He whose will, not ours, should ever be done,' be everywhere remembered and reverenced with the profoundest gratitude."[1]

On the evening of the 4th of July, the popular exultation over these successes found expression in a serenade to the President. Mr. Lincoln said: " I do most sincerely thank Almighty God for the occasion of this call; " and ever mindful of the principles of the Declaration of Independence, which were the basis of his political creed, he said: " How long ago is it ? Eighty odd years since, on the 4th of July, for the first time in the history of the world, a nation by its representatives assembled, and declared as a self-evident truth, that all men are created equal. That was the birthday of the United States of America." He then alluded to the other extraordinary events in American history which had occurred on the 4th of July—the death of Jefferson and Adams on that day, and said: "And now at this last 4th of July just passed, we have a gigantic rebellion, at the bottom of which, is an effort to overthrow the principle that all men are created equal. We have the surrender of a most important position and an army on that very day." And then he alluded proudly and gratefully to the battles in Pennsylvania, on the 1st, 2nd, and 3rd of July, as victories over the cohorts of those who opposed the Declaration of Independence.

On the 15th of July, the President issued his proclamation, breathing throughout a spirit of grateful reverence to God, of supreme love of country and of liberty, and sympathy with the afflicted and the suffering. He said:

" It has pleased Almighty God to hearken to the supplications and prayers of an afflicted people, and to vouchsafe to the army and the navy of the United States, victories on the land and on the sea, so signal and so effective, as to furnish reasonable ground for augmented confidence

1. Military and Naval History of the War, p. 505.

that the Union of these States will be maintained, their Constitution preserved, and their peace and prosperity permanently restored. But these victories have been accorded not without sacrifice of life, limb, health, and liberty, incurred by brave, loyal, and patriotic citizens. Domestic affliction, in every part of the country, follows in the train of these fearful bereavements. It is meet and right to recognize and confess the presence of the Almighty Father, and the power of His hand, equally in these triumphs and these sorrows." [1]

He then invited the people to assemble on the 4th of August, for thanksgiving, praise, and prayer, and to render homage to the Divine Majesty, for the wonderful things He had done in the nation's behalf; and he called upon the people to invoke His Holy Spirit to subdue the anger which had produced and so long sustained a needless and cruel rebellion; to change the hearts of the insurgents; to guide the councils of the government with wisdom, and to visit with tender care and consolation those who through the vicissitudes of battles and sieges had been brought to suffer in mind, body, or estate, and finally to lead the whole nation through the paths of repentance and submission to the Divine Will, to unity and fraternal peace.

With these most important victories East and West, a load was lifted from the troubled heart of the President. His form, bowed and almost broken with anxiety, once more was erect; his eye grew visibly brighter, and his whole aspect became again hopeful. But it is not proper to suppress the fact that he was greatly chagrined that Meade permitted Lee and his army again to escape across the Potomac.

In the autumn of this year of battles and of Union victories, the ground adjoining the village cemetery of Gettysburg, a part of the field on which this great battle was fought, was purchased, and prepared for consecration as a national burying ground for the gallant soldiers who fell in that conflict. Here in this little grave yard,

> "The rude forefathers of the hamlet sleep."

Here, too, slept the hosts of dead of one of the great battles

1. Military and Naval History, p. 408.

of the world; a battle which saved the republic, and in which heroes and patriots worthy of Thermopylæ or Marathon had given life for their country.

Here, on the 19th of November, with solemn, touching, and most impressive ceremonies, this ground was consecrated to its pious purpose. The President, his Cabinet, the officials of the state of Pennsylvania, governors of states, foreign ministers, officers of the army and navy, soldiers and citizens, gathered in great numbers to witness the proceedings. Edward Everett, late Secretary of State, and Senator from Massachusetts, an orator and scholar whose renown had extended over the world, was selected to pronounce the oration. He was a polished and graceful speaker, and worthy of the theme and the occasion. President Lincoln, while in the cars on his way from the White House to the battlefield, was notified that he would be expected to make some remarks also. Asking for some paper, a rough sheet of foolscap was handed to him, and, retiring to a seat by himself, with a pencil, he wrote the address which has become so celebrated; an address which for appropriateness and eloquence, for pathos and beauty, for sublimity in sentiment and expression, has hardly its equal in English or American literature. Everett's oration was a polished specimen of consummate oratorical skill. It was memorized, and recited without recurring to a note. It was perhaps too artistic; so much so, that the audience sometimes during its delivery forgot the heroic dead to admire the skill of the speaker before them. When at length the New England orator closed, and the cheers in his honor had subsided, an earnest call for Lincoln was heard through the vast crowd in attendance. Slowly, and very deliberately, the tall, homely form of the President rose; simple, rude, his careworn face now lighted and glowing with intense feeling. All unconscious of himself, absorbed with recollections of the heroic dead, he adjusted his spectacles, and read with the most profound feeling the following address:

"Fourscore and seven years ago our fathers brought forth upon this continent a new nation, conceived in liberty, and dedicated to the proposition that all men are created equal.

"Now we are engaged in a great civil war, testing whether that nation, or any nation so conceived and so dedicated, can long endure. We are met on a great battle-field of that war. We are met to dedicate a portion of it as the final resting-place of those who here gave their lives that that nation might live. It is altogether fitting and proper that we should do this.

"But, in a larger sense, we cannot dedicate—we cannot consecrate —we cannot hallow this ground. The brave men, living and dead, who struggled here, have consecrated it far above our power to add or detract. The world will little note, nor long remember what we *say* here, but it can never forget what they *did* here. It is for us, the living, rather to be dedicated here to the unfinished work that they have thus far so nobly carried on. It is rather for us to be here dedicated to the great task remaining before us, that from these honored dead we take increased devotion to the cause for which they here gave the last full measure of devotion, that we here highly resolve that the dead shall not have died in vain; that the nation shall, under God, have a new birth of freedom; and that government of the people, by the people, and for the people shall not perish from the earth."

Before the first sentence was completed, a thrill of feeling, like an electric shock, pervaded the crowd. That mysterious influence called magnetism, which sometimes so affects a popular assembly, spread to every heart. The vast audience was instantly hushed, and hung upon his every word and syllable. When he uttered the sentence: "the world will little *note* nor long remember what we *say* here, but it can never forget what they *did* here," every one felt that it was not the " honored dead" only, but the living actor and speaker, that the world for all time to come would note and remember, and that he, the speaker, in the thrilling words he was uttering, was linking his name forever with the glory of the dead. He seemed so absorbed in honoring the " heroic sacrifices" of the soldiers, as utterly to forget himself, but all his hearers realized that the great actor in the drama stood before them, and that the words he was speaking would live as long as the language; that they were words which would be recalled in all future ages, among all peoples ; as often as men should be called upon to die for liberty and country.

Thus were the immortal deeds of the dead commemorated in immortal words. There have been four instances in history in which great deeds have been celebrated in words as immortal as themselves ; the well-known epitaph upon the Spartans who perished at Thermopylæ, the words of Demosthenes on those who fell at Marathon, the speech of Webster in memory of those who died at Bunker Hill, and these words of Lincoln in honor of those who laid down their lives on the field of Gettysburg.

As he closed, and the tears, and sobs, and cheers which expressed the emotions of the people subsided, he turned to Everett, and grasping his hand, said : "I congratulate you on your success." The orator gracefully replied : " Ah, Mr. President, how gladly would I exchange all my hundred pages to have been the author of your twenty lines." [1]

1. The author is indebted to Governor Dennison, the Postmaster General and an eye-witness, for some of the incidents detailed in the text.

CHAPTER XIX.

AFTER GETTYSBURG.

THE battle of Gettysburg, and the capture of Vicksburg, were in their results more decisive than any which
had preceded them. The army of Lee, naturally elated by
their brilliant victory at Chancellorsville, had invaded Maryland and Pennsylvania, with the most sanguine hopes of success, and with the determination to carry the war into the
free states. They boasted that they would water their horses
in the Susquehanna and the Delaware. The rich grain
fields, the stock farms, and big barns of Pennsylvania and
New Jersey, should furnish them with abundant supplies.
The vast stores and the wealth of the great Northern cities
were passing vividly before the gloating imaginations of these
soldiers. The savage threats made by Jefferson Davis, on
his way to Montgomery to assume the presidency, when he
said : " We will carry the war where it is easy to advance ;
where food for the sword and the torch wait our army in the
densely populated cities," [1] were now, they believed, to be
realized. But this arrogant host, proud and elated with their
successes, were met on the rocky hills of Gettysburg, and
hurled back, never again in force to cross the border.

By the brilliant capture of Vicksburg the rebel territory
was severed, and the "great Father of Waters, went unvexed

1. Greeley's Conflict, Vol. 1, p. 415.

to the sea." No rebel flag was again to float over the majestic stream. The rebel power west of the great river was broken, never to be re-established. Before the end of 1863, fully one hundred thousand negroes, emancipated slaves, were in the military service of the United States. [1]

Lincoln entertained sanguine hopes that Lee's army would never be permitted to recross the Potomac, and its destruction, he believed, would bring the war to a close. It seems to have been quite within the power of General Meade to annihilate the enemy that he had so signally defeated at Gettysburg. He had a much larger force, and abundant supplies. Lee's three days fight had nearly exhausted his ammunition, and when he reached the Potomac he had the swollen waters of that river in his front, with no means of crossing his artillery, and another defeat must have caused the surrender of his whole army. But Meade allowed him to collect lumber from canal boats and ruined wooden houses, to construct a bridge and cross the river. On the 14th of July, Meade telegraphed to Halleck : "The enemy are all across the Potomac." It would seem as though Meade thought his duty was performed when he drove the enemy back to Virginia, forgetting that Virginia was as much a part of the republic as Pennsylvania. He displayed so little enterprise that Lee thought it safe to send Longstreet to Tennessee, to the aid of Bragg against Rosecrans.

On September 19th and 20th, was fought the battle of Chickamauga, in which the gallant Thomas, commanding the center of Rosecrans's army, firmly withstood and beat back the rebels under Bragg. He did this after the rebels had turned the Union right, and Rosecrans had been driven from the field. Thomas, the loyal Virginian, by his heroism and good conduct on this occasion saved the army, and acquired the name of the "Rock of Chickamauga." Garfield, chief of staff of Rosecrans, especially distinguished himself in this battle.

1. President's Message, December 8th, 1863.

On the 19th of October, General Grant arrived at Louisville, and assumed command of the military division of the Mississippi, into which the departments of the Ohio and the Cumberland were now merged. This brought unity of action into this important field. Rosecrans was relieved, and Thomas became commander of the army of the Cumberland.

When Thomas retired to Chattanooga, after the battle of Chickamauga, the rebels advanced and occupied the passes and heights of Lookout Mountain and Missionary Ridge, and prepared to invest Chattanooga. Longstreet had been sent to drive Burnside out of East Tennessee. In the meanwhile, Hooker had been dispatched from the East to the West with fifteen thousand men.

Grant reached Thomas on the 22d of October, and the next morning made a reconnoissance with a view of driving the enemy out of the overlooking mountains, and regaining the use of the Tennessee River, to bring to his army much needed supplies. He had ordered Sherman and his corps to join him at Chattanooga. Grant never had better lieutenants than the gallant officers who now surrounded him. Sherman, sagacious and rapid ; Thomas, ever reliable, the hero of Chickamauga ; Sheridan, the impetuous and indefatigable, and Hooker, who, while not equal to the command of a great army, was well able to lead a division or army corps ; and now, with these and their gallant associates, and an army hardy and well disciplined, Grant determined to storm and carry the heights of Lookout Mountain and Missionary Ridge.

It was a bold and difficult undertaking. Sherman's forces crossed the Tennessee, and, on the 24th of November, gained possession of the north end of Missionary Ridge. Thomas attacked in the center, and drove the enemy back to the hills. Hooker pushed round Lookout Mountain, and drove the enemy up its western slope, capturing their rifle pits, and following them with impetuous ardor through the forests and up the sides of the mountain, until he reached the summit, above the smoke and vapor of the hills, and then the spectators from the valley beheld the dramatic spectacle of Hooker's battle-flags waving in triumph from the top of the mountain and above the clouds. The next day, the army of the Cumberland assailed the field works at the foot of Missionary Ridge, captured them at the point of the bayonet, and then pressed bravely up the ridge and captured the summit; while Sherman and Hooker pressed the enemy so vigorously, that long before the day was spent, Lookout Mountain, Chattanooga Valley, and Missionary Ridge were in possession of the Union troops, and Bragg was in rapid retreat. Many prisoners and guns were captured. Thomas pursued Bragg, fought him again at Ringgold, and drove him to Tunnel Hill, twenty miles from Chattanooga.

Meanwhile, Burnside was at Knoxville, confronted by Longstreet, and Sherman was sent by forced marches to his relief. His approach sent Longstreet retreating back to Virginia, and thus closed in triumph the campaign in Tennessee. The relief of Eastern Tennessee, where, among the mountains, attachment to the Union had been general and strong, and where, in the absence of national protection, the loyal people had been most cruelly persecuted, was very grateful to the President. He issued a proclamation appointing a day of thanksgiving and gratitude to God for this signal triumph of the national cause.

It will be remembered that on the 3d of March, 1863, a law was passed for the enrollment of the entire military force of the United States. The enrollment having been completed, in June a draft for three hundred thousand men was ordered. Time was, however, given to each state to fill up its quota, and thus prevent a resort to drafting. While there was in the loyal states a considerable party opposed to the war, and many who openly or secretly opposed volunteering to fill up the ranks of the army, the great majority were loyal, and active in promoting the success of the national cause. There had been, and there was still, great pride and emulation in the towns, cities, and states, as to which should fill up its quota of troops first, and there was everywhere manifested a desire that each locality should fill its quota without the draft. Large local bounties were offered, and much the larger proportion of the men called for were obtained without drafting. All who were opposed to the war, and all who sympathized with the rebels, availed themselves of the draft to excite prejudice against and opposition to the administration. Every means was resorted to to oppose enlistments and to stir up, if possible, resistance to the draft.

But the loyalty and patriotism of the people were too strong to be subdued, and no formidable opposition to the law was manifested, except in the city of New York. Here were a large number of Southern immigrants and Southern sympathizers, and a large population foreign by birth, whose attachment to the republic was so slight that the emissaries of the rebellion succeeded in creating a formidable opposition to the law. When orders were issued to proceed with the draft, on the 11th of July, threats of opposition were made, and, on the 13th, the proceedings were arrested by a furious mob, which broke into and set fire to the building in which the marshal's office was situated. The mob prevented the firemen from extinguishing the flames, and a whole block was burned. The police were attacked and overpowered. There was no considerable force of regular troops on hand, and many of the state militia were absent in Pennsylvania, to aid in resisting the invasion of Lee, so that it was found difficult immediately to raise a force adequate to suppress the riot. It was joined by the criminal classes, and the worst elements of a great city, and for a time it went from street to street, murdering, pillaging, and burning. Hatred of the negro was the animus of the infuriated mob. They set fire to the half-orphan asylum for colored children, and, with the spirit of devils, abused and scattered the orphans, burned the building, and caught and hung every negro they could find. The police did their duty manfully, but were overpowered. Governor Seymour, of New York, was in the city, and addressed the rioters in the park, eloquently urging forbearance. But musket balls, grape shot, and cold steel, rather than civil words, were needed. Troops were recalled from Pennsylvania and elsewhere and the riot suppressed, but not until the most cruel outrages had been perpetrated.

When the President first heard of the disturbance, and before it had assumed formidable proportions, he was told that there was danger of an Irish riot in New York, in opposition to the draft, and it was suggested that he should send an efficient officer there to preserve order. He said: " I think I will send General Kilpatrick," a dashing cavalry officer. " His very name may be sufficient." But he soon learned that something more stern than words or names was needed to put down the frenzied mob.

On the 3d of September, 1863, a great meeting of the Union men of all parties was called to meet at the Capital of Illinois. The President was most earnestly and affectionately invited to attend, " to meet his old friends at his old home." He had left that old home in February, 1861, conscious that he had a task before him far more difficult than that which had devolved upon " any other man since the days of Washington," and, in parting from his neighbors, he had humbly, sincerely, and hopefully asked his old friends to pray that he might receive the " divine assistance of that Almighty Being," in whom he placed his reliance. Two and a half years had passed in the midst of the convulsions of this tremendous civil war. The young men of Illinois and the Northwest, the sons of his old friends, were in the Union armies ; some of them in soldiers' graves. It had become very obvious that his task was far more difficult than that which had devolved upon Washington. His comrades, the pioneers of Illinois, had watched his career with deep solicitude and anxiety. Could he succeed in saving his country, and redeeming it from the curse of slavery? They had talked of him around their firesides. In their log cabins and humble chapels they had prayed for his success; they had freely sent their sons to the field to fight, and now they yearned to see him again face to face, to see how he bore himself, and to hear his familiar voice.

To this meeting Lincoln wished very much to go, but he could not leave the helm, and so he sent them a kind letter. This letter to his neighbors contains such a simple, clear, and frank exposition of his policy, and is so characteristic, that it is inserted here in full. He says:

EXECUTIVE MANSION,
WASHINGTON, August 26, 1863.

HON. JAMES C. CONKLING.— *My Dear Sir :* Your letter inviting me to attend a mass meeting of unconditional Union men, to be held at the capital of Illinois, on the 3d day of September, has been received. It would be very agreeable for me thus to meet my old friends at my own home ; but I cannot just now be absent from here so long as a visit there would require.

The meeting is to be of all those who maintain unconditional devotion to the Union ; and I am sure that my old political friends will thank me for tendering, as I do, the nation's gratitude to those other noble men whom no partisan malice or partisan hope can make false to the nation's life.

There are those who are dissatisfied with me. To such I would say : You desire peace, and you blame me that we do not have it. But how can we attain it ? There are but three conceivable ways : First— to suppress the rebellion by force of arms. This I am trying to do. Are you for it ? If you are, so far we are agreed. If you are not for it, a *second* way is to give up the Union. I am against this. Are you for it ? If you are, you should say so plainly. If you are not for *force*, nor yet for *dissolution*, there only remains some imaginable *compromise*.

I do not believe that any compromise embracing the maintenance of the Union is now possible. All that I learn leads to a directly opposite belief. The strength of the rebellion is its military, its army. That army dominates all the country, and all the people within its range. Any offer of terms made by any man or men within that range, in opposition to that army, is simply nothing for the present ; because such man or men have no power whatever to enforce their side of a compromise, if one were made with them.

To illustrate : Suppose refugees from the South and peace men of

22

the North get together in convention, and frame and proclaim a compromise embracing a restoration of the Union. In what way can that compromise be used to keep Lee's army out of Pennsylvania ? Meade's army can keep Lee's army out of Pennsylvania, and, I think, can ultimately drive it out of existence. But no paper compromise to which the controllers of Lee's army are not agreed, can at all affect that army. In an effort at such compromise we would waste time, which the enemy would improve to our disadvantage; and that would be all.

A compromise, to be effective, must be made either with those who control the rebel army, or with the people, first liberated from the domination of that army by the success of our own army. Now, allow me to assure you that no word or intimation from that rebel army, or from any of the men controlling it, in relation to any peace compromise, has ever come to my knowledge or belief. All charges and insinuations to the contrary are deceptive and groundless. And I promise you that if any such proposition shall hereafter come, it shall not be rejected and kept a secret from you. I freely acknowledge myself to be the servant of the people, according to the bond of service, the United States Constitution ; and that, as such, I am responsible to them.

But, to be plain. You are dissatisfied with me about the negro. Quite likely there is a difference of opinion between you and myself upon that subject. I certainly wish that all men could be free, while you, I suppose, do not. Yet, I have neither adopted nor proposed any measure which is not consistent with even your view, provided that you are for the Union. I suggested compensated emancipation ; to which you replied you wished not to be taxed to buy negroes. But I had not asked you to be taxed to buy negroes, except in such a way as to save you from greater taxation to save the Union exclusively by other means.

You dislike the emancipation proclamation, and perhaps would have it retracted. You say it is unconstitutional. I think differently. I think the Constitution invests its Commander in Chief with the law of war in time of war. The most that can be said, if so much, is, that slaves are property. Is there, has there ever been, any question that by the law of war, property, both of enemies and friends, may be taken when needed ? And is it not needed whenever it helps us and hurts the enemy ? Armies, the world over, destroy enemies' property when they cannot use it ; and even destroy their own to keep it from the enemy. Civilized belligerents do all in their power to help themselves or hurt the enemy, except a few things regarded as barbarous or cruel. Among the exceptions are the massacre of vanquished foes and non-combatants, male and female.

But the proclamation, as law, either is valid or is not valid. If it is not valid, it needs no retraction. If it is valid, it cannot be retracted, any more than the dead can be brought to life. Some of you profess to think its retraction would operate favorably for the Union. Why better *after* the retraction than *before* the issue ? There was more than a year and a half of trial to suppress the rebellion before the proclamation was issued, the last one hundred days of which passed under an explicit notice that it was coming, unless averted by those in revolt returning to their allegiance. The war has certainly progressed as favorably for us since the issue of the proclamation as before.

I know as fully as one can know the opinion of others, that some of the commanders of our armies in the field, who have given us our most important victories, believe the emancipation policy and the use of colored troops constitute the heaviest blows yet dealt to the rebellion, and that at least one of those important successes could not have been achieved when it was, but for the aid of the black soldiers.

Among the commanders who hold these views are some who have never had an affinity with what is called " abolitionism," or with " republican party politics," but who hold them purely as military opinions. I submit their opinions as entitled to some weight against the objections often urged that emancipation and arming the blacks are unwise as military measures, and were not adopted as such in good faith.

You say that you will not fight to free negroes. Some of them seem willing to fight for you ; but no matter. Fight you, then, exclusively, to save the Union. I issued the proclamation on purpose to aid you in saving the Union. Whenever you shall have conquered all resistance to the Union, if I shall urge you to continue fighting, it will be an apt time then for you to declare you will not fight to free negroes. I thought that in your struggle for the Union, to whatever extent the negroes shall cease helping the enemy, to that extent it weakened the enemy in his resistance to you. Do you think differently? I thought whatever negroes can be got to do as soldiers, leaves just so much less for white soldiers to do in saving the Union. Does it appear otherwise to you ? But negroes, like other people, act upon motives. Why should they do anything for us if we will do nothing for them ? If they stake their lives for us, they must be prompted by the strongest motives, even the promise of freedom. And the promise, being made, must be kept.

The signs look better. The Father of Waters again goes unvexed to the sea. Thanks to the great Northwest for it ; nor yet wholly to them. Three hundred miles up they met New England, Empire, Keystone, and Jersey, hewing their way right and left. The sunny South, too, in more colors than one, also lent a helping hand. On the spot, their part of the history was jotted down in black and white. The job was a great national one, and let none be slighted who bore an honorable part in it. And while those who have cleared the great river may well be proud, even that is not all. It is hard to say that anything has been more bravely and well done than at Antietam, Murfreesboro, Gettysburg, and on many fields of less note. Nor must Uncle Sam's web feet be forgotten. At all the watery margins they have been present, not only on the deep sea, the broad bay, and the rapid river, but also up the narrow, muddy bayou, and wherever the ground was a little damp, they have been and made their tracks. Thanks to all. For the great Republic—for the principle it lives by and keeps alive—for man's vast future—thanks to all.

Peace does not appear so distant as it did. I hope it will come soon and come to stay; and so come as to be worth the keeping in all future time. It will then have been proved that among freemen there can be no successful appeal from the ballot to the bullet, and that they who take such appeal are sure to lose their case and pay the cost. And there will be some black men who can remember that with silent tongue, and clenched teeth, and steady eye, and well-poised bayonet, they have helped mankind on to this great consummation, while I fear there will be some white ones unable to forget that with malignant heart and deceitful speech they have striven to hinder it.

Still, let us not be over-sanguine of a speedy, final triumph. Let us be quite sober. Let us diligently apply the means, never doubting that a just God, in his own good time, will give us the rightful result.

Yours, very truly,   A. LINCOLN.

This honest and manly explanation of his policy was received with the most enthusiastic satisfaction and applause. His reasons for the emancipation proclamation, and all other acts for which he had been criticised, were approved, and when his words of hope and faith in final success were read, beginning: "The signs look better. The Father of Waters goes unvexed to the sea, thanks to the great Northwest, nor yet not wholly to them," etc., the people felt that nature itself, the great rivers and prairies of the West, were rejoicing in the triumphs of the Union cause. The people had such faith in his sagacity and honesty that they felt assured of final victory, and were ready to make any sacrifice which he should ask to secure it. And so Illinois sent back her greetings and congratulations to the White House. The people joined with the President in thanks to God that no longer did any rebel flag float over any part of the Mississippi; that the national capital and all national territories were now free; that the border states were all becoming free states, and that the triumph of the national arms would, under the influence of the proclamation of emancipation, abolish slavery everywhere throughout the republic. The people rejoiced that as slavery had drawn the sword, it was doomed to die by the sword; that having plunged the nation into war, slavery was to perish by the laws of war.

The elections in the autumn of 1863 indicated the confidence of the people in the President, and their unanimity in support of his administration. Every state in which elections were held, except New Jersey, gave great majorities for the administration; and in Ohio, where the democrats had nominated Vallandigham for governor, he was in a minority of nearly one hundred thousand votes.

CHAPTER XX.

THE AMENDMENT PROPOSED.

DEBATE IN THE SENATE.—SPEECHES OF TRUMBULL, WILSON, JOHN-
SON, HOWARD, AND OTHERS.—A NEW YEAR'S CALL ON THE
PRESIDENT.—DEBATE IN THE HOUSE.—TEST VOTE.—SPEECHES OF
WILSON, ARNOLD, RANDALL, PENDLETON, AND OTHERS.—THE
AMENDMENT FAILS.

IN the early part of this book we have seen that Lincoln
in his younger days dreamed of being an emancipator. In
what way this day dream or presentiment entered his mind,
whether it was due to the prophecy of the Voudou on his
visit to New Orleans, or whether it was one of those
mysterious impressions which come from no one knows
where, it is impossible to tell. A careful reading of his
speeches and writings will indicate that in some way there
had been impressed upon his mind a premonition that he
was to be an agent in freeing the slaves.

So early as January, 1837, when he was a very obscure
man, in his lecture to the young men's association at Springfield, on " The Perpetuation of Our Political Institutions,"
he spoke of the glory and distinction to be gained by the
" emancipation of slaves." "Many great and good men
may be found," he said, " whose ambition would aspire to
nothing beyond a seat in Congress, a gubernatorial or presidential chair, but such belong not to the family of the lion
or the tribe of the eagle." In the same year, as a member
of the Illinois Legislature, he joined one other member (they
being the only members who would sign it) in a protest
against pro-slavery resolutions. A Kentuckian by birth, and

representing a district very hostile to abolition, he introduced into Congress, in 1849, a bill to abolish slavery in the District of Columbia. In June, 1858, he made the speech in which he said: "A house divided against itself cannot stand." In that most thoughtful, sagacious, and philosophic address he anticipated Governor Seward's "irrepressible conflict" speech, which was delivered at Rochester, in New York, October 25th, 1858. In this June speech of the then little known philosophic statesman, he said: "Either the opponents of slavery will arrest the further spread of it, and place it where the public mind shall rest in the belief that it is in the course of ultimate extinction, or its advocates will push it forward, till it shall become alike lawful in all the states, old as well as new—North as well as South." *   * "To meet and overcome the power of the dynasty (slavery)   *   *   * is what we have to do," and he concludes with these solemn words: "The result is not doubtful. Wise counsels may accelerate or mistakes delay, but sooner or later the victory is sure to come." There are few if any words more expressive of the character of Lincoln than those with which he concluded his great speech at Cooper Institute: "Let us have faith that right makes might, and in that faith let us to the end do our duty, as we understand it." [1]

It was this faith, and the courage to do his duty as he understood it, that sustained and carried him through the darkest days of his administration. As to slavery, and his action in relation to it, he said in his letter to Hodges, of Kentucky, April 4, 1864:

"I am naturally anti-slavery. If slavery is not wrong, nothing is wrong. I cannot remember when I did not so think and feel, and yet I have never understood that the Presidency conferred upon me an unrestricted right to act officially upon this judgment and feeling. * * * When, early in the war, General Fremont attempted military emancipation, I forbade it, because I did not then think it an indispensable necessity. When still later, General Cameron, then Secretary of War, sug-

1. Observe the number of words of one syllable in this and all his writings and speeches.

gested the arming of the blacks, I objected, because I did not yet think it an indispensable necessity. When, still later, General Hunter attempted military emancipation, I again forbade it, because I did not yet think the indispensable necessity had come. When in March, and May, and July, 1862, I made earnest and successive appeals to the border states to favor compensated emancipation, I believed the indispensable necessity for military emancipation and arming the blacks would come, unless averted by that measure. They declined the proposition, and I was, in my best judgment, driven to the alternative of either surrendering the Union, and with it, the Constitution, or of laying strong hands upon the colored element. I chose the latter. In choosing it, I hoped for greater gain than loss, but of this I was not entirely confident. More than a year of trial now shows no loss by it in our foreign relations, none in our home popular sentiment, none in our white military force, no loss by it anyhow or anywhere. On the contrary, it shows a gain of quite a hundred and thirty thousand soldiers, seamen, and laborers. These are palpable facts, about which, as facts, there can be no cavilling. We have the men; and we could not have had them without the measure. *   *

"I add a word which was not in the verbal conversation. In telling this tale, I attempt no compliment to my own sagacity. I claim not to have controlled events, but confess plainly that events have controlled me. Now, at the end of three years' struggle, the nation's condition is not what either party or any man devised or expected. God alone can claim it. Whither it is tending seems plain. If God now wills the removal of a great wrong, and wills also that we of the North, as well as you of the South, shall pay fairly for our complicity in that wrong, impartial history will find therein new causes to attest and revere the justice and goodness of God."[1]

The history of the emancipation proclamation has already been told. It had been issued by him with the sincere belief that it was "an act of justice warranted by the Constitution, and, upon military necessity," and upon it he had invoked "the considerate judgment of mankind, and the gracious favor of Almighty God." Congress had abolished slavery at the capital, prohibited it in the territories, and had declared all negro soldiers in the Union army, and their families, free ; repealed the fugitive slave laws, and indeed all laws which recognized or sanctioned slavery, and it had approved the proclamation. The states not embraced in this proclamation had emancipated their slaves, so that slavery

1. McPherson's History of the Rebellion, p. 336.

existed only within the rebel lines, and only on territory over which the rebels had military control. The abolition of slavery in the republic so far as it could be done by Congress and the Commander in Chief was an accomplished fact. It existed within the rebel lines alone, and there the slaves were held by force. Lincoln was by nature a conservative, and he had always wished to emancipate the negroes, but he desired to accomplish it by gradual and compensated emancipation. He wished the change to "come gently as the dews of heaven, not rending or wrecking anything." [1]

These efforts failed, and he was compelled to resort to the proclamation, under the laws of war. From the day of its issue, he labored by pen and voice, and personal and official influence, to make that proclamation effective. After all that had been done by Congress, by war, and by the Executive, one thing alone remained, to complete and make permanently effective these great anti-slavery measures. This was to introduce into the Constitution itself a provision to abolish slavery in the United States, and prohibit its existence in every part thereof forever. To accomplish this required the adoption, by a two-thirds vote of each House of Congress, of a joint resolution to be submitted to, and ratified by three-fourths of the states. To use the homely but expressive phrase of Mr. Lincoln, "this would finish the job," and to this he now devoted his constant efforts. "We cannot," says he, "escape history. We will be remembered in spite of ourselves. * * * * The fiery trial through which we pass will light us down in honor or dishonor to the latest generation." [2]

In the midst of the war, we pause to give a history of this thirteenth, and far most important of all amendments to the Constitution. The debates thereon, in both branches of Congress, were the most important in American history. Indeed it would be difficult to find any others so important

1. McPherson's History of the Rebellion, p. 256.
2. McPherson's History of the Rebellion, p. 224.

in the history of the world. They ran through two sessions of Congress, and in eloquence and ability equal the discussions of any deliberative assembly ever held. The speeches were fully reported, which was not the case in other great debates of earlier date. We are indebted to the imagination of Webster for the speeches in the Continental Congress on the Declaration of Independence. The greatest debate in the Senate, prior to this, was the memorable one between Webster and Hayne, and their associates, on nullification.

On the 14th of December, 1863, as soon as the Speaker had announced the standing committees of the House, he proceeded in regular order of business to call the states for resolutions. As Ohio, the first state organized under the great Ordinance of 1787, was called, one of her representatives, James M. Ashley, introduced a joint resolution, submitting to the states a proposition to amend the Constitution, by abolishing and prohibiting slavery. When Iowa was called, James F. Wilson, Chairman of the Committee on the Judiciary, introduced a joint resolution providing for the submission to the states of an amendment to the Constitution for the same purpose. On the 11th of January, 1864, Senators Henderson, of Missouri, and Sumner, of Massachusetts, presented joint resolutions with the same object, and they were referred to the Committee on the Judiciary, of which Lyman Trumbull, of Illinois, was chairman. Trumbull had been elected to the Senate in 1856, by the personal influence of Mr. Lincoln. He was a ready speaker, an able debater, and in the discussions in the Senate had been a worthy rival of his great associate, Douglas. He was probably, without exception, the best practical legislator in the Senate, and, as Chairman of the Judiciary Committee, did more than any one else to frame the various acts of Congress which became laws during the war.

On the 10th of February, 1864, he reported from the Judiciary Committee a substitute for the resolutions which had been offered by Henderson and Sumner. Adopting the language of the celebrated Ordinance of 1787, he reported the proposed amendment in these words :

"*Art. XIII, Sec. 1.* Neither slavery nor involuntary servitude, except as a punishment for crime, whereof the party shall have been duly convicted, shall exist within the United States, or any place subject to their jurisdiction.

"*Sec. 2.* Congress shall have power to enforce this article by appropriate legislation."

On the 28th of March the Senate proceeded to consider the question, and the debate was opened by Senator Trumbull. He sketched with great clearness and force the struggle between freedom and slavery during the last seventy years, and showed how slavery was at the bottom of all our difficulties. He said :[1]

"If these halls have resounded from our earliest recollections with the strifes and contests of sections, ending sometimes in blood, it was slavery which almost always occasioned them. No superficial observer even of our history, North or South, or of any party, can doubt that slavery lies at the bottom of our present troubles. Our fathers who made the Constitution regarded it as an evil, and looked forward to its early extinction. They felt the inconsistency of their position, while proclaiming the equal rights of all to life, liberty, and happiness, they denied liberty, happiness, and life itself to a whole race, except in subordination to them. It was impossible in the nature of things, that a government based on such antagonistic principles could permanently and peacefully endure, nor did its founders expect it would. They looked forward to the not distant nor, as they supposed, uncertain period, when slavery should be abolished, and the government become in fact what they made it in name, one securing the blessings of liberty to all. The history of the last seventy years has proved that the founders of the republic were mistaken in their expectations ; and slavery, so far from gradually disappearing as they had anticipated, had so strengthened itself, that in 1860, its advocates demanded the control of the nation in its interests, failing in which, they attempted its overthrow. This attempt brought into hostile collision the slaveholding aristocracy, who made the right to live by the toil of others the chief article of their faith, and the free laboring masses of the North, who believed in the right of every man to eat the bread his own hands had earned."

He then reviewed the action of Congress and of the

[1]. Congressional Globe, vol. 51, p. 1313.

Executive on the subject of slavery during the war, and closed the review by showing that the only way of ridding the country forever of slavery so that it could never be resuscitated, either by state or congressional action, was by a Constitutional amendment, prohibiting it forever everywhere within the United States. His practical mind then discussed the probability of the adoption of the amendment, and on that point came to this conclusion :

"I think, then, it is reasonable to suppose, that if this proposed amendment passes Congress, it will within a year receive the ratification of the requisite number of states to make it a part of the Constitution. That accomplished, and we are forever freed of this troublesome question. We accomplish then what the statesmen of this country have been struggling to accomplish for years. We take this question entirely away from the politics of the country. We relieve Congress of sectional strife, and what is better than all, we restore to a whole race that freedom which is theirs by the gift of God, but which we for generations have wickedly denied them."[1]

Trumbull was followed by Senator Wilson, of Massachusetts, who said:[2]

"Why is it, Mr. President, that this magnificent continental republic is now rent, torn, dissevered by civil war? Why is it that the land resounds with the measured tread of a million of armed men? Why is it that our bright waters are stained, and our green fields reddened with fraternal blood? Why is it that the young men of America, in the pride and bloom of early manhood, are summoned from homes, from the mothers who bore them, from the wives and sisters who love them, to the fields of bloody strife? *   *   *   *   *

"Sir, this gigantic crime against the peace, the unity, and the life of the nation, is to make eternal the hateful domination of man over the souls and bodies of his fellow men. These sacrifices of property, of health, and of life, these appalling sorrows and agonies now upon us, are all the merciless inflictions of slavery, in its gigantic effort to found its empire, and make its hateful power forever dominant in Christian America.   *   *   *   *   *   *   *

"Sir, under the new Constitution, framed to secure the blessings of liberty, slavery strode into the chambers of legislation, the halls of justice, the mansion of the Executive, and with menaces in the one hand

1. Congressional Globe. vol. 51, p. 1314.

2. Congressional Globe, vol. 51, pp. 1320, 1323-4.

and bribes in the other, it awed the timid and seduced the weak. Marching on from conquest to conquest, crushing where it could not awe, seduce, or corrupt, slavery saw institutions of learning, benevolence, and religion, political organizations and public men, aye, and the people too, bend before it and acknowledge its iron rule. Seizing on the needed acquisitions of Louisiana and of Florida, to extend its boundaries, consolidate its power, and enlarge its sway, slavery crossed the Mississippi, and there established its barbarous dominion against the too feeble resistance of a not yet conquered people. Controlling absolutely the policy of the South, swaying the policy of the nation, impressing itself upon the legislation, the sentiments, and opinions of the North, slavery moved on to assured dominion. Under its aggressive advances, emancipation societies, organized by the men of the revolutionary era in the first bright ardor of secured liberty, one by one disappeared, presses and churches forgot to remember those in bonds as bound with them, and recreant sons disowned the sentiments, opinions, and principles of a glorious ancestry."

He then rapidly sketched the anti-slavery legislation of Congress and the action of the Executive, and thus alluded to the proclamation of emancipation :

"The enforcement of this proclamation will give peace and order, freedom and unity, to a now distracted country ; the failure to enforce it will bring with it discord and anarchy, a dissevered Union, and a broken nation. * * * But, sir, the crowning act in this series of acts for the restriction and extinction of slavery in America, is this proposed amendment to the Constitution, prohibiting the existence of slavery forevermore in the republic of the United States."

The amendment was vigorously opposed by the senators from Kentucky, by Saulsbury, of Delaware, and others.

On the 5th of April, a memorable speech in favor of the amendment was made by Reverdy Johnson, of Maryland. He was a lawyer of great learning, had been Attorney General, was a contemporary of Webster, Clay, and Calhoun, and an experienced statesman, and represented a state not included in the emancipation proclamation, but which was by its own action throwing off the burden of slavery. His speech attracted marked attention in the Senate and throughout the nation. He said, among other things :

"I concurred, and concur still, in the judgment of the great apostle of American liberty, the author of that declaration which is to live through all time as the Magna Charta of human rights, that in a contest between the slave to throw off his thralldom, and the master who holds him to it, the God of justice could take no part in favor of the latter." * * *

" God and nature, judging by the history of the past, intend us to be one. Our unity is written in the mountains and rivers in which we all have an interest. The very difference of climate renders each important to the other, and alike important. That mighty horde, which from time to time have gone from the Atlantic imbued with the principles of human freedom which animated their fathers in running the perils of the mighty deep, and seeking liberty here, are now there, and, as they have said, they will continue to say until time shall be no more: ' We mean that the government in future shall be as in the past, an example of human freedom for the light and example of the world, and illustrating in the blessings and happiness it confers, the truth of the principles incorporated into the Declaration of Independence ; that life and liberty are man's inalienable rights.' " [1]

As to the power of the President to free the slaves, he said :

" I believe that it is the rightful exercise of a belligerent power to emancipate the slaves of the enemy, if we can get possession of them, just as it is the rightful exercise of a belligerent right to take any other property belonging to the enemy, which may be taken under the civilized rules of modern warfare, or as it is a belligerent right to capture any other person of the enemy." [2]

Charles Sumner closed the debate in the Senate, bringing to the discussion rich stores of historic illustration, and quoting largely from the poets, historians, and statesmen of the past against slavery. " The amendment," said he " will give completeness and permanence to emancipation, and bring the Constitution into harmony with the Declaration of Independence." He desired to change the phraseology of the amendment, so that, instead of using the language of the Ordinance of 1787, the resolution should declare the "*equality of all persons before the law*," and he referred to the constitutions of France as precedents.[3] Senator Howard, of Michigan, said : " I prefer to dismiss all reference to French constitutions or French codes, and to go back to the good

1. Congressional Globe, vol. 51, p. 1424.

2. Congressional Globe, April 5th, 1864.

3. Congressional Globe, April 8th, 1864.

old Anglo-Saxon language employed by our fathers in the Ordinance of 1787—language well understood, and which has been adjudicated upon repeatedly, and, I may add, near and dear to the people of the Northwestern territory, from whose soil slavery was excluded." [1]

Mr. Sumner withdrew the amendment he had proposed, and the resolution, on the 8th of April, 1864, passed the Senate, in the language in which it had been reported by Mr. Trumbull; ayes, thirty-eight; noes, six. Senators Hendricks, of Indiana, and McDougall, of California, were the only senators from the free states who voted against it.

The honor of having been the author of the Ordinance of 1787, has been claimed by Virginia, for Jefferson, and by Massachusetts, through Daniel Webster, for "one Nathan Dane," but it has been settled by a very accurate historical student [2] that its real author was Dr. Cutler.

No one will ever dispute that Senator Trumbull is entitled to the honor of framing, reporting, and carrying through the Senate, the thirteenth Amendment to the Constitution of the United States, a measure as much more important when compared with the Ordinance, as the whole country is more important than the Northwest territory. The honor of this great service would, in most countries of the world, have been rewarded with a title of high nobility, and pecuniary independence. This republic will not be so ungrateful as to forget to whom this great honor is due.

The resolution having passed the Senate, the main difficulty was to come in the House of Representatives. There, it was well known, the vote would be close, and the result uncertain.

On the 1st of January, 1864, while the resolution was pending in both houses of Congress, a friend [3] of the President called at the White House to pay his respects and the

1. Congressional Globe, April 8th, 1864.

2. Mr. Poole, librarian of the Chicago Public Library. See his paper on the Ordinance of 1787, read before the Chicago Historical Society.

3. The Author.

compliments of the season. After congratulating the President on the great victories which had been achieved in the East and in the West, and the brightening prospects of peace, the visitor said:

" I hope, Mr. President, that on next New Year's day I may have the pleasure of congratulating you on three events which now seem very probable."

" What are they ? " said he.

" *First*, That the war may be ended by the complete triumph of the Union forces.

" *Second*, That slavery may be abolished and prohibited throughout the Union by an amendment of the Constitution.

" *Third*, That Abraham Lincoln may have been re-elected President."

" I think," replied he, with a smile, " I think, my friend, I would be willing to accept the first two by way of compromise."

It has already been stated that propositions for the amendment had been offered in the House by Ashley, of Ohio, and Wilson, of Iowa. The President was extremely anxious about the vote in the House, and very often, with the friends of the measure, canvassed the House to see if the requisite number could be obtained, but we could never count a two-thirds vote. One day, after we had been speculating on the probabilities of the passage of the resolution, the author said: " I will test our strength. I will introduce a resolution as a feeler. I will make it just as simple as I can, and we will have a test vote ; " and so, on the 15th of February, 1864, the author had the honor to introduce into the House the following:

" *Resolved*, That the Constitution should be so amended as to abolish slavery in the United States wherever it now exists, and to prohibit its existence in every part thereof forever." [1] This resolution was adopted by a decided majority, but not by a majority of two-thirds, and it is.

1. Congressional Globe, vol. 50, p. 659.

believed that it was the first resolution ever adopted for the entire abolition of slavery. But, although it did not pass by two-thirds, yet it enabled us to know our strength, and just how many votes were needed to carry us through.

The discussion in the House began on the 19th of March, and a vote was not reached until the 15th of June. Mr. Wilson, of Iowa, who on the first day of the session had given notice of his Constitutional amendment, and who had introduced a joint resolution for that purpose, made a very able and logical argument in favor of its adoption. His proposition was that "slavery is incompatible with a free government," and he demonstrated that proposition. He said: "What are the thunders of this war but the voice of God calling upon the nation to return from the evil paths, made rough by errors and misfortunes, blunders and crimes, made slippery by the warm, smoking blood of our brothers and friends, to the grand highway of prosperity, happiness, glory, and peace in which He planted the feet of the fathers. Can we not hear amid the awful rushing roar of this war-storm the voice of Him who rides upon the whirlwind, and rules the tempest, saying: 'You cannot have peace until you secure liberty to all who are subject to your laws.'" [1]

On the same day, Mr. Arnold, of Illinois, spoke in favor of the resolution. Among other things he said :

"Our aim is national unity without slavery. Not 'the Union as it was, and the Constitution as it is,' but a nation without slavery, the Constitution the Magna Charta which shall secure liberty to all.   *   * The wandering stars must be brought back with their lustre brightened by the ordeal through which they have passed.   *   * We can have no national harmony and union without freedom. The fearful error of uniting free and slave states, we shall never repeat. But if the grand idea can be realized of a free, homogeneous people, united in a great continental republic based on liberty for all, and retaining the great principles of Magna Charta, we shall see realized the noblest structure of government and national polity ever organized on earth.   *   *   * It is the duty of the Executive, by the sword, and by war, to destroy all armed opposition. Everything necessary to accomplish this, consistent

1. Congressional Globe, March 19th, 1864, 1st Session 38th Congress, p. 1203.

23

with the rules of war as recognized by civilized nations, he may rightfully do.   He may emancipate and arm slaves, arrest and confine dangerous enemies, and thus prevent the execution of treasonable designs, and suppress, for the time, treasonable publications.   All this may be done under the rules of war, and in the exercise of the powers vested in the Executive of carrying the war against public enemies and traitors." [1]
*   *   *   " Slavery is the soul, body, and spirit of the rebellion. It is slavery which marshals yonder rebel hosts which confront the armies of Grant and Sherman.   *   *   *

" In view of all the long catalogue of wrongs which slavery has inflicted upon the country, I demand to-day of the Congress of the United States, the death of African slavery.   We can have no permanent peace while slavery lives.   It now reels and staggers towards its last death struggle.   Let us strike the monster this last decisive blow.

" The Thirty-seventh Congress will live in history as the Congress which prohibited slavery in all the territories of the Union, and abolished it at the national capital.   The President of the United States will be remembered as the author of the proclamation of emancipation, as the liberator of a race, the apostle of freedom, the great emancipator of his country.   The Thirty-eighth Congress, if we pass this joint resolution, will live in history as that which consummated the great work of freeing a continent from the curse of human bondage.   Never, since the day when John Adams plead for the Declaration of Independence, has so important a question been submitted to an American Congress, as that upon which you are now about to vote.   The signing of the immortal Declaration is a familiar picture in every log cabin and home all over the land.   Pass this resolution, and the vote which knocks off the fetters of a whole race, will make this scene immortal.   Live a century, nay a thousand years, and no such opportunity to do a great deed for humanity, for liberty, for peace and for your country, will ever again present itself. Pass this joint resolution, and you will win a victory over wrong and injustice, lasting as eternity.   The whole world will rise up to do you honor.   Every lover of liberty in Germany, France, Italy, Great Britain, the world, will rise up and call you blessed.   The gallant soldiers in the field who are giving their lives for liberty and union, will call down upon you the blessings of heaven.   Let the lightnings of God (fit instruments for the glorious message) transmit to the toiling and struggling soldiers of Sherman, and Hunter, and Grant, the thrilling words, ' slavery abolished forever,' and their joyous shouts will echo over the land and strike terror into the ranks of the rebels and traitors fighting for tyranny and bondage.   The thousands of wounded in the hospitals around this capital,

1. Congressional Globe, 1st Session 38th Congress, pp 1196–7.

would hail the intelligence as a battle fought, and a great victory won."
* * * " The people and the states are eager and impatient to ratify it.
Will those who claim to represent the ancient democracy refuse to give
the people an opportunity to vote upon it ? Is this your confidence in
the loyal masses ? The passage of this resolution will strike the rebellion
at the heart. I appeal to border state men, and democrats of the free
states ; look over your country ; see the bloody footsteps of slavery. See
the ruin and desolation which it has brought upon our once happy land ;
and I ask, why stay the hand now ready to strike down to death the
cause of all these evils ? Why seek to prolong the life, to restore to vigor,
the institution of slavery, now needing but this last act to doom it to everlasting death and damnation ? Gentlemen may flatter themselves with the
hope of a restoration of the slave power in this country. ' The Union
as it was !' It is a dream never again to be realized. The America of
the past is gone forever ! A new nation is to be born from the agony
through which the people are now passing. This new nation is to be
wholly free. Liberty, *equality before the law*, is to be the great corner
stone. Much yet remains to be done to secure this. Many a battle on
the field has yet to be fought and won against the mighty power which
fights for slavery, the barbarous system of the past. Many a battle has
yet to be won in the higher sphere of moral conflict. While our gallant
soldiers are subduing the rebels in the field, let us second their efforts by
sweeping from the statute book every stay, and prop, and shield, of
human slavery—the scourge of our country—and let us crown all by
incorporating into our organic law, the law of universal liberty." [1]

Randall, of Pennsylvania, a leading democrat from that
state, opposed the resolution. He said: " Let the Constitution alone. It is good enough. Let the old Constitutional
tree stand in all its fulness and beauty, and not a bough
lopped off, and under its green branches there will yet
repose a united, a happy, and a prosperous people. * *

> ' " Woodman, spare that tree !
> Touch not a single bough.
> In youth it sheltered me,
> And I'll protect it now.' " [2]

Pendleton, of Ohio, closed the debate with an able
speech in opposition to the resolution. On the 15th of June,
1864, the vote was taken, amidst the most intense solicitude

1. Congressional Globe, vol. 53, p. 2988–89.

2. Congressional Globe, 1st Session 38th Congress, p. 2991.

as to the result. The vote was: ayes, ninety-three, noes, sixty-five—not a majority of two-thirds. Thereupon Ashley, of Ohio, changed his vote from aye to no, to enable him to move a reconsideration, which he did, and pending this the resolution went over to the next session. Lincoln was chagrined and disappointed, but not discouraged by the vote; as Henry Clay once said to his friends, the pioneer hunters of Kentucky, "We must pick our flints and try again."

CHAPTER XXI.

PASSAGE OF THE AMENDMENT.

WHEN Congress convened on the 5th of December, 1864, the President, in his annual message, earnestly recommended and urged the passage of the Constitutional amendment. Alluding to the elections which had lately been held, he said: "They show almost certainly that the next Congress will pass the measure if this does not. Hence there is only a question of time as to when the proposed amendment will go to the states for their action. And as it is to so go, at all events may we not agree that the sooner the better." He closed by saying: "While I remain in my present position I shall not attempt to retract or modify the emancipation proclamation, nor shall I return to slavery any person who is free by the terms of that proclamation, or by any of the acts of Congress. If the people should, by whatever mode or means, make it an Executive duty to re-enslave such persons; another, and not I must be their instrument to perform it." He thus linked his fortunes with the cause of emancipation: "'Sink or swim, live or die, survive or perish,' I give my heart and my hand to this measure."

Just before the meeting of the national convention at Baltimore, in 1864, to nominate candidates for President and

Vice President—which will be more fully described hereafter—Senator Morgan, of New York, chairman of the
national republican committee, at the request of the President called at the White House, and Mr. Lincoln said to him:
" Senator Morgan, I want you to mention in your speech
when you call the convention to order, as its key note, and
to put into the platform as the key-stone, the amendment of
the Constitution abolishing and prohibiting slavery forever."
This was done, the amendment was thus made the prominent issue, and was sanctioned by the people.

Mr. Lincoln hoped to induce some of the border state
members, and war democrats who had at the last session
voted against the proposition, to change their votes. To
this end he sought interviews with them, and urged them to
vote for the amendment. Among them was Mr. Rollins, a
distinguished member of Congress from Missouri, and a
warm personal friend. Mr. Rollins says:

" The President had several times in my presence expressed his deep
anxiety in favor of the passage of this great measure. He and others
had repeatedly counted votes in order to ascertain, as far as they could,
the strength of the measure upon a second trial in the House. He was
doubtful about its passage, and some ten days or two weeks before it
came up for consideration in the House, I received a note from him,
written in pencil on a card, while sitting at my desk in the House, stating that he wished to see me, and asking that I call on him at the White
House. I responded that I would be there the next morning at nine
o'clock. I was prompt in calling upon him and found him alone in his
office. He received me in the most cordial manner, and said in his usual
familiar way: ' Rollins, I have been wanting to talk to you for sometime about the thirteenth amendment proposed to the Constitution of
the United States, which will have to be voted on now, before a great
while.' I said : ' Well, I am here, and ready to talk upon that subject.'
He said : ' You and I were old whigs, both of us followers of that
great statesman, Henry Clay, and I tell you I never had an opinion
upon the subject of slavery in my life that I did not get from him. I
am very anxious that the war should be brought to a close at the earliest
possible date, and I don't believe this can be accomplished as long as those
fellows down South can rely upon the border states to help them; but if
the members from the border states would unite, at least enough of them
to pass the thirteenth amendment to the Constitution, they would soon

see that they could not expect much help from that quarter, and be willing to give up their opposition and quit their war upon the government; this is my chief hope and main reliance to bring the war to a speedy close, and I have sent for you as an old whig friend to come and see me, that I might make an appeal to you to vote for this amendment. It is going to be very close, a few votes one way or the other will decide it.'

"To this I responded: ' Mr. President, so far as I am concerned you need not have sent for me to ascertain my views on this subject, for although I represent perhaps the strongest slave district in Missouri, and have the misfortune to be one of the largest slave-owners in the county where I reside, I had already determined to vote for the thirteenth amendment.' He arose from his chair, and grasping me by the hand, gave it a hearty shake, and said: ' I am most delighted to hear that.'

"He asked me how many more of the Missouri delegates in the House would vote for it. I said I could not tell; the republicans of course would; General Loan, Mr. Blow, Mr. Boyd, and Colonel McClurg. He said: ' Won't General Price vote for it? He is a good Union man.' I said I could not answer. ' Well, what about Governor King?' I told him I did not know. He then asked about Judges Hall and Norton. I said they would both vote against it, I thought.

" ' Well,' he said, ' are you on good terms with Price and King?' I responded in the affirmative, and that I was on easy terms with the entire delegation. He then asked me if I would not talk with those who might be persuaded to vote for the amendment, and report to him as soon as I could find out what the prospect was. I answered that I would do so with pleasure, and remarked at the same time, that when I was a young man, in 1848, I was the whig competitor of King for Governor of Missouri and as he beat me very badly, I thought now he should pay me back by voting as I desired him on this important question. I promised the President I would talk to this gentleman upon the subject. He said: ' I would like you to talk to all the border state men whom you can approach properly, and tell them of my anxiety to have the measure pass; and let me know the prospect of the border state vote,' which I promised to do. He again said: ' The passage of this amendment will clinch the whole subject; it will bring the war, I have no doubt, rapidly to a close.'" [1]

The debate on the subject in the House began on the 6th of January, 1865. Ashley of Ohio and Orth of Indiana spoke in its favor. Voorhees of Indiana opposed it, saying:

1. Lincoln Memorial Album, pp. 491, 2, 3.

" When the sky shall again be clear over our heads, a peaceful sun illuminating the land, and our great household of states all at home in harmony once more, then will be the time to consider what changes, if any, this generation desire to make in the work of Washington, Madison, and the revered sages of our antiquity." [1]

Mr. Kasson, of Iowa, said :

" I would rather stand solitary, with my name recorded for this amendment, than to have all the honors which could be heaped upon me by any party in opposition to this proposition." [2]

Mr. Woodbridge, of Vermont, said:

"Coming from the Green Mountain state, where a good old judge fifty years ago said to a claimant, who claimed and presented a bill of sale for a slave: ' Show me a bill of sale from God Almighty, and your title will be recognized,' it is not necessary for me to say that in my judgment there can be no property in man. * * * I want this resolution to pass, and then, when it (the war) does end, the beautiful statue of liberty which now crowns the majestic dome above our heads may look north and south, east and west, upon a free nation, untarnished by aught inconsistent with freedom ; redeemed, regenerated, and disenthralled by the genius of universal emancipation." [3]

As has been said, one of the very ablest speeches in favor of the amendment was made by Rollins of Missouri. He said :

" The convention which recently assembled in my state, I learned from a telegram a morning or two ago, had adopted an amendment to our present state constitution, for the immediate emancipation of all the slaves in the state. I am no longer the owner of a slave, and I thank God for it. If the giving up of my slaves without complaint shall be a contribution upon my part, to promote the public good, to uphold the Constitution of the United States, to restore peace and preserve this Union, *if I had owned a thousand slaves, they would most cheerfully have been given up.* I say with all my heart, let them go ; but let them not go without a sense of feeling and a proper regard on my part for the future of themselves and their offspring." [4]

Of the power of the slaveholders in ruling the republic, he used the following language :

1. Congressional Globe, 2d Session 38th Congress, p. 141.

2. Congressional Globe, 2d Session 38th Congress, p. 193.

3. Congressional Globe, 2d Session 38th Congress, pp. 243-4.

4. Congressional Globe, 2d Session 38th Congress, pp. 258-60.

"Sir, the peculiar friends of slavery have controlled the government for much the greater part of the time since its establishment, and but for their own wickedness and folly might have saved the institution, and had their full share in its management for many years to come. If they have lost the political control, all are blameless save themselves !

> " ' But yesterday, the word of Cæsar might
> Have stood against the world; now lies he there,
> And none so poor to do him reverence.' "

Of the necessity of abolishing slavery to secure permanent peace, he said : [1]

"We never can have an entire peace as long as the institution of slavery remains as one of the recognized institutions of the country. It occurs to me that the surest way to obtain peace is to dispose of the institution now."

Of Mr. Lincoln's proposition for compensated emancipation, he said :

"And, sir, if ever a people made a mistake on earth, it was the men of Kentucky, by whom I was somewhat governed myself, when three years ago they rejected the offer of the President of the United States, who, wiser than we were, seeing the difficulties before us, but seeing the bow of promise set in the sky, and knowing what was to come, proposed to us to sweep the institution of slavery from the border states, offering the assistance of the United States, to aid in compensating the loyal men of those states for their losses in labor and property."

Of the effects of slavery upon Missouri, he eloquently said :

"I come now to speak a word in reference to my own state of Missouri. She came into the Union as it were in the midst of a revolution. For the purpose only of having a few thousand slaves there, the whole continent shook with the agitation of this Missouri question. We were fighting for the privilege of holding a few slaves in bondage in that great state. We forgot the paramount good in this miserable struggle. * * Look at Illinois, just across the Father of Waters. She came into the Union in 1818, two years before Missouri, and with less population, fewer mineral resources, not so many rivers, no better facilities for commerce, yet she has four thousand miles of railroad, while Missouri has only twelve hundred. Illinois has a prosperous, happy, and peaceful population of two millions; while we have only half this number, and our people are leaving in every direction, seeking homes in the terri-

1. Congressional Globe, 2d Session 38th Congress, pp. 260-61.

tories, in the distant mountains, in South America, in Mexico, in Illinois, flying away from the horrible spectre of this infernal rebellion. Why is this? I know of but one real, substantial, specific reason, and that is that the framers of the Missouri Constitution allowed slavery to remain, while Illinois was made forever free by the Ordinance of 1787, penned by Thomas Jefferson, a son of Virginia, and by which Virginia ceded an empire within itself (the Northwestern territory) to the United States."

He then indulged in the following predictions of the future:

"When the poor and humble farmers and mechanics of Alabama and Mississippi shall have left the bloody trials in which they are now engaged to tear down this temple of human liberty; when they will return perhaps to their desolated homes; when they shall look once more upon and hug to their bosoms the wives and children whom they love, in poverty and in rags; when they will go, perhaps, without an arm, or without an eye, or without a leg, and in poverty, to those who are dependent upon them for support in life; taught by experience, they will ask the question of themselves: 'Why all this? What have we been fighting for?' They will bring to mind the sweet memories of other days. They will remember the peaceful and happy home which they were induced to leave, and which they enjoyed under the benign influences of wholesome and liberal laws passed here, and they will inquire: 'By what sophistry, by what appeal, by what force, by what maddening influence is it that we have been induced to enter into this terrible rebellion?' Not to promote any interest of wife and children, but to destroy all the blessings vouchsafed to us and to them by a free government and equitable laws; and they will further ask: 'Who has been the author of my misfortunes, and the ruin of my family, my all?' Sir, they will point to those who hold the power at Richmond; they will direct their vengeance against them; and Davis and his traitorous crew, as I have said upon a former occasion, will, like Actæon of old, be in the end destroyed by their own friends."

The speech of Garfield of Ohio, afterwards President, was especially able and interesting. As a soldier he had already won the rank and laurels of a Major General. His victory over Humphrey Marshall, at Middle Creek, and the brilliant record he made at Chickamauga, had been rewarded by the President with the commission of Major General, dated on the day of that battle. He now represented the district in Ohio known as the Giddings district, and his manly appearance, his ruddy complexion, bronzed by exposure and hardship as a soldier, as well as his fervid eloquence, attracted general attention. His speech was mainly in reply to his colleague, Pendleton, was full of classical allusions, and gave evidence of scholarship and culture. He said :

"Who does not remember that thirty years ago, a short period in the life of a nation, but little could be said with impunity in these halls on the subject of slavery? How well do gentlemen here remember the history of that distinguished predecessor of mine, Joshua R. Giddings, lately gone to his rest, who, with his forlorn hope of faithful men, took his life in his hands, and in the name of justice protested against the great crime, and who stood bravely in his place until his white locks, like the plume of Henry of Navarre, marked where the battle of freedom raged fiercest? We can hardly realize that this is the same people, and these the same halls, where now scarcely a man can be found who will venture to do more than falter out an apology for slavery, protesting at the same time that he has no love for the dying tyrant. None, I believe, but that man of more than supernal boldness from the city of New York [Mr. Fernando Wood] has ventured this session to raise his voice in favor of slavery for its own sake. He still sees in its features the reflection of divinity and beauty, and only he. 'How art thou fallen from heaven, O Lucifer, son of the morning? How art thou cut down to the ground, which didst weaken the nations !' Many mighty men have been slain by thee ; many proud ones have humbled themselves at thy feet ! All along the coast of the political sea they lie like stranded wrecks, broken on the headlands of freedom. How lately did its advocates with impious boldness maintain it as ' God's own,' to be venerated and cherished as divine. It was another and higher form of civilization. It was the holy evangel of America, dispensing its blessings to the wilderness of the West. In its mad arrogance it lifted its hands to strike down the fabric of the Union, and since that fatal day, it has been a fugitive and a vagabond upon the earth, and like the spirit that Jesus cast out, it has since then been 'seeking rest, and finding none.'" [1]

And now, on the 13th of January, came Thaddeus Stevens, Chairman of the Committee of Ways and Means, and the recognized leader of the House, to close the debate. As he came limping with his club foot along down the aisle from his committee room, the members gathered thickly around him. He was tall and commanding in person, and although venerable with years, his form was unbent and his intellect undimmed. The galleries had already been filled

1. Congressional Globe, 2d Session 38th Congress, p. 263.

with the most distinguished people in Washington. As the word ran through the Capitol that Stevens was speaking on the Constitutional Amendment, senators came over from the Senate, lawyers and judges from the court rooms, and distinguished soldiers and citizens filled every available seat, to hear the eloquent old man speak on a measure that was to consummate the warfare of forty years against slavery.

Reviewing the past, he said :

"When, fifteen years ago, I was honored with a seat in this body, it was dangerous to talk against this institution, a danger which gentlemen now here will never be able to appreciate. Some of us, however, have experienced it ; my friend from Illinois on my right [Mr. Washburne] has. And yet, sir, I did not hesitate, in the midst of bowie knives and revolvers, and howling demons upon the other side of the House, to stand here and denounce this infamous institution in language which possibly now, on looking at it, I might deem intemperate, but which I then deemed necessary to rouse the public attention, and cast odium upon the worst institution upon earth, one which is a disgrace to man, and would be an annoyance to the infernal spirits 　　*　　*

"Perhaps I ought not to occupy so much time, and I will only say one word further. So far as the appeals of the learned gentleman [Mr. Pendleton] are concerned, his pathetic winding up, I will be willing to take my chance when we all molder in the dust. He may have his epitaph written, if it be truly written, ' Here rests the ablest and most pertinacious defender of slavery and opponent of liberty,' and I will be satisfied if my epitaph shall be written thus : ' Here lies one who never rose to any eminence, and who only courted the low ambition to have it said that he had striven to ameliorate the condition of the poor, the lowly, the downtrodden of every race and language and color.'

"I shall be content, with such an eulogy on his lofty tomb, and such an inscription on my humble grave, to trust our memories to the judgment of other ages.

"We have suffered for slavery more than all the plagues of Egypt. More than the first born of every household has been taken. We still harden our hearts, and refuse to let the people go. The scourge still continues, nor do I expect it to cease until we obey the behests of the Father of men. We are about to ascertain the national will by an amendment to the Constitution. If the gentlemen opposite will yield to the voice of God and humanity and vote for it, I verily believe the sword of the destroying angel will be stayed, and this people be re-united. If we still harden our hearts, and blood must still flow, may the ghosts of the slaughtered victims sit heavily upon the souls of those who cause it." [1]

The vote on the passage of the resolution was taken amidst the most intense anxiety and solicitude. Up to the last roll call no one knew what the result would be. Democratic votes were needed to carry the measure. We knew we should get some, but whether enough none could tell. The most intense anxiety was felt, and as the clerk called the names of members, so perfect was the silence that the sound of a hundred pencils, keeping tally as the names were called and recorded, could be heard. When the name of Governor English, a democrat from Connecticut, was called, and he voted *aye*, there was great applause on the floor and in the crowded galleries, and this was repeated when Ganson, Nelson, Odell, and other democrats from New York responded *aye*. The clerk handed the vote to the speaker, Colfax, who announced in breathless silence the result: ayes, one hundred and nineteen; noes, fifty-six. Every negative vote was given by a democrat.

When the speaker made the formal announcement: "The constitutional majority of two thirds having voted in the affirmative, the joint resolution is passed," it was received with an uncontrollable outburst of enthusiasm. The republican members, regardless of the rules, instantly sprang to their feet and applauded with cheers. The example was followed by the spectators in the galleries, who waved their hats and their handkerchiefs, and cheers and congratulations continued for many minutes. Finally, Mr. Ingersoll of Illinois, representing the district of Owen Lovejoy, in honor, as he said, of the sublime event, moved that the House adjourn. The motion was carried, but before the members left their seats the roar of artillery from Capitol Hill announced to the people of Washington that the amendment had passed Congress. The personal friends of Mr. Lincoln, hastening to the White House, exchanged congratulations with him on the auspicious result. The pass-

1. Congressional Globe, 2d Session 38th Congress, p. 124.

age of the resolution filled his heart with joy. He saw in it the complete consummation of his own great work, the emancipation proclamation.

On the following evening a vast crowd of rejoicing and enthusiastic friends, with music, marched to the White House, publicly to congratulate the President on the passage of the joint resolution. Arriving at the Executive Mansion, the band played national airs, and as Mr. Lincoln appeared at a window over the portico he was greeted with the greatest enthusiasm. When the cheering had subsided, he raised his arm, and, with every feature radiant with joy slowly said:

"The great job is ended." * * "The occasion is one of congratulation, and I cannot but congratulate all present, myself, the country, and the whole world upon this great moral victory. The amendment," he continued, "has already been ratified by Illinois, and Maryland is half through, but I feel proud," said he, "that Illinois is a little ahead. * * This ends the job."

Yes, and it was the brave heart, the clear, sagacious brain, the indomitable but patient will of Abraham Lincoln that carried through the great revolution. There remained now but a few more battles, a few more victories, and all would be won, and a free and united republic established from the lakes to the gulf, and then the work of the prairie statesman would be finished. He would have fully vindicated his right to be called one "of the family of the lion and the tribe of the eagle." The dream of his youth, the prophecy of his manhood would be realized. As yet no dark shadow, no presentiment of death rose on the landscape of the future.

When in June, 1858, at his home in Springfield, Abraham Lincoln startled the people by the declaration: "This nation cannot endure permanently half slave and half free," and when in concluding that very remarkable speech, with prophetic voice, uplifted eye, and the inspired mien of a seer, he exclaimed: "We shall not fail ; if we stand firm *we shall not fail.* Wise counsels may accelerate, or mistakes delay, but sooner or later the victory is sure to come." He looked to long years of political controversy; he expected a severe struggle and a final triumph through the use of all the agencies by which public opinion is influenced and formed; and he anticipated the final triumph through the ballot box. But he did not foresee, unless in those mysterious, dim shadows which sometimes startle by half revealing the future, his own elevation to the Presidency; he did not foresee that he should be chosen by God and the people to lead on to that victory which he then felt was sure to come; that he should speak the word which should emancipate a race and free his country. Nor did he foresee that a martyr's death would crown a life which was so consecrated to duty, a life which was to be from that day forth so filled with unselfish, untiring devotion to country and to liberty, that his example will be everlasting, growing brighter with years; forever to inspire the patriot, and give courage to those who labor, and struggle, and die, for the poor and the oppressed; until in all the world, there shall be left no slave to be freed, no oppressor to be overthrown.

As has been stated, Illinois, under the inspiration of Lincoln, took the lead of all the states in ratifying the amendment. Then followed Rhode Island and Michigan, and on the same day, the 2nd·of February, regenerated Maryland; on the 3rd, and keeping pace with her, were New York and West Virginia. Then Maine and Kansas, Massachusetts and Pennsylvania; and then old Virginia and Ohio and redeemed Missouri; and then Nevada and Indiana, and Louisiana and the other states followed, until more than three-fourths of all ratified the amendment.

It was a proud moment when William H. Seward, on the 18th of November, 1865, as Secretary of State, officially proclaimed the ratification of the amendment and certified [1]

1. The following correspondence gives in a semi-official form the dates of the ratification:

"that the same had become to all intents and purposes valid as a part of the Constitution of the United States."

WASHINGTON, July 23, 1866.

Hon. W. H. SEWARD, *Secretary of State.*

My Dear Sir: * * * May I trouble you to furnish me the dates at which the several states adopted the Constitutional amendment prohibiting slavery forever throughout the republic, and a copy of your official certificate or proclamation, announcing such ratification by the requisite number of states? I cannot forbear congratulating you on the part you have taken in this great revolution. Few have had the felicity of living to witness such glorious results from their labors. How few could have anticipated when you began your anti-slavery labors, that you would live to officially proclaim that " *slavery is no more.*"

Very Respectfully Yours,

ISAAC N. ARNOLD.

DEPARTMENT OF STATE, WASHINGTON, August 22, 1866.

ISAAC N. ARNOLD, ESQ.,

Sir: Your letter of the 23d ultimo, asking to be furnished the dates at which the several states adopted the amendment to the Constitution prohibiting slavery, etc., was duly received; but owing to the exigencies of public business in this Department, it has not been convenient to answer it until now.

The dates of ratification by the several states, up to this time, are as follows : Illinois, February 1st, 1865; Rhode Island, February 2d, 1865; Michigan, February 2d, 1865; Maryland, February 1st and 3d, 1865; New York, February 2d and 3d, 1865; West Virginia, February 3d, 1865; Maine, February 7th, 1865; Kansas, February 7th, 1865; Massachusetts, February 8th, 1865; Pennsylvania, February 8th, 1865; Virginia, February 9th, 1865; Ohio, February 10th, 1865; Missouri, February 10th, 1865; Nevada, February 16th, 1865; Indiana, February 16th, 1865; Louisiana, February 17th, 1865; Minnesota, February 8th and 23d, 1865; Wisconsin, March 1st, 1865; Vermont, March 9th, 1865; Tennessee, April 5th and 7th, 1865; Arkansas, April 20th, 1865; Connecticut, May 5th, 1865; New Hampshire, July 1st, 1865; South Carolina, November 13th, 1865; Alabama, December 2d, 1865; North Carolina, December 4th, 1865; Georgia, December 9th, 1865; Oregon, December 11th, 1865; California, December 20th, 1865; Florida, December 28th, 1865; New Jersey, January 23d, 1866; Iowa, January 24th, 1866.

I transmit a copy of the certificate of ratification, agreeably to your request. Thanking you for the congratulations with which you conclude your letter.

I am, Your Obedient Servant,

WILLIAM H. SEWARD.

CHAPTER XXII.

GRANT AND SHERMAN.

General Grant Comes to the Potomac.— Sherman Goes Through Dixie to the Ocean.—Fort McAllister Taken.— Savannah Falls.—The Alabama is Sunk.—Farragut Captures Mobile.

Again must the reader return with us to the fields of war. Grand marches are yet to be made, bloody battles to be fought, carnage, suffering, desolation, and death must yet be encountered in their utmost horror before the end of the great drama is reached. But the result of it all is, to the intelligent reader, no longer doubtful.

In the West, victory had of late everywhere attended the Union flag, the capture of Vicksburg and Port Hudson having been followed by the brilliant victory of Missionary Ridge and Lookout Mountain. But in the East, the case was far different. The defeat of the rebel forces at Gettysburg had been so crushing that, had the Union armies followed up their advantages, the war might have been brought to a more speedy termination. Instead of this, Lee was permitted, to the great mortification and grief of the President, to recover from his defeat, to re-cross the Potomac, and to occupy his former lines. But the time was near when the conduct of military operations was to be entrusted to the able hands of the hero of Vicksburg, and when reverses would no longer alternate with the successes of the Northern armies.

Early after the opening of the Thirty-eighth Congress, Washburne, of Illinois, the ever faithful friend of Grant, and to whom this great soldier was more indebted for opportunities to serve his country than to any other man, brought forward a bill creating the office of Lieutenant General. It was the wish of the friends of that law that the great soldier who had achieved such signal success in the valley of the Mississippi should take the high position of commander, under the President, of all the armies of the United States. On the 22d of February, 1864, the President approved the act, and sent the name of Grant to the Senate as Lieutenant General. On the 2d of March the nomination was confirmed, and the President immediately requested the General's presence at Washington. Up to this time Grant had not, during the war, visited the capital. He was personally unknown to the President, the Secretary of War, and most of the members of Congress. This unsolicited appointment found him at his post of duty, and, with a modesty and generosity towards his most trusted lieutenant, General Sherman, as rare as it was honorable, he said : " I think Sherman better entitled to the position than I am." He arrived at the capital on the 8th of March, and in the evening attended a levee at the White House. He entered the reception room unannounced, and almost a stranger. He was instantly recognized by the President, and the Western soldier was never more cordially welcomed. As soon as it was known that he was present, the pressure of the crowd to see the hero of Vicksburg was so great, that he was forced to shelter himself behind a sofa. So irrepressible was the desire to see him, that Secretary Seward finally induced him to mount a sofa, that this curiosity might be gratified. When parting from the President, he said, " This has been rather the warmest campaign I have witnessed during the war."

On the next day, at the Executive Mansion, the President in person, and in the presence of a few friends, presented him his commission, saying :

" General Grant : The nation's appreciation of what you have done, and its reliance upon you for what remains to be done in the existing great struggle, are now presented with this commission, constituting you Lieutenant General in the army of the United States. With this high honor devolves upon you also a corresponding responsibility. As the country herein trusts you, so, under God, it will sustain you. I scarcely need to add, that with what I here speak for the nation, goes my own hearty personal concurrence." To this General Grant made the following reply :

" MR. PRESIDENT : I accept the commission with gratitude for the high honor conferred. With the aid of the noble armies that have fought on so many fields for our common country, it will be my earnest endeavor not to disappoint your expectations. I feel the full weight of the responsibilities now devolving on me, and I know that if they are met, it will be due to those armies, and above all to the favor of that Providence which leads both nations and men."

After visiting the army of the Potomac, he returned to Washington, and after an interview with the President and Secretary of War in regard to his plans, prepared to leave for the West. Mrs. Lincoln, sharing in the universal gratitude and admiration felt for him, and desirous of showing him some attention, invited him to meet a brilliant party at dinner that evening. He received the invitation at the close of this important interview with the President. The General said : " Mrs. Lincoln must excuse me. I must be in Tennessee at a given time." " But we can't excuse you," said the President. " Mrs. Lincoln's dinner without you, would be Hamlet with Hamlet left out." " I appreciate the honor Mrs. Lincoln would do me," said the General, " but time is very important now—and really—Mr. Lincoln, I have had enough of this show business." This was a remark Mr. Lincoln could well appreciate and with which he could fully sympathize. General Grant went to the West without waiting for the dinner.

General Sherman, on the recommendation of General Grant, was assigned to the command of the military division of Mississippi. General Grant, on the 17th of March, assumed command of the armies of the United States, and announced that his headquarters would be in the field, and until further orders, with the army of the Potomac. From this time there was unity of purpose—each army coöperating and acting under one far-seeing executive head. From this time on, there was energy in attack, rapidity in pursuit, and everywhere a fit man in the fittest place for him. Grant had the very great advantage of having subordinates who enjoyed his most perfect confidence, and who reposed the most perfect faith in him. Henceforth rivalries and jealousies were, to a great extent, banished from the armies of the republic. Nothing had given Mr. Lincoln more anxiety than the rivalries and quarrels among his generals. From the time that Grant assumed command as Lieutenant General, this annoyance to a great extent ceased. Sherman was justly regarded as Grant's right arm. Grant and Sherman, at the head of the armies of the East and the West, had perfect confidence in each other and in the President, and he in them. A great load of responsibility was lifted from his shoulders.

On the 30th of April, the President wrote a letter to Grant, in which he says:

"You are vigilant and self-reliant, and pleased with this, I wish not to obtrude any restraints or constraints upon you.   *   *   *
If there be anything wanting in my power to give, do not fail to let me know.   And now, with a brave army and a just cause, may God sustain you." [1]

With these words Lincoln sent Grant to the field. General Grant's plan is clearly and simply stated by him. He said :

"The armies in the East and West acted independently and without concert, like a balky team, no two ever pulling together; enabling the enemy to use to a great advantage his interior lines of communication for transporting troops from East to West, re-enforcing the army most vigorously pressed, and to furlough large numbers, during seasons of inactivity on our part, to go to their homes and do the work of producing for the support of their armies.   It was a question whether our

1. McPherson's History of the Rebellion, p. 425.

numerical strength and resources were not more than balanced by these disadvantages and the enemy's superior position."

" From the first I was firm in the conviction that no peace could be had that would be stable and conducive to the happiness of the people, both North and South, until the military power of the rebellion was entirely broken, I therefore determined; *first*, to use the greatest number of troops practicable against the armed force of the enemy; preventing him from using the same force at different seasons against first one and then another of our armies, and the possibility of repose for refitting and producing necessary supplies for carrying on resistance. *Second*, to hammer continuously against the armed force of the enemy and his resources, until by mere attrition, if in no other way, there should be nothing left to him but an equal submission with the loyal section of our common country to the Constitution and laws of the land."

The campaign in Virginia opened on the 4th of May. With the army of the Potomac under Meade, re-enforced by the Ninth Corps, under Burnside, Grant started by the overland route for Richmond. When he pitched his tent on the banks of the Rapidan, he found the two hostile armies grimly and proudly confronting each other. Each army was in high spirits. Each could look with pride upon a long list of victories inscribed on its battle flags. Every one realized that the rebel army of Northern Virginia carried upon its standard the fate of the Confederacy, and now there came from the valley of the Mississippi the brilliant and hitherto invincible hero of the West, to test his genius and his fortunes against the great leader of the rebellion. It was believed the crisis was at hand. But while the Confederates were nearly exhausted in men and money and credit, the military resources of the Union did not seem to be seriously lessened. Men swarmed in Northern towns, cities, and states; and labor, and every branch of industry was stimulated to the utmost activity by the war. Meade, as has been stated, had under Grant the immediate command of the army of the Potomac, which was divided into three corps, under Hancock, commanding the Second ; Warren, the Fifth, and Sedgwick, the Sixth. Hancock, perhaps the most capable and brilliant of all McClellan's subordinates, was the model of a hero. He had that fine martial bearing, that personal gallantry

and magnetism which made him the idol of his soldiers. Warren was a rapid, clear thinker, and ready alike on the field
and in council. Sedgwick was an able, experienced, steadfast soldier, perfectly certain to do his whole duty wherever
placed. Under them was a long list of brave and intelligent officers, whose names will live in history.

At midnight, on the 3d of May, the Union troops began
to move, and on the 4th the whole army was across the Rapidan. On the 5th and 6th were fought the bloody battles of
the Wilderness. On the 7th, Grant began to move by the
flank towards Spottsylvania Court House. Lee, being on the
inner and shorter line, reached there first. On the 9th, 10th
and 11th, there was continual maneuvering and fighting.
On the 11th Grant sent to Washington a dispatch, saying :
"Our losses have been heavy, as well as those of the
enemy, and I propose to fight it out on this line if it takes
all summer."

The armies fought again on the 12th, and again at North
Anna, and at Cold Harbor. During these weeks of May and
early June, there was constant fighting and marching, and
great loss of life, and during all these furious and persistent
struggles, the losses were greater to the Union than to the
rebel forces. Lee was on the inner and shorter line, knew
the ground perfectly, and could choose the time and place
of attack. Grant had fought his way to the Chickahominy,
but he had not taken Richmond, nor destroyed the brave
army of Northern Virginia.

Those of the wounded of the Union army who could be
moved were brought on steamboats to Washington, where a
large number of great field hospitals covered the hills overlooking the capital. These wounded came in appalling
numbers. The line of ambulances, moving from the steamers to the hospitals, was often one and two miles long, and
unbroken from wharf to hospital. The President, whose
sympathy for human suffering was most tender, could often
be seen with Mrs. Lincoln in his carriage driving slowly
along this line of sufferers, speaking kind and cheering

words, and personally seeing that every want and need was
supplied.

During these long days of terrible slaughter the face of
the President was grave and anxious, and he looked like one
who had lost the dearest member of his own family. I
recall one evening late in May, when I met the President in
his carriage driving slowly towards the Soldiers' Home.
He had just parted from one of those long lines of ambulances. The sun was just sinking behind the desolate and
deserted hills of Virginia; the flags from the forts, hospitals,
and camps drooped sadly. Arlington, with its white colonnade, looked like what it was—a hospital. Far down the
Potomac, towards Mount Vernon, the haze of evening was
gathering over the landscape, and when I met the President
his attitude and expression spoke the deepest sadness. He
paused as we met, and pointing his hand towards the line of
wounded men, he said: " Look yonder at those poor fellows. I cannot bear it. This suffering, this loss of life is
dreadful." Recalling a letter he had written years before to
a suffering friend whose grief he had sought to console, I
reminded him of the incident, and asked him: " Do you
remember writing to your sorrowing friend these words:
' And this too shall pass away. Never fear. Victory will
come.' " " Yes," replied he, "victory will come, but it
comes slowly."

General Butler commanded a force on the James River.
On the 5th of May he took possession of City Point and
Bermuda Hundred. On the 16th, he was attacked, and
forced back between the James and the Appomattox. Here,
the enemy erecting fortifications in his front, he was, as
General Grant said, "bottled up."

Grant now resolved to move his army to the south of the
James. Meanwhile, General Hunter had marched up the
valley of the Shenandoah, routed the enemy at Piedmont,
and from thence marched on Lynchburg, which he reached
on the 16th of June. Lee had sent a large force from Richmond to meet Hunter. Breckenridge occupied the defences

of Lynchburg, and was joined by Early, and they compelled
Hunter to retreat by way of the Kanawha.   General Early
then, with twelve thousand veterans, marched down the
valley towards Maryland.   General Lew Wallace gathered a
small force and placed himself at Monocacy in Early's front,
to protect Baltimore and Washington.   Wallace could only
delay the advance of Early, but Grant had despatched the
Sixth Corps under Wright, and the Nineteenth from Fortress Monroe, and they arrived in time to prevent an attack
upon the capital.   But so near were the enemy that the
country home of Montgomery Blair, the Postmaster General,
was plundered and burned, and "Silver Spring," the residence of Francis P. Blair, was for a short time occupied by
the rebel General Breckenridge.   These residences were
only about seven miles from the White House.   Lincoln,
from Fort Stevens, witnessed the repulse of Early's troops,
and this was the last attempt of the rebels to capture the
capital.   They retired into their old retreat, and there
remained a menace to Washington.

Grant now determined to drive Early out of this rich and
productive valley, and leave it in a condition to be no longer
useful in furnishing supplies to the enemy.   There had
been many Union commanders in the Shenandoah, but none
who had achieved a complete success.   Grant now selected
Sheridan to execute the decisive campaign he had planned.
On the 19th of September, Sheridan attacked Early at
Opequan, and drove him from the field with a loss of four
thousand men.   From this day Maryland was never more in
danger of invasion.   Sheridan pursued Early to the passes
of the Blue Ridge Mountains, destroying the railroads, and
on his return destroyed everything in the way of provisions
and forage, drove off the stock, and left the rich and beautiful valley a desolate waste.   Rendering, in his own words,
"the whole country from the Blue Ridge" untenable for a
rebel army.

On the morning of the 19th of October, Early crossed
the mountains, and, in the absence of Sheridan, surprised

and drove from the field the left of the Union army.* Retreating in confusion, and with heavy loss, the Union troops were rallied near Middletown, and made a stand. At this juncture, Sheridan, who had been at Winchester, and there heard the heavy guns, came dashing forward at the full speed of his horse. Arriving on the field, his magnetic presence, heroic bearing, and indomitable will, inspired his troops with fresh courage and enthusiasm. Passing rapidly along his lines, he arranged them in time to repel a heavy attack. Immediately following the repulse, he attacked with great impetuosity in turn, recapturing the guns and prisoners that Early had taken. The rebel army was broken, routed, and destroyed, the remnants of it only escaping during the night. Thus ended the war in the Shenandoah, and Sheridan's victory at Cedar Creek was the last of the many battles fought in the valley.

Sheridan's ride to the battle-field, and the battle itself, have been made the theme of one of the most spirited poems of the war.[1] No name on the records of either army of those who fought in this famed valley can compare with Sheridan's, unless it be that of Stonewall Jackson.

We will leave Grant preparing to invest Petersburg, and follow the victorious standards of Sherman on the other side of the Alleghanies. He opened the campaign on the 6th of May, 1864, and on the 2d of September entered Atlanta. In the graphic language of his report dated September 8th, he says : "On the first of May our armies were lying in garrison seemingly quiet, from Knoxville to Huntsville, and our enemy lay behind his Rocky-Faced barrier at Dalton, proud, defiant, and exultant."

The rebels had recovered from their defeat at Mission Ridge, their ranks were again filled up, and a new commander, General Johnston, second to none for skill and sagacity, was now at the head of their army. " All at once," says Sherman, " our armies assumed life and action, and appeared before Dalton. Threatening Rocky Face, we

1. Sheridan's Ride, by Thomas Buchanan Read.

threw ourselves upon Resaca, and the rebel army escaped by the rapidity of his retreat." * * * * " He took post at Allatoona, but we gave him no rest, and by our circuit towards Dallas and subsequent movement, gained the Allatoona Pass. Then followed the eventful battles about Kenesaw, and the escape of the enemy across the Chattahooche; the crossing of the Chattahooche, and the breaking of the Augusta Road was most handsomely executed. At this stage of our game, our enemies became dissatisfied with their old and skillful commander, and selected one (Hood) more rash and bold. New tactics were adopted. Hood boldly, on the 20th of July, fell on our right at Peach Tree Creek, and lost. On the 22d, he struck our extreme left, and was severely punished, and finally, on the 28th, he repeated the attempt on our right, and this time must have become satisfied, for since that time he has remained on the defensive." Sherman then drew his lines about Atlanta, and, on the 2d of September, obtained possession of that important railroad and military position. In this short, brilliant, and decisive campaign, in an attack by Hood on the 22d of July, the brave and accomplished McPherson was killed. The President, who had watched these successful movements with the greatest interest, issued a general order of thanks to Sherman and his gallant officers and soldiers, in which he justly says: " This campaign will be ever famous in the annals of war."

Far from his base of supplies, General Sherman deemed it a military necessity to remove the inhabitants of Atlanta so that it should be occupied exclusively for military purposes. General Hood and the mayor of Atlanta protested against this order for removal. In reply, General Sherman said:

" The use of Atlanta for warlike purposes is inconsistent with its character as a home for families. There will be no manufactures, commerce, or agriculture here for the maintenance of families, and sooner or later, want will compel the inhabitants to go. Why not go now, when all the arrangements are completed for the transfer, instead of waiting till the plunging shot of contending armies will renew the scenes of the past month. * * * You cannot qualify war in harsher terms than I will. War is cruelty, and you cannot refine it; and those who brought war on our country, deserve all the curses and maledictions a people can pour out. I know I had no hand in making this war, and I know I will make more sacrifices to-day than any of you to secure peace. But you cannot have peace and a division of our country. If the United States submits to a division now, it will not stop, but will go on till we reap the fate of Mexico, which is eternal war. The United States does and must assert its authority wherever it has power; if it relaxes one bit to pressure, it is gone, and I know that such is not the national feeling. This feeling assumes various shapes, but always comes back to that of the Union; once admit the Union; once more acknowledge the authority of the national government, and instead of devoting your houses, and streets, and roads to the dread uses of war, I and this army become at once your protectors and supporters, shielding you from danger, let it come from whatever quarter it may."

This reply of Sherman is written with great vigor, and shows that he could use the pen with as much ability as the sword. Meanwhile, Hood, with the hope of compelling Sherman to retire to the North, moved to the right of Atlanta, towards Tennessee. But Sherman proposed to Grant to destroy Atlanta and the railroads leading to it, and boldly strike through the enemy's country to the sea. Grant evidently at first thought the enterprise very hazardous, if not rash, and in reply, on the 11th of October, he telegraphed to Sherman: "Hood will probably strike for Nashville. * * If there is any way of getting at Hood's army I would prefer that, but I must trust to your judgment. * * * I am afraid Thomas, with such lines of road as he has to protect, could not prevent Hood from going North." On the same day, Sherman telegraphed to Grant from Kingston, Georgia: "We cannot remain here on the defensive. * * * I would prefer making a wreck of the roads and the country from Chattanooga to Atlanta, including the latter city, sending back my wounded, and with my effective army move through Georgia, *smashing things to the sea.*" To this Grant on the same day replied: "If you are satisfied the trip to the sea can be made, holding the line of the Tennessee River firmly, you may make it." And so the bold and adventurous Sherman cut loose from his communications in the rear, cut the wires of the telegraph and started for the sea, which he must reach or perish.

But before we follow the path of this enterprising soldier, let us see what were the fortunes of Hood. Thomas was being strengthened. Hood, following Schofield, who was marching towards Thomas, attacked him at Franklin, but was repulsed with serious loss. Thomas and Schofield formed a line of battle in front of Nashville, and, on the 15th of January, Thomas attacked Hood, and after a fierce and bloody conflict, continuing through two days, the Confederates broke and fled in confusion, the Union army capturing several thousand prisoners, and a vast amount of small arms and artillery. The soldiers of Hood were scattered or captured, and never again appeared in the field as an army organization. Some fragments of his army escaped, and under Johnston, surrendered to Sherman in the spring of 1865, at the final surrender of Johnston.

Where now was Sherman? Jefferson Davis prophesied that Sherman's army, then in the heart of the Confederacy, would meet the fate of the army of Napoleon when it invaded Russia. "Our cavalry and our people," said the rebel leader, "will harass and destroy this army, as did the Cossacks that of the French, and the Yankee General, like Napoleon, will escape with only a body guard."

But this "Yankee General," at whom Davis so arrogantly sneered, marched at pleasure through his Confederacy, and soon Davis himself, as the result, became first a fugitive, and then a captive, and his empire based on slavery crumbled into ruins.

Sherman marched eastward towards Macon, destroying railroads and everything which could be of service to the Confederacy. He reached Milledgeville, the capital of Georgia, in November, without any serious opposition. By the 12th of December he had reached and invested Savannah. Lincoln had sent Admiral Dahlgren with a fleet, to find and coöperate with Sherman. To open communication with the fleet it was necessary to capture Fort McAllister, which commanded the approaches from the sea on the south side of the city. On the 13th of December, General Hazen assaulted and captured the Fort, a boat was sent to the fleet, General Sherman went on board, and sent a despatch to Washington announcing his arrival and his complete success. On the 20th, Hardee, in command of Savannah, abandoned the city, Sherman took possession, and sent to the President a despatch saying: "I present to you as a Christmas gift the City of Savannah, with one hundred and fifty guns, plenty of ammunition, and about twenty-five thousand bales of cotton."

Thus ended this grand march to the sea, a part of the romance of history. With the overwhelming force of the avalanche Sherman descended from the North, crushing everything in his path from the mountains to the sea. And now it only remained for this Northwestern army to turn again to the North, and, coöperating with the veterans of Grant, to crush the remaining fragments of the rebellion.

Nothing occurred during the war which more incensed the American people than the ravages upon their commerce by English built cruisers sailing under the rebel flag. Avoiding armed antagonists, they long roamed the sea with impunity, robbing and destroying American merchantmen, and finding refuge and protection, and often supplies, in neutral ports, especially those of Great Britain. Among the most destructive of these cruisers were the Alabama, the Florida, and the Georgia. Early in June, 1864, the Alabama, after a successful cruise, put in to Cherbourg, France. The Kearsarge, Captain John A. Winslow, immediately sailed for that port, and waited for the Alabama to put to sea. The Alabama, having made the most careful preparation for the conflict, on the 19th of June steamed out of the harbor to meet her foe. As she came out she opened fire at long range. The Kearsarge made no reply, but steamed directly for her antagonist. Arriving at close quarters, she opened a tremendous fire, and in a short time the Alabama surrendered. Captain Semmes, her commander, and her other officers abandoned their ship, and were picked up and carried to England by the English yacht Deerhound. The Alabama in a few moments went down, even before all the wounded could be saved. Of this gallant fight, Admiral Farragut, in a letter to his son, says: " It was fought like a tournament in full view of thousands of French and English, with full confidence on the part of all but the Union people that we would be whipped. * * * I would sooner have fought that fight than any ever fought on the ocean." [1] The Florida and the Georgia were both captured during the year. Neither the sinking of the Alabama, nor the payment by the English government to the Americans of the Alabama claims, have entirely removed from the people of this republic their indignation towards the English for their unfriendly conduct in permitting, while professing friendship to our government, the Alabama and other rebel cruisers to be fitted out in their ports.

In the same summer of 1864, Admiral Farragut was in command of the national squadron off Mobile. The city was supposed to be able to defy any attack. It was defended by Forts Gaines, Morgan, and Powell, by water batteries and earth-works, by torpedoes, and by the iron-clad ram Tennessee, which it was supposed could destroy any fleet which should attempt its capture. But with Farragut there was nothing impossible. He made his preparations for attack on the 5th of August. " Strip your vessels and prepare for the conflict," said he. As he went into close action, the grand old Admiral stood in the port-rigging of the flag-ship, a few ratlins up, standing on, and steadying himself by the ropes, and, as the smoke increased, he ascended the rigging step by step, until he found himself above the futtock-bands, and holding on to the shrouds. Captain Drayton, seeing the perilous position of the Admiral, and seeing that if wounded he would fall into the sea, sent a sailor with a line to secure him. The sailor took a lead line, and fastening it around the Admiral, made it fast to the shrouds. "For," said the

1. See Life of Farragut, p. 403.

sailor, " I feared he would fall overboard if anything should carry away, or he should be struck." And thus lashed to the shrouds, in a position above the smoke, and where he could see the fight, the Admiral fought the most brilliant naval battle of the war. Captain Craven, of the Tecumseh, eager to engage the Tennessee, pressed rapidly on, struck a torpedo, and went down with nearly all on board. Farragut, from his lofty position, saw his brave comrades go down by his side, and at the same moment the Brooklyn, leading the fleet, and discovering the line of torpedoes across the channel, began to back water.

" What's the trouble ? " was shouted through a trumpet to the Brooklyn.

" Torpedoes," was shouted back in reply.

"Damn the torpedoes ! " said Farragut.

" Go ahead, full speed," he shouted to his own captain. And away went the flag-ship, the Hartford, passing the Brooklyn, and leading the fleet to victory,[1] at a moment when hesitation would have been fatal. This brilliant victory by Farragut was followed by the surrender of Mobile, and the forts, on being invested by General Granger, soon also surrendered.

The President issued a proclamation of thanksgiving and gratitude to God. He was now buoyant with hope, and began to expect an early termination of the war.

1. Life of Farragut, p. 417.

CHAPTER XXIII.

THE SECOND TERM.

Lincoln Renominated and Re-Elected.— His Administration. — Peace Conference.— Greeley and the Rebel Emissaries. — Blair's Visit to Richmond.— Hampton Roads Conference.— Second Inauguration.

In the meanwhile, time and tide, and Presidential elections, wait for no man. Lincoln's first term was approaching its end, and the people began to prepare for the election.

There was not only an active, hostile party organization against the President, eager to obtain power, ready to seize upon and magnify the faults and errors of the administration, but there were also many ambitious men in the Union party, who, with their friends and followers, believed the best interests of the republic required a change. There were candidates for the Presidency among the generals, whom the President had been compelled by his sense of duty to relieve of command, and even in his Cabinet was an eager aspirant for the White House. The attention of all the world was directed to this approaching election.

Occurring in the midst of this tremendous civil war, it was regarded as the most fearful ordeal to which our institutions could be subjected. Many candid and intelligent men did not believe we could pass through its dangers without anarchy and revolution. There were also elements of danger in secret and factious organizations which bold, ambitious, and unscrupulous men, sympathizing with the rebels, were ready to use for dangerous purposes. All thoughtful observers know that in time of war, and especially civil war, the passions, prejudices, and convictions of men become strongly excited and difficult to control. The people are easily led to throw off the restraints of law, and to adopt questionable means to secure their ends. There was danger, grave danger, in this election.

The safety and triumph of law, order, and the Constitution were largely due to the forbearance, the patriotism, and the personal character of the President. He was so modest, so calm, so just, so truthful, so magnaminous to others, so sincerely honest, and so clearly and obviously unselfish and patriotic, that faction and personal hostility were calmed and quieted. With "malice towards none, and charity for all," he could not be provoked to do any act of personal injury or wrong; and faction stood disarmed by his transparent truth, and honest desire to do right. He would not be provoked into personal controversy. The great mass of the people stood firmly by him. They trusted him fully, and while the politicians, a majority of both Houses of Congress, and the great leaders of the press in the great cities, were not favorable to his re-election, the people, with the instinctive good sense which characterized them during the war, were almost universally in his favor. The prominent men who opposed him in Congress, and out of it, could get no following. In vain Mr. Horace Greeley, through the New York Tribune, and over his name, in the Independent, opposed the renomination. [1] In vain an organization was gotten up at Washington in opposition to him, composed of a large number of able, eloquent, and influential senators and members of Congress, and in vain were secret circulars issued, and speeches made opposing him. [2] The people would

1. See Letter of Horace Greeley in The Independent of February 25th, 1864. See also New York Daily Tribune, February 13th, 1864, and other issues during the winter and spring of that year.

2. See Secret Circular issued by Senator Pomeroy and others. As an illustration of the opinion of Congress, the following incident is recalled. A prominent editor from the interior of Pennsylvania, a warm friend of the President, came to Washington in the winter of 1864, and, going to the Congressional leader, Mr. Thaddeus Stevens, said : " Introduce me to some member of Congress friendly to Mr. Lincoln's renomination." " Come with me," replied Stevens. They came to the seat of the

not respond to their appeals. They said: "We know and trust Lincoln, and we will not change pilots in the midst of the storm." To use his own homely but expressive illustration, they said: "We will not swap horses while fording the stream."

The opposition to him was divided in its preferences. Some were for General Fremont, and more for Salmon P. Chase, the Secretary of the Treasury. He had been a trusted leader in the anti-slavery movement, a distinguished senator, an able secretary, but he had the fault of many great men ; he was ambitious, he wished to be President. And, while holding a position in Mr. Lincoln's Cabinet, he not only permitted, but encouraged his friends to seek his elevation over the man in whose political family he held a position so confidential. He was not loyal to his chief. He used the power which the President gave him to place his own partisans in office. They did not scruple to use this power to pull Lincoln down and set Chase up. The President was fully conscious of this, but permitted it to go on, saying : "It will all come out right in the end." But when Ohio, Mr. Chase's own state, declared for Mr. Lincoln, he withdrew from the canvass. Lincoln was so magnanimous that a short time thereafter, when a vacancy occurred in the great office of Chief Justice of the United States, he appointed Mr. Chase to that high position.

The people were satisfied with the President, and they were so engrossed with the contest for national existence, and the overthrow of slavery, that they were impatient of divisions and controversies among the Union leaders. So

member from the Chicago District in Illinois. Addressing him, Mr. Stevens said : " Here is a man who wants to find a Lincoln member of Congress. You are the only one I know, and I have come over to introduce my friend to you." "Thank you," said the member. " I know a good many such, and I will present your friend to them, and I wish you, Mr. Stevens, were with us."

But Stevens was quite right in supposing a large majority to be opposed to the President. In January, 1865, Mr. Stevens said : " If the question could be submitted to the people of the United States, whom they would elect for the next President, a majority would vote for General Butler." Cong. Globe, 2nd Session 38th Congress, part 1, p. 400.

much so, that the opposition to Mr. Lincoln, talented, eloquent, zealous, and active, and supported by many of the leading journals of the country, produced hardly a ripple upon the wave of public sentiment, which rolled on in favor of his renomination. The voters at home, and the soldiers in the field, had learned to trust him fully and absolutely. They knew his hands were clean, and that his heart was thoroughly honest ; that he was bold and sagacious. They knew that there was no bribe big enough, no temptation of wealth or power sufficient to seduce his integrity. Hence their instinctive sagacity settled the presidential question, and the politicians and the editors, after vain efforts to turn the tide, acquiesced.

The convention was called to meet at Baltimore, on the 8th of June, 1864. The opposition to Mr. Lincoln made a great effort to have it postponed until autumn, but failed.[1]

1. The following letter will show the manner in which the President's friends met this effort, and the spirit of the canvass.

" *To the Editors of the Evening Post:*

"I have received a printed circular to which several distinguished names are attached, urging the postponement of the national convention.

"Believing that such postponement would be most unwise and dangerous to the loyal cause, I ask the privilege, through the columns of the Evening Post, very briefly to give my reasons for such belief.

"I concur most fully with the gentlemen who signed the paper referred to, that it is very important that all parties friendly to the government should be united in support of a single candidate (for President), and that when a selection shall be made it shall be acquiesced in by all sections of the country, and all branches of the loyal party.

"I am perfectly convinced that the best means of securing a result so essential to success is an early convention, and that nothing would be more likely to prevent such union than its postponement.

"The postponement would be the signal for the organization of the friends of the various aspirants for the Presidency, and for the most earnest and zealous canvass of the claims, merits, and demerits of those candidates.

"If the time should be changed to September, we should see the most violent controversy within the Union ranks known in the history of politics.

"Is such a controversy desirable, and shall we encourage and stimulate it by postponing the convention?

"I think I am fully warranted in stating that up to this time there has been no considerable difference of opinion among the people on the Presidential question. It is a most significant fact that, notwithstanding the efforts made in this city and elsewhere in behalf of prominent and able men in military and civil life; notwithstanding a thoroughly organized, able, ardent, and zealous opposition to President Lincoln here, embodying great abilities and abundant means; with the co-operation of some of the

A few disappointed members of the party met at Cleveland, Ohio, and nominated General Fremont for President, but this nomination was so obviously without popular support that Fremont withdrew, and his friends generally voted for Lincoln. An attempt was made to bring out General Grant

great leading newspapers of the Union, and with the aid of some of the distinguished names of trusted national leaders attached to your petition; yet all this has produced no perceptible effect upon public opinion. The minds of the people are fixed upon the great contest for national existence, and are impatient of quarrels and controversies among ourselves. The opposition to the President in our own party, talented, eloquent, zealous, and active as it is, has scarcely produced a ripple on the wave of public sentiment which is so strongly running in favor of Mr. Lincoln's re-election.

"There is no organization among the friends of the President, they are doing nothing; but this action of the people is spontaneous, unprompted, earnest, and sincere. State after state holds its convention, appoints its delegates, and without a dissenting voice instructs them to vote for Mr. Lincoln. This popularity of the President, this unanimity of the people, is confined to no section, but East as well as West, middle state and border state, they all speak one voice, 'Let us have Lincoln for our candidate.' Do I exaggerate? Maine speaks for him on the Atlantic, and her voice is echoed by California from the Pacific, New Hampshire and Kansas, Connecticut and Minnesota, Wisconsin and West Virginia, and now comes the great state of Pennsylvania, seconding Maryland; one after another, all declare for the re-election of the President. Is it not wiser to recognize and accept this great fact than to struggle against it?

"The truth is, the masses of the people, and the soldiers everywhere, trust and love the President. They know his hands are clean and his heart is honest and pure. They know that the devil has no bribe big enough, no temptation of wealth or power, which can seduce the integrity of Abraham Lincoln.

" Hence the people—the brave, honest, self-denying people—the people who have furnished the men, and who are ready to pay the taxes necessary to crush the rebellion, and who are determined to establish national unity based on liberty—they are more wise, less factious, and more disinterested than the politicians. Their instinctive sagacity and good sense have already settled the Presidential question. It cannot be unsettled without a convulsion which will endanger the Union cause. A postponement of the convention would not prevent Mr. Lincoln's renomination; it might possibly endanger his election.

"Acquiescence, union, and harmony will follow the June convention. Delay encourages faction, controversy, and division. I say harmony will follow the June convention. I say this because I believe General Fremont and his friends are loyal to liberty and will not endanger its triumph by dividing the friends of freedom. I say this because I believe the radical Germans who support Fremont, who have done so much in this contest to sustain free institutions, cannot be induced by their enthusiasm for a man to desert or endanger the triumph of their principles.

"The hour is critical. We approach the very crisis of our fate as a nation. With union and harmony our success is certain.

"The Presidential election rapidly approaches. We cannot divert attention from it by postponing the convention. We cannot safely change our leaders in the midst of the storm raging around us.

"The people have no time for the discussions which must precede and follow such a change.

as a candidate, but the people saw that he was more useful at the head of their armies. General Grant himself, with the good sense, fidelity, and integrity which marked his career, refused to have his name used to divide the Union party. Mr. Lincoln said to a friend in regard to this movement: "If General Grant could be more useful as President in putting down the rebellion, I would be content. He is pledged to our policy of emancipation and the employment of negro soldiers, and if this policy is carried out, it won't make much difference who is President."

The national convention met on the 8th of June, and was organized by the election of the Rev. Robert J. Breckenridge, of Kentucky, as temporary chairman. He was a stern old Presbyterian clergyman, and, although the uncle of General John C. Breckenridge of the rebel army, a determined Unionist and an emancipationist. In a bold and fervid speech, and amidst the applause of the convention, he declared slavery to be " contrary to the spirit of the Christian religion, and incompatible with the natural rights of man," and he continued: " I fervently pray God that the day may come when throughout the whole land every man may be as free as you are, and as capable of enjoying regulated liberty." [1]

Ex-Governor William Dennison, of Ohio, was made President. After endorsing the administration, and approving the anti-slavery acts of Congress and the Executive, and especially the proclamation of emancipation, the convention declared in favor of amending the Constitution so as to abolish and prohibit slavery forever throughout the republic. Lincoln was unanimously nominated for President, and Andrew Johnson, of Tennessee, for Vice-President. Han-

" I repeat, we cannot safely or wisely change our leader in the midst of the great events which will not wait for conventions. Such is the instinctive, nearly universal judgment of the people. Let, then, the convention meet and ratify the choice which the people have already so clearly indicated.

" I am, very truly and respectfully yours,

" ISAAC N. ARNOLD.

" *Washington, May 2, 1864.*"

1. McPherson's History of the Rebellion, p. 505.

nibal Hamlin, the incumbent, an able man of unquestionable
integrity, and in every way unexceptionable, was dropped,
and from motives of policy, Johnson was nominated in his
place. Johnson's heroic fidelity to the Union, as senator
from Tennessee, when so many of his associates proved
faithless, his bold and stern denunciation of traitors and
treason on the floor of the Senate, had secured for him the
admiration of the loyal people, and by many it was thought
expedient to take one who was a war democrat for the position of Vice-President.

Among the members of Mr. Lincoln's Cabinet, Montgomery Blair, the Postmaster General, was especially noted
as his personal and political friend. The Blair family had
made a bitter war upon Fremont, and Francis P. Blair had
made a severe attack upon him in the House of Representatives. The hostility between the Blairs and Fremont and
his friends was mutual. The latter sought by every means
in their power to get Montgomery Blair out of the Cabinet.
Finally, after the Presidential nominations had been made,
Fremont's friends made the removal or retirement of Montgomery Blair a condition of Fremont's declining the Cleveland nomination for the Presidency. They induced the
Union national committee, or a part of it, to agree that if
Fremont would decline, the Postmaster General should
resign. They succeeded in making the committee believe
that Fremont would so divide the Union vote in some of
the states as to endanger the success of the Union party.
They tried in vain to induce the President to ask Mr. Blair
to retire. The President was satisfied with Blair as a member of his Cabinet; did not believe there was any serious
danger of defeat; and consequently refused, but finally, the
national committee sent for Judge Ebenezer Peck, of
Illinois, a warm friend of the Blairs, and devoted to Mr.
Lincoln, to visit Washington. He went, and said to the
President: "Your reëlection is necessary to save the Union,
and no man must stand in the way of that success. Mr.
Blair himself," continued Judge Peck, "will gladly retire to

strengthen the ticket." [1]   By these arguments, Judge Peck and others finally induced the President to ask the resignation of Mr. Blair, which he did in a note of great kindness and friendship. Mr. Blair promptly sent his resignation, and Governor William Dennison, of Ohio, was appointed his successor.

Mr. Lincoln gratefully and modestly accepted the nomination, saying: "I view this call to a second term as in no wise more flattering to myself than as an expression of the public judgment, that I may better finish a difficult work than could any one less severely schooled to the task." In relation to the great question of the impending Constitutional amendment, he said: "Such an amendment as is now proposed becomes a fitting and necessary conclusion to the final success of the Union cause. Such alone can meet all cavils. The unconditional Union men, North and South, perceive its importance, and embrace it. In the joint names of Liberty and Union let us labor to give it legal form and practical effect." [2]

The democratic convention met at Chicago, on the 29th of August, and nominated George B. McClellan for President, and George H. Pendleton, of Ohio, for Vice-President. Clement L. Vallandigham, having returned to Ohio from the rebel lines to which he had been sent in pursuance of the sentence of a court-martial, was an active and prominent member, and chairman of the committee on resolutions. The second resolution declared "that after four years of failure to restore the Union by war   *   *   immediate efforts should be made for a cessation of hostilities with a view to an ultimate convention of the states or other practicable means, to the end that peace may be restored on the basis of the Federal Union of the states." [3]

1. Judge Peck to the author.

2. Lincoln's response to the committee, which announced his renomination. McPherson's History of the Rebellion, p. 408.

3. The following is the resolution:
"*Resolved*, That this convention explicitly declare, as the sense of the American people, that after four years of failure to restore the Union by the experiment of

The issue was thus distinctly presented. The union republican party declared for the most vigorous prosecution of the war to the complete suppression of the rebellion, the utter and complete extinction of slavery—approving of the anti-slavery measures of Congress and the Executive, and the pending anti-slavery amendment to the Constitution. The democratic convention denounced the action of Congress and the Executive, declared the war "a failure," and that peace should be sought through a national convention, or other feasible means.

A most exciting canvass followed. The people longed for peace, but they believed peace could only be secured by successful war. In the language of Mr. Lincoln, they "hoped it would come soon, and come to stay, and so come as to be worth keeping in all future time." The President looked for it, and the people expected it, from some great battle-field in Virginia, a field in which the hosts of the rebellious slaveholders would be crushed and overthrown. They believed that the path which it should take was through Richmond, and that the best agents to bring it were not Vallandigham, nor Seymour, nor McClellan, but Grant and Sherman, Sheridan, Thomas, and Farragut. Such a peace as they would bring would be based on union and a restored nationality; liberty for all and a continental republic. It would harmonize and mould into one homogeneous people, a territory stretching from sunrise to sunset, from where the water never thaws to where it never freezes. The brilliant successes of Sherman and Schofield in the West, of Sheridan under Grant in the East, and of Farragut at Mobile in the summer and autumn of 1864, rendered cer-

---

war, during which, under the pretense of a military necessity, or war power higher than the Constitution, the Constitution itself has been disregarded in every part, and public liberty and private right alike trodden down, and the material prosperity of the country essentially impaired; justice, humanity, liberty, and the public welfare demand that immediate efforts be made for a cessation of hostilities, with a view to an ultimate convention of the states, or other peaceful means, to the end that at the earliest practicable moment peace may be restored on the basis of the Federal Union of the states."

tain the success of the Union ticket in November, and indicated an early triumph of the Union cause.

Early in July, Mr. Chase resigned the position of the Secretary of the Treasury, and William Pitt Fessenden, the very able Chairman of the Committee of Finance of the Senate, was appointed his successor. Mr. Chase had been a very able secretary, and in his management of the finances during his administration had rendered great service to the country. Senator Fessenden was reluctant to accept the position, and he expressed this reluctance very frankly to the President. Mr. Lincoln would not excuse him, and playfully said to him : "Fessenden, it is your duty to accept, and if you don't, I'll send you to Fort Lafayette as a prisoner."

During the canvass made by the friends of the President for his nomination and election, he never used his power or his patronage to secure success.[1]

The closing paragraph refers to his own nomination for the Presidency. Indeed, such was his scrupulous delicacy on this point, that Preston King, Senator from New York, was sent by the New York politicians to enquire, as King himself humorously said, "whether Lincoln intended to support the ticket nominated at Baltimore."

Lincoln was re-elected almost by acclamation, receiving every electoral vote, except those of New Jersey, Delaware, and Kentucky. His majority of the popular vote was nearly

---

1. The following note, written in behalf of a friend in Illinois to an officeholder who was charged with using his power against his friend, will illustrate the views of the President:

"EXECUTIVE MANSION, Washington, July 4th, 1864.

"To ————Esq.

"*Dear Sir:* Complaint is made to me that you are using your official power to defeat Mr. ————'s nomination to Congress. I am well satisfied with Mr.————, as a member of Congress, and I do not know that the man who might supplant him would be as satisfactory. But the correct principle I think is, that all our friends should have *absolute freedom* of choice among our friends. My wish therefore is, that you will do just as you think fit with your own suffrage in the case, and not constrain any of your subordinates to do other than he thinks fit with his. This is precisely the rule I inculcated and adhered to on my part, when a certain other nomination now recently made was being canvassed for.

"Yours very truly,

"A. LINCOLN"

half a million, a majority greater than has been given before or since for any presidential candidate. Those who feared the ordeal of a popular election amidst the excitement and passion of civil war, were compelled to acknowledge the calmness, the sobriety, the wisdom and dignity with which the people passed through the crisis.

As soon as the result was known, General Grant telegraphed from City Point his congratulations, and added that " the election having passed off quietly * * * is a victory worth more to the country than a battle won." At a late hour on the evening of the election, Mr. Lincoln, in response to a serenade, said: " I am thankful to God for this approval of the people. But while deeply grateful for this mark of their confidence in me, if I know my own heart, my gratitude is free from any taint of personal triumph. * * It is not in my nature to triumph over any one, but I give thanks to Almighty God for this evidence of the people's resolution to stand by free government and the rights of humanity."

The autumn of 1864 and winter of 1865 were eventful, and changes were rapid. The success of the national armies, the undiminished ability of the government to carry on the war, and its unflinching determination to do so until its objects were fully accomplished, inspired a constantly increasing confidence in the loyal people, and the rebels became more and more desperate and disheartened. Loyal state governments, with constitutions securing freedom to all, had been organized in Arkansas and Louisiana, and movements in the same direction were in progress, and soon to be successful, in Missouri, Kentucky, and Tennessee. Maryland was at peace under a free government.

Chief Justice Taney, who will go down to posterity as the author of the decision of the Supreme Court pronounced in favor of slavery in the notable Dred Scott case, died October 12th, 1864. Salmon P. Chase was immediately suggested as his successor, but the hostility of his friends to Mr. Lincoln's renomination, and his abrupt retirement from the Cab-

inet, led those who did not know Lincoln's magnanimity to
believe that he would not be nominated. The President
himself, however, declared that he early determined to nominate Mr. Chase, and had never changed that determination.
His only hesitation arose from a conviction that Mr. Chase,
even after he had taken a seat on the bench, would not abandon his aspirations for the Presidency. Salmon P. Chase,
the abolitionist, as Chief Justice of the Supreme Court, and
the successor of Roger B. Taney, marked the completion of
the revolution on the subject of slavery.

Meanwhile the cause of the insurgents was growing
more and more desperate. They had no credit. They
could not fill up their armies. They were discussing the
project of arming their negroes, and giving them liberty as
the reward of military service. And, as their cause became
more and more dark and uncertain, schemes of desperation,
involving the burning of Northern cities, murder, robbery,
and assassination, were being discussed and organized by the
desperate men who began to despair of success in civilized
warfare.

The emissaries of the rebels, in the summer of 1864,
succeeded in creating the conviction in the mind of that
good but credulous and sometimes indiscreet man, Horace
Greeley, that certain Southern agents in Canada were anxious for peace, and that it would be wise for the President
to confer with them. On the 7th of July, 1864, Greeley
wrote to the President a letter, in which he said : "I venture to remind you that our bleeding, bankrupt, almost dying
country also longs for peace — shudders at the prospect of
fresh conscriptions, of future wholesale devastations, and of
rivers of human blood. * * I fear, Mr. President, you do
not realize how intensely the people desire any peace consistent with national integrity and honor." He begged
Mr. Lincoln to extend safe conduct to certain rebel
agents then at Niagara, that they might submit their
propositions. The President was in a position to know, and
did know, far better than Mr. Greeley or any private indi-

vidual, the views of the insurgents. Their object, especially of the emissaries in behalf of whom Greeley wrote, was to aid the democratic party to divide the loyal states, and they made a dupe of good Mr. Greeley. The President knew that the best means of securing peace was to destroy the rebel armies, and that Grant and Sherman and Farragut were doing more to bring it than any negotiations. He doubted whether these agents had any authority. But as Mr. Greeley was a prominent editor, and a man of the best and purest motives, Lincoln, with his usual sagacity, determined to convince him, not only of his own desire for peace, but to expose what he believed to be the deceptive character of these agents. In reply to Mr. Greeley, he said: "If you can find any person anywhere, professing to have any proposition of Jefferson Davis, in writing, for peace, embracing the restoration of the Union and abandonment of slavery, whatever else it embraces, say to him he may come to me with you." In another letter, the President said to Mr. Greeley: "I not only intend a sincere effort for peace, but you shall be a personal witness that it is made."

Messrs. Clay, Sanders, and Holcombe, the persons, alluded to by Mr. Greeley, had no authority whatever to treat for peace; they declared that they were in the confidential employment of their government, but for what purpose they were discreetly silent. They asked for a safe conduct to and from Washington, which Mr. Greeley urged the President to give. This application was met by the following passport, or safe conduct, under the hand of the President:

"July 18th, 1864.

" *To whom it may concern :*

"Any proposition which embraces the restoration of peace, the integrity of the whole Union, and the abandonment of slavery, and which comes by and with an authority that can control the armies now at war against the United States, will be received and considered by the Executive Government of the United States, and will be met by liberal terms on substantial and collateral points; and the bearer or bearers thereof shall have safe conduct both ways.

" ABRAHAM LINCOLN."

This put an end to the intrigues with which these men, Clay and his associates, had entrapped Mr. Greeley.

Another prominent editor from the West visited Washington soon after the November election, to urge upon the Executive that he should make peace. He said, in substance :

"Assuming that Grant is baffled and delayed in his efforts to take Richmond, will it not be better to accept peace on favorable terms, than to prolong the war ? Have not nearly four years of war demonstrated that, as against a divided North, a united South can make a successful defence ? The South is a unit, made so, it is conceded, by despotic power. We of the North cannot afford to secure unity by giving up our constitutional government ; we cannot secure unity without despotism. * * * The rebels will fill up their exhausted armies by three hundred thousand negroes ; these negroes, under the training and discipline of white officers, and with freedom as their reward, will fight for them. The Union armies will be very greatly reduced next year by the expiration of the term of service of many of the men. How will you fill up the ranks ? The people are divided ; one-third or more, as the election shows, are positively and unalterably for carrying it on until the rebellion is thoroughly subjugated ; the remainder of the people, when the clouds gather black and threatening again, when another draft comes, and increased taxation, the peace men, and the timid, facile, doubtful men, will go over to the opposition, and make it a majority. You can now secure any terms you please, by granting to the rebels recognition. You can fix your own boundary. You can hold all within your own lines—the Mississippi River, and all west of it, and Louisiana. You can retain Maryland, West Virginia, and Tennessee. Take this—make peace. Is not this as much territory, which was formerly slave territory, as the republic can digest, and assimilate to freedom at once. Make this a homogeneous country—make it free, and then improve and develope the mighty empire you have left. If you succeed in subduing the entire territory in rebellion, can the nation assimilate and make it homogeneous ? Are the people in the Gulf states sufficiently intelligent to make freedom a blessing ? You can people, educate, and bring up to the capability of self-government, the territory you have within your lines. But taking it all—with its people accustomed to slavery, with the ignorance and vice resulting therefrom, is it clear that it is worth the blood and treasure it may cost ? "

The President was unmoved by these representations. His reply was brief and emphatic. " There are," said he,

" just two indispensable conditions to peace—*national unity* and *national liberty*. The national authority must be restored through all the states, and I will *never* recede from the position I have taken on the slavery question. The people have the courage, the self-denial, the persistence, to go *through*, and before another year goes by, it is reasonably certain, we shall bring all the rebel territory within our lines. We are neither exhausted nor in process of exhaustion. We are really stronger than when we began the war. The purpose of the people to maintain the integrity of the republic has never been shaken."

For the purpose of learning the views of the Confederate leaders, Francis P. Blair, a private citizen, but a man of large political experience and great influence with many family and personal friends among the rebels, on the 28th day of December, 1864, obtained from the President permission to pass through the military lines South, and return. The President was informed that he intended to use the pass as a means of getting to Richmond, but no authority to speak or act for the government was conferred upon him. On his return, he brought Mr. Lincoln a letter from Jefferson Davis, addressed to himself, the contents of which he had been authorized by Davis to communicate to the President, and in which Davis stated that he was now, as he had always been, willing to send commissioners or receive them, and " to enter into a conference with a view to secure peace to the *two countries*." Thereupon, the President addressed a note to Mr. Blair, dated January 18th, 1865, in which, after stating that he had read the note of Davis, he said he had been, was now, and should continue, ready to receive any agent whom Davis, or other influential person resisting the national authority, might informally send to him, with a view of securing peace to the people of " *our common country*." This note was delivered by Mr. Blair to Jefferson Davis. The visit of Mr. Blair resulted in the appointment by Davis, of Alexander H. Stephens, R. M. T. Hunter, and John A. Campbell, to confer with the President on the subject of peace, on the basis of his letter to Mr. Blair. When their arrival at the camp of General Grant was announced, Secretary Seward was charged by the President with representing the government at the proposed informal conference. With the frankness which was characteristic of Mr. Lincoln, he instructed Mr. Seward to make known to Messrs. Stephens, Hunter, and Campbell, that three things were indispensable, to-wit:

First, The restoration of the national authority throughout all the states.

Second, No receding by the Executive of the United States, on the slavery question, from the position assumed thereon in the late annual message to Congress, and in preceding documents.

Third, No cessation of hostilities, short of an end of the war, and the disbanding of all forces hostile to the government.

He was further instructed to inform them that all propositions of theirs not inconsistent with the above, would be considered and passed upon in a spirit of sincere liberality. He was further instructed "to hear and report, but not to consummate anything."

Before any conference was held, however, the President joined Secretary Seward at Fortress Monroe, and, on the 3rd of February, Messrs. Stephens, Hunter, and Campbell came on board the steamer of the President, and had an interview of several hours with him. The conditions contained in the President's instructions to Mr. Seward were stated and insisted upon. Those conditions, it will be observed, contained an explicit statement that the Executive would not recede from the emancipation proclamation, nor from any of the positions which he had taken in regard to the abolition of slavery. The agents of Davis were also informed that Congress had, by a constitutional majority, adopted the joint resolution, submitting to the states the proposition to abolish slavery throughout the Union, and that there was every reason to believe it would be adopted by three-fourths of the states, so as to become a part of the Constitution. The rebel agents earnestly desired a temporary cessation of hostilities, and a postponement of the questions, but to this the President would not listen. So far from it, Mr. Lincoln said to General Grant: "Let nothing that is transpiring change, hinder, or delay your military movements or plans." The conference ended without accomplishing anything. [1]

In their extremity, General Lee was, on the 2d of February, 1865, made commander of all the rebel forces, and in their desperate fortunes, the rebel authorities resolved to call upon their negroes for aid. Judah P. Benjamin, their Secretary of State, in a public meeting after the Hampton Roads conference, said that the Confederates had six hundred and eighty thousand black men, and expressed regret that they had not been called into service as soldiers. He added: "Let us now say to every negro who wishes to go into the ranks on condition of being free: 'Go and fight; you are free.'" "My own negroes," continued he, "have been

---

1. Mr. Stephens is stated by a Georgia paper to have repeated the following characteristic anecdote of what occurred during the interview : "The three Southern gentlemen met Mr. Lincoln and Mr. Seward, and after some preliminary remarks, the subject of peace was opened. Mr. Stephens, well aware that one who asks much may get more than he who confesses to humble wishes at the outset, urged the claims of his section with that skill and address for which the Northern papers have given him credit. Mr. Lincoln, holding the vantage ground of conscious power, was, however, perfectly frank, and submitted his views almost in the form of an argument. * * * Davis had, on this occasion, as on that of Mr. Stephens's visit to Washington, made it a condition that no conference should be had, unless his rank as Commander or President should first be recognized. Mr. Lincoln declared that the only ground on which he could rest the justice of war—either with his own people, or with foreign powers— was that it was not a war for conquest, for that the states have never been separated from the Union. Consequently he could not recognize another government inside of the one of which he alone was President ; nor admit the separate independence of states that were yet a part of the Union. 'That,' said he, ' would be doing what you have so long asked Europe to do in vain, and be resigning the only thing the armies of the Union have been fighting for.'

"Mr. Hunter made a long reply to this, insisting that the recognition of Davis's power to make a treaty was the first and indispensable step to peace, and referred to the correspondence between King Charles I. and his Parliament, as a trustworthy precedent of a constitutional ruler treating with rebels. Mr. Lincoln's face then wore that indescribable expression which generally preceded his hardest hits, and he remarked : ' Upon questions of history I must refer you to Mr. Seward, for he is posted in such things, and I don't pretend to be bright. My only distinct recollection of the matter is that Charles lost his head.' That settled Mr. Hunter for a while."

to me and said: 'Master, set us free, and we will fight for you.' You must make up your mind to try this or see your army withdrawn from before your town. * * I know not where white men can be found." General Lee had long before recommended this policy. But it was too late, if indeed it could ever have been successful.

Meanwhile the ides of March had come, the term of the Thirty-eighth Congress expired, and Mr. Lincoln, on the eve of final triumph, was to be inaugurated President. The morning of the 4th of March was stormy and cloudy, but as the hour of twelve approached, the rain ceased, the clouds disappeared, and the sun came forth in all its splendor. Crowds of people, the best, the noblest, the most patriotic, those who had given time and means and offered life to save the republic, gathered at the Capitol to witness the second inauguration of a man now recognized as the savior of his country. As the great procession started from the White House for the Capitol, a brilliant star made its appearance in the sky, and was by many regarded as an omen of approaching peace. The two houses of Congress had adjourned at twelve, but a special session of the Senate had been called, at which Andrew Johnson, the Vice-President, appeared, took the oath of office, and became presiding officer of that august and dignified body. Mr. Lincoln was attended by the judges of the Supreme Court in their official robes, by the diplomatic corps, brilliant in the court costumes of the nations they represented, and by a crowd of distinguished officers of the army and navy in full uniform, prominent citizens, scholars, statesmen, governors, judges, editors, clergy, from all parts of the Union. The galleries were filled with ladies, and with soldiers who had come in from the camp and hospitals around Washington to witness the inauguration of their beloved chief. Striking was the contrast between this audience and that which had greeted him four years before at his first inauguration.

As the President, followed by the brilliant assembly from

26

the Senate, was conducted to the eastern portico of the
Capitol, the vast crowd met him in front of the colonnade ;
a crowd of citizens and soldiers who would willingly have
died for their Chief Magistrate.   It was touching to see the
long lines of invalid and wounded soldiers in the national
blue, some on crutches, some who had lost limbs, many pale
from unhealed wounds, who had sought permission to witness the scene.   As the President reached the platform, and
his tall form, high above his associates, was recognized,
cheers and shouts of welcome filled the air ; and not until he
raised his arm in token that he would speak, could they be
hushed.   He paused a moment, and, looking over the brilliant scene, still hesitated.   What thronging memories passed
through his mind !   Here, four years ago, he had stood on
this colonnade, pleading earnestly with his " dissatisfied fellow countrymen" for peace, but they would not heed him.
He had there solemnly told them that in their hands, and
not in his was the momentous issue of civil war.   He had
told them they could have no conflict without being themselves the "aggressors " ; and even while he was pleading
for peace, they had taken up the sword and compelled him
to "accept war."   Now, four long, weary years of wretched,
desolating, cruel war had passed ; those who had made that
war were everywhere being overthrown ; that cruel institution
which had caused the war had been destroyed, and the
dawn of peace was already brightening the sky behind the
clouds of the storm.

Chief Justice Chase administered the oath.[1]   Then, with

---

1. Two or three days after the inauguration, the author called at the White
House, and Mrs. Lincoln showed him the Bible used by the Chief Justice in adminis-
tering the oath to the President. The 27th and the 28th verses of the 5th chapter
of Isaiah were marked as the verses which the lips of Mr. Lincoln touched in kissing
the book. She seemed to think the text admonished him to be on his guard, and not
to relax at all in his efforts. The words marked are these :

"None shall be weary, nor stumble among them; none shall slumber nor sleep;
neither shall the girdle of their loins be loosed, nor the latchet of their shoes be broken.

"Whose arrows are sharp, and all their bows bent, their horses' hoofs shall be
counted like flint, their wheels like a whirlwind."

Chief Justice Chase had given this Bible to Mrs. Lincoln so marked.

a clear but at times saddened voice, President Lincoln pronounced his second and last inaugural.

"Fellow Countrymen :—At this second appearing to take the oath of the Presidential office, there is less occasion for an extended address than there was at the first. Then, a statement somewhat in detail of a course to be pursued, seemed very fitting and proper. Now, at the expiration of four years, during which public declarations have been constantly called forth on every point and phase of the great contest which still absorbs the attention and engrosses the energies of the nation, little that is new could be presented. The progress of our arms, upon which all else chiefly depends, is as well known to the public as to myself, and it is, I trust, reasonably satisfactory and encouraging to all. With high hope for the future, no prediction in regard to it is ventured.

"On the occasion corresponding to this, four years ago, all thoughts were anxiously directed to an impending civil war. All dreaded it, all sought to avoid it. While the inaugural address was being delivered from this place, devoted altogether to saving the Union without war,—insurgent agents were in the city, seeking to destroy it with war,—seeking to dissolve the Union, and divide the effects by negotiation. Both parties deprecated war, but one of them would make war rather than let the nation survive, and the other would accept war rather than let it perish; and the war came. One-eighth of the whole population were colored slaves, not distributed generally over the Union, but localized in the southern part of it. These slaves constituted a peculiar and powerful interest. All knew that this interest was somehow the cause of the war. To strengthen, perpetuate, and extend this interest, was the object for which the insurgents would rend the Union by war, while the government claimed no right to do more than to restrict the territorial enlargement of it.

"Neither party expected for the war the magnitude or the duration which it has already attained. Neither anticipated that the cause of the conflict might cease with, or even before the conflict itself should cease. Each looked for an easier triumph, and a result less fundamental and astounding.

"Both read the same Bible, and pray to the same God, and each invokes His aid against the other. It may seem strange that any men should dare to ask a just God's assistance in wringing their bread from the sweat of other men's faces. But let us judge not, that we be not judged. The prayer of both could not be answered. That of neither has been answered fully. The Almighty has his own purposes. 'Woe unto the world because of offenses, for it must needs be that offenses come, but woe to that man by whom the offense cometh.' If we shall suppose that American slavery is one of these offenses, which in the providence of God must needs come, but which, having continued through his appointed time, he now wills to remove, and that he gives to both North and South this terrible war as the woe due to those by whom the offense came, shall we discern there any departure from those divine attributes which the believers in a living God always ascribe to him ? Fondly do we hope, fervently do we pray, that this mighty scourge of war may speedily pass away. Yet if God wills that it continue until all the wealth piled by the bondsman's two hundred and fifty years of unrequited toil shall be sunk, and until every drop of blood drawn with the lash shall be paid by another drawn by the sword, as was said three thousand years ago, so still it must be said, that ' the judgments of the Lord are true and righteous altogether.'

" With malice towards none, with charity for all, with firmness in the right as God gives us to see the right, let us finish the work we are in, to bind up the nation's wounds, to care for him who shall have borne the battle, and for his widow and his orphans, to do all which may achieve and cherish a just and a lasting peace among ourselves and with all nations."

Since the days of Christ's sermon on the mount, where is the speech of emperor, king, or ruler, which can compare with this? May we not, without irreverence, say that passages of this address are worthy of that holy book which daily he read, and from which, during his long days of trial, he had drawn inspiration and guidance? Where else, but from the teachings of the Son of God, could he have drawn that Christian charity which pervades the last sentence, in which he so unconsciously describes his own moral nature: " *With malice towards none, with charity for all, with firmness in the right as God gives us to see the right.*" No other state paper in American annals, not even Washington's farewell address, has made so deep an impression upon the people as this.

A distinguished divine, coming down from the Capitol, said: " The President's inaugural is the finest state paper in all history." A distinguished statesman from New York said in reply: " Yes, and as Washington's name grows brighter with time, so it will be with Lincoln's. A century from to-day that inaugural will be read as one of the most sublime utterances ever spoken by man. Washington is the great man of the era of the Revolution. So will Lincoln be of this, but Lincoln will reach the higher position in history."

This paper, in its solemn recognition of the justice of Almighty God, reminds us of the words of the old Hebrew prophets. The paper was read in Europe with the most profound attention, and from this time all thinking men recognized the intellectual and moral greatness of its author.

CHAPTER XXIV.

THE APPROACHING END.

IN following the currents of great events at the capital
and at the theatre of war, some facts of minor importance,
but of great interest, have not been noticed. Among them
were the great organizations for the relief, health, and comfort of the soldiers, known as the Sanitary and Christian
Commissions. These organizations were novel, and indicate an advance in humanity and civilization; they relieved war of half the horrors and of much of the suffering
incident to its destruction of human life. The tenderness
and sympathy of the President with all forms of suffering
was apparent in all his life, and the stern soldiers of the war
often regarded his humane spirit as a weakness. They
claimed that his clemency was often abused, and that his
reluctance to inflict punishment interfered with rigid discipline. There were some grounds for these complaints.

When, therefore, in the summer of 1861, Dr. Henry W.
Bellows, of New York, visited Washington, and laid before
the President a plan for organizing the Sanitary Commission, he was listened to with the most careful consideration,
and he found in Mr. Lincoln one as zealous as himself to
carry out his humane purposes. The project was to organ-

ize a commission of the most intelligent, highly respected, and best citizens of the country, whose special duty it should be, in connection with the regular medical officers of the army, to look after and improve the sanitary condition of the soldiers, including their food and their medical and surgical treatment. The President organized this commission by naming Dr. Bellows as its president, and associating with him some of the leading citizens of the great cities of the Union. Its object was to bring the wealth and social influence, and the highest intelligence, skill, and culture of the republic, to secure to the soldier every possible means of preserving and maintaining his health, and the very best possible treatment when wounded or sick. The attention of the very best experts was directed to securing for them the best and most wholesome food, and especially to the comfort and hygiene of camps and hospitals. Voluntary associations, composed of the best men and women of the republic, were organized all over the loyal states, and all the people, with generous and patriotic liberality, placed in the hands of this commission, and in those of a kindred association called the Christian Commission, money, medicines, food, clothing, wine, fruit, and every delicacy for the hospitals; secular and religious reading, trained nurses, and everything which could contribute to the welfare and relieve the wants of the soldiers. Sanitary stores, the most skillful surgeons, and kind and well-trained nurses, followed the soldiers to every battle-field. The wounded of both armies were tenderly cared for and nursed, the dying soothed, and their last messages carefully sent to family and friends. By such means the battle-field was robbed of half its horrors, and the soldier realized that kindness, skill, and care would attend him; that everything would be done to relieve his sufferings and restore him to health. And if it was his fate to die for his country, he knew that his last hours would be soothed by affection and Christian sympathy, and that he would be honored and cherished as a patriot, by his family and friends. For objects so noble and purposes so holy, no appeal for aid was ever made in vain. From the widow's mite and the orphan's pittance, from the day laborer's dollar, the products of the farm and the shop, the gold and jewels of the rich, the means flowed in so lavishly that the resources of the commissions were never exhausted, and many millions were freely given during the war. In further-ance of these objects, a series of great Sanitary Fairs was inaugurated at Chicago, and extended to Philadelphia, New York, Baltimore, Boston, Pittsburgh, and all the great cities and towns of the Union. The President attended many of these fairs, and made many speeches recommending them and urging the most liberal contributions. To the great Northwestern Fair held at Chicago in September, 1863, he sent the original draft of the proclamation of emancipation, to be sold for the benefit of the soldiers, as has already been stated.

The women of the nation, in every social position, were the most active and efficient agents in these enterprises. With a power of organization rivalling that which organized armies, with a tireless energy and executive ability which knew no pause nor rest, many noble women, and especially the widows, mothers, and sisters of soldiers who had been killed, consecrated their time and sacrificed their lives to these noble and patriotic purposes. Party, sect, creed, and social distinction melted away before the holy influence of these objects, and all, rich and poor, laborer and millionaire, laid their gifts upon the altar of patriotism. Here was a universal brotherhood. These institutions were the fruits of religious inspiration, and the fairest flowers of Christian civilization. The Christian Commission expended more than six millions of these generous contributions, and sent five thousand clergymen, from among the very best and ablest, to the camps and battle-fields of the war. The Sani-tary Commission had seven thousand associated societies, and, through an unpaid board of directors, distributed with skill and discretion fifteen millions of dollars in supplies and money.

In this connection may be mentioned the extreme tenderness and sympathy of Mr. Lincoln for all forms of suffering. One day in November, 1864, his attention was called to the fact that a widow of Boston, Massachusetts, had lost five sons in battle. He immediately wrote to her from the White House, saying:

" I feel how weak and fruitless must be any word of mine which should attempt to beguile you from the grief of a loss so overwhelming, but I cannot refrain from tendering to you the consolation that may be found in the thanks of the republic they died to save.

" I pray our Heavenly Father may assuage the anguish of your bereavements and leave only the cherished memory of the loved and lost, and the solemn pride that must be yours to have laid so costly a sacrifice upon the altar of freedom.

"Yours, very sincerely and respectfully,

"A. LINCOLN." [1]

Incidents illustrating the same feeling might be multiplied without number.[2]

1. McPherson's History of the Rebellion, p. 606.

2. I venture to add the following, which came under my personal observation. In the early spring of 1862, a young lad, who had lost his right hand at the battle of Belmont, came to Washington to obtain an appointment as assistant quartermaster. He arrived on Saturday, and calling at my house found that I was out of the city. With the confidence of youth, he did not wait my return, but, having very strong recommendations, went to the Secretary of War, and was greatly disappointed when Mr. Stanton refused to appoint him. In the evening he came to me in great distress, and stated his case. I told him I would go with him on Monday to the War Office, but that his case was injured by his having been once rejected. On Monday we called on Mr. Stanton, who was receiving and dispatching a multitude of suitors. I noticed that the Secretary was in an ill humor; however, we took our turn, and I stated the case. Turning to the young soldier, Stanton said: " Were not you here Saturday, and did I not refuse to appoint you? And now here you are again on Monday, troubling me again. I cannot and will not have my time wasted in this way."

I said: "Mr. Stanton, I am responsible for this second application." But he would not listen to me, and continued to scold at the young soldier. I thought him rude and uncivil, but seeing his irritability, retired as soon as possible, saying to the young soldier: " We will stop at the White House, and see what the President has to say to this."

We found Mr. Lincoln alone in his office, and I had scarcely stated the case, when he took a card and wrote on it: " Let —— be appointed Assistant Quartermaster, etc. A. Lincoln." He had not then become familiar with one-armed and one-legged soldiers, and he seemed touched by the empty sleeve of the fine-looking young man. Putting the card in my pocket, I went to the Capitol. In the course of the day, Stanton came on the floor of the House, and as he seemed in good humor, I went to him and said: " Mr. Stanton, you seemed very harsh and rude to my friend and constituent this morning. It seems to me that those who lose their right hands in the service of

Great dissatisfaction was expressed at one time because Mr. Lincoln hesitated, or seemed to hesitate, in ordering retaliation for cruelties and barbarities practiced by the rebels on Union soldiers and prisoners. The story of the terrible cruelties inflicted upon Union prisoners at Andersonville, and at other places, and the alleged massacre of colored soldiers at Fort Pillow, filled all the people with horror. The committee on the conduct of the war reported that the statements were true, and, on the 16th of January, 1865, Senator Wade offered a resolution directing retaliation in kind, with unflinching severity.[1] But Senator Sumner replied : " We cannot be cruel, or barbarous, or savage, because the rebels, whom we are meeting in war, are cruel, barbarous, and savage." He quoted Dr. Lieber as saying : " If we fight with Indians, who slowly roast their prisoners, we cannot roast in turn the Indians whom we may capture." When reports of these barbarities, and the official report of the committee on the conduct of the war, were brought to the attention of Mr. Lincoln, and he was urged to retaliate *in kind*, he said : " No, I never can. I can never starve men like that." Edward Everett, speaking, however, of the conduct of the rebels at Andersonville and elsewhere, said : " You have no more right to starve than to poison a prisoner of war." Senator Chandler advocated retaliation in kind, declaring that Sumner's " sublimated humanitarianism would not do for 'these accursed rebels.'" McDougall, of

the country should at least be entitled to kindness and courtesy from the Secretary of War."

" Well, well," he replied, " I was vexed and annoyed this morning. Take your young friend to the President. He always does anything you ask him, and he will, I doubt not, appoint him."

" Mr. Stanton," I replied, " if the President grants my requests, I take care never to ask anything but what I am sure is right; but in this instance you do the President no more than justice. He has already directed the appointment, and I beg you will not interpose any obstacle or delay, as you sometimes do."

Taking the card, Mr. Stanton said: "I will send you the commission as soon as I get to the War Department." An hour later a messenger brought the commission.

1. See the debate in the Senate. Cong. Globe, 2d Session 38th Congress, pp. 364, 411–12.

California, a man of rare eloquence and genius, spoke against the resolution, comparing the proposal with the wild outrages and cruelties of the French Revolution, and which had no parallel save in the barbarities of the dark ages. But it was the eloquent voice of Sumner, appealing to the nobler and more humane feelings of our nature, which restrained the just indignation, and the fierce and terrible demands for retaliation in kind; and the resolution was so modified as to require "retaliation according to the laws and usages of war among civilized nations."

Mr. Sumner had become the sincere and confidential adviser of Mr. Lincoln. These two men, in many respects so unlike, became the most ardent and affectionate personal friends. They rode and walked together, and seemed to enjoy each other's society like brothers. Sumner, the scholar and the man of conventionality, the favorite American of the English aristocracy, found in Lincoln one that he admired and confided in above all others.

The employment of negroes as soldiers in the Union armies had created intense excitement and bitterness in the rebellious states. The Confederate press and members of the Confederate Congress, at first, in their angry fury, proposed to execute all slaves found in arms, and to put their officers to death. Conscious that such acts of atrocity would bring severe retaliation, the whole subject was referred to Jefferson Davis, with power to act. He issued a proclamation declaring that negro troops and their white officers would, if captured, not be treated as prisoners of war, but would be turned over to state authority for punishment, and that all free negroes captured with arms should be sold into slavery. In reply to this, the President issued an order directing "that for every soldier of the United States killed in violation of the laws of war, a rebel soldier shall be executed ; and for every one enslaved or sold into slavery, a rebel soldier shall be placed at hard labor on public works, and continued at such labor until the other shall be released and receive the treatment due to a prisoner of war." [1]

At the Sanitary Fair at Baltimore, Mr. Lincoln said: "The black soldier shall have the same protection as the white soldier. If the reports relative to this massacre [at Fort Pillow] are substantiated, retribution will be surely given." [2] In accordance with the order of the President, certain rebel prisoners were, in 1864, placed at hard labor on the Dutch Gap Canal, in retaliation for certain negro soldiers captured by the rebels and employed at work in the trenches of the rebels at Fort Gilmer. General Grant, in his correspondence with General Lee on the subject, laid down the rule which governed the Union authorities, based on the order of the President, saying: "I shall always regret the necessity for retaliating for wrongs done our soldiers, but regard it my duty to protect all persons received into the army of the United States, regardless of color or nationality." [3] The firmness of the President and General Grant resulted in compelling the Confederates to accord the negro soldiers, when captured, the rights of prisoners of war.

This visit to the Baltimore Fair was the occasion of an exhibition of love and veneration towards Mr. Lincoln on the part of the negro race, almost without a parallel in history. They crowded around the Washington depot, and so filled the streets along which he was to pass that it was difficult for him to make his way. Hundreds of negro women kneeled on the sidewalks, holding up their children that they might see him and be blessed by him. They seemed to feel that to look at him was a privilege, and that to be touched by him would bring a blessing. Their feeling recalled the old superstition that the touch of the king would heal all disease. But he was to them more than king, more than mortal.

1. McPherson's History of the Rebellion, p. 280.

2. McPherson's History of the Rebellion, p. 281.

3. See correspondence of Grant and Lee on the subject. McPherson's History of the Rebellion, p. 445.

He was to these simple, sincere worshipers something super-
naturally good and great. The scene at Baltimore might
without irreverence be compared to that when Christ rode
into Jerusalem. The negroes, ignorant, simple, and earnest,
looked upon him as their savior, their deliverer, and they
were ready " to spread their garments in his way ; to cut
down branches of the trees and strew them in his path."
"And they that went before, and they that followed after,
cried, ' Hosanna. Blessed be he that cometh in the name of
the Lord.' " To the negro race he had passed into mythol-
ogy, and already become a great historic figure, free from all
human infirmity.

The subject of reconstruction, of restoring the rebel
states to their former relations with the national government,
was one of difficulty, and one in relation to which there was
a wide difference of opinion. Upon no question of statesmanship was Mr. Lincoln's sagacity and practical good
sense more strikingly illustrated. There were many theories
on the subject, which were advocated with great vehemence
and passion. Mr. Lincoln did not adopt any particular
theory as to any one mode by which the national authority
could be restored. Daniel Webster, speaking of the secession of the states and of the dissolution of the Union,
sadly said : " If these columns fall, they will be raised not
again. Like the Colosseum and the Parthenon, they will be
destined to a mournful and melancholy immortality. Bit-
terer tears, however, will flow over them than were ever
shed over Grecian or Roman art, for they will be the ruins
of a more glorious edifice than Greece or Rome ever saw—
the edifice of constitutional American freedom." [1] It was
the difficult but not impossible work of Lincoln to raise
again and reconstruct the shattered fragments of the republic ; to rear again the broken and prostrate columns of the
seceding states ; but this time, their foundation was to be
on the rock of liberty. As has been said before, he was no
mere theorist, but a practical statesman, looking ever for the

1. Webster's Speeches, vol. 1, p. 231.

wisest means to secure the end. One indispensable condition—emancipation, the freedom of the colored race—he
made the condition of every act of reconstruction. This
he repeatedly declared in his messages to Congress, in his
instructions to Mr. Seward at the time of the Hampton
Roads conference, and in many speeches. Loyalty and
fidelity to the national government and the Constitution,
including the proclamation of emancipation and the amendment prohibiting slavery, were the conditions of reconstruction. He appointed provisional governors over rebellious states, and recommended Congress to provide by law for
the establishment of courts for " all such parts of the insurgent states and territories as may be under the control of
the government, whether by voluntary return to its allegiance
and order, or by the power of our armies."

The rebel state governments he regarded as public enemies to be subdued, while a new government, republican in
form, was to be established in their place. In initiating steps
to organize new, loyal, and republican state governments, he,
as the Executive and Commander in Chief, and in the
absence of the action of Congress, prescribed the qualifications of voters, requiring all to be loyal to the Constitution.
These proceedings he regarded as preliminary, and subject
to the action and approval of Congress, before the new state
government should be entitled to representation in Congress
or to vote in the electoral college. He treated the Confederates as public enemies ; all acts of the Confederate government, and of the rebel states while in rebellion, were void,
and these organizations were to be overthrown and subjugated, and the territory from which they were expelled to be
governed, until otherwise provided, by martial law. The
states in rebellion were not entitled to vote in the electoral
college.[2]

The question as to whether the loyal negro was to vote
had not been definitely settled at the time of Mr. Lincoln's

1. Message of December, 1861. Also message of December, 1863.

2. See President's Message of February 8th, 1865, and resolutions of Congress.

death. As early as March 13th, 1864, the President, writing to Michael Hahn, Governor of Louisiana, said : " Now you are about to have a convention, which, among other things, will probably define the elective franchise. I barely suggest for your private consideration whether some of the colored people might not be let in, as, for instance, the very intelligent, and especially those who have fought gallantly in our ranks." In his speech of April 11th, 1865, four days before his assassination, speaking of the new constitution in Louisiana, he said : " It is unsatisfactory to some that the elective franchise is not given to the colored man. I would myself prefer that it were now conferred on the very intelligent, and on those who serve our cause as soldiers. Still the question is not whether the Louisiana government is quite all that is desirable. The question is, will it be wiser to take it as it is, and help to improve it, or to reject it."[1]

In a letter to General Wadsworth, Mr. Lincoln says: " I cannot see, if universal amnesty is granted, how, under the circumstances, I can avoid exacting, in return, universal suffrage, or at least suffrage on the basis of intelligence and military service."[2] It may be assumed as settled, that Mr.

1. McPherson's History of the Rebellion, p. 609. He adds :

" We encourage the hearts and nerve the arms of the twelve thousand to adhere to their work, and argue for it, and proselyte for it, and fight for it, and feed it and grow it, and ripen it to complete success. The colored man, too, seeing all uniting for him, is inspired with vigilance and energy and daring to the same end. Grant that he desires the elective franchise, will he not obtain it sooner by saving the already advanced steps towards it, than by running backward over them ? Concede that the new government of Louisiana is only to what it should be, as the egg to the fowl ; we shall sooner have the fowl by hatching the egg than by smashing it. Again, if we reject Louisiana, we also reject one vote in favor of the proposed amendment to the national constitution. To meet this proposition it has been argued that no more than three-fourths of those states which have not attempted secession are necessary to validly ratify this amendment. I do not commit myself against this farther than to say that such a ratification would be questionable, and sure to be persistently questioned ; whilst a ratification by three-fourths of all the states would be unquestioned and unquestionable."

2. The following is an extract from the Wadsworth letter. I have never seen the authenticity of this letter denied, and it bears internal evidence of being genuine. Mr. Lincoln says :

" Your desire to know, in the event of our complete success in the field, the same being followed by a loyal and cheerful submission on the part of the South, if universal amnesty should not be accompanied with universal suffrage. Now, since you

Lincoln favored negro suffrage " on the basis of intelligence and military service " at least, but it is not clearly proved that he would have made it universal.

He was a man of great evenness of temper, rarely excited to anger. Personal abuse, injustice, and indignity offered to himself did not disturb him, but gross injustice and bad faith towards others made him indignant, and when such were brought to his knowledge, his eyes would blaze with indignation, and his denunciation few could endure. When some one dared to suggest to him that he might placate the rebel masters, and secure peace, by abandoning the freedmen, he exclaimed: " Why, it would be an astounding breach of faith ! If I should do it, I ought to be damned in time and eternity." To this day, the South does not appreciate, nor does the world know, how much the Confederates were indebted to the humane, kind, almost divine spirit of Lincoln. The key-note of his policy towards the rebels was

know my private inclinations as to what terms should be granted to the South in the contingency mentioned, I will here add, that if our success should thus be realized, followed by such desired results, I cannot see, if universal amnesty is granted, how, under the circumstances, I can avoid exacting in return universal suffrage, or, at least, suffrage on the basis of intelligence and military service. How to better the condition of the colored race has long been a study which has attracted my serious and careful attention ; hence I think I am clear and decided as to what course I shall pursue in the premises, regarding it as a religious duty, as the nation's guardian of those people who have so heroically vindicated their manhood on the battle-field, where, in assisting to save the life of the republic, they have demonstrated their right to the ballot, which is but the humane protection of the flag they have so fearlessly defended."

The following note from the Hon. Charles A. Dana, Assistant Secretary of War during the last two years of Mr. Lincoln's administration, will throw some light on Mr. Lincoln's views:

" NEW YORK, November 13, 1866.

" *My Dear Sir:* In a speech here before the election, I stated that at the time of Mr. Lincoln's death, a printed paper was under consideration in the Cabinet, providing ways and means for restoring state government in Virginia. In that paper it was stated that all loyal men, *white or black*, were to be called upon to vote in holding a state convention, while all rebels were to be excluded. I said that I could not affirm that Mr. Lincoln had definitively adopted that policy with respect to black suffrage, but that I knew his mind was tending to it, and that I was morally certain he would have finally adhered to it. After Mr. Johnson's accession, all the provisions of the paper were incorporated in the presidential proclamation respecting the reorganization of state governments, with the single exception of this one making all loyal men voters, whether white or black.   *   *   Yours very truly,

" *Hon. Isaac Arnold.*   CHARLES A. DANA."

boldly struck in his second inaugural, when he declared "with malice towards none, with charity for all, with firmness in the right as God gives us to see the right, let us finish the work we are in, to bind up the nation's wounds,   *   * to do all which may achieve a just and lasting peace among ourselves and among all nations."

In the midst of the fierce passions and bitter animosities growing out of the war, many thought him too mild and too forbearing; but his conviction was clear, and his determination firm, that when there was a sincere repentance, then there should be pardon and amnesty.   In the face of those who sternly demanded punishment and confiscation, and the death of traitors and conspirators, he declared: " When a man is sincerely penitent for his misdeeds, and gives satisfactory evidence of it, he can safely be pardoned."

When the fiery and eloquent Henry Winter Davis, the stern, blunt, downright Ben Wade, and the unforgiving Thaddeus Stevens, demanded retaliation, confiscation, death, desolation, and bloody execution, the voice of Lincoln rose clear above the storm, firm, gentle, but powerful, like the voice of God. " With malice towards none, with charity for all, with firmness in the right as God gives us to see the right," he hushed the raging storm of passion, and brought back peace and reconciliation.

CHAPTER XXV.

VICTORY AND DEATH.

Conference of Lincoln, Grant, and Sherman.—Richmond
Falls.—Lee Surrenders.—Jefferson Davis Captured.—Lincoln's Visit to Richmond.—The Last Day of His Life.—His
Assassination.—Funeral.—The World's Grief.—Mrs. Lincoln Distracted.—Injustice to Her.—Her Death.

Let us resume the narration of the progress of the
Union arms. Fort Fisher, which guards the harbor of Wilmington, North Carolina, was captured by General Terry,
on the 15th of January, 1865. Sherman, moving from Savannah, entered Columbia, the capital of South Carolina, on the
17th of February. From thence he moved to Goldsboro,
North Carolina, and opened communication with General
Schofield, who had, after the destruction of Hood's army at
Nashville, been ordered east. The rebels under Hardee
abandoned Charleston, and Admiral Dahlgren and General
Foster took possession of the capital of South Carolina.
General Lee appointed General Joe Johnston to command
the forces which were trying to oppose the advance of Sherman, and at Bentonville there was a severe battle, but Johnston was compelled to retire; and now the Union forces
were concentrating around Lee, and the end was rapidly
approaching.

On the 3d of March, 1865, as is usual on the last night
of the sessions of Congress, the Executive with the Cabinet
was in the President's room at the Capitol, to receive and
act upon the numerous bills which pass during the last hurried hours of the session. Congress continued in session

from seven o'clock in the evening to eight o'clock on the morning of the 4th. It was a stormy, snowy night, but within all was bright, cheerful, and full of hope. While the President was thus waiting, and receiving the congratulations of senators, members of Congress, and other friends, a telegram came from General Grant to the Secretary of War, informing him that Lee had at last sought an interview, with the purpose of seeing whether any terms of peace could be agreed upon. The despatch was handed to the President. Reflecting a few moments, he wrote the following reply, which was then submitted to the Cabinet and sent:

"WASHINGTON, March 3, 1865, 12 P. M.

"LIEUTENANT GENERAL GRANT:—The President directs me to say to you that he wishes you to have no conference with General Lee, unless it be for the capitulation of General Lee's army, or on some other minor and purely military matter. He instructs me to say that you are not to decide, discuss, or confer upon any political question. Such questions the President holds in his own hands, and will submit them to no military conferences or conventions. Meanwhile you are to press to the utmost your military advantages. EDWIN M. STANTON,

"Secretary of War."

On the 27th of March, the President, by appointment, met Generals Grant and Sherman in the cabin of the steamer "Ocean Queen," lying in the James River, and not far from the headquarters of General Grant. This meeting has been appropriately made the subject of a great historical painting called "The Peace Makers," and the artist has very felicitously represented the prophetic rainbow spanning the boat, and shining in at the windows, where these remarkable men held their last conference. [1]

The perfect harmony, earnest and cordial coöperation, and brotherly friendship between the great military leaders, Grant and Sherman, Sheridan and Meade, and their subordinates, was in striking contrast with the jealousy and quarrels of some of the President's earlier generals. He could not but recall the days of McClellan and others, when such

1. This painting by Healy was made for E. B. McCagg, Esq., of Chicago, and now hangs on the walls of the Calumet Club of that city.

quarrels were among the heaviest burdens he had to bear. It would be difficult to find in history three men more unlike physically and mentally, and yet of greater historic interest or more distinguished ability, than the statesman President, and Grant and Sherman. And, although so entirely unlike one another, each was a type of American character, and all had peculiarities not only distinctively American, but Western. Lincoln's towering form had been given dignity and repose by the great deeds and great thoughts to which he had given such eloquent expression. His rugged and strongly marked features, lately so deeply furrowed with care, anxiety, over-work, and responsibility, were now full of hope and confidence. He met the two great soldiers with the most grateful cordiality. With clear intelligence, he grasped the military situation, and listened with the most eager and profound attention to the details of the final moves which it was hoped would end the terrible game of war.

Contrasting with the tall, towering form of Lincoln, was the short, sturdy, firm figure of the hero of Vicksburg, every feature and every movement expressing inflexible will and resolute determination. Also strikingly in contrast with these was Sherman, with his intellectual head, his keen restless eye, his nervous energy, his sharply outlined features, bronzed by that magnificent campaign from Chattanooga to Savannah, and now fresh from the conquest of North and South Carolina. "Hold Lee," he said to Grant, "in his fortified lines for two weeks; our wagons will be loaded, and we will start for Burksville. If Lee will remain in Richmond until I can reach Burksville, we will have him between our thumb and fingers." [1]

1. The following most interesting letter from General Sherman to the author gives the details of this interview :

"WASHINGTON, D. C., November 28th, 1872.
"THANKSGIVING DAY.

" Hon. I. N. ARNOLD, Chicago, Ill.

"*My Dear Sir :* I have just received your letter of November 26th, and it so happens that it comes to me on an official holiday, when I am at leisure, and at my house, where I keep the books of letters written by me during and since the civil war.

Sherman, with his army of eighty thousand men, as hardy and as brave as Cæsar's Gallic Legion, once in close communication with Grant, Lee would be " shut up in Richmond

My records during the war are quite complete, but since the war I have only retained copies of letters on purely official business, and I find no copy of the one you describe as having been lost in the great fire of Chicago last year. I regret this extremely, as in my official records I find but a bare allusion to the interview with Mr. Lincoln at City Point, in March, 1865, an account of which was contained in my former letter, and which you now desire me to repeat. I must do so entirely from memory, and you must make all allowances, for nearly eight eventful years have intervened.

" On the 21st of March, 1865, the army which I commanded reached Goldsboro, North Carolina, and there made junction with the forces of Generals Schofield and Terry, which had come up from the coast at Newbern and Wilmington.

" My army was hard up for food and clothing, which could only reach us from the coast, and my chief attention was given to the reconstruction of the two railroads which meet at Goldsboro, from Newbern and Wilmington, so as to re-clothe the men, and get provisions enough with which to continue our march to Burksville, Virginia, where we would come into communication with General Grant's army, then investing Richmond and Petersburg. I had written to General Grant several times, and had received letters from him, but it seemed to me all important that I should have a personal interview. Accordingly, on the 25th of March, leaving General Schofield in command, I took the first locomotive which had come over the repaired railroad, back to Newbern and Morehead City, where I got the small steamer ' Russia' to convey me to City Point. We arrived during the afternoon of March 27th, and I found General Grant and staff occupying a neat set of log huts, on a bluff overlooking the James River. The General's family was with him. We had quite a long and friendly talk, when he remarked that the President, Mr. Lincoln, was near by in a steamer lying at the dock, and he proposed that we should call at once. We did so, and found Mr. Lincoln on board the ' Ocean Queen.' We had met in the early part of the war, and he recognized me, and received me with a warmth of manner and expression that was most grateful. We then sat some time in the after-cabin, and Mr. Lincoln made many inquiries about the events which attended the march from Savannah to Goldsboro, and seemed to enjoy the humorous stories about 'our bummers,' of which he had heard much. When in lively conversation, his face brightened wonderfully; but if the conversation flagged, his face assumed a sad and sorrowful expression.

" General Grant and I explained to him that my next move from Goldsboro would bring my army, increased to eighty thousand men by Schofield's and Terry's reinforcements, in close communication with General Grant's army, then investing Lee in Richmond, and that unless Lee could effect his escape, and make junction with Johnston in North Carolina, he would soon be shut up in Richmond with no possibility of supplies, and would have to surrender. Mr. Lincoln was extremely interested in this view of the case, and when we explained that Lee's only chance was to escape, join Johnston, and, being then between me in North Carolina and Grant in Virginia, could choose which to fight. Mr. Lincoln seemed unusually impressed with this, but General Grant explained that at the very moment of our conversation, General Sheridan was passing his cavalry across James River from the north to the south, that he would, with this cavalry, so extend his left below Petersburg as to meet the South Shore Road, and that if Lee should ' let go' his fortified lines, he (Grant) would follow him so close that he could not possibly fall on me alone in North Carolina. I, in like manner, expressed the fullest confidence that my army in North Carolina was willing to cope with Lee and Johnston combined, till Grant could come up. But we both with no possibility of obtaining supplies, and would have to surrender." Lincoln, when told that "one more bloody battle was likely to occur before the close of the war," with

agreed that one more bloody battle was likely to occur before the close of the war.

"Mr. Lincoln repeatedly inquired as to General Schofield's ability, in my absence, and seemed anxious that I should return to North Carolina, and more than once exclaimed: 'Must more blood be shed? Cannot'this last bloody battle be avoided?' We explained that we had to presume that General Lee was a real general; that he must see that Johnston alone was no barrier to my progress, and that if my army of eighty thousand veterans should reach Burksville, he was lost in Richmond, and that we were forced to believe he would not await that inevitable conclusion, but make one more desperate effort.

"I think we were with Mr. Lincoln an hour or more, and then returned to General Grant's quarters, where Mrs. Grant had prepared us some coffee, or tea. During this meal, Mrs. Grant inquired if we had seen Mrs. Lincoln. I answered: 'No. I did not know she was on board.' 'Now,' said Mrs. Grant, 'you are a pretty pair,' and went on to explain that we had been guilty of a piece of unpardonable rudeness; but the General said, 'Never mind. We will repeat the visit to-morrow, and can then see Mrs. Lincoln.'

"The next morning a good many officers called to see me, among them Generals Meade and Ord, also Admiral Porter. The latter inquired as to the 'Russia,' in which I had come up from Morehead City, and explained that she was a slow tub, and he would send me back in the steamer 'Bat,' Captain Barnes, U. S. Navy, because she was very fleet, and could make seventeen knots an hour. Of course I did not object, and fixed that afternoon to start back.

"Meantime we had to repeat our call on Mr. Lincoln on board the 'Ocean Queen,' then anchored out in the stream at some distance from the wharf. Admiral Porter went along, and we took a tug at the wharf, which conveyed us off to the 'Ocean Queen.' Mr. Lincoln met us all in the same hearty manner as on the previous occasion, and this time we did not forget Mrs. Lincoln. General Grant inquired for her, and the President explained that she was not well, but he stepped to her state-room and returned to us asking us to excuse her. We all took seats in the after-cabin, and the conversation became general. I explained to Mr. Lincoln that Admiral Porter had given me the 'Bat,' a very fleet vessel, to carry me back to Newbern, and that I was ready to start back then. It seemed to relieve him, as he was afraid that something might go wrong at Goldsboro in my absence. I had no such fears, and the most perfect confidence in General Schofield, and doubt not I said as much.

"I ought not, and must not, attempt to recall the words of that conversation. Of course none of us then foresaw the tragic end of the principal figure of that group so near at hand ; and none of us saw the exact manner in which the war was to close; but I knew that I felt, and I believe the others did, that the end of the war was near.

"The imminent danger was, that Lee, seeing the meshes closing surely around him, would not remain passive, but would make one more desperate effort ; and General Grant was providing for it, by getting General Sheridan's cavalry well to his left flank, so as to watch the first symptoms, and to bring the rebel army to bay till the infantry could come up. Meantime I only asked two weeks delay, the *status quo*, when we would have our wagons loaded, and would start from Goldsboro for Burksville, via Raleigh. Though I cannot attempt to recall the words spoken by any one of the persons present on that occasion, I know we talked generally about what was to characteristic humanity exclaimed: 'Must more blood be shed? Cannot this bloody battle be avoided?'" And even while they were consulting, Sheridan, the embodiment of energy and rapidity of movement, was marching with the utmost celerity far to Grant's left, to seize and cut off the only available route for Lee's escape. Ten days of incessant marching and fighting, with Sheridan in the lead and Grant closely following, finished the campaign. The line of intrenchments around Richmond and Petersburg extended

be done when Lee's and Johnston's armies were beaten and dispersed. On this point Mr. Lincoln was very full. He said that he had long thought of it, that he hoped this end could be reached without more bloodshed, but in any event he wanted us to get the deluded men of the rebel armies disarmed and back to their homes ; that he contemplated no revenge; no harsh measures, but quite the contrary, and that their suffering and hardships during the war would make them the more submissive to law. I cannot say that Mr. Lincoln, or any body else, used this language; but I know I left his presence with the conviction that he had in his mind, or that his Cabinet had, some plan of settlement ready for application, the moment Lee and Johnston were defeated.

" In Chicago, about June or July of that year, when all the facts were fresh in my mind, I told them to Geo. P. A. Healy, the artist, who was casting about for a subject for an historical painting, and he adopted this interview. Mr. Lincoln was then dead, but Healy had a portrait which he himself had made at Springfield, some five or six years before. With this portrait, some existent photographs, and the strong resemblance in form of Mr. Swett, of Chicago, to Mr. Lincoln, he made the picture of Mr. Lincoln seen in this group. For General Grant, Admiral Porter, and myself, he had actual sittings, and I am satisfied the fine portraits in this group of Healy's are the best extant. The original picture, life size, is, I believe, now in Chicago, the property of Mr. McCagg; but Healy afterwards, in Rome, painted ten smaller copies, about 18x24 inches, one of which I now have, and it is now within view. I think the likeness of Mr. Lincoln by far the best of the many I have seen elsewhere, and those of General Grant, Admiral Porter, and myself, equally good and faithful. I think Admiral Porter gave Healy a written description of our relative positions in that interview, also the dimensions, shape, and furniture of the cabin of the 'Ocean Queen ' but the rainbow is Healy's—typical, of course, of the coming peace. In this picture I seem to be talking, the others attentively listening. Whether Healy made this combination from Admiral Porter's letter or not, I cannot say ; but I thought that he caught the idea from what I told him had occurred, when saying 'that if Lee would only remain in Richmond until I could reach Burksville, we would have him between our thumb and fingers,' suiting the action to the word. It matters little what Healy meant by his historic group, but it is certain we four sat pretty much as represented, and were engaged in an important conversation, during the forenoon of March 28th, 1865, and that we parted never to meet again.

" That afternoon I embarked on the ' Bat,' and we steamed down the coast to Hatteras Inlet, which we entered, and proceeded to Newbern, and from Newbern to Goldsboro by rail, which I reached the night of March 30th.

" I hope this letter covers the points of your inquiry.

" With great respect, " Yours truly,

" W. T. SHERMAN, General."

Hon. I. N. Arnold, Chicago, Ill.

some forty miles. Grant had resolved to interpose Sheridan between Lee and retreat. On the 29th, he wrote to Sheridan: "I now feel like ending the matter, if it be possible, before going back. * * Push round the enemy, and get on his right rear; we will act as one army here, until it is seen what can be done with the enemy."

The rain fell in torrents, the soil was deep mud, and the roads were nearly impassable; but nothing could stop or stay Sheridan. He pushed on over all obstacles to Five Forks. On the morning of March 31st, Lee, struggling to escape, had eighteen thousand men in front of Sheridan's ten thousand. While he fought, Sheridan sent word to Grant: "I will hold Dinwiddie until I am compelled to leave." Grant promptly sent an entire corps to his aid. Fighting and marching, and preventing Lee from making his escape, nothing could exceed the activity and energy of Sheridan. On the morning of the 2d of April, the works in front of Petersburg were carried. Lee fled westward, his object being to reach Burksville Junction, where two roads met, and from thence either to join Johnston, or escape to the mountains. Sheridan captured a telegraphic message, not yet sent, ordering three hundred thousand rations to feed Lee's famishing army. Sheridan forwarded the message, with the hope that the rations would be sent forward and fall into the hands of the Union army. Such was the result. And now Sheridan had seized and occupied the only road by which Lee could obtain supplies. The rebel army was without food, with Sheridan and his cavalry and the Fifth Army Corps in its front, while Grant was behind, at its heels and on its flank, with his eager and victorious troops. Lee made desperate efforts to escape, to cut his way through, but in vain. The remains of the proud and often victorious Army of Northern Virginia struggled and fought gallantly, but were hemmed in, and everywhere met by a force which they could not break through. On Sunday, the 2d of April, Longstreet, who had held the lines north of the James, was ordered to join Lee.

The bells of Richmond tolled the knell of the Confederacy. The drums beat, calling on the citizens and militia to man the lines from which Longstreet was retiring. The rebellion was at its last gasp. At 11 A. M. of that Sunday morning, Lee sent a message to Jefferson Davis, saying that Richmond and Petersburg could no longer be held. Davis hurriedly fled, and on the dawn of Monday, the 3d, General Weitzel sent forward a party of Union cavalry, who hoisted the national flag on the State House, and took possession of the rebel capital. But not for Richmond and Petersburg did the iron will of Grant for one moment turn aside from his determination to "end the matter" then and there, by the destruction of the army of Lee. Pushing on with all possible speed, the army of the James, under General Ord, on one side of the Appomattox, and that of Grant on the other, and Sheridan on his front, there was left no escape possible. The chase was up. On the 9th of April, after one last desperate effort to cut his way through, Lee sent a white flag, asking a suspension of hostilities, pending negotiations for terms of surrender. An interview was held between Grant and Lee, and generous terms of capitulation agreed upon. The arms, artillery, and public property were given up; officers and soldiers were paroled not to take up arms against the United States until properly exchanged, and the officers and men were allowed to return to their homes, not to be disturbed so long as they observed their parole and the laws.

Lee had many qualities which created sympathy, and the scene after the surrender was sadly pathetic. Riding through the ranks of his ragged and half-starved soldiers, he said, in a voice broken with grief: "Men, we have fought through the war together; I have done the best I could for you." It was not in the heart of his generous and victorious foe to exact severe terms, and his misfortunes almost disarmed justice. The meeting of the rank and file, and of the officers of the two armies, was cordial. They had learned to respect each other. The rebels were really starving. The Union soldiers grasped the hands of their late enemies, made them their guests, divided with them their rations, supplied them with clothing, and loaned them money with which to go to their homes.

The surrender of Lee was regarded by the other rebel leaders as fatal. They deemed it useless to prolong the struggle. On the 5th of April, Grant had requested Sherman to push forward against Johnston. "Let us," said he, "see if we cannot finish the job." On the 13th of April, Sherman occupied Raleigh, and on the 14th, intelligence of the surrender of Lee reached him, and a correspondence was opened between him and Johnston for the disbandment of the rebel army, and to propose a basis of peace, subject to the approval of the President. The terms were not approved. On the 24th, General Grant arrived at the headquarters of Sherman, and immediately Sherman notified Johnston that the terms were disapproved, and a demand was made for the surrender of his army. A meeting between Sherman and Johnston was had on the 26th of April, which resulted in the surrender of Johnston and his army, on the same terms substantially as those which Lee had accepted. The surrender of all the organized rebel forces everywhere soon followed. On the 11th of May, Jefferson Davis, fleeing in disguise, was captured in Georgia.

After the meeting of the President with Grant and Sherman, before described, Lincoln, anxious to be near the scene of action, where he could keep in constant communication with Grant, remained at City Point. General Grant telegraphed to him from day to day and hour to hour the progress of the movements, and these despatches were forwarded by Mr. Lincoln to the Secretary of War at Washington, and by him to the exulting people of the loyal states. The brilliant and decisive successes of the army filled the nation with joy and gratitude.

When, on the morning of the 4th of April, the Union troops took possession of Richmond, they found a terrific fire raging, which had been caused by the rebels setting fire to the great tobacco warehouses, ordnance foundries, and other public property, which they had burned to prevent its falling into the hands of the Union army. These were destroyed, and with them, before the fire could be extinguished, fully one-third of the beautiful city.

On the day of its capture, the President, leading his youngest son Thomas (Tad) by the hand, and accompanied by Admiral Porter and a few others, visited Richmond. Leading his son—then twelve years old—he walked from the wharf near Libby prison to the headquarters of General Weitzel, which had been the residence of Jefferson Davis, and from which he had so lately fled. The coming of the President had been unannounced, but the news of his presence spread through the city, and immediately the exulting negroes came running from every direction to see their deliverer. They danced, shouted, and cried for joy; for their enthusiasm was uncontrollable. He held a brief reception in the room lately occupied by the rebel President, took a drive about the town, saw that the fire was being subdued, and returned the same evening to City Point.

On the Thursday following, with Mrs. Lincoln, the Vice-President, and several senators and friends, he again visited Richmond. On this occasion he was called upon by several prominent citizens of Virginia, anxious to learn what the policy of the government towards them would be. Without committing himself to specific details, he satisfied them that his policy would be magnanimous, forgiving, and generous. He told these Virginians they must learn loyalty and devotion to the nation. They need not love Virginia less, but they must love the republic more.

On the 9th of April, the President returned to Washington, and he had scarcely settled at the White House before the news of Lee's surrender reached him. Robert T. Lincoln, his oldest son, was on the staff of General Grant, and in the field at the front. When the intelligence of Lee's surrender reached the President, no language can express the joy and gratitude to Almighty God which filled his heart and that of the people.

On the evening of the 11th, a great crowd, exultant and happy, went to the White House to congratulate him, and with him rejoice over the triumph. Again his tall form stood at the window of the Executive Mansion, and looked out on the happy multitude. How often during the past four years had he stood there. In times of disaster and of danger, when all was dark and uncertain, how often had he cheered and encouraged his hearers with words of hope and confidence; how often had he cheered the soldiers marching to the field. Now the great work was done. The rebellion was crushed, and throughout the republic there was not a slave. To him, more than to any other; to him more than to all others; to him under God were these grand results due. But there was no selfish exultation. Modest, just, and grateful to others, he said: "We meet this evening in gladness of heart. The surrender of the insurgent army gives hopes of a righteous and speedy peace.   *   *   *   * In the midst of this, He from whom all blessings flow must not be forgotten.   *   *   *   I was near the front,   * *   *   but no part of the honor for plan or execution is mine. To General Grant, his skillful officers and brave men, all belongs." [1]

From the 11th to the 14th were eventful, memorable days. The surrender of all the rebel armies followed in rapid succession. The whole country, every city, town, village, and neighborhood, was intoxicated with joy. All the houses, even the houses of mourning, were bright with Union flags. Every window in every home was illuminated. Bells were rung and salutes fired. Bands of music played, patriotic songs were sung, and the voice of praise and thanksgiving to Almighty God went up from every house of worship, and from every home and fireside. No one was more joyous and happy than Mr. Lincoln. The dark clouds had disappeared. Full of hope and happiness, with the consciousness of great difficulties overcome, of great duties well and successfully performed, his heart was filled, and

1. McPherson's History of the Rebellion, p. 609.

now visions of days of peace and happiness were rising
before him. He was considering plans of reconciliation;
how he could best bind up and heal the wounds of the whole
country, and how obliterate the scars of war and restore
good feeling and friendship to every section. There was in
his heart no bitterness, no desire for revenge. He wished
to frighten the leading rebels out of the country, that there
might be no executions.

On the morning of the 14th, his son Robert, just returned
from the front, where he had witnessed the surrender of
Lee, breakfasted with his father. The family passed a
happy hour together, Mr. and Mrs. Lincoln listening to the
details of the events witnessed by Robert. After breakfast,
the President spent an hour with Mr. Speaker Colfax. Then
followed a happy meeting and exchange of congratulations
with a party of Illinois friends. At 12 m. there was a meeting of the Cabinet, at which General Grant was present, and
all remarked the hopeful, happy spirits of the President, and
his kindly disposition towards those lately in arms against
him. While waiting for the Secretary of War, Mr. Lincoln
was observed to look very grave, and said : " Gentlemen,
something serious is going to happen. I have had a strange
dream, and have a presentiment such as I have had several
times before, and always just before some important event.
But," he added abruptly as Mr. Stanton came in, " let us
proceed to business."

After the Cabinet meeting he went to drive with Mrs.
Lincoln, expressing a wish that no one should accompany
them, and evidently desiring to converse alone with her.[1]
" Mary," said he, " we have had a hard time of it since
we came to Washington, but the war is over, and with God's
blessing we may hope for four years of peace and happiness, and then we will go back to Illinois and pass the rest
of our lives in quiet." He spoke of his old Springfield
home, and recollections of his early days, his little brown
cottage, the law office, the court room, the green bag for his

1. I state this conversation from memory, as related by Mrs. Lincoln.

briefs and law papers, his adventures when riding the circuit, came thronging back to him. The tension under which he had for so long been kept was removed, and he was like a boy out of school. "We have laid by," said he to his wife, "some money, and during this term we will try and save up more, but shall not have enough to support us. We will go back to Illinois, and I will open a law-office at Springfield or Chicago, and practice law, and at least do enough to help give us a livelihood." Such were the dreams, the day-dreams of Lincoln, the last day of his life.[1] In imagination he was again in his prairie home, among his law books, and in the courts with his old friends. A picture of a prairie farm on the banks of the Sangamon or the Rock River rose before him, and once more the plough and the axe were to become as familiar to his hands as in the days of his youth.

In the early evening he had another interview with Mr. Colfax, and with George Ashmun, the president of the convention at Chicago which had nominated him for the Presidency. It had been announced by the newspapers that he and General Grant would attend Ford's theatre that evening. General Grant was prevented by some other engagement from attending, and Mr. Lincoln, though for some reason reluctant to go that night, was persuaded to attend, that the people might not be disappointed. Mr. Colfax walked from the parlor to the door with him, and there bade him good-bye, declining an invitation to accompany him to the play. On

---

1. If he had lived and carried out these plans, what would have been his future ? Would he have passed, like other Ex-Presidents and great soldiers and statesmen, into comparative obscurity ? The proverbial ingratitude of republics is verified by our own, not towards the pensioned private soldier, but to the leaders. In almost every state to-day are living men who have rendered the country inestimable service, earning their living in pursuit of various branches of industry, unknown, unappreciated, and nearly forgotten. How differently great public services are rewarded on the other side of the Atlantic. There, titles and wealth are sure to follow great public service in civil and military life. Blenheim Palace and the Dukedom of Marlborough were very substantial rewards for the victory of Blenheim. Apsley House, and its contents, and the title of Duke of Wellington, were well earned by the conqueror of Waterloo. Would Lincoln, the savior of his country, had he lived, been left to earn his living by the practice of a *nisi prius* and Supreme Court lawyer, or would the republic have honored him and itself by honors and wealth ?

the steps of the White House, just as he was stepping into his carriage, the author met him, and he said : " Excuse me now. I am going to the theatre. Come and see me in the morning."

From the time of his election to his death, many threats had been made to assassinate him. He had received many letters warning him against assassination. An attempt to murder him at Baltimore, in 1861, would undoubtedly have been made, but for the discovery of the plot, and his passing through that city without the knowledge of and before the time expected by the conspirators. Lincoln was constitutionally brave, and assassination is a crime so entirely foreign and abhorrent to the American character, that he regarded all these threats as idle words, and his friends could never induce him to take precautions. He walked unguarded and unconscious of danger through the streets of Richmond on the day of its capture.

The President, Mrs. Lincoln, and their party, reached the theatre at nine o'clock. On his entry, he was received with acclamation. As he reached the door of the box reserved for him, he turned, smiled, and bowed his acknowledgment of the greeting which welcomed him, and then followed Mrs. Lincoln into the box. This was at the right of the stage, and not many feet from the floor. In the corner nearest the stage sat Miss Harris, a daughter of Senator Harris, of New York; next her was Mrs. Lincoln, Major Rathbone being seated on a sofa behind the ladies, and the President nearest the door. The box was draped and festooned with the national colors. The play was the " American Cousin."

It is painful to have to mention the name of the man who had attained some distinction in the representation of the mimic tragedies of the drama ; the name of one henceforth to be more infamous than any of the villains whose parts he had assumed, and which the genius of Shakspeare had conceived. John Wilkes Booth, the assassin, visited the theatre behind the scenes and saw the President sitting in the box. He had a fleet horse in the alley behind the building, all saddled and ready to aid him in his escape, and saw that the door to this alley was open.   The arrangements for the murder being completed, at 10:30 P. M. a pistol shot, startling and sharp, was heard, and a man holding a dagger dripping with blood leaped from the President's box to the stage, exclaiming : " *Sic semper tyrannis ;* the South is avenged." As the assassin struck the floor of the stage he fell on his knee, breaking a bone, the spur on his boot having caught in the folds of the flag as he leaped.   Instantly rising, he brandished his bloody dagger, darted across the stage through the door he had left open, sprung upon his horse, and galloped away.   Major Rathbone, at the sound of the pistol, and as the assassin rushed towards the stage, had attempted to seize him, and received a severe cut in the arm. The audience and actors, startled and stupefied with horror, were for a few seconds spell-bound.   Some one then cried out, " *John Wilkes Booth !*" and the audience realized that the well-known actor had been the author of the deed. Booth had passed around to the front of the theatre, entered, passed to the President's box, gone in at the open and unguarded door, and, stealing noiselessly up behind the President, who was intent upon the play, had placed his pistol close to the back of the head of Mr. Lincoln at the base of the brain, and fired.   The ball penetrated the brain, the President fell forward unconscious and mortally wounded. [1]

1. The following is the sworn statement of the actor on the stage at the moment: " I was playing ' Asa Trenchard ' in the ' American Cousin.'   The ' old lady ' of the theatre had just gone off the stage, and I was answering her exit speech when I heard the shot fired.   I turned, looked up at the President's box, heard the man exclaim, ' *Sic semper tyrannis*,' saw him jump from the box, seize the flag on the staff, and drop to the stage; he slipped when he gained the stage, but he got upon his feet in a moment, brandished a large knife, saying, ' The South shall be free,' turned his face in the direction I stood, and I recognized him as John Wilkes Booth.   He ran towards me, and I, seeing the knife, thought I was the one he was after, and ran off the stage and up a flight of stairs.   He made his escape out of a door directly in the rear of the theatre, mounted a horse and rode off.   The above all occurred in the space of a quarter of a minute, and at the time I did not know the President was shot, although, if I had tried to stop him, he would have stabbed me."

Major Rathbone testified :   " The distance between the President, as he sat, and the door, was about four or five feet.   The door, according to the recollection of this

No words can describe the horror and the anguish of Mrs. Lincoln. Her heart was broken, and her mind so shattered by the shock that she was never quite herself thereafter. When told that her husband must die, she prayed for death herself. The insensible body was moved across the street to the house of Mr. Peterson. Robert T. Lincoln, personal friends, and members of the Cabinet, soon arrived and filled the rooms. The strong constitution of the President struggled with death until twenty-two minutes past seven of the next morning, when his heart ceased to beat. It would be idle to attempt to describe the agony of that fearful night. The manly efforts of the son to control his own suffering, that he might soothe and comfort his mother, can never be forgotten. At the rising of the sun on the morning of the 15th, the remains of the President were borne back to the White House. [1] The assassin was pursued, overtaken, and, on the 21st of April, refusing to surrender, he was shot by a soldier named Boston Corbett.

On the same night of the murder of the President, accomplices of Booth attempted to kill the Secretary of State, Mr. Seward. He had been confined to his house by severe injuries received from being thrown from his carriage. He was fearfully wounded, and his life was saved by the heroic efforts of his sons and daughter, and a nurse named Robinson. Frederick Seward, his son, in attempting to prevent the entrance of the ruffian into his father's room, was

deponent, was not closed during the evening. When the second scene of the third act was being performed, and while the deponent was intently observing the proceedings upon the stage, with his back towards the door, he heard the discharge of a pistol behind him, and looking around saw, through the smoke, a man between the door and the President. * * This deponent instantly sprang towards him and seized him; he wrested himself from the grasp and made a violent thrust at the breast of deponent with a large knife. Deponent parried the blow by striking it up, and received a wound several inches deep in his left arm, between the elbow and the shoulder. The orifice of the wound is about an inch and a half in length, and extends upwards towards the shoulder several inches. The man rushed to the front of the box, and deponent endeavored to seize him again, but only caught his clothes as he was leaping over the railing of the box."

1. The author was one of the sad procession which followed the corpse to the Executive Mansion.

28

struck on the head with a pistol, and his skull fractured. Some of the accomplices of Booth, including Mrs. Surratt, were arrested, convicted, and hung, but whether they were the tools and instruments of more guilty instigators, has never been clearly proved.

Andrew Johnson, Vice-President, was immediately, on the morning of Mr. Lincoln's death, sworn into office as President. The terrible intelligence of Mr. Lincoln's death was early on the morning of the 15th borne by telegraph to every part of the republic. Coming in the midst of universal rejoicing over the fall of Richmond and the surrender of Lee, no language can adequately express the horror and grief of the people. A whole nation shouting for joy was in one moment struck dumb with horror, and the next bathed in tears. Persons who had not heard of the event, entering crowded cities, were appalled by the strange aspect of the mourning people. All business, by common impulse, was instantly suspended, and gloom and grief were on every face. The national flag which had been floating in triumph over every roof, every public building, spire, and mast, was lowered to half mast, and before the sun went down, the people, by a common impulse, each family by itself, began to drape their houses in mourning, so that before darkness closed over the land, every house was shrouded in black. If every family in the republic had lost its first born, the emblems of grief could hardly have been more universal. There were none whose grief was more demonstrative than that of the soldiers and freedmen. The vast armies not yet disbanded looked upon and loved Lincoln as a father. They knew that his heart had been with them in all their marches and battles, and in all their sufferings. Grief and vengeance filled all their hearts. But the poor negroes wept and mourned over a loss which they instinctively felt was irreparable. On the Sunday following his death, the people gathered in every place of public worship, and mingled their tears.

On Monday, the 17th, a meeting of the members of Congress then in Washington was held at the Capitol to arrange for the funeral. A committee of one member from each state and territory, and the entire delegation from Illinois, was appointed to attend the remains to Springfield. The fact was recalled that a vault had been prepared under the dome of the Capitol for the remains of Washington, which had never been used, because the Washington family and Virginia desired that the body of the father of his country should rest at Mount Vernon. It was now suggested that it would be peculiarly appropriate that the body of Lincoln should be placed under the Capitol of the republic he had saved. The family of Lincoln would have consented to this, but the governor of Illinois, her senators, and others, were so urgent that the remains should be taken to his old home, that it was finally decided that this should be done.

A short time before his death, on the visit of the President and Mrs. Lincoln to City Point and Richmond before spoken of, as they were taking a drive on the banks of James River, they came to an old country graveyard. It was a retired place, shaded with trees, and early spring flowers were opening on nearly every grave. It was so quiet and attractive that they stopped the carriage and walked through it. Mr. Lincoln seemed thoughtful and impressed. He said: " Mary, you are younger than I. You will survive me. When I am gone, lay my remains in some quiet place ·like this." [1]

The funeral took place on Wednesday, the 19th, and the religious services were held in the east room of the Executive Mansion. This was the third funeral which had taken place at the White House, while occupied by the family of Mr. Lincoln. First, that of Colonel Ellsworth, at whose death the President was deeply grieved; then that of his own son William, whom Mr. Lincoln idolized; and now that of the Presi-

---

1. Mrs. Lincoln told this incident to the author in October, 1874. She was speaking of his grave at Oak Ridge. Some of his Illinois friends had desired that he should be buried near the State House, that his monument should be near the Capitol. She said she preferred Oak Ridge, because it was more retired, and she gave the above incident as expressing his own wishes on the subject.

dent. The services were solemn and touching. The new President, the Cabinet, the Chief Justice and his associates, General Grant, Admiral Farragut, senators and members of Congress, the diplomatic corps, a great number of military and naval officers, and citizens from every part of the country attended. After the religious ceremonies, the body was taken to the rotunda of the Capitol, tenderly guarded by sad and sorrowing soldiers. The coffin was kept constantly covered with a profusion of sweet spring flowers, while the placid face was exposed, and thousands came to take a last look before the remains should start for their final resting place on the distant prairies. The features were natural, gentle, and seemed yet to express the Christ-like sentiments which he had uttered from the colonnade of the Capitol in his last inaugural. Non-commissioned officers of the Veteran Reserve Corps were detailed to act as a body-guard, and major generals of the army were directed to attend the train and keep watch, so that at all times during the journey the coffin should be under their special guardianship. It was ordered that the funeral train should take nearly the same route that Mr. Lincoln had taken when he came from Springfield to Washington to enter upon his duties as President.

The train left the capital on Friday the 21st, and was to halt and stay for a short time at Baltimore, Philadelphia, New York, Albany, Cleveland, Columbus, Indianapolis, and Chicago, and thence was to proceed to Springfield ; thus traversing the states of Maryland, Pennsylvania, New Jersey, New York, Ohio, and Indiana, to Illinois. It was one long pilgrimage of sorrow. The people of every state, city, town, village, and hamlet came with uncovered heads, with streaming eyes, with wreaths of flowers, to witness the passing train. Minute guns, the tolling of bells, mournful music, dirges, draped flags at half mast, with black hanging from every public building and private house, marked this long line of two thousand miles. Nowhere were the manifestations of grief more impressive than at Baltimore, and especially from the negroes. Their coarse, homely features were convulsed with a grief they could not control, and sobs, cries, and tears told how deeply they mourned their deliverer. At Philadelphia, the remains lay in state in old Independence Hall. Four years before, in that same hall, when on his way to the capital, he had declared he would sooner be assassinated than give up the principles of the Declaration of Independence. He had been assassinated because of his fidelity to those principles. The old historic bell, which had rung out the peal announcing the adoption of the Declaration of Independence, and on which had been engraved the words : "Proclaim liberty throughout the land to all the inhabitants thereof," stood at the head of the coffin of Lincoln—who had made and maintained that proclamation. The procession reached New York on the 24th, and remained until the 25th. Every house, from pavement to roof, all the way from the Battery to Central Park, was draped in black. Here came the venerable old soldier, General Scott, to take his last look at the President whose inauguration he had helped to secure.

As the train passed up the Hudson towards Albany, near one of the towns lying in the shadow of the mountains, a tableau of picturesque beauty had been arranged. Just as the evening sun was sinking behind the Catskills, the train was seen slowly approaching. A great crowd had gathered near the banks of the river. An open space encircled with evergreens was seen, and, as the train came still nearer, sad, slow, melancholy music was heard, and a beautiful woman representing Liberty was discovered kneeling over the grave of Lincoln, with a crown of laurels, and the flag draped in mourning.

And thus the sad procession moved on, reaching Chicago on the first of May. Here every one had personally known Mr. Lincoln. Here he had made his speeches to courts and juries. Here he had often debated with his great rival, Douglas, and here he had been nominated for President. Here, from all parts of Illinois now thronged his old friends and neighbors. Here, as everywhere, mottoes expressive of the grief of the people were everywhere displayed. On the 3d of May, the funeral train reached Springfield, and his remains were taken to the State House, which had so often echoed with his eloquence. Over the door of the entrance, in allusion to the last words spoken by him when he bade his neighbors good-bye, were the lines:

> " He left us borne up by our prayers;
> He returns embalmed in our tears."

The whole world hastened to express sympathy with the American people. From Windsor Castle and from the cottage of the humblest day-laborer, came the voice of sorrow. England's widowed queen, under her own hand, expressed the deepest sympathy with the widow at the White House. The English speaking race, from every part of its magnificent empire, from Parliament and Westminster Abbey, and from India, and Australia, Canada, and the Islands of the Sea, everywhere came forward with the expression of its profound regret. Indeed, all nations and all peoples vied with each other in the expression of their sorrow. These utterances were communicated to our State department. Mr. Seward felicitously called them " The Tribute of the Nations to Abraham Lincoln." They were printed, and constitute a quarto volume of nearly a thousand pages, unique in its character, and a tribute never before in any age paid to any man.

His body was taken to Oak Ridge Cemetery, and there, surrounded by his old friends and neighbors, his clients and constituents, among whom was here and there an old Clary Grove companion—there, with the nation and the world for his mourners—he was buried.

He left, as has been stated, a heart-broken widow, a woman whose intellect was shattered by a shock so awful as scarcely to have had a parallel in history. For a time she was beside herself with grief. She so far lost the control of her mind that she dwelt constantly on the incidents of the last day of her husband's life, and she lost the ability, by any effort of her will, to think of other and less painful things.[1]

As time passed she partly recovered, and her friends hoped that change of scene and new faces would bring her back to a more sound and healthful mental condition. But the death of her son Thomas, to whom she was fondly attached, made her still worse. He died at Chicago, July 15th, 1871, and after this bereavement she became still more morbid, and from that time, Mrs. Lincoln, in the judgment of her most intimate friends, was never entirely responsible for her conduct. She was peculiar and eccentric, and had various hallucinations. These at one time assumed such a form, that her devoted son and her family friends thought it safer and more wise that she should be under treatment for her physical and mental maladies. She was removed to the quiet of the country, where she received every possible kindness and attention, and in a few months so far improved that her elder sister, Mrs. Ninian Edwards, took her to her pleasant home in Springfield, where she lingered until her death, which took place on July 16th, 1882.

Mrs. Lincoln has been treated harshly—nay, most cruelly abused and misrepresented by a portion of the press. That love of scandal and of personality, unfortunately too general, induced reporters to hang around her doors, to dog her steps, to chronicle and exaggerate her impulsive words, her indiscretions, and her eccentricities. There is nothing in American history so unmanly, so devoid of every chivalric impulse, as the treatment of this poor, broken hearted woman,

---

1. The author called upon her a few days after her husband's death, and she narrated to him the incidents of the last day of Mr. Lincoln's life. The next day, and the next, and every time the author met her, she would go over these painful details, until she would be convulsed with sorrow. When entreated not to speak on such a painful subject, and when an effort was made to divert her to others less sad, she would apparently try to turn her thoughts elsewhere, but directly and unconsciously, she would return to these incidents, forgetful that she had told them to her visitor again and again, and she apparently had lost all power of choice in the subjects of her conversation.

whose reason was shattered by the great tragedy of her life. One would have supposed it to be sufficient to secure the forbearance, the charitable construction, or the silence of the press, to remember that she was the widow of Abraham Lincoln. When the Duke of Burgundy was uttering his coarse and idle jests concerning Margaret of Anjou, the Earl of Oxford rebuked and silenced him by saying: "My Lord, whatever may have been the defects of my mistress, she is in distress, and almost in desolation." [1]

The abuse which a portion of the American press so pitilessly poured upon the head of Mary Lincoln, recalls that splendid outburst of eloquence on the part of Burke, when, speaking of the Queen of France, he said: "Little did I dream that I should live to see such disasters fall upon her in a nation of gallant men ; a nation of men of honor, cavaliers. I thought ten thousand swords must have leaped from their scabbards to avenge even a look that threatened her with insult. But the age of chivalry has gone." Charles Sumner was true to the widow of his friend to the last. Largely through his influence, Congress passed a law giving to Mrs. Lincoln a pension, and conferring upon her the franking privilege for life.

1. Sir Walter Scott's " Anne of Geierstein."

CHAPTER XXVI.

CONCLUSION.

THOSE who have read these pages thus far, have obtained the means of forming a more correct judgment of Abraham Lincoln than can be obtained from any attempt at description or word painting. He can be best studied and understood from his speeches, writings, acts, and conduct. And yet while conscious of his inability to do justice to his great subject, the author, who knew him from early manhood to his death, at the bar, on the stump, in private and in public life, cannot forbear the attempt to sketch and portray him as he saw and knew him.

Physically, as has been stated, he was a tall, spare man, with large bones, and towering up to six feet and four inches in height. He leaned forward, and stooped as he walked. He was very athletic, with long limbs, large hands and feet, and of great physical strength. There was no grace in his movements, but an expression of awkwardness, combined with force and vigor. By nature he was diffident, and when in crowds, not speaking and conscious of being observed, he seemed to shrink with bashfulness. When he spoke or listened, he immediately became absorbed in the subject, and all appearances of self-consciousness left him. His forehead was broad and high, his hair was rather stiff and coarse, and nearly black, his eye-brows heavy, his eyes dark grey, clear, very expressive, and varying with every mood, now sparkling with humor and fun, then flashing with wit; stern with indignation at wrong and injustice, then kind and genial, and then again dreamy and melancholy, and at times with that almost superhuman sadness which it has been said is the sign and seal of those who are to be martyrs. His nose was large, clearly defined, and well shaped; his cheek bones high and projecting. His mouth was large, but indicated firmness and decision. Ordinarily, his manner and greeting to his friends was most cordial, kind, and familiar. The glance of his eye, the genial smile on his face, the friendly tone, the hearty grasp of the hand, all indicated a man brotherly to his associates. He would have been pointed out in any crowd as a man from the Northwest. There is expression and character in handwriting. Lincoln's was plain, clear, and simple, as legible as that of Washington, but, unlike Washington's, it was without ornament. He was in one sense " the truest gentleman that ever lived." Awkward, sometimes unconventional, he was always just, unselfish, brave, and true ; to the weak and to his inferiors, always considerate, gentle, and respectful. Neither at the bar, nor in public life, was he ever charged with anything dishonest, or false, or tricky, but he was always open, manly, sincere. The ruggedness of a rude age and a very imperfect education was never entirely obliterated, but he became a very intelligent and well informed man, and with the roughness of his early years there was blended a homely integrity, simplicity, and honesty, apparent in all the events of his life. He was the most magnanimous of men, always just to those who injured or sought to injure him ; and if he ever did an injustice, no one was so ready to make reparation. He was a most faithful friend, and most affectionate in all his family relations. To his children he was warmly devoted.

The tenderness of his heart was apparent in all the actions of his life. He loved, and trusted, and confided in the people to a degree rarely known in a statesman. He had faith in the common every-day folk, with a yearning for their happiness almost paternal. The people seemed to feel instinctively how thoroughly he trusted them, and they revered and trusted him in turn. He was ever loyal to them, and they to him. Some have doubted whether he would have had this confident faith, if it had been his fortune to live in great cities and become familiar with the vicious and criminal classes as there exhibited. There is often seen in history an instinctive sagacity in the popular appreciation of character. The people never misunderstood, nor were they ever in the least suspicious of Lincoln.

In the endeavor to analyze his intellectual and moral character, and to state those qualities which made him so great, and which led to his success, his love of truth should be mentioned. His mental eye was clear and accurate. The question with him was not how can a good argument be made on this or that side, but what is the truth. He had a sagacity which seemed almost instinctive in sifting the true and real from the false. Extraneous circumstances, coloring, association, the accidents, did not mislead him. His mind ever went to what lawyers call the gist of a question. He was ever seeking the right, the real, and the true. He had a passion for this. He analyzed well, was exact, careful, and accurate in his statements, so that the statement was often a demonstration. What has been said implies not only sound judgment, but also the ability to present clearly the reasons for his conclusions. His memory was strong, ready, and tenacious. Although his reading was not extensive, yet his memory was so retentive and so ready, that in history, poetry, and in general literature, few, if any, marked any deficiency. As an illustration of the powers of his memory, may be related the following: A gentleman called at the White House one day, and introduced to him two officers serving in the army, one a Swede and the other a Norwegian. Immediately he repeated, to their delight, a poem of some eight or ten verses descriptive of Scandinavian scenery, and an old Norse legend. He said he had read the poem in a newspaper some years before, and liked it, but it had passed out of his memory until their visit had recalled it.

The two books which he read most were the Bible and Shakespeare. With these he was perfectly familiar. From the Bible, as has before been stated, he quoted frequently, and he read it daily, while Shakespeare was his constant companion. He took a copy with him almost always when traveling, and read it at leisure moments. He had a great love for poetry and eloquence, and his taste and judgment were excellent. Next to Shakespeare among the poets was Burns. There was a lecture of his upon Burns full of favorite quotations and sound criticism. He sympathized thoroughly with the poem, " A Man's a Man for a' That." He was very fond of simple ballads, of simple, old-fashioned, sad, and plantive music. He loved to hear Scotch ballads sung, and negro melodies, and camp-meeting hymns. Holmes's poem of " The Last Leaf " was with him a great favorite. He recited and read works of poetry and elo-quence with great simplicity, but with much expression and effect. When visiting the army, or on a journey on a steamer or by rail, as well as when at home, he would take up his copy of Shakespeare and would often read aloud to his companions. He would remark: " What do you say now to a scene from Hamlet or Macbeth ? " And then he would read aloud with the greatest pleasure scene after scene and favorite passages, never seeming to tire of the enjoy-ment. On the last Sunday of his life, as he was on the steamer returning from his visit to Richmond and City Point, he read aloud many extracts from Shakespeare.[1] He read among other passages the following from Macbeth:

> " Duncan is in his grave ;
> After life's fitful fever he sleeps well;
> Treason has done his worst: nor steel, nor poison,
> Malice domestic, foreign levy, nothing,
> Can touch him further."

Senator Sumner said that " impressed by its beauty, or by something else, he read the passage a second time." [2] His tone, manner, and accent, were so impressive, that after his

1. The author has a quarto edition of Shakespeare, with the name of Lincoln on a blank page, and believes it to be that from which he then read.

2. See Sumner's Eulogy on Lincoln, at Boston, June 1st, 1865.

assassination his friends recalled the incident, and with it this passage from the same play:

> " This Duncan
> Hath borne his faculties so meek, hath been
> So clear in his great office, that his virtues
> Will plead like angels, trumpet-tongued, against
> The deep damnation of his taking-off."

In conversation he was most interesting. Few were so well informed, and fewer still so original, so impressive, and so fascinating. On every subject he had something new and striking to say; and with this there was so much genial humor, that he was attractive beyond comparison. Mirthfulness and melancholy, hilarity and sadness, were strangely combined in him. His mirth was sometimes exuberant. It sparkled in jest, story, and anecdote, while at the next moment, his peculiarly sad, pathetic, melancholy eyes would seem to wander far away, and one realized that he was a man "familiar with sorrow and acquainted with grief." This peculiar look often suggested the thought: " What has made this joyous, merry man so sad ? What great sorrow lies at his heart?" Statesmen, great soldiers, scholars, and distinguished foreigners all agreed that as a conversationalist he had no equal. As a public speaker, he was the most effective of the great speakers of his day. That is, he brought more of his hearers to his conclusions than any other. There are more of his sayings, more extracts from his writings and speeches, generally familiar, than of any other American. Great as were his services as President, the influence upon the future of his words, his acts, and his character, in shaping the nation's character, will be scarcely less important. "Honest Abe" will help to make his countrymen honest. His patriotism, his integrity, his purity, his moderation, will contribute largely to make the American people patriotic, honest, and upright. He was brought by many qualities in such close sympathy with the masses of the people, that it is not extravagant to say that the national character will be more influenced by him than by any other man in our history. Greater in some things than Washington, he had far more in common with the people than the founder of the republic, and his influence will be greater. And yet, who can measure this influence? who can estimate the power of "Aristides the Just"? who can measure the formative influence of Shakespeare?

We hear Lincoln's words in every school-house and college, in every cabin and at every public meeting. We read them in every newspaper, school-book, and magazine; and they are all in favor of right, and liberty, and truth, and of honesty and reverence for God. His words, becoming some of them as familiar as the Bible, are on the tongues of all the people, shaping the national character, and thus "though dead he yet speaketh." His life, his teaching, and his character will prolong the life of the republic. If Providence sends us other Lincolns, and enough of them, the republic may continue forever.

Lincoln was not a scholar, but where is there a speech more completely exhaustive in argument than his Cooper Institute speech? Where anything more touching and pathetic than his farewell to his neighbors at Springfield? Where anything more eloquent than the appeal for peace and union in his first inaugural? Where anything finer than his defense of the Declaration of Independence in the Douglas debates? Where the equal in moral sublimity of his speech at Gettysburg? Where anything stronger than the argument on arrests in his letter to the Albany meeting? Where anything finer than his letter to the Illinois State Convention? Where is there, in simple grandeur of thought and sentiment, the equal of his last inaugural?

It is very strange that any reader of Lincoln's speeches and writings should have the hardihood to charge him with a want of religious feeling. No more reverent Christian than he ever sat in the executive chair, not excepting Washington. He was by nature religious; full of religious sentiment. The veil between him and the supernatural was very thin. It is not claimed that he was orthodox. For creeds and dogmas he cared little. But in the great fundamental principles of religion, of the Christian religion, he was a firm believer. Belief in the existence of God, the immortality of the soul, in the Bible as the revelation of God to man, in the efficacy and duty of prayer, in reverence towards the Almighty, and in love and charity to man, was the basis of his religion. From the time he left Springfield to his death he not only himself continually prayed for divine assistance, but constantly asked the prayers of his friends for himself and his country. Declarations of his trust in God and his belief in the efficacy of prayer pervade his state papers, letters, and speeches. Pages of quotations showing this might be furnished. His reply to the negroes of Baltimore when they, in 1864, presented him with a magnificent Bible, ought to silence forever those who charge him with unbelief. He said : " In regard to the Great Book I have only to say, that it is the best gift which God has given to man. All the good from the Savior of the world is communicated through this Book." [1]

In a letter written January 12th, 1851, when his father was dangerously ill, he says: " I sincerely hope father may yet recover his health, but at all events tell him to remember to call upon and confide in our great and good and merciful Maker, who will not turn any from Him in any extremity. He notes the fall of a sparrow, and numbers the hairs of our heads. He will not forget the dying man who puts his trust in Him. * * Say to him if it be his lot to go now, he will soon have a joyous meeting with loved ones gone before, and where the rest of us, through the help of God, hope ere long to join him." [2] To a friend, who inquired

1. See the speech, in McPherson's History of the Rebellion, p. 424. Also, Washington Chronicle, September 5, 1864, where it is printed entire. A full account of the presentation is to be found in Carpenter's Six Months at the White House, and Lincoln's speech in full on p. 199.

2. This letter is quoted in full in a letter of W. H. Herndon, dated February 18th, 1870, in which he says, speaking of the letter: " I hold a letter of Mr. Lincoln in my hand, dated January 12th, 1851, from which the above paragraphs are taken."

why, with his marked religious character, he did not unite with some church organization,[1] Lincoln replied: " I have never united myself to any church, because I found difficulty in giving my assent, without mental reservation, to the long and complicated statements of Christian doctrine which characterize their articles of belief and confessions of faith. When any church will inscribe over its altar, as its sole qualification for membership, the Savior's condensed statement of the substance of both law and gospel: ' Thou shalt love the Lord thy God with all thy heart, with all thy soul, and with all thy mind, and thy neighbor as thyself,' that church shall I join with all my heart and soul."

His statements to Mr. Bateman, in the form which Mr. Bateman declared to be substantially correct, have been quoted already.

But it is not necessary to debate the subject. All his writings prove that he was a religious man, reverent, humble, prayerful, charitable, conscientious; otherwise his whole life was a sham, and he himself a hypocrite. Doubtless, like many others, he passed through periods of doubt and perplexity; but his faith in a divine Providence began at his mother's knee, and ran through all the changes of his life. Not orthodox, not a man of creeds, he was a man of simple trust in God, living in the consciousness of the presence of the great Creator, and one whose heart was ever open to the impressions of the unseen world. He was one whom no sectarian could claim as a partisan, yet one whom every true Christian could recognize as a brother. To the poor widow, five of whose sons had been killed in battle, and the sixth severely wounded, he said: " I pray our Heavenly Father may assuage the anguish of your bereavement." These pages might be filled with quotations of a similar character, but surely this is not necessary. When the unbeliever shall convince the people that this man, whose whole life was straightforward, truthful, clear, and honest, was a sham and

1. Mr. Deming, member of Congress from Connecticut. See his Eulogy of Lincoln, p. 42.

a hypocrite, then, but not before, may he make the world doubt his Christianity.

Let us now for a moment try to appreciate the greatness of his work and the value of his services. What did he accomplish in the four years of his administration ?

When he became President, the ship of state was tossing among the rocks, driven hither and thither by a fearful tornado. He found the treasury empty, the national credit gone, the little nucleus of an army and navy scattered and disarmed, many of the officers rebels, and those who were loyal strangers. The party which elected him was in a minority, he having received but a plurality of the popular vote. The old democratic party, which had ruled most of the time for half a century, was hostile, and a large portion of it, even in the North, in sympathy with the insurgents; while his own party was made up of discordant elements. Nor had he or his party then acquired prestige and the confidence of the people. It is the exact truth to say that when he entered the White House, he was the object of personal and unfavorable prejudice with a majority of the people, and of contempt to a powerful minority. He entered upon his work of restoring the Union without sympathy from any of the great powers of Western Europe. Those which were not open enemies manifested a cold neutrality, or a secret hostility, and none of them extended to him and his administration any cordial good-will or moral aid. The London Times gave expression to the hope and belief of the ruling classes, not only of Great Britain but of France, when it said exultingly: " The great republic is no more. The bubble is burst." Yet in spite of all this inexperienced man of the prairies, by his sagacity, his sound judgment, his wisdom, his integrity, and his trust in God, crushed the most stupendous of rebellions, and one supported by armies more vast, resources greater, and an organization more perfect than any which ever before undertook the dismemberment of a nation. He not only united and held together, against bitter and contending factions, his own party, but strengthened it by

29

winning the confidence and support of the best part of all parties. He composed the bitter quarrels of rival military leaders, and at length discovered and placed at the head of his armies the skill and ability which secured military success. Gradually he won the respect, the confidence, the good-will and sympathy of all nations and peoples. His own countrymen learned that he was honest and patriotic, that he was as unselfish and magnanimous as he was true, and they re-elected him almost by acclamation; and after a series of brilliant victories, he overcame and destroyed all armed opposition. Ever keeping pace with public sentiment, he struck blow after blow at the institution of slavery, until he proclaimed emancipation, and crowned his work by an amendment of the Constitution, prohibiting slavery throughout the republic, thus realizing the dream of his early years. And all this he accomplished within the brief period of four years.

Those who think he lacked boldness and firmness, do not know and appreciate the man. He had no vanity in the exhibition of power, but what he thought it his duty to do, he did with a quiet firmness. What bolder act than the surrender of Mason and Slidell, against the resolution of Congress and the intense public sentiment prevailing? No member of his Cabinet, nor all of them, nor Congress itself, could induce him to swerve from his convictions of duty. The whole Senate did not succeed in coercing him to remove Mr. Seward as Secretary of State. And this man, when the hour of supreme victory came, made it not the hour of vengeance, but of reconciliation and forgiveness. No words of bitterness or of denunciation can be found in his writings or speeches. He had the almost divine power of separating the crime from the criminal. There is no doubt that he had a deep, profound conviction, a superstition, a presentiment —call it what you please—a belief that he was called and set apart for a great purpose, and that he was an instrument in the hands of God for the work he had to do. Hence his faith, his trust that right makes might. Believing this, he did his duty as God enabled him to see it, and he never in the darkest hour despaired.

Mr. Lincoln has been charged with telling coarse and indecent anecdotes. The charge, so far as it indicates any taste for indecency, is untrue. His love for the humorous was so strong,that if a story had this quality, and was racy or pointed, he did not always refrain from narrating it because the incidents were coarse. But it was always clear to the listener that the story was told for its wit and not for its vulgarity. "To the pure all things are pure," and Lincoln was a man of purity of thought as well as of life. [1]

It will interest those who did not see him at the White House, and who have come on the stage since his death, to know something of his life and habits while he lived in the Executive Mansion. At Springfield, his home was a small, modest, comfortable wooden cottage, such as is found everywhere in the villages of our country. Here he lived in a quiet, unostentatious manner, without any pretension, and dispensed to his personal friends and members of the bar and judges, a cordial but very simple hospitality. At the White House, he was compelled by custom and usage to have large receptions, to give dinners, and to adopt a life of conventional form and ceremony, to which it was not easy for him to conform, and which was far less agreeable than the simple and easy life he had led before. His reception-room—which he called his office—was on the second floor on the south side of the White House, and the second apartment from the southeast corner, the corner room looking east towards the treasury being occupied by his private secretary.

---

1. Carpenter, in his "Six Months at the White House," pp. 80-81, says: "It is but simple justice to his (Lincoln's) memory, that I should state that during the entire period of my stay in Washington, after witnessing his intercourse with all classes of men, * * * I cannot recollect to have heard him relate a circumstance to any of them which would have been out of place in a lady's drawing-room." Dr. Stone, his family physician, said : "Lincoln is the purest-hearted man with whom I ever came in contact." My own personal observation and intercourse, extending through a period of over twenty years, enables me to endorse these statements. The truth is that scores of stories of this character have been falsely attributed to Mr. Lincoln.

It was about twenty-five by forty feet in size. In the center, on the west, was a large white marble fire-place, with big old-fashioned brass andirons, and a large and high brass fender. A wood fire was burning in cool weather. The large windows opened on the beautiful lawn to the south, with a view of the unfinished Washington Monument, the Smithsonian Institute, the Potomac, Alexandria, and down the river towards Mt. Vernon. Across the Potomac were Arlington Heights, and Arlington House, late the residence of Robert E. Lee. On the hills around, during nearly all of his administration, were the white tents of soldiers, and field fortifications and camps, and in every direction could be seen the brilliant colors of the national flag. The furniture of this room consisted of a large oak table covered with cloth, extending north and south, and it was around this table that the Cabinet sat when it held its meetings. Near the end of the table, and between the windows, was another table, on the west side of which the President sat in a large arm chair, and at this table he wrote. A tall desk with pigeon-holes for papers stood against the south wall. The only books usually found in this room were the Bible, the United States Statutes, and a copy of Shakespeare. There were a few chairs, and two plain hair-covered sofas. There were two or three map frames, from which hung military maps on which the position and movements of the armies were traced. There was an old and discolored engraving of General Jackson on the mantel, and later a photograph of John Bright. Doors opened into this room from the room of the secretary, and from the outside hall running east and west across the House. A bell cord within reach of his hand extended to the secretary's office. A messenger stood at the door opening from the hall, who took in the cards and names of visitors. Here, in this plain room, Mr. Lincoln spent most of his time while President. Here he received every one, from the Chief Justice and Lieutenant General to the private soldier and humblest citizen. Custom had fixed certain rules of precedence, and the order in which officials should be received. Members of the Cabinet and the high officers of the army and navy were generally promptly admitted. Senators and members of Congress were received in the order of their arrival. Sometimes there would be a crowd of senators and members of Congress waiting their turn. While thus waiting, the loud ringing laugh of Mr. Lincoln—in which he would be joined by those *inside*, but which was rather provoking to those *outside* —would be heard by the waiting and impatient crowd. Here, day after day, often from early morning to late at night, Lincoln sat, listened, talked, and decided. He was patient, just, considerate, and hopeful. The people came to him as to a father. He saw everyone, and many wasted his precious time. Governors, senators, congressmen, officers, clergymen, bankers, merchants—all classes approached him with familiarity. This incessant labor, the study of the great problems he had to decide, the worry of constant importunity, the quarrels of officers of the army, the care, anxiety, and responsibility of his position, wore upon his vigorous frame.

His friends and his family, and especially Mrs. Lincoln, watched his careworn and anxious face with the greatest solicitude. She and they sometimes took him from his labors almost in spite of himself. He walked and rode about Washington and its picturesque surroundings. He visited the hospitals, and, with his friends, and in conversation, and visits to the theatre, he sought to divert his mind from the pressure upon it. He often rode with Secretary Seward, with Senator Sumner, and others. But his greatest relief was when he was visited by his old Illinois friends, and for a while, by anecdotes and reminiscences of the past, his mind was beguiled from the constant strain upon it. These old friends were sometimes shocked with the change in his appearance. They had known him at his home, and at the courts in Illinois, with a frame of iron and nerves of steel; as a man who hardly knew what illness was, ever genial and sparkling with frolic and fun, nearly always cheery and bright. Now, as the months of the war went slowly on, they saw the wrinkles on his face and forehead deepen into furrows, the laugh of old days was less frequent, and it did not seem to come from the heart.   Anxiety, responsibility, care, thought, disasters, defeats, the injustice of friends, wore upon his giant frame, and his nerves of steel became at times irritable.   He said one day, with a pathos which language cannot describe : " I feel as though I shall never be glad any more." During these four years, he had no respite, no holidays. When others fled away from the heat and dust of the capital, he remained.   He would not leave the helm until all danger was passed, and the good ship of state had weathered the storm.   At last his labors were crowned with complete success.   His great work was done, and while the shouts of victory were resounding in his ears and echoing over the land, he was assassinated.

There is but one other name in American history which can be mentioned with his as that of a peer—the name of Washington.   Lincoln was as pure, as just, as patriotic, as the father of his country.   He had more faith in the people, and was more hopeful for the future.   Both have been so associated with our history that time will only brighten the lustre of their fame.

THE END.

INDEX.